Textual Analysis

Some Readers Reading

Edited by

MARY ANN CAWS

The Modern Language Association of America
New York, New York

Library of Congress Cataloging in Publication Data

Main entry under title:

Textual Analysis.

  Bibliography: p.
  1. Literature, Modern—Explication. I. Caws,
Mary Ann.
PN710.T467   1986   801'.959   85-18808
ISBN 0-87352-140-4
ISBN 0-87352-141-2 (pbk.)

Published by The Modern Language Association of America
10 Astor Place, New York, New York 10003

Contents

When we read too quickly or too slowly, we understand nothing.

(Pascal, qtd. in Paul de Man, *Allegories of Reading* v)

Preface

I shall endeavour for the future to put my self-contradictions in short sentences and direct terms, in order to save sagacious persons the trouble of looking for them.
(John Ruskin, "Modern Manufacture" 150n)

Of the difficult and controversial craft called, at various times, close reading, explication de texte, or textual commentary, these two dozen samples—each of which demonstrates a different kind of reading—render an account by illustration. Their contradictory viewpoints were chosen to represent a wide range of current reading practices, applied to a relatively wide range of literatures (American, Danish, English, French, German, Italian, Japanese, Latin American, and Spanish).

This shared endeavor looks back to the traditional forms of explication or exfoliation, as well as to the close reading of a more recent time, and also around and forward to other and conflicting forms of interpretation and to its present and future undoing. The book offers itself as a fair sampling of trends—along lines both conservative and less so—in the area of what I would call intensive rather than close reading; it represents as many aspects as possible of the textual question—a vexed but challenging one. Different generations meet here, with their styles of reading: historical and perspectival, analytic and psychoanalytic, thematic and semiotic, rhetorical and deconstructive, political and feminist, willingly textual and intertextual in several senses.

By opening ourselves to readings less familiar in our own experience, we encounter, in the text, what Thomas Greene describes as the vulnerability of one culture to incision by others:

> Contact with another culture is dangerous precisely because acculturation betrays the arbitrary particularity of each myth and code. Culture exists partly to shield the individual by imposing mythical patterns on the random chaos of history, but culture is not itself shielded from fortuitous violence, neither from the violence of the field of battle nor from the violence of skepticism.

Even when the exterior world is only implicit, there remains within the text sufficient material for conflict between the deconstructionists and their detractors, or between formal and substantial readings, phenomenological and perspectival ones. Here are assembled close, middle, and distant interpretations, cognitive and structural, with a split visible between those that apply independently of historical limitations and those that do not.

The participants in this work were asked first to sketch out a way of tackling a text and then to exemplify it with a specific analysis, from any literature and period each might choose. Some surprises ensued: specialists did not necessarily stick to their own well-mapped domains. A practical consequence of what I am calling here intensive reading is that in being so engaged, one forgets, at least temporarily, one's label—or may choose to ignore it.

Since so many of these essays are concerned with textuality and intertextuality, the discussions by Riffaterre and Greene on those topics begin the volume. Traditional or "organic" analysis, in the essays by Kneller and Lawler on French poetry and Warnke and Jackson on German and American poetry, is followed by the phenomenologically and subjectively oriented essays by Martinez-Bonati and Alazraki on Spanish and Latin American literature. Epistemological or cognitive criticism is represented by Miner on Bashō and by Cohn on Baudelaire, whereas Mazzotta's reading of Petrarch and Vendler's of Whitman merge traditional and open viewpoints. A perspectival viewing of Woolf by Mendelson, from near and far distances, retains the openness, but with a twist.

Deconstruction's challenge is represented in several ways, including the modes called up by Chambers, Chase, Esch, Johnson, and Miller. These modes include the psychoanalytic and the feminist, leading directly to Gilbert's invocation of the feminist field of letters and to the politically oriented essays of Rice-Sayre and Eagleton, which remind us that the signifying practices we engage in are often, consciously or not, forms of rhetorical power play. "All criticism is in some sense political," as Eagleton points out, and the "energy, urgency, and enthusiasm" he calls for may waken the implicit drama he suggests in his final image of the sleeping lion.

Finally, lest we take ourselves too seriously in all our contentious conversation, ironic distance is represented by Harrison's rendering of Kierkegaard, while a coda by Fletcher and Stewart rounds out the image of our reading in an energetically idiosyncratic mode.

MARY ANN CAWS

Textuality

W. H. Auden's "Musée des Beaux Arts"

MICHAEL RIFFATERRE

No critical approach can be relevant without being centered on what constitutes the literariness of literature. Analysts must first make sure that the literary work of art under study exhibits features common to all literary phenomena—the universals of literature. Secondly, they must gear their analyses to these universals, using them to put together in logical and interpretable form the accumulation of data known as reader response.

But when they attempt to differentiate between the ordinary day-to-day use of language and its manipulation into a verbal work of art, by simply listing special generic or stylistic features such as tropes and figures, they soon recognize that any device empirically felt to be literary can be found occasionally in common usage and in nonliterary texts. Such devices therefore define literary discourse only, and it remains to be shown what makes sequences of literary discourse into actual works of art. Only one universal of literariness, it seems to me, can provide the answer, namely textuality. By textuality I mean the complex of formal and semantic factors that characterize a self-sufficient, coherent, unified text and legitimize its forms, however aberrant they may be, by removing any hint of the gratuitous. These factors are the idiolect, that is, the special rules of grammar and lexical distribution valid only for the text; closure; and an all-encompassing significance that supersedes the discrete meanings of the successive parts or components of the text.[1] None of these can be defined except by opposition to its homologue in the free-floating universe of potential linguistic expression. Idiolect is inseparable from the sociolect (language not just as grammar and lexicon but as the repository of society's myths and commonplace representation of reality) that it challenges. Closure as a physical fact and as a limitation to the number of possible interpretive strategies the text allows is inseparable from the open-endedness of the verbal associations it puts an end to. And significance is the product of the relation between the text and its intertext. To put it otherwise, significance (the semiotic face of textuality) results from intertextuality.

This much abused term designates the relation that connects the work of art with other works.[2] It is not to be confused with the link a learned critic may perceive between a work and its source, nor should the term be used as a synonym for literary influence, or for thematic or generic kinship. Intertextuality is that form of reference experienced when the reader finds that a text presupposes another and that the latter provides the former with the means of interpreting it and of justifying its formal and semantic peculiarities. This is not to say the intertext glosses or paraphrases the text, clarifying and making explicit what may be obscure or implicit in it. Rather the intertext is another text, or a corpus of other texts (or textlike segments of the sociolect), that shares its lexicon and its structures with the one we are reading. This intertext represents a model on which the text builds its own variations. It is a kind of ad hoc norm (ad hoc in the sense that it is valid only within the bipolar twinning of the two texts, as opposed to a linguistic norm from which a given literary utterance may depart). Consequently a departure from usage may define an instance of literary discourse, whereas a departure from a text defines, and brings to the reader's consciousness, the textuality of a finite verbal sequence, whether or not it is also characterized by traits of literary discourse. To the reader's eye the text's variations on the intertext tend to appear as disconcerting, obscure, unmotivated, or downright ungrammatical because their referents are elsewhere, and they remain so as long as we fail to connect them with their intertextual model. They thus make for the text's originality, its uniqueness, and quite literally (not just in the commonplace sense of the term) for its difference. Even as it is challenged this norm still stands as the referent and as the authority against which the text now makes its claim. The implicit presence of that authority, the frame of that reference, once perceived or actualized by the reader's recognition of them, save the text's idiolectic deviance from any appearance of gratuitousness.

Intertextuality is therefore the reader's awareness of the structural variants—namely, the text's deviant versions of their homologues in the intertext.

Textual deviances from the intertext run the gamut from reversals of the model's meanings (i.e., stating contraries) or its markers (i.e., changing connotations from positive to negative) to mere translations of the model into a different and generally incompatible lexical code or stylistic register (i.e., parody).

At first, readers perceive anomalies or peculiarities in the text—precisely the kind that, more often than not, they alternately frown on as gratuitous or tolerate as "poetic license" (a revealing phrase). In a second step, they make the connection with the intertext's models, the "grammatical" versions of the text's ungrammaticalities. Thus, while intertextuality is an operation of readers' minds, it is an obligatory one: the readers' unavoidable realization that their grasp of what the text means is incomplete and frustrated so long as they do not go through the detour of the intertext. Textuality in short is the fact that a literary piece owes its significance to its complementary or contradictory intertextual homologue.

Significance comes from constant features, when a sense of the formal and semantic consistency compels the reader's attention, although nothing seems to detract from the variety of the details or the multiple meanings suggested in the course of the narrative. This consistency stems from the realization that while the mimesis adds various details and the narrative progresses to new elements, these additions never-

theless repeat the same thing. For, whether content or form, they are also variants
of an invariant, of a structure that constitutes the poem's overall significance. Now
perceived as variants they contribute to textuality by providing this unity or tautology
within the changing successivity of narrative and mimesis. The structure that generates them is the matrix of the text,[3] from which the variants are derived sequen-
tially, to the very clausula that visibly represents the conclusive apex of the tautological
paradigm. So far as empirical observation can tell, the matrix owes it power to a
departure, to the shock, scandal, or mere novelty violating a structure well established in the sociolect, such as the shock created when an equivalency is changed
into an opposition. As for the derivation itself, its lexical "stuff"—the words that
actualize the matricial variants—is supplied by the intertext.

I shall use these concepts for the analysis of the following poem by W. H. Auden:

Musée des Beaux Arts

About suffering they were never wrong,
The Old Masters: how well they understood
Its human position; how it takes place
While someone else is eating or opening a window or just walking dully along;
5   How, when the aged are reverently, passionately waiting
For the miraculous birth, there always must be
Children who did not specially want it to happen, skating
On a pond at the edge of the wood:
They never forgot
10 That even the dreadful martyrdom must run its course
Anyhow in a corner, some untidy spot
Where the dogs go on with their doggy life and the torturer's horse
Scratches its innocent behind on a tree.

In Breughel's *Icarus*, for instance: how everything turns away
15 Quite leisurely from the disaster; the ploughman may
Have heard the splash, the forsaken cry,
But for him it was not an important failure; the sun shone
As it had to on the white legs disappearing into the green
Water; and the expensive delicate ship that must have seen
20 Something amazing, a boy falling out of the sky,
Had somewhere to get to and sailed calmly on.

December 1938
(*Collected Poems* 146–47)

The poem's significance is hardly in doubt. It is in fact because the piece makes
its point quite directly in the first part (lines 1–13) that I chose it, the better to
show what verbal mechanisms are at work here.

The poem is about the true horror of evil, that is, its very banality and ordinariness.
As Edward Mendelson puts it, this banality entails, in the poem as it did in the
Old Masters, the "inversion of the principle [of classical rhetoric] that the most
important subjects require the highest style" (363).

The normalcy of evil is stated directly and indirectly. Its direct expression is in the first "stanza," which speaks of the world's equanimity toward evil. Evil is taken as a matter of fact, greeted with indifference. The indirect statement of significance is more hidden than obvious in the poem's second part, which describes the painting, in art-criticism fashion.

The poem is built on two intertexts, the painting and Ovid's *Metamorphoses* (which is also Breughel's intertext). In the former, intertextuality may seem a straightforward case of ekphrasis. But the perception of a textual constant changes ekphrasis from objective representation to representation in which the emphasis on the genre itself, on the ekphrastic trope, makes it a hypersign[4] for the poem's significance rather than a representation whose effectiveness only depends on reproducing Breughel so faithfully that the reader surmises what the painter was trying to achieve. Needless to say, even if the ekphrasis were not thus oriented it would not exhaust the painting's text. Auden selects, and underlines by selecting, those elements of the picture that may buttress his own interpretation, his rewrite, of Breughel. As for intertextuality with Ovid, it provides Auden with the textual constant mentioned above.

As I said before, Ovid initially serves as an intertext to Breughel. But Auden bypasses Breughel and makes straight for book 8 of the *Metamorphoses*, in order to underscore the pathos of the event. Merely reporting Icarus's headlong plunge as Breughel paints it could otherwise easily suggest an almost comical demise. The "splash" (16), for instance, may be inferred from Breughel, less so the "forsaken cry" (16). Ovid does echo the child's piteous cry for help, vainly uttered: "Oraque cærulea patrium clamantia nomen / Excipiuntur aqua" 'His mouth is still calling his father's name when the azure water drowns it' (8.229; trans. mine). Suppose we may credit Auden with enough imagination to think of a death scream by himself. The fact remains that nothing in Breughel would lead to the specific half line "a boy falling out of the sky," for the painting shows only one leg sticking out of the water; no viewer could tell it is a teenager's, and there is nothing in the legend, save that Icarus was Dædalus's son, to make his age worth mentioning. Whereas Ovid insists on the victim's tender years ("teneram prolem" [8.214]) and childish, irresponsible playfulness, details that become relevant if one's subject is the suffering of the innocent.

But the Ovid intertext fulfills a more important function. The representation of indifference among the witnesses of evil owes its impact not to the mere accuracy or expressiveness in the portrayal of these bystanders so callously turning away from the disaster but to an intertextual reversal of a depiction of the opposite of indifference. Indeed, this indifference is not just a question of physical representation, a choice made by Breughel and approved by Auden, a narrative proairesis[5] from two equally possible attitudes (interest and lack of interest) and two equally possible narrative developments from the given: Icarus's fall. The impact of this indifference is that it cancels out and challenges Ovid's original version of the story, an intertext of rapt attention. In Ovid, Icarus's flight was made into a poetic experience, a *mirabile*, a *thauma*, by the amazement of these same characters. For the characters in Breughel's picture, and in Auden's reproduction, are all of them in Ovid, where they are gaping, admiring spectators ("vidit et obstipuit" 'he saw and remained dumbfounded' [8.219]) who conclude that Icarus and Daedalus are gods winging skywards. Their gazing faces define the miracle; they are the literary means of pointing to an exemplum. Now their backs, suddenly turned, intertextually define not just a disaster but the reverse of a positive miracle.[6] They are the sign of its opposite, of a negative exemplum.

The act of the same nonwitnesses, who avert their gaze from Icarus's plight, is made into a symbolic act, therefore a literary structure of the poem, by the fact that the witnesses who had lifted their gaze towards the flight of Icarus are here turned inside out. Just imagine a reverse variant of the Passion, in which the witnesses whose mourning draws the lesson of the Crucifixion in so many paintings were suddenly shown with their backs to the cross.

As for Breughel's initial motive in upsetting the Ovidian cart, it must not be connected directly with an individual pessimism, with a cynical view of the ways of the world. This would not necessarily strike a chord in all viewers. What does is that Breughel's motivation has the authority of the sociolect. It is to be found in yet another intertext. The artist's moral stance expresses itself through the mediation of another sign system. This mediating intertext, the third component in any semiotic operation, is the interpretant[7] that links the sign and its object and constitutes the interpreter's reaction to perceiving the link. This interpretant is for Breughel the German proverb "No plough is stopped for the sake of a dying man" (Stechow 55; cf. Praz 75 and n. 25). In Auden's case, the other paintings, the ones alluded to in the first thirteen lines of the poem, provide the "indifference" motif and are the interpretant to his verbal rewording of Breughel's subversion of Ovid.

The matrix generating this reversal may be drawn from the very semantic configuration of the word *witness*. If a dictionary definition of a witness is a tautological derivation, someone who saw something and can or must testify about it, then a witness who refuses to see or hear produces a powerful oxymoron, or, in structural terms, a function canceling itself out. The poem does nothing more than translate this oxymoron into visual terms and human shapes.

Thus the unified significance of the text comes into being. Thus the mimesis—detail by detail, character by character, sentence by sentence—is replaced with the constant common to all these details, a constant verified in every sentence. Separately, these are indicators of verisimilitude. Recognized as components of a text, as the cumulative, repetitive variants of one invariant, this factor—their common function, their textuality—transforms their status, valorizes them, makes them into one semiotic system; because of this systematic integration, the mimesis becomes exemplary, and the exemplary becomes symbolic.

That such is indeed the working of the Ovid intertext can be verified by comparing Auden and two other poems for which Breughel is the only intertext. In both instances significance issues from ekphrasis only, objective or "pure," but still selective, still manipulative in its selectiveness.

One objective ekphrasis is William Carlos Williams's "Landscape with the Fall of Icarus":[8]

> According to Brueghel
> when Icarus fell
> it was spring
>
> a farmer was ploughing
> 5 his field
> the whole pageantry
>
> of the year was
> awake tingling
> near
>
> 10 the edge of the sea
> concerned
> with itself
>
> sweating in the sun
> that melted
> 15 the wings' wax
>
> unsignificantly
> off the coast
> there was
>
> a splash quite unnoticed
> 20 this was
> Icarus drowning

No trace here of the witnesses: the farmer is represented all by himself, as if Breughel's painting had been empty except for him and the falling man. Furthermore, the sentence does not relate the farmer to Icarus, not even negatively, as would be the case if his attention were said to be elsewhere. Four stanzas isolate him from the fall, and Icarus is not even visible but is introduced as the narrator's explanation for the splash, as a footnote to the tableau rather than as a character in it.

Indifference to the tragedy is expressed by objective ekphrasis, simply by focusing on the landscape, with a lyrical, paeanlike salute to a glorious spring ("the whole pageantry / of the year was / awake"), and by contrasting this luminous glimpse with a dreary repetitious series of abstract prosaic statements of unconcern ("concerned / with itself," "unsignificantly," "quite unnoticed"). The witnesses' apathy is erased, displaced by the monotonous voice of the art critic reading the picture.[9]

The second objective ekphrasis is in a prose poem by Philippe Jaccottet:[10]

> J'ai pensé . . . à ce *Paysage avec la Chute d'Icare*, de Breughel, où le laboureur est si proche, et le héros presque indiscernable; et j'ai cru voir commencer maintenant une nouvelle ère du regard, où nos travaux quotidiens et nos rêves les plus hardis

ne seraient plus, sur l'écran du monde, que vagues de labours, chute d'une larme lumineuse et sillons dans les eaux tombales.

I thought . . . of Breughel's *Landscape with the Fall of Icarus*, in which the plough-man stands so close to us and where the main character can hardly be seen. I thought this was then the beginning of a new way of seeing things, when our daily labors and our boldest dreams alike would appear on the world's screen as no more than the waves of tilled fields, a luminous tear falling, and furrows in the watery grave. (34; trans. mine)

Despite the images at the end, the language and the attitude here are those of an art critic. The gaze itself has become quite conceptual, a way of interpreting a *paysage moralisé* (to parody Auden, parodying didactic landscape poetry)—a setting entirely subservient to the lesson it symbolizes. This lesson depends on the respective sizes of the farmer and of Icarus, the farmer looming large, filling the foreground, Icarus a dot far off center. Finally a kind of descriptive fusion reiterates the message. The tilled furrows that symbolize normal life are used to depict the briny deep where the fall occurred, Icarus's watery grave translated, defused of its drama, by the tillage code into which it is translated ("sillons dans les eaux tombales").[11]

I shall now discuss Auden's other intertext, the one he shares with Williams and Jaccottet: the relation between his text about life's cruelty and Breughel's painting. The second part of Auden's poem is different from the first in that, instead of allusions to unnamed works of art ("The Numbering at Bethlehem" and "The Massacre of the Innocents"), instead of allusions that are in fact invisible, for the events described could have been directly drawn from reality, we have an overt description of Breughel's painting. The poem has shifted from the direct expression of sentiment to a representation of a symbolic representation of sentiment. Auden has moved from an overt form of poetry of the self to a covert form of it, translated as it were into ekphrastic discourse.

But the reader is not immediately aware of this change in the semiotic function of that discourse. The reader's response, the ultimate realization that indeed such a change has taken place, is both delayed and triggered by his perceiving that, besides the fact that it is reoriented by the input from Ovid, this ekphrasis is more than a copy from the original.

To begin with, the title has an aloofness about it that seems to privilege a preoccupation with aesthetics over the pathos that nonetheless remains the poem's obvious center. And then, the specifics—*white* legs, *green* water (18)—seem unrelated to the tragic immediacy of the sketch they complete. In fact, the drowning man undergoes the same objectifying, the same pictorial freezing up, as does William Carlos Williams's wheelbarrow, and through similar tampering with metrical lin-eation: "a red wheel / barrow . . . beside the white / chickens" (*Spring and All* 21, *Poems* 127). Finally there is the discrepancy between Auden's treatment of the ship as a witness, as a live presence, and his deliberate description of it as a representation of the ship rather than as an actual vessel—"expensive delicate" (19): these adjectives suggest more a scale model, a reproduction within its bottle on the mantelpiece, than a participant in a maritime drama.[12] The reader is first bothered by a gap between two functions, by the fact that the mimesis of a painting and the mimesis of the very drama it depicts do not jibe, and then comes to realize that indifference to suffering is expressed consistently, without harming the poem's unity, through two signifying systems: first, the listing of bystanders united in their refusal to admit that there is anything to see (thus canceling out the most essential semantic feature of the word "martyrdom" (10), an act whereby you bear witness to a truth); second, the ekphrasis that distances the mimesis from the pathos. In other words, the text is generated by the unfolding of two verbal sequences: the indifference sequence that expresses its object plainly and the ekphrastic sequence that expresses it figuratively by making the aesthete's stance entail a denial that suffering should have a special place in the scale of values, or its own scale of ethical values.

The text's clausula confirms that such is indeed the verbal mechanism at work, since the ship sailing by, undeterred by a boy's drowning, is the culminating hyperbole, the most exemplary passerby in the indifference sequence (leaving as it were the scene of the accident, an apt image of irresponsibility). And the same ship happens to be the culminating point of the detached aesthetician's sequence. Auden's title was what had, up to now, remained remote. Its validity as a metonymic title was tenuous, consisting in a roundabout way of designating a whole collection in terms so general that they seem irrelevant. The title metonymically designates one picture only from the whole Brussels Royal Collection, a picture whose pictorial, museum-level value has little to do with the significance Auden finds in it, for he uses it as his text, to be sure, but only in the sense that a preacher refers to the text of his sermon. This indirectness or irrelevance that the reader could only interpret as a conceit is now changing in the light of the clausula, the physical, verbal actualization of closure. Seen from the angle of the image that constitutes that clausula, the words "Musée des Beaux Arts" stop referring to a place so designated or to a class among the species of museums. They now function in terms of what the words "Musée" and "Beaux Arts" would have in common if they were just side by side, if instead of being subordinated to each other syntactically so as to form a toponym they were just a fragment of a paradigm of synonyms. For if they were, they would now continue a series beginning with the adjectives that modify "ship" in the final image of the clausula. What "expensive," "delicate," "museum," and "beaux arts" have in common, as we have seen, is that from the viewpoint of representation they are all askew, irrelevant on the plane of factual, discrete bits of information, and that is what now makes them relevant on the higher plane of united, unified textuality. For as a paradigm, they all refer to a detached aesthetic distance, to a preference for form, to an ideal of beauty, that presupposes elitism and the trappings of social privilege, collecting fine arts, taste, and money lavished on artifacts. They all function as variants of *academic*. They now translate into artistic code the decision to relegate suffering not to a secondary place but to a place in an aesthetic that is not geared toward ethical questions. Art treats evil as one component among others, far from privileging it as morals would; as such, evil is truth and reflects the order of nature.[13]

In technical terms the title now appears to the reader as the prolepsis[14] that anticipated the clausula. Reread in the light of this kinship (the clausula being now the title's analepsis in the process of retroactive, summative, conclusion-drawing reading), the title finalizes the closure and makes the poem a significant self-sufficient system, impervious to the distracting sociolect it has shut out.

The intertextual underpinnings of the poem are thus twofold. The first basic transformation reverses the markers of the Ovidian mimesis, making Ovid's episode (epyllion) stand on its head as it were, forcing it into a representation of the contrary of what it meant in the Latin model. Authority and exemplariness do remain unaltered, however, retaining as they do their power, despite the denotative reversal. The second fundamental transformation modifies the markers of the ekphrasis: instead of symbolizing separately, and each time differently, the precision or realism or interpretive stances entailed by the transfer from one art medium to the other, these markers—now unified as one hypersign—focus on the indifference to pathos and on the detachment from human sympathy that art for art's sake presupposes.

Three points must be emphasized in conclusion. First, the radical nature of semiosis. The transformation we observe in this ekphrasis has the impact of a paradox, for its significance reverses its meaning, without impairing its faithfulness as a description. While for Breughel the landscape belittles Icarus, that the eternal order of things might prevail, Auden's description of the pictorial scheme and figures that achieve this belittling effect, merely spelling out that such is the economy of the painting, magnifies Icarus and the enormity of the notion that suffering should be in the order of things. Pointing to what is hidden in the landscape makes the description of the landscape a pretext to show what it is hiding, a textual periphrasis around the existential core. Auden adheres here to his own poetic principles:

> To me Art's subject is the human clay
> And landscape but a background to a torso.
> ("Letter to Lord Byron," pt. 4; *English Auden* 185)

Second point: the agent that controls reader response and ensures the ultimate discovery of the poem's significance is precisely the element in the text that seems to weaken textuality. A baffling discrepancy or apparent lack of unity, a seemingly gratuitous departure from the idiolect's own norms at the very moment the reader becomes conscious of these ad hoc rules—these factors annoy or disturb and keep readers on their toes until they uncover the twist that makes the self-same components the cornerstones of a new sign system. Here Auden's act of injecting the literalness of ekphrasis into a moral allegory appears as an indulgence, the temptation to describe merely for the sake of vying with pictorial art. Such appears to be the case until another reading makes the ekphrastic discourse another variant (in Old Masters code, appropriately) of the world's indifference to suffering. Ekphrasis has hardly fulfilled its surface role as a hyperbole of the mimesis, when its textual function as an agent of semiosis becomes manifest. The whole landscape is now a circuitous, dilatory hide-and-seek way of pointing to the essential, that is to say, to what jars us in this panorama of country peace in the autumn, or better, to the one element that is not the landscape: someone's misery. The whole of Breughel and the manipulation of Ovid, which has until now seemed a gratuitous *contresens*, are now revealed in their textual function: a vast tortuous periphrasis around the real subject matter. It would be difficult to find a more distracting and therefore exemplary instance of the indirection of meaning, the figurative parti-pris, and the all-pervasive catachresis that characterize literariness.

Third point: textuality as a literary function is a restrictive process that places narrow limitations on the reader's flights of fancy, and more especially on the tendency to use the text as a springboard for open-ended mental associations. This tendency is encouraged by two factors: one, the text's difficulty, or even its obscurity, which impels the reader to grasp at every verbal straw offered by the sociolect that might remotely echo the perplexing verbal sequence. Two, the reader's own culture or linguistic competence, which proffers the straw. That is, every possible meaning that the problem word may have in the dictionary, every possible context that word may have entered in known literary works, will be invoked as an explanation. Which means it will be substituted for the special use of the word in the text. This practice, however, flouts textuality itself by separating the problem word from the textual continuum, whereas this continuum should lead to the significance unique to our poem. This kind of error, the bane of traditional criticism, has affected our text: Richard Johnson, for instance, injects the romantic appropriation of Icarus into Auden, writing "Icarus can be seen as the figure of the aesthete who use[d] his art to try to escape the world of immediacy . . . and ended, pictorially, as a quick stroke of the brush" (41). But textuality does not include the whole dictionary; it manifests itself by eliminating every item but one in the definition and connotations of the name or noun that actualizes the text's matrix (here, Auden's melodramatic focusing on a child's death eliminates the artist symbolism).

Closure expels the sociolect, replaces the commonplaces of language and preexistent, pertinent (i.e., comparable) texts with the idiolect. The semantic equivalencies that govern rhetorical amplification and indeed any generating of verbal sequences in the sociolect are replaced with new equivalencies that make sense only inasmuch as they presuppose the ones they replace. Closure is thus achieved by an implied reference to what it excludes; this shutting out is realized by creating and integrating into the text the reverse image of what the text is not, by making textuality the other face of intertextuality.

Notes

[1] On the distinction between multiple, successive meanings and one unifying, simultaneously perceived significance, see my *Semiotics*, esp. 11–13, 46, 164–66, and *Text Production*, esp. 43–61, 109–24; cf. de Man, "Hypogram."

[2] Intertextuality has developed from Bakhtin's dialogism: see Tzvetan Todorov,

Mikhail Bakhtine. For a historical, somewhat biased survey of the evolution of the concept, see Angenot. I have developed a typology of intertextuality in the books quoted in n. 1. See also my "Syllepsis," "La trace," "Intertextualité," and "Interpretation." In the last three, I distinguish between obligatory and aleatory intertextuality. Obligatory intertextuality is necessary to the text's interpretation; even if a reader cannot quite identify the intertext as a literary piece, he will still perceive its presence in the text as a system of presuppositions.

[3] On textual matrices, see my *Semiotics*, esp. 19–21: a text results from the transformation of the matrix, a minimal and literal sentence, into a longer and nonliteral periphrasis. The text actualizes an equivalence between this minimal given and the periphrasis. The matrix itself modifies a structure that more often than not corresponds to the semic system and to the presuppositions of one word.

[4] *Hypersign*, a complex formal unit (such as a compound word, a sentence, or a trope that may generate derivations of variants extending to the full text) that despite its complexity carries one global or overall meaning, or one marking.

[5] *Proairesis*, the choice between possible actions that reveals the inner self of the character in a narrative. At every point of the narrative sequence such a choice must be made, dictating the reader's understanding of the character's motivations and therefore of the lesson, or "message," symbolized by the character. *Proairesis* is an Aristotelian concept (see Aristotle, *Poetics* 6.50.a.9 and 15.54.a.19); on Roland Barthes's application of it to narrative analysis, see his *S/Z* 25.

[6] Revealingly, Auden omits two characters, the angler and the shepherd, the latter being in fact looking at the sky even in Breughel, and the former standing on the shore from which he cannot help seeing Icarus. His function as the witness who cannot evade the spectacle is transferred to the ship. The reason for this is that the ship lends itself much better than an angler to the ekphrastic stylization I discuss below.

[7] *Interpretant*, a concept evolved from C. S. Peirce's (a sign stands for an object, conveys its meaning and gives rise to an idea, the interpretant): a mediating text that contains a model of the equivalences, transferrals, or reversals from the intertext to the text (see my *Semiotics* 81–114).

[8] The second of his *Pictures from Brueghel* (3). Irene Fairley has demonstrated how the "stylistic isomorphism between poem and painting" (that is, ekphrasis alone) is the organizing principle of significance in this text (68).

[9] Cf. Caws, "Double Reading," esp. 325–26. Caws admirably emphasizes the importance of a linguistic frame (the series of present participles, from the initial recounting impulse to the hero's fall), which stresses its own reading: the reader, by reading, replays or rewrites the downgrading of the heroic attempt, the "human failure at transcendence" (326). I cannot agree, however, that "the painting reads like a tale of three gazes: the worker's at the soil, his companion's at the sky, and our own, at Icarus" (326). Our own gaze, certainly, that is quite sufficient to uncover the imbalance between "the whole pageantry" and an individual's "drowning"; this keen remark would be just as apposite in the case of the Jaccottet prose discussed

below. But the other two gazes can be inferred only from Breughel: Williams shows the ploughman not looking away or looking at his tillage but simply tilling it, in other words minding his business. Likewise the shepherd looking at the sky (a traditional attribute of literary and pictorial shepherds, by the way, not just Breughel's) is not mentioned.

[10] The title of the collection, *Paysages avec figures absentes*, seems to be meant as an ad hoc commentary on Auden's slanted reading of Breughel. This impression stems from the very ungrammaticality of "landscapes with absent characters," where logic and grammar (in agreement for once) both demand "landscapes without characters," so long as we understand a genre of landscape painting in which figures are an expected and necessary human component. Jaccottet wishes to suggest that certain natural landscapes, especially those fraught with traces of human history, speak for themselves. Whatever interpretation they demand and whatever emotion they elicit are experienced without the help of the mythological figures Renaissance painters found necessary to justify and complete their landscapes. They found they needed such figures "in order to express more explicitly what in fact was quite well expressed by certain light effects" (34). Further proof of the intertextual inversion is that Jaccottet, in the same breath in which he states that these figures were not really necessary, describes them as the key to the pictures, symbolizing as they do the appeal of the landscape ("they were like the eternal symbols of Desire" [33]).

[11] The interpretant here is the commonplace that represents the waves of the sea as the furrows of a field and vice versa (see Rimbaud's "Marine," in *Illuminations*).

[12] For a similar transformation of a mimesis of nature into ekphrasis see again Jaccottet: "sur la rive opposée, délimités avec précision par des files de peupliers, il y avait des prés, très verts, . . . et dans ces prés des chevaux, des chars, des faneurs; chaque élément de cette scène aussi net que si l'on avait eu sous les yeux une miniature de Livre d'heures représentant la Fenaison" 'On the opposite shore, there were meadows precisely delimited by ranks of poplars, deep green meadows, . . . and in these there were horses, carts, and haymakers; each element of the spectacle was as clearly delineated as if you had been looking at a Book of Hours picture depicting Haymaking' (127; my trans.). Precise, visual details, exemplary colors, and natural geometry—in short, features meant to represent reality—end up suggesting an artifact and become the picture of a picture of reality.

[13] This interpretation may seem close to Mary Ann Caws's: "the disaster is not, we are told, really very important, if we compare it with the aesthetic stress of the picture: ship and sea in their splendor, dwarfing the human fate" ("Double Reading" 327–28). That stress is ultimately redeeming in her view, because of the continuity it suggests, "the way the universal may triumph over individual failure, simply by continuing past each human disaster" (a view bolstered by the final "on" of the poem). We differ, however, on a crucial point. Caws founds her reading on the semantic content: accordingly the title is locative, the ship displaces the focus from the drowning boy, telling us where to look, and so on. She thus privileges the painting referred to, its sensory visual message being the authority for any interpre-

tive decision. My reading is on the contrary dictated by the formal or stylistic features, or markers common to certain words; these forms privilege a connotation (aesthetic distance, or rather aestheticism). The title therefore is locative as meaning, but "moral" as significance. Moreover it seems to me the referent authorizing an interpretation is the ekphrasis. Its authority displaces that of the painting: Auden's words focus on the disaster by stressing that the intertext pretends to ignore it.

[14] *Prolepsis*, any component of a narrative that either announces a future event or is perceived ex post facto (when this event has taken place) as having been an allusion to its coming or a verbal anticipation of it. *Analepsis* (not to be confused with *epanalepsis*), the point at which this realization takes place, usually thanks to a repetition of or an allusion to the prolepsis. These definitions are narrower, but perhaps more specific, than the ones first proposed by Gérard Genette (*Figures III* 82–83, 111–12).

Rescue from the Abyss

Scève's Dizain 378

THOMAS M. GREENE

This reading of a dizain from the *Délie* of Maurice Scève rests on the conception of a literary text as *vulnerable*, and perhaps the most useful preface to my reading would be an explanation of the ways this term seems to me pertinent to textual analysis. As an epigram or subtext I want to cite Valéry's poem "Aurore," which like Scève's dizain describes a return to consciousness. This liminary or auroral preface to the volume *Charmes* evokes the awakening of the poetic intelligence and its simultaneous recognition of a host of analogies and ideas at its disposal. They have been close to the poet, they tell him, throughout the night of his slumber.

> Nous étions non éloignées,
> Mais secrètes araignées
> Dans les ténèbres de toi! . . .
> Regarde ce que nous fîmes:
> Nous avons sur tes abîmes
> Tendu nos fils primitifs.

> We were not far off, but were secret spiders in your shadows. . . . See what we have done: we have stretched our crude threads over your abysses. (112)[1]

The sleeping mind of the poet has been an abyss across which the spider metaphor has woven its fragile network ("une trame ténue") of threads. The poet then enters a "sensual forest" of being where every vine and tree offers images ripe for plucking, though surrounded by thorns.

> Je ne crains pas les épines!
> L'éveil est bon, même dur!
> Ces idéales rapines
> Ne veulent pas qu'on soit sûr:
> Il n'est pour ravir un monde
> De blessure si profonde
> Qui ne soit au ravisseur
> Une féconde blessure,

Et son propre sang l'assure
D'être le vrai possesseur.

I don't fear the thorns! Waking is good, even if harsh! These ideal plunderings do
not permit one to be certain. To carry off a world, no wound is so deep that it is
not for the pillager a fecund wound, and his own blood assures him that he is the
true possessor.   (113)

The paradoxical "féconde blessure," the wound whose blood is a sign of fertility
and power, can serve to emblematize the character of poetry this analysis will assume.
Valéry is thinking primarily of the creative consciousness, but his thought will not
be seriously falsified if his image is transferred to the structure of the poem itself.
The text wins its privileged status as poem, as literary text, partly because it accepts
a beneficent incision.

The vulnerability of poetry stems from four basic conditions of language: its
historicity, its dialogic function, its referential function, and its dependence on
figuration. We can approach the first of these conditions by considering how unprotected, at a macrocosmic level, are a given culture and all that it produces. This
is to say not only that cultures are subject to change and decay, nor even that they
are incipiently threatened by contact with other cultures, although this latter threat
is not without its importance. But more fundamentally, the very role of a culture—
as provider of rationales and myths, liturgies and symbols, in response to the
individual's quest for identity and purpose—rests on fictions that can always be
exposed as ungrounded by a demystifying mind. Culture as a product of history
partakes of historical contingency and can create only constructs, ad hoc fabrications,
including those codes, images, forms, and metaphors that will govern its works of
art. Contact with another culture is dangerous precisely because acculturation betrays
the arbitrary particularity of each myth and code. Culture exists partly to shield the
individual by imposing mythical patterns on the random chaos of history, but culture
is not itself shielded from fortuitous violence, neither from the violence of the field
of battle nor from the violence of skepticism.

Books are often praised for outlasting violence, but to pretend that their survival
exacts no price is to sentimentalize their "immortality." In fact they reach us as
vestigial fragments of a once living civilization we are unable to reconstruct in its
dynamic fullness. We must labor to restore a power to the symbols and a density
to the codes of an inherited text that will never fully overcome its estrangement.
Thus the text is vulnerable simply through the historicity of its signifiers. The
reader who hopes to bypass this historicity and to appropriate the remote text
immediately as modern will only flounder in the bog of hermeneutic narcissism.
Historicity is a fact that makes the text vulnerable to a slippage of understanding,
just as its origin and the fabricated, arbitrary character of its code or codes have
exposed it to the challenge of alternative codes. One can define this exposure most
simply by noting that any literary text, possessing as it does a specific historical
origin and specific moral style, is always potentially subject to parody.

An analogous vulnerability stems from the involvement of any text in a perennial series of exchanges, allusions, and responses, an involvement that constitutes that dialogic character which in our century has been studied most searchingly by Mikhail Bakhtin. Bakhtin has shown how speech in the novel and other novelistic modes is never pure but is always to some degree invaded by voices other than the speaker's, even if the speaker is the narrator. The resultant interplay of voices within a given discourse always carries with it alternative or antithetical discourses. Bakhtin associates this interplay with what he calls the novelistic, but this category in fact expands to embrace a large part of the canon. Indeed Bakhtin may not have allowed it to expand far enough; arguably, every literary work contains a dialogic element. Every poem contained in a collection maintains a dialogic relation with the other poems surrounding it[2] and also with the antecedent poems of its tradition. This admission of dialogue is an admission of vulnerability, since the poetic discourse is open to the challenge of divergent or opposing utterances, reminding the reader of alternatives, pointing to potential weaknesses, underscoring the partiality of the ostensibly unflawed and complete statement. Although the poetic text may appear to withdraw from the dialogues that make up our daily life, although it may appear to isolate itself from the ongoing extratextual dialogues of history, it only exchanges one dialogue for another. In this exchange, if it deserves our attention, it will neither swerve from its exposure to the alien nor be capable of deconstructing its subtexts; it will remain toward them in a state of dialectical tension. Intertextuality imposes vulnerability.

In a different sense the referential function of language also imposes risks on the poetic text. Poems call into being entities for which no names exist and for which no single term can adequately be coined, since that term would require a definition still to be supplied. Poems thus intensify a problem that seems inherent in language: the signifier tends to possess sharper clarity and firmer presence than the signified. The invisible arrow from signifier to signified is itself a cultural construct, fabricated within history and subject to historical distortion. Poems are commonly located near the border of the ineffable, and in that location lies a willed heightening of the problem of signifying; there lies the danger that the border may be overstepped and the act of reference may fail. The poem participates—and invites the reader to participate—in the quintessentially human quest to fix meanings behind representations, and it characteristically chooses meanings closest to the unrepresentable. Some poems allude to this proximity by invoking the ineffability topos, as though to call attention to their flirtation with failure. Poems act out the noble, persistent struggle to win through to the unnamable, to that which resists reference, and in this struggle they reveal a conative character that excludes absolute fulfillment.

To carry on this struggle, poetry attempts to control and elaborate a fourth condition of language, its involvement in figuration. Poetry employs metaphor and other figures in order to denominate more finely, but in this employment there lies a further risk, since a figure is a kind of wound; commonly it introduces what is a literal non-sense. The poem misuses deliberately the names that exist in order to evoke the unnamable, but in doing this it courts the perilous obliquity of figuration.

The metaphor is perhaps the riskiest of all figures, since it violates literal sense most visibly and since its interpretation requires sensitivity to the particular force of its expressed or unexpressed copula. The metaphor may raise the level of discourse to a "higher" plane, but it also introduces nodes of uncertainty, centers of explosive resonance whose precise overtones may have to remain indeterminate. In the potent metaphor that closes Scève's dizain 378 lies a large (fatal?) degree of hermeneutic indeterminacy. The poetic structure must contain as best it can the violent outbreaks of its tropes.

To speak of the vulnerability inherent in a poem's cultural origin, in its historicity, in its dialogic and intertextual character, in its effort to refer and to name, in its involvement with figuration, is not to exhaust all the sources of potential damage. Each poem runs its own risks. But what distinguishes those poems that deserve our interest is their survival in spite of—or perhaps because of—their risks. Exposure to subversion does not necessarily doom a poem to collapse, chaos, or aporia. We tend to underestimate of late its tolerance of dissonance. A wounding may confer, in Valéry's language, a waking alertness, a power, a fecundity. Thus the analytic phase that registers a text's exposure has to be followed by a phase that asks whether and how the text survives. The reader should be sensitive to the rewards that textual courage can win, the strategies of containment, the harmony beyond dissonance. The idea of a vulnerable text does not exclude it from the tragic hazards, divisions, fragmentations of human experience; the idea assumes rather what might be called the text's humanity. But it also recognizes the possibility of a paradox that is not self-destructive, a tension that is not aporetic, an oxymoron that produces fresh meaning, such as "une féconde blessure." It would be possible to deconstruct that antithesis and the poem that rests on it, but not without the danger of reduction. It might be more rewarding to ask how the oxymoron could hold together, how it could justify itself and justify poetry. The successful poem can be regarded as a linguistic structure in which limits and specificities reveal their profundity, the explosive reveals its brilliance, and oppositions reveal their tensile strength. The poem's vulnerability is not the authorial, Philoctetean neurosis Edmund Wilson analyzed; it is not psychologistic. It might be compared to the relative weakness of the Aristotelian enthymeme in relation to the syllogism. The enthymeme, the principal tool of rhetoric, deals with probabilities and contingencies where the syllogism deals with certainties.[3] Each literary text—also resting on probabilities and contingencies, always failing to achieve the unflawed precision of logic—produces at best a construct, reaches at best a microcosmic, relative stability of which the macrocosm is the relatively stable culture standing as its vulnerable matrix.

The *Délie* of Maurice Scève is a sequence of 449 poems, each composed of ten decasyllabic lines. Most are love poems showing the influence of Petrarch and his Italian imitators. A prefatory poem of eight lines entitled "A sa Délie" is followed by a motto that also follows the concluding poem: "Souffrir non souffrir." Beginning with dizain 6, every ninth poem is preceded by an impresa or device, conventionally if misleadingly referred to as an "emblem." The "emblem" consists of a woodcut picture accompanied by a motto; the motto is then echoed in the final line of the following dizain. Thus emblem 42 represents a bat, with the motto "Quand tout repose point ie ne cesse" 'When all is at rest I do not stop.' This motto is echoed by the close of the following dizain 375.

> Et sur la nuict tacite, & sommeillante,
> Quand tout repose, encor moins elle cesse.

> And during the silent and sleeping night, when all is at rest, still less does it [the poet's soul] stop [admiring and praying to the remembered image of the lady Délie].

Although it is rare for the eight poems following the emblem poem to refer back to the emblem, the dizain to be analyzed, 378, does contain a common element—a troubled night. Although this retrospective reference is not an essential aspect of 378, it deserves to be noted because it involves that poem directly with a dated semiotic construction.

I quote 378 in its original version of 1544.

> La blanche Aurore a peine finyssoit
> D'orner son chef d'or luisant, & de roses,
> Quand mon Esprit, qui du tout perissoit
> 4 Au fons confus de tant diuerses choses,
> Reuint a moy soubz les Custodes closes
> Pour plus me rendre enuers Mort inuincible.
>   Mais toy, qui as (toy seule) le possible
> 8 De donner heur a ma fatalité,
> Tu me seras la Myrrhe incorruptible
> Contre les vers de ma mortalité.

> The white Dawn had scarcely finished adorning her head with gleaming gold and roses when my Mind, which was perishing altogether in the turbid depths of many multifarious things, returned to me under the closed curtains to render me more invincible against Death.
> But you who have (you alone) the capacity to bring favor to my destiny, you will be to me the incorruptible myrrh against the worms of my mortality.

Analysis can begin by clarifying a difficulty at the literal level. Line 6 is somewhat obscure and has led to some scholarly controversy. I follow Dorothy Coleman in reading the return to waking consciousness in line 5 as a return to relative security from death. The sleeping mind has been perishing totally ("du tout perissoit") while unconscious. Wakefulness renders the poet less subject to this psychic foundering, somewhat safer ("plus invincible") in the face of death, but only to a degree. It is the woman alone, "Délie," as the final four lines affirm, who offers a form of absolute protection.[4] Thus Scève's poem is itself about vulnerability; it distinguishes three degrees of exposure to mortality.

This poem is also, like Valéry's, about an awakening, a dawn of consciousness, and in fact certain images associated with sleep in "Aurore" are found in Scève. Valéry writes of the inner darkness ("ténèbres") and gulfs ("abîmes") over which his "Ideas" have spun their webs, spiderlike, during his sleep. The *Délie* is haunted by the fear of an experience of psychic dissolution, the dissipation in confusion of lines 3–4 above, an experience for which the commonest metaphor is *abysme*. Another metaphor is *tenebres*. Often the two appear together, as in another dizain of sleep and awakening, 79, where consciousness is at first swallowed up in

> . . . le profond des tenebreux Abysmes,
> Ou mon penser par ses fascheux ennuyz
> Me fait souvent percer les longues nuictz . . .

> . . . the depth of the shadowy abysses, where my mind through its grievous torments often causes me to pass long nights . . .

Here as in the "fons confus" of 378, the experience of the abyss seems to consist of a disintegration into multiplicity, a psychic unravelment. In Scève there is no counterpart to Valéry's "trame ténue," the fragile web over the abyss that anticipates the fragile texture of the poem. In the *Délie* the *abysme* is naked and fearful. The chasm can swallow the poet even when, paradoxically, he receives from the woman a spiritual illumination: ". . . plus m'allume, & plus, dont m'esmerueille, / Elle m'abysme en profondes tenebres" 'The more she illumines me, the more (I marvel at it) she engulfs me in deep shadows' (dizain 7). Dizain 164 recounts a kind of equivocal awakening from a bitter vortex of consciousness, a "Gouffre amer," which in this case is not bodily sleep but a slough of listless self-abandonment.

> Lors toy, Espoir, qui en ce poinct te fondes
> Sur le confus de mes vaines merueilles,
> Soudain au nom d'elle tu me resueilles
> De cest abysme, auquel ie perissoys.

> Then you, Hope, who at this moment base yourself on the confusion of my futile imaginings, suddenly, hearing her name, you wake me from that abyss where I was perishing.

The substantivized adjective "confus" and the verb "perissoit" link this experience with the disintegration of our original poem 378. The ominous repetition of this motif in the *Délie* and its extension beyond mere physiological sleep permit us to identify the experience of the *abysme* as the dominant traumatism of the work. The abyss of nonbeing is the ontological opposite of that reality incarnated by the female presence called "Délie." The final line of the entire sequence—"Non offensé d'aulcun mortel Letharge" 'unravaged by any mortal lethargy'—seems to affirm at last the speaker's freedom from the abyss of somnolent dissolution. All these passages can be read as a gloss on lines 3–4 of 378. The epithets *confus* (confused, disorderly, uncertain, obscure) and *diverses* (various, far-off, inconstant, strange, painful) evoke a recurrent danger threatening the speaker with cognitive fragmentation. In view of this danger, the image of the bat—emblematic of the soul's nocturnal anguished restlessness—assumes a more sinister coloring. A certain kind of sleep may resemble a certain kind of sleeplessness.

This danger to the speaker can be construed as a danger to the poem as well, since the poem's coherence would normally depend on the speaker's own cognitive coherence. Because the return from the death of confusion is presented as only a relative return, we may ask whether his regained consciousness is firm enough or reliable enough to build a poem on. If psychic incoherence remains a recurrent experience in the *Délie*, then perhaps its poetry reflects a failed struggle for personal integration. Under this interpretation, the speaker's vulnerability would become the work's, and in particular this dizain's. It is significant that the heraldic term *mise en abyme* has been appropriated by modern criticism to mean any structure containing a smaller representation of itself that in turn contains an infinite series of progressively smaller representations. The deconstructive school of criticism has associated this series with the semantic vortex that is alleged to engulf all texts. Perhaps Scève was self-conscious enough to thematize his own text's vortex in his own obsessive *abysme*. To raise this possibility is not to affirm it but to suggest the degree of potential disturbance inherent in line 4 of 378.

The implication of fragmentation is intensified by the quasi-allegorical figure of "mon Esprit," represented as distinguishable from the speaker's selfhood and even relatively independent. The region of confusion where the Esprit is languishing seems to lie outside the essential self, since the Esprit is said to return in line 5. The phrasing suggests that it (he?) has made a conscious decision to return that is not the poet's decision. Does the voice we hear speak for a self into which the Esprit is integrated? We cannot immediately be sure. In one sense, the confused depths lie within the self; in another, they lie outside. We have to strain to intuit the implied epistemology, as we strain to grasp the semiallegorized world that also includes a vaguely personified "Mort" and, in a somewhat different rhetorical register, the mythographic "Aurore." The same world also includes a Petrarchan "toy" apart from these personifications and a "moy" who exists both in their world and in hers. A historical explanation for this commingling of codes would note Scève's transitional position between an older poetic rhetoric dependent on allegoresis and an emergent rhetoric mingling mythography with Petrarchan topoi. Analysis thus leads us to confront the historicity of this poem's eclectic language. The poetry of the *Délie* commonly formulates sophisticated insights through the dramatic interplay of shadowy faculties: le Coeur, l'Ame, Espoir, le Sens, le Desir, Vouloir, and, inevitably, Amour. Sometimes, as in 378, the psychomachias lie in a gray area between weak allegory and sustained metaphor. The vulnerability of the poetry is made more acute by a rhetorical irresolution connected with the inner irresolution of the speaking self.

Our impression of this self is further qualified by the remarkable detail of the "Custodes closes" in line 5. These can be taken as "bed-curtains," as in the translation above and in McFarlane's gloss. This reading is inevitable, but it may also be incomplete. A second reading might be "eyelids." A third would locate the "Custodes" within the speaker to imply a kind of mental curtaining or closing off. There may be a suggestion of protection anticipating the "plus . . . invincible" of the following line (Latin *custos*: guardian, watchman). But there surely emerges as well a sense of occlusion from the external world, and specifically from the gorgeous brilliance of Dawn. The evocation of Dawn at the opening gathers together all that the curtained self must lose. The temporal coincidence presented as the ostensible link between outer and inner world (". . . a peine finyssoit . . . quand . . .") conceals a more important discontinuity. The poet is removed, voluntarily or involuntarily, behind his "Custodes," limited to shades of black and grey, their sobriety set off by the threefold repetition of the syllable *or* (gold) in lines 1–2: "La blanche Aur*or*e a peine finyssoit / D'*or*ner son chef d'*or* luisant, & de roses. . . ." The cosmic coquetry of Aurore, in her gleaming and youthful vitality, draws both on natural adornments ("roses") and precious artifacts ("or luisant") to heighten her seductiveness. Of this immense polychromatic effulgence the poet is deprived, as the poem itself turns away, underscoring the contrast of its own drama, drawing so to speak its *custodes* about itself. Its solution to the threat of mortality will necessarily exclude that universal, periodic, inhuman dynamism but will reach at the end an intuition of eternity that implicitly belittles the brevity of the precise moment when the first glow of auroral white first turns to pink and gold. The criticism works in both directions: the cosmic vitality is excluded from the drama of mortality that follows, but it remains in the poem to set limits to the drama. It is neither rejected nor vindicated; it exists in tension with its antitheses, the mortal man and the immortalizing woman.

At the affective and imagistic pole from auroral brilliance, the Esprit returns to the dormant self, curtained off from all that light. The prepositional phrase "soubz les Custodes closes" can be taken to modify both the pronoun "moy" and the verb "revint"; taken with the verb, it hints at an added effort by the Esprit to pass through a barrier. This return constitutes a kind of reunion, a homecoming that averts, at least on this occasion, a drowning in confusion. It implies a recapture of clear-sighted self-possession by the poet and thus a provisional salvation from dissolution. In the struggle with Death that occupies life, a struggle that ebbs and flows irregularly, this homecoming represents a modest victory; it strengthens the living human's defenses, though not without an ambiguity stemming from the application of the adverb "plus" to an adjective, "invincible," that does not commonly admit distinctions of degree. Line 6 leaves the reader hesitating uncertainly between a comparative and an absolute invulnerability.

The verb "revint" also represents a modest victory in another, obscurer struggle, which might be described as a striving with Petrarch. The verb is actually anti-Petrarchan. The basic pattern of movement in all Petrarchan poetry is a continuous, incomplete repetition of suffering, or a repetitive cycle of suffering and illusory hope. Frequently this cycle spins so fast that it produces oxymorons (such as Scève's "agreables terreurs," an oxymoron in dizain 1 that accompanies his initial wounding by love and authenticates, so to speak, its Petrarchan character). This incomplete experience of suffering may sometimes be evoked in the imperfect tense ("J'errois flottant parmy ce Gouffre amer"), but its commonest vehicle is the iterative present: Petrarch's "Vegghio, penso, ardo, piango" 'I wake, think, burn, weep,' Scève's "Mon mal se paist de mon propre dommage" 'my suffering feeds upon its own injury,' Sidney's "My youth doth waste, my knowledge brings forth toys." This iterative present, with its associations of entrapment, frustration, and (frequently) narcissism, is fundamental to Petrarchan poetry and to the *Délie* (I discuss the iterative present in "Styles" 68–69 and *Light* 119–26). Lines 3–4 of dizain 378, read out of context, would seem to perpetuate a Petrarchan indefinite repetition, depending as they do on a verb in the imperfect tense ("perissoit"), which lacks precise limits. But in the *Délie* this repetition is intermittently interrupted by single, detachable events that are embedded in it but that provide a kind of surcease from it. This is the case with the "revint" of line 5; it offers a salutary specificity. It even offers a glimpsed alternative to the endless cycle of the claustrophobic Petrarchan consciousness—a willed choice of independent, lucid consciousness. The *Délie* assumes a certain vulnerability by admitting these agonistic patterns of experience, but it averts collapse by hierarchizing the patterns. In the first six lines of 378, the specific event overcomes repetition, both in the cosmos and within the poet. Here Scève might be said to tip the balance against Petrarch and thus to make it possible for his sequence as a whole to reach some kind of closure, as the *Canzoniere* totally fails to do.

But from the perspective of the last four lines, the relative victory of reunion and specificity in lines 5–6 proves, uncharacteristically, to have been inadequate. The closing lines go on to present still another pattern of experience, which supersedes the temporary repossession of the self. This new pattern is introduced by the hinge conjunction "Mais" in line 7. It shifts the poetic focus away from the private, curtained interior of the poet's consciousness to an interpersonal relation between him and Délie, here named simply "toy." Délie enters the poem dramatically with the reiterated pronouns of line 7 and the pronoun of line 9, all of which receive accentual stress; the two strong syllables of the parenthetical "toy seule" are adroitly placed to receive particular stress, creating a dramatic spondee that the following mute *e* helps to isolate and lengthen further. This shift of focus, which also exchanges allegoresis for metaphor, does not however split the poem altogether, since the contest with death remains to provide thematic continuity.

The abrupt entry of Délie is also related to the textual striving with Petrarch. Petrarch's Augustinian self-rejection led him, as supposed lover, to an almost total self-involvement. A counterpart of Petrarchan repetition is a certain haziness or even unreality of the woman, who figures in the lover's narcissistic sensibility chiefly as fantasy, memory, angel, or dream. Thus the struggle in the *Délie* against the oxymoronic circularity of Petrarch is also a struggle to make contact with an actual woman. Here in 378 she is suddenly revealed, as the work's subtitle describes her, as an "obiect de plus haulte vertu" (a "source of the highest power"). She is not a fantasy; she has an actual talismanic potency. It is she who will bring "heur" ("favor, good fortune") to his "fatalité" (his "lot" or "destiny"), a word normally lacking in sixteenth-century usage the modern meaning of doom but in this context unmistakably including death. She will not utterly transform this human lot; she will confer an aura of felicity on a course of life whose outlines may remain unchanged. After his death her existence will act as a kind of myrrh, a preservative balm, against the worms devouring his body. This affirmation does not state, as I read it, that there will be no worms, just as line 8 does not cancel fatality. We are left simultaneously with the myrrh and the worms in the state of opposition denoted by the preposition "contre." The copula, which appears here in a very rare (for Scève) and strongly affirmative future tense ("seras"), leaves room for mystery and indeed creates it. But with their mystery these final two lines do offer a stable (though always vulnerable) image of redemption, all the more credible because it includes decay. They offer a continuity that is not Petrarchan.

The pattern of experience of the last four lines might best be described as simultaneity of opposites. The Italian Neoplatonic tradition in which Scève was steeped contained theories of a coincidence of antitheses (Pico della Mirandola: "Contradictoria coincidunt in natura uniali"). Scève stops short of a coincidence to affirm a mutuality of opposed forces, deepening and arresting the Petrarchan oxymoronic cycle to produce, as here, an equilibrated metaphoric paradox. The "seras" of line 9 is really a magical copula, affirming a talismanic and transformative power, a copula that displays its own power by asserting the counterlogical identity of Délie with myrrh. The metaphor resting on this strong copula creates a space for reflection, for exploration and inquisition. It constructs a myth, a fabricated, mysterious assertion of a human power equal no longer to an allegorized external "Mort" but to a personal, bodily, intimate "mortalité." Any single answer to the question of how Délie protects the poet against death—by her exemplary character, by her role as poetic muse—any attempt to salve the textual incision of this metaphoric non-sense would only reduce the space that the metaphor opens for meditation.

The final line is vulnerable of course to a second interpretation, which would read "vers" as lines of poetry. Few readers will fail to weigh this interpretive option, but the decision to adopt it is not easily made. Our contemporary obsession with textual autoreferentiality should not lead us to project thoughtlessly an anachronistic meaning on a work that resists it. Scève as love poet does not thematize consistently and explicitly the act of poetic composition as do Petrarch, Ronsard, Sidney, and Shakespeare. In 378 nothing before the last line would lead the reader to expect this kind of autoreferentiality. It is possible, though not easy, to devise a conceivable interpretation taking "vers" as lines of verse. These last lines might mean that the lover's poetry is destined to oblivion without the saving honor and power of the woman they celebrate. Without her, the poetry could be imagined as languishing, like the Esprit, in a gulf of turbid incoherence. This interpretation *may* be appropriate to lines 9–10, but it has to be forced a little. The metaphor that closes this little poem may be a node of exceptional semantic resonance, but it is also a node of uncertainty. It offers a possible secondary meaning that is difficult either to reject or to adopt, and in this ambiguity it demonstrates one type of vulnerability inherent in figurative language.

What is not ambiguous in the last four lines is the tone of awed reverence attained by a voice whose spiritual serenity is conveyed with luminous expressivity. Tone in any poem is governed by what I have called moral style, that area of meaning where verbal style becomes synecdochic of a recognizable, existential posture, a style of experiencing. The moral style of the *Délie* emanates from the density and economy of its language, from the intensity of the alternating pain and joy, from a certain abstract dryness occasionally shot through with images of sensuous immediacy, from its intricate, sometimes crabbed syntax, from a play with pointed antithesis that can lapse into sterility, but also from a spiritual seriousness that survives despair and engulfment. The stretches of verbal and affective dryness augment the intensity of those privileged moments that reward the patience of both speaker and reader. Dizain 378 concludes with one of these moments, replacing the somewhat jagged hypotaxis and cool manner of the first sentence with the extraordinarily harmonious, warm, tranquil, and voluptuous fluency of the second. The closing lines represent at once a marvelous achievement of rhythm, trope, and tone.

Tone is the slightest of poetic elements: it does not lend itself to structural and diagrammatic analysis; it is easily neglected and easily mistaken. But it plays nonetheless a critical structural role: it hierarchizes conflicting forces through its delicate and subtle pressures. Here in Scève's dizain it validates the final metaphor as a spiritual attainment, privileging it above the initial cosmic brilliance and the repossession of integrated selfhood. The role of Délie in this poem as in the sequence is always vulnerable to a hermeneutic of suspicion; we know her after all only through figures; she might arguably be regarded as merely a Petrarchan fantasy. For her to become what she is affirmed to be, a source of real power, the poetry has to manifest its own *vertu*, its own transformative magic. If we are to believe in the poet's recovery from incoherence, his language must assume a credible coherence. The poem does in fact achieve these things, does deal with its vulnerabilities and dissonances, by means of the calm solemnity that informs its resolution. It does not of course dispel the dissonances it has admitted. As a time-specific construct of codes and fictions, it is always exposed to demystifying skepticism. Its effort to formulate an ineffable and mysterious relationship may always be charged with obscurantism. Its *vers* may prove *mortels*. But it has avoided that equality of polarized components leading to the aporetic *abyme*. It has succeeded in this because its modulations of tone and intensity have made distinctions, have assigned hierarchical values. It has also dealt with the historicity of its inherited traditions by privileging a metaphor over mythography and allegoresis, recognizing and organizing its own cultural past.

A printer's device on the 1544 title page portrays a great rock battered by sea and wind with the motto "Adversis duro," which seems not unfitting to the volume that follows. The phrase would normally be translated, "I endure against adversities." But in the case of Scève's book the more appropriate rendering might be, "I endure because of adversities"; I endure, that is, because of oppositions, antitheses, subversions, paradoxes. Scève's book begins and ends with the simplest and briefest expression of paradoxical simultaneity, "Souffrir non souffrir," which means essentially, "To suffer through contact with transformative power is not to suffer." That is the kernel of unreason at the heart of *Délie*. Perhaps in a larger sense it is the unreason of poetry, fecundated by its wounds. Great poetry assumes the parochialisms, the contradictions, the tensions of the semiotic world from which it issues; it takes them on itself and from them it acquires its tensile strength. Even its violations of its inherited codes pay a kind of homage. If it were to repress the contingencies of its historical moment, the modalities of its particular signifiers, the illogic of its particular tropes, it would interest us less. Each poem is a wager of the mind struggling for mastery over its babble, its obsessions and anxieties, its organizing metaphors, its divergent rhetorics, the expressive limitations of its cultural vocabulary, its distance from its subtexts and its readers, its resistances to closure. The wager is won when the text proves its own tolerance of subversions and its strength of containment, its capacity to confront without reducing. The wager is lost when the text fails to contain, when it fails to organize and distinguish, or when it contains too strictly, leaving no room for the play of meditation. Dizain 378 involves a wager that its construct can rest on a power and a presence known only through an ambiguous analogy. If the analogy collapses, the poem sinks to a confused depth with so many other jumbled things. If the analogy holds, in its oracular and hieratic dignity, the poem remains exposed but coherent, a fragile web, humanly, precariously, sufficiently coherent, enduring within and through its adversities.

Notes

[1] All translations of Valéry and Scève are mine.

[2] This is clear in the case of Valéry's *Charmes*, where "Aurore" and its follower "Au platane" stand in a sharply dialogic relation to the final poem "Palme."

[3] "Rhetoric seeks to discover the means of coming as near such success as the circumstances of each particular case allow." Aristotle, *Rhetoric* 1355b. For the enthymeme's dependence on the contingent, the probable and the fallible, see 1357 a-b, 1396a, 1402b.

[4] Coleman 157–60. McFarlane in a note to 378 suggests that the return to consciousness renders the speaker unprotected, since he had previously been in a trance and thus immune from death (Scève 446). This reading assumes that "plus" should be read "ne . . . plus." Aside from the doubtfulness of that assumption, the interpretation is surely refuted by the statement that the Esprit has been perishing while asleep.

Nerval's "Artémis"

JOHN W. KNELLER

The approaches to *Les chimères* of Gérard de Nerval have followed rather than anticipated the successive stages of literary criticism in France, Great Britain, and the
United States. In brief, they have been extrinsic, intrinsic, and structural. For
current purposes, extrinsic method will be synonymous with projection; intrinsic
procedure will also go by the name of explication or commentary; and structural
system will include not only structuralism but also semiotics and theories of reading.

After the thunderous silence of late nineteenth- and early twentieth-century Lan-
sonian literary historians, who hardly mentioned Nerval in their manuals, practitioners of extrinsic methods prevailed after World War II and took two different
courses. Some applied techniques of other fields, such as psychiatry, biography,
astrology, and alchemy. Others attempted to use texts or parts of texts as a means
of obtaining access to obscure parts of the poet's life. The first group, in their
procrustean determination to make the evidence fit the theory, often stretched the
text to death or cut off its head and feet. The second, by resolving a word, phrase,
or sentence into an antecedent person, object, or event, fell into the genetic fallacy.

In the fifties, following the centennial of Nerval's death, intrinsic approaches took
over and summoned their practitioners to eschew genetic, affective, intentional, and
historical fallacies, to affirm the interiority of the text, and to illuminate its meaning
and form. Projection was clearly put to rout by explication and structuralism. In
1960, I characterized "El Desdichado" as "a coherent, unified statement of an
experience. . . . [It] is complete in itself; it contains its own meaning" (402, 409).
Three years later, studying the same sonnet, Albert S. Gérard wrote: "le poème,
pour être valable, doit contenir une signification perceptible sans références excessives
à autre chose qu'à lui-même" (507). Eight years after the 1963 study by Jakobson
and Lévi-Strauss of Baudelaire's "Les chats," Jacques Geninasca, inspired by Jakobson, published his *Analyse structurale des* Chimères de Nerval.[1] For Geninasca, analyzing a text meant dismantling its system to expose its literary devices, while
respecting the specific character of its poetic language and symbolic thought. His
ultimate goal was to arrive at the author's total system through the properties of
literary discourse uncovered in the process. Thanks to him and to other structuralists

and semioticians, it was no longer necessary to plead for the validity and value of detailed poetic analysis.

Today everyone treats projection with the neglect it deserves. Two generations of Americans schooled in the methodology of the New Criticism and many more generations of French reared on explications de texte have seen to that. Some Nervalists now prefer structural approaches; others continue to practice explication. When most successful, the former have shown that it is possible to be systematic without being totally scientific, and the latter have demonstrated their ability to be interpretive without being utterly intuitive. All, let us presume, would agree that no one can really appreciate a work of art without understanding its form and its matter. For my part, I am willing to be called eclectic. Like explicators and semioticians, I am swayed most of all by the imperatives of the text itself, but I would insist that these imperatives include not only careful analysis of each word or symbol but a respect for the order in which they were written.

Since "Artémis," like the other sonnets of *Les chimères*, is a coherent, ordered statement, I shall try to elucidate its words, images, and devices in the order set forth by the poet. Beginning with the circumstances surrounding its publication, I propose to discuss the title and then take the poem from top to bottom, the way it was written.

Artémis

La Treizième revient . . . C'est encore la première;
Et c'est toujours la seule,—ou c'est le seul moment:
Car es-tu reine, o toi! la première ou dernière?
Es-tu roi, toi le seul ou le dernier amant? . . .

Aimez qui vous aima du berceau dans la bière;
Celle que j'aimai seul m'aime encore tendrement:
C'est la mort—ou la morte . . . O délice! o tourment!
La rose qu'elle tient, c'est la *Rose trémière*.

Sainte napolitaine aux mains pleines de feux,
Rose au coeur violet, fleur de sainte Gudule:
As-tu trouvé ta croix dans le désert des cieux?

Roses blanches, tombez! vous insultez nos dieux:
Tombez fantômes blanches de votre ciel qui brûle:
—La sainte de l'abîme est plus sainte à mes yeux. (Guillaume 18)

"Artémis" was first published, with other sonnets, in *Les filles du feu*, in 1854, while the poet was still alive. Although the manuscript of this version has not come to light, the text, as it appeared, was undoubtedly reviewed by Nerval and is therefore definitive.[2]

The original title of *Aurélia* was *Artémis ou le rêve et la vie*. This datum not only invites us to link the sonnet with the récit but also eliminates any remote possibility that "Artémis" could be an invented masculine form of "Artémise."[3] True, the speaker of "El Desdichado" thinks of himself as a widower ("Je suis le ténébreux, le veuf . . ." [Guillaume 13]). True, the gloss "olim mausole" appears in the margin of the Eluard manuscript next to the word "veuf" of that sonnet. But even if El Desdichado's widowerhood could be compared, mutatis mutandis, to that of Artemisia—the widow of Mausoleus, in whose memory she erected the mausoleum of Halicarnassus, one of the seven wonders of the ancient world—there can be no question about the sex of Artemis or Aurelia. This Artemis is an avatar of the moon deity, a new being whose identity and essential qualities are determined not by classical antiquity but by the sonnet that bears her name. She is "La Treizième" and "la première" of the first line; "la seule" of the second; "la première ou dernière" of the third. She is the one that the speaker loves and "la morte" of the second quatrain. She is, above all, "la sainte de l'abîme" of the last line.

> The Thirteenth One returns . . . once more she is the first;
> And she is still the only one—or this is the only moment:
> For are you queen, oh you! the first or last?
> Are you king, the sole or last lover? . . .[4]

The Eluard manuscript bears a reference near "Treizième" to a note in Nerval's own handwriting: "La XIIIᵉ heure (pivotale)." It is tempting to let this note be an exclusive identification of the "Thirteenth One." Doing so, however, would rob the poem of its inherent richness and complexity. "La Treizième" unfolds the major themes of the sonnet—love, time, number, death, and religion—all at once. The ordinary language of analysis will force us to take them up seriatim, but this simultaneity is fundamental, not only here but elsewhere in the text.

"La Treizième" calls forth a woman. Obviously not anybody's thirteenth mistress, she is the heroine of this poem, already named in the title. She is thirteenth because she is "unique" and "fated." She is endowed, further on, with the common love superlatives "first," "last," "always," and "only": Nerval used these superlatives in the ninth letter to Jenny Colon and in the third chapter of *Sylvie*, and he repeats them here as a kind of exorcism to bring back together the myriad aspects of love that have disintegrated in the inexorable course of time.

Since adjectival nouns in French are more effective in presenting poetic ambiguity than is any possible English equivalent, "La Treizième" not only evokes the goddess and queen but also introduces the "thirteenth hour," because time and love are considered indissoluble. Science easily relates time to space; poetry can, as it does here, relate time to love. Instructive in this matter are two passages in Nerval's *Sylvie*. In this récit, the speaker pauses in the third chapter to describe a tortoise-shell Renaissance clock, whose gilded dome is topped by the figure of Time. On the face of this clock, in bas-relief, Diana, leaning on her stag, is surrounded by the enameled figures of the hours. The clock has not been rewound for two centuries and was not acquired to tell the time (247–48). In the first chapter of *Sylvie*, the speaker, describing the actress with whom he is infatuated, extols her perfections and compares her to the "divine Hours, which stand out so clearly, with stars on their foreheads, against the brown backgrounds of the Herculaneum frescoes" (241). If we bear in mind that "Artémis" was published in the same volume as *Sylvie*, we cannot doubt that Nerval was preoccupied with the reckoning of time and that he associated it with the goddess Artemis when he wrote this poem.

The Lombard manuscript of "Artémis" bears the title "Ballet des heures." This fact makes some examination of the word *heures* essential. The Greek and Latin *Horae* were divinities of the seasons; only by an improper translation from Latin to French have they come to be confused with the hours of the day. The Hours, as they appear in art and the dance, may depict the seasons, the day, or parts of the day: they do not depict any particular hour. In Ponchielli's *La gioconda*, for example, the Hours portray the first faint glimmerings of dawn, then high noon, twilight, and finally night; victory goes to the Hours representing light over the Hours representing darkness. Nerval could well have been unaware of the etymology of this word; he was no scholar. He certainly did not know Ponchielli's opera, which was first performed at La Scala in Milan in 1876, long after his death. But as an enthusiastic and informed devotee of music, dance, and theater, he could not have ignored the meaning of the Hours for the arts. Nor should we.

If the Thirteenth One is nobody's mistress, it is certainly not one o'clock in the afternoon. Rather, it is the pivotal hour, season, or year. Like the small hand on the old Renaissance clock or the shadow on a sundial, time completes one span at a certain instant, then passes on to the next. Depending on whether it is seen ending a cycle or beginning a new one, it is the thirteenth hour or the first—or both.

In the history of humanity, time has been reckoned on the basis of either the solar or the lunar cycle. As early as the fifth millenium BC, in matriarchal Sumer, time was based on lunations, or lunar months—the time from one full moon to another. This period was approximately twenty-eight days. Analogies with the menstrual cycle are inescapable. There were thirteen lunations, or thirteen times twenty-eight days, in a year. To that total (364) was added the extra day between the thirteenth and first month—a unique day that was both the end and the beginning. In the ancient lunar calendar, thirteen was the number of the sun's death month, when the days are the shortest of the year. As a result, it has always had ominous overtones for the superstitious. In fortune-telling tarots, thirteen is the death card. This pivotal, fated, and mysterious number is central in importance and function in "Artémis"; the symbols and themes revolve around it, as the planets revolve around the sun.

The exact meaning of "ou," which appears three times in the first stanza and once in the second, invites scrutiny. It does not indicate an alternative between different or unlike things (the only moment, but not the only woman). It indicates, rather, the synonymous, equivalent, and substitutive character of two ideas (the only woman *is* the only moment). "Ou" enriches the polysemous nature of the entire sonnet. For the thirteenth woman is also the first, as the thirteenth hour is the first. First and thirteenth merge with last and, with the help of "encore" and "toujours," introduce the themes of cyclic movement, recurrence, and permanence.

The suspension points after "revient" and "amant" ask the reader to pause and wonder what is left out, signaling a change of thought. They emphasize the importance of the Thirteenth One, relate her or it to the title, and invite us to ponder all the resonances of meaning that this woman, this period in time, and this number beget. Time fades in the third and fourth lines, as love takes over again. Opposite this "queen"—the multiple Artemis of the poem—the speaker looks at a projection of himself and asks whether he is "king," the first, the last, the unique love, the hero of this drama.

Paradoxically, these complex ideas are expressed in simple language. The stanza contains only two verbs: "revenir," which, followed by the suspension points, evokes cyclic movement, and "être," which appears five times, expressing permanence and essential being. The rhyme scheme (abab) departs from the traditional sonnet form (abba) and emphasizes the oscillation of themes in this quatrain.[5]

> Love the one who loved you from the cradle to the grave;
> The one I alone loved still loves me tenderly;
> She is death—or the dead one. . . . Oh delight! Oh torment!
> The rose that she holds is the *Rose mallow*.

In the first line of the second stanza, taking an aphoristic tone, the speaker tells all living beings to love the unique woman of many names and attributes who figures in this sonnet. To the boldness of simplicity and repetition in the first stanza is added the temerity of the cliché in the first line of the second. The time-worn locution "from the cradle to the grave" relates the apparent polarities of "first" and "last" to human existence, as the speaker strives to resolve them into eternal principles.[6]

This unique woman resides in the realm of the dead. She is the personification of death ("la mort") or the incarnation of death ("la morte"). This juxtaposition is matched by another ("délice" and "tourment"), and the pairs can be shuffled: "La mort-tourment" may be death without expectation of survival of soul; "la morte-délice" may portray the deceased beloved who, as in *Aurélia*, will guide the speaker through a series of trials to salvation. The pair "mort-délice" bespeaks physical death, a joy, with certainty of afterlife; "mort-tourment," physical death, an intense suffering, if not perceived as a transition to another life. Pervading all the couplings is the painful uncertainty concerning death.

This woman, whether death itself, or the deceased beloved, appears in line 8 holding a flower in her hand. The flower she holds is the very one held by Aurélia in the garden scene of the récit that bears her name. Coming at the end in italics, "*Rose trémière*" recalls "bière," with which it forms a rich rhyme—as well as with "première" and "dernière" in the first stanza. Unlike many saints in Christian iconography and many heroines in German romanticism, the bearer of this flower must be associated with the multiple Artemis of this poem, who opposes them. That is the significance of "*Rose trémière*."[7] Standing midway in the sonnet, the one who holds it embodies the themes presented in the first part and those that will appear in the second.

A frequent attribute of saints in Christian iconography, "rose" appears four times in the sonnet: twice here; once in line 10; once, in the plural, in line 12. By metonymy, it is manipulated to stand for Artemis, for saints who oppose her, and ultimately for the opposing religions that those saints embrace.

> Neapolitan saint with hands full of fires,
> Violet-hearted rose, flower of Saint Gudula:
> Have you found your cross in the wilderness of heaven?

In Nerval's sonnets, the first two lines of the sestet often contain the key to the entire poem. These two are perhaps the most famous that he ever wrote. Maurice Barrès supposedly took delight in repeating them; Tristan Derême honored them with a poetic "garland"; François Constans considered them to be at the heart of Nerval's thought.[8] The repetition of vowel sounds ("*sainte-mains*," "napolit*aine*-pl*eines*") explains some of that charm, but to appreciate the verses fully, one must read them in context.

The "Neapolitan saint" cannot possibly be the one who holds the rose mallow in line 8, nor can she be the saint of the abyss in the last line. On the Eluard manuscript—which, let us recall, is not the basis for the final version of this poem—the name "Rosalie" appears next to "la sainte de l'abîme" of line 14, leading some commentators to assume that the Neapolitan saint, the saint of the abyss, and Saint Rosalie were all one and the same. Such an interpretation pushes poetic ambiguity to the brink of chaos. The memories that might have gone into the making of these tercets are legion. Rosalie (in reality a Sicilian saint) appears in works that Nerval read, as well as in works that he wrote. But even if my approach did not exclude extrinsic matters of this sort, except where they are essential to an understanding of the text itself, I could not avoid the observation that if Nerval had wanted Rosalie in this poem, he would not have taken such pains to keep her out.

The Neapolitan saint is, on the contrary, a person consecrated in this poem to arouse devotional memories or feelings of holiness. Instead of bearing a flower, as one might expect, she holds a lantern, or lights. This is a nice twist, because Gudula, patron saint of Brussels, is usually represented with a lantern. According to tradition, this lantern, symbolizing the faith, went out and was then miraculously relit by Gudula's prayer. On the Lombard manuscript, Nerval originally wrote "soeur de Sainte Gudule." By replacing "soeur" with "fleur," he not only avoided sibilant cacophony but also achieved a synthesis of the two saints, the Latin and the Nordic. This new saint stands in opposition to the Artémis of this poem.

The eleventh line completes the apostrophe. The speaker asks the combined saint of the previous two lines whether she has found her cross (her salvation), in the wilderness of heaven. Has she been as fortunate, for example, as Saint Helena, mother of Constantine I, who, according to tradition, found a relic of the true cross near Calvary in 326 (an event usually called the invention of the cross)? Obviously not, since the heavens are empty. The ironic tone here recalls the defiance of Nerval's "Antéros," the despair of his "Le Christ aux oliviers," and Musset's 1842 satire,

"Sur la paresse": "Et, pour qui joint les mains, pour qui lève les yeux, / Une croix en poussière et le désert aux cieux . . ." (416).

Nerval originally wrote, "l'abîme des cieux." Let's be grateful for the change, for the ambiguity of associating "abîme" with a saint of heaven as well as with the saint of the last line would have been sloppy rather than poetic.

> White roses fall! You insult our gods:
> Fall, white phantoms, from your burning heaven:
> The saint of the abyss is saintlier in my eyes!

Falling roses constitute a familiar symbol of the victory of Christian faith over death. When Saint Rosalie died, cherubs are said to have rained roses upon her body. In the denouement of Goethe's *Faust*, part 2, after the death of the hero, Mephistopheles speaks ironically of his disciple's fate. The angels answer with hymns, and a shower of roses falls on the ground, signifying that Faust, who has repented at the last moment of his life, will be saved. Even Mephistopheles is moved by the scene and, for a moment, begins to doubt his own denial of faith. The sense of this sonnet is, however, quite different. The speaker doubts the efficacy of forgiveness symbolized by falling roses. For him they are "white ghosts" ("fantômes blancs"), and they insult his gods—that is, the gods who preceded monotheism. It is Artemis, the saint of the abyss, who is holier in his eyes, for she has twofold saintliness: she is the symbol of pre-Christian, polytheistic faith and the embodiment of an eternal beloved woman.

Some of Nerval's works lie close to the events that he witnessed, encountered, underwent, or lived through as he wrote them, but this poem does not. "Artémis" is not the transcript of a particular poetic experience, nor is it a "song without words" or "pure poetry," as some readers have suggested. It is a profound meditation on time, love, faith, life, and death. Not a word in it is haphazard or empty of meaning. In my view, it is the most ambitious, the most carefully elaborated, and the most beautiful of this great poet's writings.

Notes

[1] Following this brilliant study, Geninasca produced another, *Les chimères de Nerval*, in which he furthered his intention to arrive at the author's total system. In this second book, he gives a detailed history of the exegetical approaches to Nerval's sonnets and evaluates Gérard's method and mine (66–70). These two books followed a study in the Archives des Lettres modernes, *Une lecture d' "El Desdichado,"* where he also considers our methods (10–14, 66–70).

[2] Two earlier versions of this sonnet exist in what are known as the Lombard and the Eluard manuscripts (included in Guillaume). Since they have been discussed many times and in detail by others, I shall mention them only where they shed light on a particular passage.

With the exception of "El Desdichado," "Artémis" has received more commentaries than has any other sonnet of Nerval. I shall not attempt to deal with all of them. The studies by Geninasca, mentioned above, and Rinsler are not only well informed but perceptive. Constans's article is still important and useful. Jean Richer devotes an entire chapter to this sonnet. He stresses the exemplary fidelity of Catherine de Médicis and Marie-Félice des Ursins (Orsini), immortalized in famous monumental tombs to their husbands, King Henry II (at Saint-Denis), and the Duke of Montmorency (at Moulins). Nerval compared these illustrious women to Artemisia.

[3] Lebois would like us to consider whether Nerval did in fact play on words and invent a masculine for Artemisia: "Il serait, lui, Artémis, le veuf, l'inconsolé" (21). The idea is farfetched, if not ridiculous.

[4] All translations are mine unless otherwise noted.

[5] After a rapid analysis of the rhyme scheme in this sonnet, Geninasca, quoting Jakobson, concludes:

> These facts are interpretable to the extent that one may wish to refer them to the poetic function which 'projects the principle of the equivalence of the axis of selection on the axis of combination.' The semantic oppositions, which join the words of given verse or syntagm, are more surely perceived if they are indexed by the phonic-positional parallelism of the rhyme. (*Analyse* 107–08)

[6] It is idle to speculate on the source of this common expression. The sentence from *Faust*, "Dass von Wiege bis sur Bahre / Kein Mensch den alten Sauerteig verdaut" (Nerval's translation: "Depuis le berceau jusqu'à la bière / Aucun homme ne peut digérer le vieux levain" [Goethe, *Faust: Les textes en deux langues* 134–35]) simply uses the trite phrase as the equivalent of "during his lifetime."

[7] As for the note "Philomème" written by Nerval on the Eluard manuscript next to "*Rose trémière*," André Rousseaux and others after him have correctly concluded that Saint Philomena, the virgin martyr, whose tomb was discovered in 1802 in the catacombs, has nothing to do with the woman who figures here ("Sur trois manuscrits" 163–65). It is likewise unnecessary to elaborate further on what roses meant to Nerval or whether he possessed any knowledge of the false etymology of "trémière" (*trans mare*: "outremer").

[8] Rousseaux, "Un déjeuner"; Constans 340. In the Lombard manuscript, Nerval wrote, "*O Sainte de Sicile* aux mains pleines de feux" (Guillaume 46; my emphasis). By opting for the final version, the poet avoided a cacophony of sibilants and an unfortunate repetition of the sound *o* ("O . . . aux").

Reading as Explication

Mallarmé's "Toast funèbre"

JAMES LAWLER

Explication, Michael Riffaterre has observed, is "a machine to tame the literary work, to take away its virtue by returning it to customary paths" (*La production* 8; trans. mine). His comment is not easy to dismiss: the traditional French method with its claims to scientific exactness has often appeared synonymous with facile demonstration. But one may consider that its procedures are not wholly misguided. It places primary emphasis on the text itself; it strives for an orderly analysis; it seeks to be answerable to the linear experience of reading; above all, it bears witness to the diverse levels of style and thought that are not reducible to a simple equation. Theoretically at least, it is as multiple as the text will allow. And if explanation suggests a naive program of critical inquiry, one can recall that explication is etymologically an unfolding—"pli selon pli," as Mallarmé writes with a view to his orphic explication of the earth—revealing patterns of significance that are substantial texture. In this perspective, I wish to apply it to a key poem of symbolism, the subtlety of which may best serve to justify such a study.

Toast Funèbre

O DE NOTRE BONHEUR, toi, le fatal emblème!

Salut de la démence et libation blême,
Ne crois pas qu'au magique espoir du corridor
J'offre ma coupe vide où souffre un monstre d'or!
5 Ton apparition ne va pas me suffire:
Car je t'ai mis, moi-même, en un lieu de porphyre.
Le rite est pour les mains d'éteindre le flambeau
Contre le fer épais des portes du tombeau:
Et l'on ignore mal, élu pour notre fête
10 Très simple de chanter l'absence du poëte,
Que ce beau monument l'enferme tout entier:
Si ce n'est que la gloire ardente du métier,
Jusqu'à l'heure commune et vile de la cendre,
Par le carreau qu'allume un soir fier d'y descendre,
15 Retourne vers les feux du pur soleil mortel!

Magnifique, total et solitaire, tel
Tremble de s'exhaler le faux orgueil des hommes.
Cette foule hagarde! elle annonce: Nous sommes
La triste opacité de nos spectres futurs.
20 Mais le blason des deuils épars sur de vains murs
J'ai méprisé l'horreur lucide d'une larme,
Quand, sourd même à mon vers sacré qui ne l'alarme,
Quelqu'un de ces passants, fier, aveugle et muet,
Hôte de son linceul vague, se transmuait
25 En le vierge héros de l'attente posthume.
Vaste gouffre apporté dans l'amas de la brume
Par l'irascible vent des mots qu'il n'a pas dits,
Le néant à cet Homme aboli de jadis:
"Souvenirs d'horizons, qu'est-ce, ô toi, que la Terre?"
30 Hurle ce songe; et, voix dont la clarté s'altère,
L'espace a pour jouet le cri: "Je ne sais pas!"

Le Maître, par un œil profond, a, sur ses pas,
Apaisé de l'éden l'inquiète merveille
Dont le frisson final, dans sa voix seule, éveille
35 Pour la Rose et le Lys le mystère d'un nom.
Est-il de ce destin rien qui demeure, non?
O vous tous, oubliez une croyance sombre.
Le splendide génie éternel n'a pas d'ombre.
Moi, de votre désir soucieux, je veux voir,
40 A qui s'évanouit, hier, dans le devoir
Idéal que nous font les jardins de cet astre,
Survivre pour l'honneur du tranquille désastre
Une agitation solennelle par l'air
De paroles, pourpre ivre et grand calice clair,
45 Que, pluie et diamant, le regard diaphane
Resté là sur ces fleurs dont nulle ne se fane,
Isole parmi l'heure et le rayon du jour!

C'est de nos vrais bosquets déjà tout le séjour,
Où le poëte pur a pour geste humble et large
50 De l'interdire au rêve, ennemi de sa charge:
Afin que le matin de son repos altier,
Quand la mort ancienne est comme pour Gautier
De n'ouvrir pas les yeux sacrés et de se taire,
Surgisse, de l'allée ornement tributaire,
55 Le sépulcre solide où gît tout ce qui luit,
Et l'avare silence et la massive nuit.

Oh you, fatal emblem of our happiness! Greeting of madness and pale libation,
do not think that I offer to the corridor's magical hope my empty cup in which a
golden monster is suffering. Your appearance will not satisfy me, for I myself put
you in a place of porphyry. The ritual is for the hands to extinguish the torch
against the thick iron of the gates of the tomb, and having been chosen for our
very simple feast of singing the poet's absence, one cannot fail to recognize that
this fine monument contains him entire. And yet the ardent glory of the craft,
until the common vile hour of ashes, returns, through the windowpane lit by an
evening proud to descend there, toward the fires of the pure mortal sun!

Magnificent, total and solitary, in such a way does men's false pride tremble to express itself. That haggard crowd! It announces: we are the sad opaqueness of our future specters. But, with the heraldry of mournings spread out on vain walls, I scorned the lucid horror of a tear when, deaf even to my sacred verse that does not stir him, one of the passers-by, proud, blind and mute, the host of his vague shroud, changed into the virgin hero of posthumous waiting. Vast gulf brought into the misty mass by the angry wind of the words he did not utter, Nothingness to this man abolished of yore: "O you, memories of horizons, what is Earth?" So howls this dream; and space, a voice whose clarity wanes, has this cry for plaything: "I do not know!"

The Master, by a profound eye, as he passed, has quieted the troubled marvel of Eden whose final shiver, in his voice alone, awakens for the Rose and the Lily the mystery of a name. Is there nothing that remains of this destiny? Oh all of you, forget a dark belief. Splendid eternal genius has no shadow. Solicitous of your desire, I wish to see, in honor of the tranquil disaster, a solemn aerial agitation of words survive him who vanished yesterday in the ideal duty prescribed to us by the gardens of this planet—drunken purple and great clear chalice that, rain and diamond, the diaphanous glance, as it remains there on those unfading flowers, isolates amid the hour and the radiance of day!

It is already the whole place of our true groves where the pure poet's broad and humble gesture wards off dream, enemy of his ordination: so that, on the morning of his high repose, when as for Gautier ancient death consists of not opening sacred eyes and remaining silent, there shall rise up, as tributary ornament of the pathway, the solid sepulchre where lies all that harms, and mean silence, and massive night. (Œuvres 54–55; trans. mine)

"Toast funèbre" is not a neglected work; on the contrary, it has received searching attention since a first critique by Thibaudet in 1912. The readings, for the most part, have been line-by-line exegeses, useful in discussing particular images and parallel texts from other writings of Mallarmé. (Lloyd J. Austin refers to more than twenty-five detailed discussions of the poem.) Though the best commentaries are meticulous, they tend to treat the poem as a puzzle to be solved and to leave its form and worth undetermined. One may, however, turn to the latest approach, which posits the "undecidability" of the text. The meaning is held to be equivocal, and this very equivocalness becomes the central value: " 'Toast funèbre,' " Leo Bersani writes, "is perhaps most interesting as an extremely oblique dismissal of the poet to whom it pays a tribute"; again: "In 'Toast funèbre' Gautier's apparent gift for seeing the world is implicitly treated as an anti-poetic illusion"; again: "The obscurity of 'Toast funèbre' may have less to do with the difficulty of specific verses than with the ultimately undecidable nature of Mallarmé's tribute to Gautier" (28, 31, 32). Bersani's analysis has the merit of bringing traditional readings into question, of suggesting a subversive intention, of facing the problem of evaluation. The following remarks are a response that seeks to read the poem in largely different terms and with particular reference to its formal aspects—genre, versification, language—which have, I think, been neglected.

One may begin with the circumstances of the writing. "Toast funèbre" was composed in 1873, in the disorder of post-Commune Paris. Mallarmé had recently returned to the capital after eight years in the provinces, which included the crisis of his Tournon years when he undertook to invent a radical poetics. He laid out in detail the plans of his future work, but "Toast funèbre," to be sure, was not yet among them. Gautier died on 22 October 1872, and within a few days his son-in-law Catulle Mendès proposed a collective volume to honor the dead poet. The pretext would be a wake during which each poet would rise to salute a facet of the dead master's talent—"l'un des côtés du talent de leur maître mort" 'one of the aspects of their dead master's talent.' Each would address an image of Gautier, using the *tu* form, at least in the beginning; each poem would be approximately sixty lines in length, arranged in stanzas; and the initial rhyme would be feminine, the last masculine, to conform to a single pattern.[1] Mallarmé had known Mendès for several years so that, not surprisingly, he was invited to submit a poem; but whereas some of the forty-two other authors were allotted specific themes—thus, Mendès asked François Coppée to develop Gautier's "tendresse"—Mallarmé chose to celebrate the seer:

> Commençant par *O toi qui* . . . et finissant par une rime masculine, je veux chanter en rimes plates une des qualités glorieuses de Gautier; le don mystérieux de voir avec les yeux (ôtez mystérieux). Je chanterai le *voyant*, qui, placé dans ce monde, l'a regardé, ce que l'on ne fait pas.

> Starting with "Oh you who . . ." and ending on a masculine rhyme, I want to praise, in couplets, one of Gautier's glorious qualities: the mysterious gift of seeing with his eyes (delete mysterious). I shall celebrate the seer who, set down in this world, has looked at it, which is something that people do not do. (*Correspondance* 2: 37)

These lines have an elliptic vagueness, as Bersani has pointed out; but is he right to find an implicit discrepancy in Mallarmé's references to Gautier as artist of the real and artist of mystery? "Voyant" tells us otherwise: it echoes Gautier's use of the word in his 1868 preface to the posthumous edition of *Les fleurs du mal*, which singles out the visionary element in Baudelaire for praise, just as in his essay of 1859 Baudelaire had hailed Gautier's visionary genius.[2] Gautier writes:

> . . . il ne faut pas oublier que Baudelaire, bien qu'on l'ait souvent accusé de matérialisme, reproche que la sottise ne manque pas de jeter au talent est, au contraire, doué à un degré éminent du don de *spiritualité*, comme dirait Swedenborg.

> . . . one must not forget that Baudelaire, although he has often been taxed with materialism, which is a reproach that fools never fail to level at talent, is on the contrary eminently endowed with the gift of *spirituality*, as Swedenborg would say.

And he pursues, making use of the biblical and gnostic term:

> Il possède aussi le don de *correspondance*, pour employer le même idiome mystique, c'est-à-dire qu'il sait découvrir par une intuition secrète des rapports invisibles à d'autres et rapprocher ainsi, par des analogies inattendues que seul le *voyant* peut

saisir, les objets les plus éloignés et les plus opposés en apparence. Tout vrai poète est doué de cette qualité plus ou moins développée, qui est l'essence même de son art.

He also has the gift of *correspondences*, to use the same mystical language; that is to say he can by a secret intuition discover relations invisible to other men and bring together, by unexpected analogies that only the *seer* can grasp, the most distant and most apparently disparate objects. Every true poet has this quality in more or less developed form, and it is the very essence of his art.   (31)[3]

Rimbaud read Gautier's preface and, in his 1871 letter to Demeny, used *voyant* to describe what was for him the supreme poetic quality. Mallarmé adopts it in a similar sense: whereas Coppée would show the warmth of Gautier's reputedly cool art, Mallarmé would treat its insightfulness, not its reputed objectivity. The theme is, then, a tribute to the talent that Gautier shares with genuine poets. The master, who described himself as "un homme *pour qui le monde visible existe*" 'a man *for whom the visible world exists*' (Goncourt and Goncourt 103), saw things as others do not, in relation to an ideal; going beyond the surface, he captured mysteriously, necessarily, the sign and sense of the visible world.

Nevertheless, given this theme, one must wonder how Mallarmé came to find the distinctive diction and form of "Toast funèbre." His art in this case does not derive from Baudelaire, although Baudelaire played a decisive role in his growth; nor does it come from Gautier, nor from Banville, nor yet from Poe, despite fugitive echoes of each of these authors. The crucial text, I believe, was Hugo's "A Théophile Gautier," which, though it appeared in 1873 in the same volume as "Toast funèbre," was written before Mallarmé's poem. Hugo dated his manuscript 2 November 1872, which was All Souls' Day, and sent a copy to Catulle Mendès from Guernsey two days later.[4] It is thus clear that, from an early stage in the preparation of the commemorative volume, Mendès had Hugo's text in hand, and nothing could be more natural than to share it with his collaborators at one of their meetings. However this may be—and certainly we have no documentary proof—the Hugo and Mallarmé poems have much in common: both are written in rhyming couplets; both are divided into five parts; both describe a pagan ritual—"la porte funéraire" of Hugo, "le fer épais des portes du tombeau" of Mallarmé—that reverses Christian imagery of personal survival; both use paradox as the central rhetorical figure (life is darkness, death is glory); both bring together certain key words such as the rhyme "Gautier"-"altier"; both identify the destiny of the dead poet with that of the self in an un-Parnassian, characteristically Hugoesque manner. But above all, a combined gravity and warmth of tone link the two poems. We remember the lines in Hugo: "Je te salue au seuil sévère du tombeau . . ."; "Car entrer dans la mort c'est entrer dans le temple . . ."; "Passons; car c'est la loi; nul ne peut s'y soustraire . . ."(105–06)—and a similar accent resonates in "Toast funèbre." Mallarmé adopts the register and develops the elevation and awe that in one or two lines of his poem—"Vaste gouffre apporté dans l'amas de la brume / Par l'irascible vent des mots qu'il n'a pas dits . . ."—can seem at first reading like pastiche.

Yet "Toast funèbre" escapes the shadow of Hugo. The vision is not one of poignant decline as Mallarmé asserts happiness, recovery, resurrection by the artwork itself. One detail may serve to point up the reversal of values: at the end of the fourth part of "A Théophile Gautier" we find an admirable line: "J'écoute ce grand vent sublime évanoui." The words have exceptional strength because of the rhythmic and semantic insistence of "grand vent," the effacement of the caesura, the positional balance and semantic contrast of "écoute" and "évanoui." The sense is one of universal pathos. But this line is also Mallarméan in that emptiness (Hugo's "évanoui") receives a positive value, not as the audible depth of silence but as the form in which the image of beauty will reveal itself (Mallarmé's "coupe *vide*," "*vains* murs," "*s'évanouit*"). To Hugo's lament for a dead friend and a vanishing age, Mallarmé responds by a poem of mortality overcome in death.

He writes in the formal tradition of the epitaph or threnody. He obeys Mendès's recommendations, conforms to the desiderata of length and arrangement of rhymes, but orients the mode along personal lines as "The Raven" had taught him—speaking of death, inhabiting the space of "Nevermore." A tension is created that takes the genre beyond dirge and panegyric to the dramatic exorcism of death by beauty, night by dawn, chaos by language, reality by mystery. A series of oppositions— turns and counterturns—sets the action in the poetic texture itself, beyond any anecdotal representation, as measure and timbre assert a visionary confidence. The funeral ode inscribes a salute to death that frees the work from the degradations of time. The alexandrine is the meter—"notre instrument si parfait . . . ," Mallarmé said (*Œuvres* 868)—of public solemnity. But the pattern is modified in ways that have been learnt from Hugo and that assume Hugo's liberties: for example, the displacement of the caesura. The mold is not broken, but in a quarter of the cases— that is, fourteen lines out of fifty-six—the accent is thrown forward in the line by an energetic thrust as dramatic rhythm contends with symmetry. (When speaking of Mallarmé's prose Claudel used an expression wholly suited to "Toast funèbre": "Le dessein en projection de votre phrase . . ." 'the forward thrust of your sentence pattern' [53].) Mallarmé's line is not that of "L'après-midi d'un faune," composed of brusque transitions and unexpected breaks; where the soliloquy is bathed in summer intoxication, "Toast funèbre" moves with deliberate impetus.

One must however speak not only of the shape of individual lines but also of the voice that Mallarmé forges for his poem. Valéry was no doubt referring to the late works when he said of Mallarmé that it is "la faculté de parler qui parle" 'the faculty of speech that speaks,'[5] for what is true of "Une dentelle s'abolit" does not apply to "Toast funèbre," in which the self strikes an apostrophic note from the start and maintains vocal timbre by repeatedly echoing the vowel of the first invocation, which is also that of the title word "Toast" ("au," "beau," "flambeau," "tombeau," "carreau," "faux," "nos," "hôte," "héros," "mots," "ô," "Rose," "nos," "repos," "au," "Gautier"). The apostrophe imposes itself as a prime phonetic means of amplifying the sonority, of creating a presence. Yet this technique is not isolated; it is reinforced by multiple orchestration. The density of the first line—its solemn vocative, the positional symmetries of "O" and "toi" and of "de" and "le" in each hemistich, the alliteration—gives way to the comparatively discursive manner of the second part, which depends on the introductory sibilance of "salut" (*s* signifies for Mallarmé "incitation"), the force of "démence" (*d*: "une action suivie et sans éclat, profonde"), the liquidity of "libation" (*l*: "tout son pouvoir d'aspiration"), the plosive strength of "blême" (*b*: "les sens . . . de production ou enfantement, de fécondité, d'amplitude, de bouffissure et de courbure . . .") (*Les mots anglais*, *Œuvres* 948, 950, 958, 929).

But after this consonantal energy and its mimological suggestions for phonetic and semantic development, besides the continuity of nasals juxtaposed to the sharp vowels, a syntactical articulation commands the vocal line, which is that of a lesson deduced from the initial imperative: "Ne crois pas . . . Car . . . Le rite est . . . Et l'on ignore mal. . . ." However, the argument turns on itself with the adversative "Si ce n'est que . . . ," which is the saving insight. The intonation falls until line 12, when the change occurs that carries the section to its lapidary resolution. The third part is introduced by three adjectives that have a superlative denotation; while the inversion is recalled structurally by the answering adjectives of line 23 ("fier, aveugle et muet"). The syntax traces thereby a concave parabola similar to that of the previous lines, although the adversative comes much earlier: "[le faux orgueil des hommes] tremble . . . Cette foule . . . annonce . . . Mais . . . j'ai méprisé. . . ." Nevertheless a second parabola occurs in the last six lines as the question put by the gulf ("qu'est-ce, ô toi, que la Terre?") is answered by the man's denial ("Je ne sais pas!"), so strong indeed that it will modify the echo of the abyss ("voix dont la clarté s'altère"). We note in this stanza the use of repeated prelusive appositions ("Hôte de son linceul vague . . . ," "Vaste gouffre apporté dans l'amas de la brume . . . ," "Souvenirs d'horizons . . .") and of an ablative absolute in line 20, both of which throw forward the weight of the phrase and at the same time highlight the metaphoricity. In the fourth section, which begins in apparently anecdotal manner, a new pattern of affirmation and counteraffirmation governs thought and voice: "Le Maître . . . a . . . apaisé . . . Est-il de ce destin . . . O vous tous, oubliez . . . Le splendide génie éternel n'a pas . . . Moi, je veux voir. . . ." The apostrophe of line 37 initiates a reversal that translates the *passé composé* of the opening into the present tense and anticipated future of the last lines. The work of the master is taken up by the disciple, and the syntax projects the center of the lines (by displaced caesuras, adverbial and adjectival phrases, appositions) and the center of the sentences (by a series of inversions, the most surprising of which, "A qui s'évanouit" in line 40, precedes the semantically contrasting infinitive, "survivre," that commands it). Finally, the fifth stanza is written as a universal truth introduced by an impersonal construction: "C'est de nos vrais bosquets . . . Où le poète . . . a pour geste . . . De l'interdire . . . Afin que . . . [le sépulcre] surgisse. . . ." These nine lines, like the nine lines of the second half of the fourth section, are a single sentence in which "surgisse" recalls the parallel articulatory force of "survivre" in line 42. As in the three previous stanzas, the syntax inscribes a concave parabola: intonation turns on the subjunctive of line 54, which, thrust at us by the intervening adverbial phrase and clause, leads the poem to its brief exultant climax.

Meter, sound, and syntax reveal much, then, of this ode to the absent poet, which is Mallarmé's attempt to create a presence in absence. The language, similarly, goes beyond normal poetic usage in order to establish a domain of its own. Whereas the poignancy of "A Théophile Gautier" comes in large measure from its intermixture of the familiar and the mythological, Mallarmé has recourse to an art of abstraction. Thus he develops the phonetic series of "bonheur," "horreur," "honneur," "heure"; of "espoir," "gloire," "devoir"; of "démence," "absence," "croyance," "silence"— a mutually reinforcing incantation that succeeds in personifying abstraction. We may look at lines 16 and 17: "Magnifique, total et solitaire, tel / Tremble de s'exhaler le faux orgueil des hommes." The abstract subject is treated with a dramatic power unlike that of any allegory. The three epithets designate an ambition that contrasts with the sham of "faux orgueil"; "tremble" and the unusual reflexive "s'exhaler," uniting "s'exprimer," "exhaler," and "expirer" in the multiple senses of an ultimate expression, provide a context of physical and emotional effort; at the same time, "orgueil" will lead to "blason des deuils" in line 20, which ironically points to an ambition that sees no further than death. One could cite many such cases, which are a prime mark of "Toast funèbre"—the idea being apprehended as an active image that is defined in relation to the whole. And this applies not only to words in phonetically allied groups but also, for instance, to the cluster of abstract terms ("néant," "souvenir," "songe," "clarté") at the end of the third stanza:

> Le néant à cet Homme aboli de jadis:
> "Souvenirs d'horizons, qu'est-ce, ô toi, que la Terre?"
> Hurle ce songe; et, voix dont la clarté s'altère,
> L'espace a pour jouet le cri: "Je ne sais pas!"

Nothingness becomes a shrieking dream, space a voice that can maintain its brightness no more, and the dead Gautier—"Souvenirs d'horizons"—an image of the creative self in whom objects recede so that their truth can be apprehended in the far depths of memory. Mallarmé has fled immediacy, and his use of periphrasis invents a linguistic space that allows thought to be envisioned in theatrical terms.

Proceeding from these initial remarks on Mallarmé's language, we find an imaginative coherence of unique intensity. For the title proposes the antithesis that embraces the text in its details, as grief is contradicted by a ritual salute. This opposition is the matrix that will be transposed by consistently subtle permutations. Thus "bonheur" and "fatal emblème" take up the preliminary contrast of the title by applying it to Gautier, who becomes the image that combines regret with rejoicing; similarly, "Salut de la démence" and "libation blême" vary the terms that serve both as vocative (Gautier is this sacred offering who has gone to the ends of unreason) and prelusive apposition (the words being spoken are themselves this solemn offering that is answerable only to an ideal). The same primary antithesis is brought to focus in the third and fourth lines: "Ne crois pas qu'au magique espoir du corridor / J'offre ma coupe vide où souffre un monstre d'or!" The language is not purely ornamental but projects the tension of festive death. The empty glass contains a golden form: poetry offers the writhing image of beauty that is written on the void. Mallarmé's method is not a more or less simple variation of terms but a concerted harmonics, a drama of ideas, a language intellectual and daring. In similar fashion, "coupe vide" and "monstre d'or" will be recalled in line 20 by the "vains murs" on which beauty emblazons a proud image; by the "linceul vague" of line 24 that clothes the poet, who, in death, heroically conquers death; by the "éden" of poetic contemplation in line 33, which like the last rays of the sun captures the world in its essence:

> Le Maître, par un œil profond, a sur ses pas,
> Apaisé de l'éden l'inquiète merveille
> Dont le frisson final, dans sa voix seule, éveille
> Pour la Rose et le Lys le mystère d'un nom.

The golden monster has become this "inquiète merveille" in its supreme moment. Instead of qualifying the dead poet, or his poetry, or the present poem, or the curtains hung on the walls of death like the tapestry of *Igitur*, the metaphorical structure tropes the workings of poetic creation, whose end is immaterial language. No less vigorously, glass and monster will echo in "pour l'honneur du tranquille désastre" of line 42, which is the muted pathos and implicit glory of Gautier's life, and in "pourpre ivre et grand calice clair" of line 44, purple being the color of royal mourning, "ivre" the inspired and agitated form, and "calice" the ritual chalice that holds this poem in which Mallarmé continues the art of Gautier.

Finally, in the last stanza, the tomb—not only Gautier's but that of all poets— conforms to the same funeral salute:

> Afin que le matin de son repos altier,
> Quand la mort ancienne est comme pour Gautier
> De n'ouvrir pas les yeux sacrés et de se taire,
> Surgisse, de l'allée ornement tributaire,
> Le sépulcre solide où gît tout ce qui luit,
> Et l'avare silence et la massive nuit.

The appositive "ornement tributaire" points up the continuity of the idea: here the champagne glass is a sepulcher that takes to itself the elements hostile to poetry and contains them, the scheme showing yet again the image of beauty and the void.

The language of "Toast funèbre" is, then, this acutely self-conscious modulation that illustrates the art it praises. Structuring form and language, the five parts compose the theme, not in any declamatory way—as in the case of Hugo—but with a severe logic. (1) The first line provocatively sets the paradox, postulating the atemporal significance of Gautier's death—"notre bonheur." (2) A series of negations ends on a strong affirmation: Gautier is indeed dead, but his art shines like the daily sacrifice of the sun. (3) Inversely, a series of affirmations ends on a negation: all humans would wish to triumph over death, but their pride is false, and they come to recognize their "triste opacité"; yet Gautier's death is of another kind that brings the speaker to new awareness: not only can he look death in the face without seeking a "magic corridor" of resurrection, but he can scorn sorrow itself ("J'ai méprisé l'horreur lucide d'une larme"). Gautier's future is assured for he has overcome the abyss of chaos and old night; his "Je ne sais pas!" is the cry of the *voyant* who sees with his imagination. (4) Poetic vision is inseparable from the art of naming: Gautier found a true language in the fateful struggle of death and beauty ("frisson final"); in complementary manner, Mallarmé celebrates Gautier in his own poem, his words a sumptuous funereal offering ("pourpre ivre et grand calice clair"), his vision the combined transparency of rain and diamond ("pluie et diamant"), at once stylized nature and art. (5) In his work, Gautier, like all true poets, continues to ward off the antagonistic dream ("rêve" echoes the vertiginous "songe" of the third section), creating an ideal garden for all to know, but the chronological progression of "un soir" (line 14), "amas de la brume" (line 27), and "hier" (line 40) leads to "le matin" (line 51) in accordance with the myth of Orpheus; at the same time the "hôte de son linceul vague" (line 24) becomes, like the Christ, the universal work of poetry, free of mortal coils. The dream will no longer be outside but within the tomb, encompassed and thereby held in check: the sepulchre, or book ("le Livre . . . tenté à son insu par quiconque a écrit, même les Génies . . .", 'the Book . . . attempted unawares by whoever has written, even writers of Genius . . . [*Œuvres complètes* 663]), will subsume the human imagination, since Gautier's efforts converge with those of his fellow poets past and future whose vision is that of the inner eye.

The argument in its bare outline enables us to grasp the imaginative and conceptual mastery of the text. Against the claim of undecidability and the supposed equivocalness of the poet's intention, I have tried to show an exceptionally achieved piece in which Gautier is held to exemplify *voyance*. Going beyond the Hugoesque and romantic lament for lost time, Mallarmé enunciates a theory of poetry that is also a theory of identity: his invocation of the seer is the poetry of the seer, both oracular and didactic. He does not dismiss Gautier in however oblique a fashion, nor does he offer a left-handed tribute: here, at the end of his crisis of faith, which coincides with the crisis of faith of his age (since, as Valéry observed, "Hugo demands Mallarmé"), he establishes his homage on a sequence of periphrases, of interconnected—indeed, concentric—tensions: the poet and personality, the poet and language, the poet and the world.[6] His resolution is proposed in the name of a visionary art that owes its fervor, its sustained gravity, to the presence of death. Before the octosyllabic lightness of his late sonnets, "Toast funèbre" is his plurivalent sign, and high expression, of the poem as mortal struggle and impersonal accomplishment.

Notes

[1] I extract these prescriptions from the letter Catulle Mendès sent to François Coppée, quoted in Monval.

[2] ". . . un maître qui sait douer de vie tout ce qu'il veut regarder" 'a master who can grant life to all he wishes to look at' (Baudelaire, *Œuvres* 2: 121).

[3] Littré calls the extended use of *voyant* a "terme de l'Ecriture Prophète."

[4] On 4 November 1872 Hugo noted in his diary: "J'envoie à M. Catulle Mendès les vers qu'il m'a demandés pour Théophile Gautier" 'I am sending M. Catulle Mendès the verse he requested for Théophile Gautier' (792).

[5] *Œuvres II* 635; likewise: "Mais au fait, qui parle dans un poème? Mallarmé voulait que ce fût le langage lui-même" 'But in reality, who speaks in a poem? Mallarmé wanted it to be language itself' (*Cahiers* 22: 442).

[6] Valéry, who looked at Mallarmé with a filial but jealous eye, saw intellectual and imaginative suppleness as the latter's prime characteristic. A few years after Mallarmé's death he wrote in an unpublished notebook of "cette intelligence disparue qui était plus vaste que la mienne, *qui voyait bien plus de choses dans la même chose . . .*" 'that intelligence has disappeared which was vaster than my own, *which saw many more things in the same thing . . .*' (emphasis added).

Rilke's *Sonette an Orpheus,* Part 1, Number 6

FRANK J. WARNKE

The assumptions underlying this essay in textual analysis have an unfashionable simplicity. I assume that a literary text, though unlike a practical language exchange in its greater complexity and higher degree of organization, resembles such an exchange in its manner of operation. Like other kinds of language utterance, it is often complex, and often ambivalent, but not a total mystery. Whatever the validity of theoretical speculation concerning signification or the limitations of language, it remains verifiably true that, in the practical sphere, language works. A query as to the time of day is understood as such and, whether or not it is truthfully or accurately answered, has an effect on behavior. Instructions conveyed in language will, if competently followed, lead to the learning of a foreign language or even to the successful opening of a cereal box.

The communication of an aesthetic experience is surely more complex than the communication of practical information, but it operates within the same system. The poem tells or questions or exhorts or performs other semantic functions, and, though readers may well and properly debate what it all adds up to, it clearly adds up to something—and not just any old thing the reader cares to make it. When Rilke asks "Ist er ein Hiesiger?," any reader who knows the language understands the question, regardless of who the "er" may be, and understands the negative answer, regardless of what the "aus beiden Reichen" may signify. Assuming a meaningful analogy (though not an identity) between a poetic utterance and a practical one, the reader may perhaps claim the right to abstain from abstract speculation and to engage in interpretation—a human activity of considerable antiquity and established utility.[1]

> Ist er ein Hiesiger? Nein, aus beiden
> Reichen erwuchs seine weite Natur.
> Kundiger böge die Zweige der Weiden,
> wer die Wurzeln der Weiden erfuhr.
>
> Geht ihr zu Bette, so lasst auf dem Tische
> Brot nicht und Milch nicht; die Toten ziehts—.

Aber er, der Beschwörende, mische
Unter der Milde des Augenlids

ihre Erscheinung in alles Geschaute;
und der Zauber von Erdrauch und Raute
sei ihm so wahr wie der klarste Bezug.

Nichts kann das gültige Bild ihm verschlimmern;
sei es aus Gräben, sei es aus Zimmern,
rühme er Fingerring, Spange und Krug.

Is he from hereabouts? No, from the two
Kingdoms his wide nature grew.
More expertly twists he the branches of willow
Who has known the roots of the willow first-hand.

When you're ready for bed, don't leave on the table
Bread or milk; they will beckon the dead—
But him the conjurer, let him compound,
Under the mildness of the eyelid,

Their appearance into everything seen;
Let the magic of earthsmoke and rue
Be to him as true as the clearest relation.

Nothing can spoil for him the valid image;
Be it from graves, be it from rooms,
Let him praise finger ring, buckle, and jug.   (Rilke 490)[2]

One's approach to the reading of any of the *Sonette an Orpheus* must depend to a large extent on one's awareness of the other poems in the sequence. The poem under consideration here is sonnet 6 of the first of the two parts that make up the work. Although it appears early in the sequence, the preceding five poems enable us to identify the "he" of the first line as Orpheus, the god who, as sonnets 1.3 and 1.5 have already informed us, moves freely between this world and the underworld, the "two kingdoms" of lines 1–2. Deriving from the land of the living and the land of the dead, he is not native to either. The unique strangeness thus attributed to him is underscored by the word "Hiesiger": I first thought of rendering this noun as the English construction "from here"; in the original, however, the force is more akin to "someone from hereabouts," "someone from our part of the world"—almost, in its colloquial flavor, "a local boy," but without the faintly rustic, faintly facetious connotation of that English equivalent. (Provincial terms have more elegance and respectability in German than they do in English—an incidental problem in German-English poetic translation.)

Not "from hereabouts," Orpheus has about him an uncanny strangeness (*unheimlich*, a German might say for "uncanny"—not from "home"). This strangeness is, in the opening quatrain, linked with his peculiar power, that of bending or twisting the branches of the willow, and that power in turn is seen as deriving from his experience of the roots of the willow. "Experienced" or "known" are both, in context, weak renderings of "erfuhr," but there's not much else one can do: the original, etymologically linked to *fahren* ("travel," "go"), suggests experience in the sense of "experience of foreign lands, experience of much life" rather than of "experience on the job, experience in handling tools." Hence my version as "has known the roots of the willow first-hand." This "traveled" kind of experience enables Orpheus to bend the branches of willow, creating thus his lyre, a metonymy for poetry or art throughout the sequence (see sonnets 1.9 and 1.19). The willow is, of course, a funerary symbol, an emblem of mourning, and it is clear that Orpheus's experience at the roots of the willow is the experience of death and loss—the underworld where he reclaimed, then definitively lost, Eurydice—and that the art epitomized in his lyre is made of that experience, has it as its very substance.[3]

The first quatrain is thus composed of complex suggestions about the relation of art to death and mourning and, beyond that, of the relation of art to life and, hence, of death to life. It is also a quasi-magical incantation, as a reading aloud of the quatrain will demonstrate:

> Ist er ein Hiesiger? Nein, aus beiden
>
> Reichen erwuchs seine weite Natur.
>
> Kundiger böge die Zweige der Weiden,
>
> wer die Wurzeln der Weiden erfuhr.

The strongly dactylic rhythm, reinforced by internal assonance and alliteration as well as by the heavy stress accent intrinsic to German, makes any oral rendition of the quatrain a kind of chant, the incantatory quality becoming especially intense in lines 3–4. It enables the reader to hear the beginning of the poem as a magic spell, a charm (i.e., *carmen*), and the question-and-answer form of the lines further emphasizes the suggestion of formalized magic ritual. English idiom requires an indicative verb for line 3; in the original, "böge" has rather the force of "might he twist (or bend)."

Magic continues to permeate the second quatrain. A warning is given against an unintended conjuring up of the dead through leaving available to them the fruits of the earth—the bread and milk that might perhaps activate their speech as the bowl of blood does for the dead in book 11 of the *Odyssey*. But, though the presence of the dead is unwelcome as an uninvited haunting, it is urged as desirable under the aegis of the lord of the two realms—Orpheus the conjurer, who is capable of transforming our eyesight so that all earthly things appear under the aspect of death. As "der Beschwörende," Orpheus is "the conjurer," but the word can also have the meaning of "the exorcist," or "one who confirms by oath." Magic powers, those learned at the willow's roots, authorize Orpheus to introduce the dead into the sensuous world, an act that might perhaps be attended by negative or fatal consequences if undertaken by one not so authorized.

Only as seen under the aspect of death do perishable earthly things become permanent and immortal. As Rilke wrote in explaining aspects of his *Duino Elegies* to his Polish translator, "we are the bees of the invisible,"[4] using imagination to transmute the visible and exterior into the invisible and interior and thus engaging in the unique activity that keeps transitory things alive forever. Sonnet 9 of part 1 is helpful as a gloss:

> Nur wer die Leier schon hob
> auch unter Schatten,
> darf das unendliche Lob
> ahnend erstatten.
>
> Nur wer mit Toten vom Mohn
> ass, von dem ihren,
> wird nicht den leisesten Ton
> wieder verlieren.
>
> Mag auch die Spieglung im Teich
> oft uns verschwimmen:
> Wisse das Bild.
>
> Erst in dem Doppelbereich
> werden die Stimmen
> ewig und mild.

> Only the one who has lifted the lyre,
> Even among shadows,
> May guessingly render
> The infinite praise.
>
> Only the one who has tasted the poppy
> Of the dead, while among them
> Will not again lose
> The most delicate tone.
>
> Though the reflection within the lake
> May often swim before us:
> Recognize the image.
>
> Only in the double realm
> Do the voices become
> Mild and eternal.   (492)

The knowledge of the "other realm" is the necessary condition for the praising of the things of this world, and such praise, as sonnet 1.7 indicates, is the essential function of poetry. (Sonnets 1.13–15, along with many other poems of the volume, exemplify this function.)

Being is only complete when nonbeing is recognized as its other half. Life is only complete—only bearable, perhaps—when death is seen as its necessary complement. Knowledge and beauty are possible only when life is kept "open towards death"

(Norton 130). There is no "hereafter," for life and death, being and nonbeing, are ever coexistent and present. One name for the total recognition of this state of affairs is art; another name is love.

The effecting of the impingement of the death-half of reality on the life-half is a magical act, and the incantatory tone and syntax of the poem under primary discussion (1.6) are thus proper, even inevitable. "Magic" ("Zauber") is overtly named in the second line of the sestet, in association with "earthsmoke and rue." "Erdrauch" (literally "earthsmoke") is fumitory (from the Latin *fumus terrae*), an herb that is, like rue, of medicinal value and, through its etymology, associated, like rue, with regret and remembrance: the presence of the dead in everything viewed endows the symbolic herbs with the kind of immediate truth experienced in the most obvious relations of daily life (Norton 142). Equipped with the magic of these herbs, which is also the magic of the willow, the god who is the lord of the two realms is enabled to bestow valid praise. Nothing can spoil for him the valid image: in the original, "spoil" is "verschlimmern" ("to turn worse," "to take a turn for the worse," in context, perhaps, "to cause to take a turn for the worse"). The connotations are appropriate to the temporal and transitory world of sneezes and sickbeds, but in the poem those connotations are no longer relevant. The valid image remains unchanged, just as, in 1.9, the image reflected in the lake remains recognizable. The god is urged to praise, in the last line of the sonnet, three objects— finger ring, buckle, and jug—humble objects of adornment and utility associated with quotidian life but, at the same time, objects frequently buried with the dead.

Whether found in the rooms of the living or in the graves of the dead, these objects elicit and are hallowed by the praise of the poet, and, transfigured by being seen in the double aspect of life and death, they hallow in turn our experience of them. As we are told in 1.8, a sonnet closely related in theme to this one, "Nur im Raum der Rühmung darf die Klage gehn . . ." (491) ("Only in the realm of praising may Lament / go . . ." [trans. Norton 31]). The relation is reciprocal: true lament and true praise condition one another and establish a unity.

The poem creates its meanings and effects its actions by claiming the status of a magical spell or charm. I have noted its heavily incantatory rhythm and the reinforcement of that incantatory effect through the use of alliteration and assonance, and I have remarked also on the magical functions taken on by most of the substantives in the poem, functions that transform images into symbols: the "Weide" of the first quatrain confers the power of creating art; the "Brot" and "Milch" of the second quatrain are capable of conjuring up the dead; the "Erdrauch" and "Raute" of the first tercet are identified with magic; and, in this context, the "Fingerring," "Spange," and "Krug" of the final line assume a numinous aura—without, however, ceasing to be simple images of everyday life. The syntax and the strategy of address of 1.6 fully articulate the magic claim. The poem opens with an interrogation addressed to us, to nobody in particular, or to the speaker himself; it is not clear which, and it is not finally relevant. The question is answered, appropriately if obscurely, in the indicative, and the statement is immediately developed in a further statement, subjunctive, concerning the actions the "er" is empowered to perform, if he so chooses. The second quatrain opens with an imperative, oracular in tone,

at once explained and justified in a brief indicative clause. From this point on the
poem remains almost entirely in the optative mood: "Let" the conjurer mix the
appearance of the dead into everything seen; "let" the magic of the funereal herbs
be real for him; nothing "can" spoil the valid image for him (the single reversion
to the indicative); whether it "be" from graves or from rooms, "let" him praise
finger ring, buckle, and jug.

It is clear, from the combination of incantatory rhythm, magically charged symbol, and oracular syntax, that the business of this poem is to bring something about.
"Poetry," as Auden has told us, "makes nothing happen." But it often *acts* as if it
does, and that is precisely what *Orpheus* 1.6, is doing—as a good many other of the
greatest lyric poems also do. What is it making happen? (Or claiming to make
happen, which is, in art, the same thing.) It is summoning a supernatural being
who is also human—Orpheus—and conjuring him to alter radically the aspect under
which earthly things are experienced. In bringing about this alteration of perception,
it decrees that the experience of the transitory be, without ceasing to be precisely
that, the experience of total being—which includes also, we must remember, nonbeing as a part of itself.[5] The "it" of these last assertions of mine is the voice of the
poem—that is to say, the voice of one Herrn Rainer Maria Rilke, slowly succumbing
to leukemia in Muzot, Switzerland, in 1926; the voice of a persona imagined by
that artist; and the voice of the god-artist Orpheus, mediator between the realms
of life and death.

The last identification becomes other than fantastic in the light of *Orpheus* 1:5,
the poem immediately preceding. Its octave is as follows:

Errichtet keinen Denkstein. Lasst die Rose
nur jedes Jahr zu seinen Gunsten blühn.
Denn Orpheus ists. Seine Metamorphose
in dem und dem. Wir sollen uns nicht mühn

um andre Namen. Ein für alle Male
ists Orpheus, wenn es singt. Er kommt und geht.
Ists nicht schon viel, wenn er die Rosenschale
um ein paar Tage manchmal übersteht?

Erect no monument. Just let the rose
Each year bloom for his sake.
For it is Orpheus. His metamorphosis
in this and that. We should not trouble ourselves

To find another name. Once and for all
It's Orpheus when there's singing. He comes and goes.
Isn't it a lot already if sometimes
He overstays a bit the bowl of roses?   (489)

"Once and for all / It's Orpheus when there's singing"—the habits of his native
language make it possible for Rilke to say, literally, "Once and for all times / It is
Orpheus when it sings." This conveys his vision, and no English translation can
catch it without ceasing to be idiomatic. "Es singt" means, of course, "there is

singing," but it also says, "it sings," suggesting that all of reality engages in singing, and the rest of the quatrain tells us that, when this occurs, the voice is that of Orpheus. All poets, then, are Orpheus, and therefore, in 1.6, the voice that does the conjuring belongs also to the being who is conjured, the being who, in turn, does the conjuring that constitutes the action of the poem. The reflexive quality of these associations is appropriate, indeed necessary, to the conceptions of song, praise, and reality that are the subject matter of the poem.

Since the author of the poem (Rilke, or whatever his mundane name is) is making a poem, he is Orpheus: "Wir sollen uns nicht mühn / um andre Namen." A yet more alarming metamorphosis occurs: the reader also becomes Orpheus, since to experience the poem—in the most simple sense of comprehending what it says— is to assume a particular kind of knowledge that alters one's identity (even if only temporarily, only in illusion—for, speaking of art, we are speaking of illusion). The roots of the willow, the magic power of the herbs, convey and bestow the valid image, and, with it, the Orphic knowledge. One of the most nearly perfect of Rilke's middle-period poems ends with the phrase "Du muss Dein Leben ändern" ("Archäischer Torso Apollos"; 313)—"You must change your life." That is, of course, expecting a bit much, and most of us respectfully ignore the command. Still, as the poet observes in another of the *Orpheus* sonnets (1.11):

> Auch die sternische Verbindung trügt.
> Doch uns freue eine Weile nun
> Der Figur zu glauben. Das genügt.

> Even the stellar relationship deceives.
> But let us now take pleasure for a while
> In believing the figure. It's enough.   (494)

The figure that 1.6 and all the other *Sonette an Orpheus* request—and require— us to believe is one that participates centrally in the lyric genre. In *Orpheus* 1.6, the figure is the god-man-artist who, having experienced nonbeing as a vital part of being, is able to imbue all sensuous and mundane phenomena with his knowledge. In so doing, he shares his knowledge and thus becomes identical with both the voice of the poem and the reader of the poem. If I contend that the experience of this lyric, like that of most great lyrics, is of a merging with the godhead, with the divine, I hope I shall not be taken as being either mystifying or religious, neither of which I am. I am speaking of a psychological phenomenon, of an illusion perhaps. It is generally accepted that the dramatic genre has its origin in religious ritual, in the enactment of the fate of the god, and that all dramatic works can be viewed as more or less extreme "realistic" displacements of that primal impulse. It has been contended by some (e.g., Frye 136–40) that the narrative genre takes its origin from myth, the chanting of the deeds of the god, and that mythic lineaments are dimly perceptible in even the most realistic of novels. Is it perhaps possible that the lyric genre has its origin in sacrament, in the consuming and consequent merging with the god? (I use the term *sacrament* as a convenient shorthand for those gestures of the poetic imagination that effect the fusion of the self with the totality of being—

or its convenient image, a god. It would be misleading to link the non-Christian Rilke with any specifically Christian sense of sacrament. It is nevertheless interesting to note that at least one minisequence within the *Sonette an Orpheus*—part 1, sonnets 12–15, celebrating the eating of the fruits bestowed by the earth and the dead—depends centrally on the sacramental motif of bodily ingestion.) The severely limited thematic concerns of the lyric throughout its history—passionate sexual love, death, mystical religious devotion, absorbed contemplation of nature, and a few others—have significantly to do with the annihilation of the self and the paradoxical and simultaneous affirmation of that self. The reconciliation of opposites that Coleridge sees as definitive for poetry (12–15) seems to have its lyric version in the reconciliation of being and nonbeing—a theme that appears in radically displaced forms in a Petrarch sonnet, in a Renaissance *blason*, or in a poem like Herrick's "Corinna's Going a-Maying" but that fully reveals its sacramental nature in many lyric poems of strikingly different idiom—Marvell's "Garden," for example, or Leopardi's "L'infinito," or Keats's "Nightingale" ode, or Rilke's *Sonette an Orpheus*. All are supremely sophisticated and artful lyric utterances, yet all remain firmly in touch with the primal sources of poetry in ritual and magic.

Notes

¹ Cf. Jules Brody:

> Soyons donc assez généreux pour consentir à ce que de nouvelles sciences—la psychanalyse, la sémiotique, l'onomastique et bien d'autres à venir—se servent *de* la littérature comme matière première de leurs expériences. Avec ou sans notre consentement d'autres que nous vont mettre à profit les romans et les poèmes dans un but parfois étranger au nôtre. Cette démarche n'est pas par ailleurs sans précédents; les philosophes, les linguistes, les psychologues et les historiens en font autant depuis longtemps. . . .
>
> Étendons notre générosité jusqu'à admettre que des aspects de la littérature soient susceptibles d'être étudiés scientifiquement, que l'étude scientifique de la littérature puisse co-exister avec la critique littéraire sans interférences et sans rivalités. Reconnaissons pourtant qu'une scission existe, qu'elle est réelle, qu'elle n'est pas sur le point de se cicatriser. Mais reconnaissons en même temps que la crise déclenchée ne vise pas seulement la substance de l'activité critique, telle qu'elle se pratique depuis Sainte-Beuve jusqu'à Starobinski, mais son identité et sa mission propres. Au carrefour où la critique se trouve actuellement, ses practiciens ne sauraient se refuser à une prise de conscience et à une confession de foi. Si la psychanalyse lacanienne et la sémiotique sont des sciences, la critique littéraire n'en reste pas moins un art. Les critiques littéraires sont des artisans qui vivent vis-à-vis de la littérature dans le même rapport que les médecins vis-à-vis de la biologie ou de la chimie. Dans la mesure où le critique littéraire ou le médicin exerce un métier, sa tâche principale consiste à constater les données de chaque cas, de s'expliquer à lui-même, puis à son client, ce qui se passe dans son champ de vision et comment il faut comprendre l'objet de son étude. Un médecin, même excellent, peut tout ignorer de la génétique et de la physique nucléaire. Il serait ridicule qu'il se reproche cette ignorance; il serait encore plus qu'il s'en voulût ou qu'il se laissât reprocher de ne pas être généticiste. Quant aux généticistes, ils feraient bien piètre figure

s'ils s'amusaient à taxer les médecins d'être traditionnalistes, réactionnaires et fas-
cistes à cause de leur refus de faire autre chose qu'ils ne savent ou qu'ils ne font:
i.e., traiter des malades. Sans eux, qui accomplirait cette tâche indispensable? . . .
    Le critique littéraire, qu'il le sache ou non, a fait un choix: il s'est donné pour
métier et pour mission de faire mieux connaître et comprendre les œuvres littéraires;
il devrait vouloir bien laisser à d'autres la gloire d'élaborer les grandes vérités
générales *sur* la littérature. Si le critique littéraire n'est rien de plus qu'un médecin
ou qu'un ingénieur de la littérature, ainsi soit-il.   (183–84)

[2] All translations in this essay are mine unless noted otherwise, but I am happy
to acknowledge a debt to M. D. Herter Norton; I have often followed her felicitous
phrasing.

[3] Norton cites Frazer's *The Golden Bough* on the willow as the passport to the
land of the dead (141–42). My colleague Katharina Wilson points out to me that
in Austria the willow is traditionally associated with Easter celebrations; one is
reminded again of the interpenetrations of death and life.

[4] Norton 133. The relevant context is as follows:

> Nature, the things we move among and use, are provisional and perishable; but,
> so long as we are here, they are *our* possession and our friendship, sharing the
> knowledge of our grief and gladness, as they have already been the confidants of
> our forebears. Hence it is important not only not to run down and degrade every-
> thing earthly, but just because of its temporariness, which it shares with us, we
> ought to grasp and transform these phenomena and these things in a most loving
> understanding. Transform? Yes; for our task is so deeply and so passionately to
> impress upon ourselves this provisional and perishable earth, that its essential being
> will arise again "invisibly" in us. We are the bees of the invisible. We frantically
> plunder the visible of its honey, to accumulate it in the great golden hive of the
> invisible. The "Elegies" show us at this work, the work of these continual con-
> versions of the beloved visible and tangible into the invisible vibration and ani-
> mation of our [own] nature, which introduces new frequencies into the vibration-
> spheres of the universe.

[5] Rilke's conceptions of life and death, being and nonbeing, are strikingly
suggestive of the attitude of the ancient Greeks, as reconstructed by Kerényi:

> The modern idea of non-existence is completely empty. For ancient religious man
> non-existence, as the enclosing framework of organic life, was both full and empty
> at the same time.
>   It is not a logically bounded, exactly defined idea, like the non-existence of the
> philosophers, but a reality bordering on all living things. It is only in its border
> region that it can be comprehended at all, for its real core remains the inconceivable.
> In its border region, however, we do approach this inconceivable. We do it by
> intermediate stages, just as we approach non-existence. . . . It was only for the
> philosopher among the Greeks, and not before him, that pure non-existence could
> be separated from existence, the *me on* from the *on*. Ancient religion worshipped
> the gods of heaven and of the underworld, the Olympic and the Chthonic deities.
> Their world was even more of a single whole than the world of later pantheistic
> philosophy. Non-existence had its place in it as a reality of the soul, a "being-
> other" for man. In it both existence and non-existence were equally powerful, and
> capable of appearing in a rout of divine figures which surrounded and penetrated
> the universal whole with radiance and meaning.   (278–79)

The Virtues of Attending

Williams's "The Corn Harvest"

THOMAS H. JACKSON

Literary criticism is of course not a science, and, except to the industrial chemist, a work of literature cannot be an object of genuinely scientific scrutiny. A literary text assumes standing as such by the regard in which it is held by an audience— though this claim is open to qualification. Quasi-scientific conceptions of literature and criticism (Northrop Frye's was perhaps the baldest, structuralism perhaps the most confused) seem to turn on a category-mistake: the assumption that literature is a category of the same sort as, say, frogs. Frogs are *there*, independent of human perception, in a way literature is not. If our age says of an earlier one, "Why, they had x, which was a delightful form of literature, and they didn't even know it," it can only mean that we call "literature" something they did not. None of this is to say that a work of literature is just anything anyone can make of it. Current preoccupations with "free play," with the decentering or deconstruction of texts, seem complicatedly wrongheaded; that a text may be only vaguely centered does not necessarily mean that it is uncentered. The idea that our day-to-day uses of, say, the verb *feel* center on an absence of any basic or core meaning—an absence that by its presence proves the absence of any stability "behind" language—is philosophically infantile.

It seems safe to say that every phenomenon we call a work of art has been in one purposeful way or another formed or set by human hands.[1] Confronting a poem is confronting a part of life, and reading the one cannot honestly be separated from reading the other. One shortcoming of the heady methods-oriented criticism of recent fashion has been its tendency to do just that—to operate as if artistic acts were not humanistic acts; it has returned to the position that text is to critic (usually a salaried academic) as kidney is to medical researcher. Poet and poetic productions are again seen as the mere raw material for academic industries.

However that may be, it seems to me that what is most profitable in the operations of literary analysis is a commitment to articulating the reasons, the logic—not the causes—of the object's being as it is. That is not the end of it, to be sure, for this logic will enable the interpretation or analysis to move outward, into culture, let us say, where, as Geoffrey Hartman has put it, it helps the artwork integrate with other structures (14). Such integration generates in turn new modes or manifestations of significance, and this interplay between our initially internalistic acts of interpretation and their cultural bearing keeps alive those works that do live era after era.

All academic analysis probably falsifies or at least constitutes unrealistic exaggeration. Perhaps only a fraction of the intense intellectual operations we perform on a text is ever actually experienced in day-to-day reading (not that all reading must be day-to-day, or academic, either)—this quite apart from such things as reader-participation theories, which must grossly oversimplify the process of reading in order to operate at all. But the operations proposed in the following pages can yield a meaningful, retainable, and, for what the term is worth, authentic understanding of poems.

The method begins, again, by taking the text as a piece of human behavior. Someone had a hand in making this poem what it is. This applies to anonymous inscriptions and to objects signed "John Ashbery" or "Mary Ann Caws." (Some thing could have been involved, of course, but it would have to be a thing, like a sophisticated computer, that can approximate what humans do, and in such a case analysis would proceed on a much lower, more merely mechanical level.) This postulate immediately suggests various parameters of response; in general it is a matter of applying, bringing to bear, whatever intellectual or emotional frameworks seem appropriate. The frameworks need not be arcane, though they might be, and I shall list a few in a moment. Criticism being the profoundly personal pursuit F. R. Leavis said it is, one hopes that the frameworks will not be arbitrary or stupid or trivial, and one hopes that they will not be stupidly applied, but sometimes they will be, naturally. Though everyone eats, few can distinguish the flavors. But barring outright and obvious zaniness, the choice of frameworks is self-limiting: no one is really likely to try to read *David Copperfield* in the light of its relation to modern manuals on dog training, for example, and if anyone insists on reading it as, say, a guide to the opinions of its author, the proper correctives will not be long in coming. That is to say, despite the appearance of informality in the method in question, verifiability and testing present no real problems outside the realm of inappropriately abstract theorizing.

The method I have in mind starts out from what used to be known to the trade as close reading—nowadays perhaps "mere close reading," or even "nothing more than mere close reading"! It is less a method than a technique, less a technique than a stance, perhaps, and it can include everything from the pleasing proposals in a good undergraduate essay to Barthes's theory of narrative structure and the most diaphanous and philosophically searching meditations of a Geoffrey Hartman. It seems abashingly commonsensical, yet it can by no means be reduced to common sense.

The first step is a perhaps rough and ready version of the overall goal of the undertaking: the pursuit of the implicit question of just how the thing should be taken. This may be the only part of the procedure that can properly be called a "step," because what follows is the adducing of a congeries of resonances or contexts that need not follow any particular order—though the first I shall mention is probably first necessarily: a consideration of the language of the text, the patterns and high-lightings it evinces. A fairly materialistic poring over the verbal features of the text—grammatical patterns, prominent features of diction, and the like—may or may not suggest correlations with certain external relations the work might enter into: philosophical implications, cultural or generic ties that seem to affect the object's significance. The general question is where or how the text fits into one's total experience, and the open-ended ambiguity of that last phrase is of course intentional. The text may impress itself—or one may catch on to it—as a manifestation of a particular genre, or as like or pointedly unlike the usual works of a genre. If there is such an appeal, one wants to account for it and to identify the relations that seem significant. Is the generic pull a comment on the text or on the genre? or even on the way texts make such appeals?

If any sort of narrative force is embedded in the text, questions of shape or narrative style may be important. Mythic associations may also be significant—in fact, it might be interesting to make them important, to seek them out; at this point, of course, the wider cultural bearing of the work comes into question, and one is released from what might be limiting anxieties over intentionality. And so for further aspects of the work's and the reader's cultural ambience—overall, how and where does the work fit in? It is helpful to consider the text in the light of recurrent features of the author's total oeuvre—a version of the principle of inter-textuality, which was a common-sense principle long before Kenneth Burke rec-ommended it in *A Rhetoric of Motives* as a special methodological tool. (That book, by the way, exemplifies what I meant by the implications of narrative style or shape in its application of the principle of isomorphism to the symbolic interplay of personal and political courtship and the courtship between author and reader—between, that is, various structures of human relations seen as governed by the question of political authority and power.) There is no reason, of course, why we should not bring in everything we know about the author as an aid to understanding.

One must ground all this material in the best attention one is capable of paying to the language of the text. I said that the technique transcends common sense, but one must be reasonably modest in one's transgressions, and there is rarely much sense in proposing interpretations that fly in the face of what is plainly said. Let us proceed to the poem, which is from William Carlos Williams's *Pictures from Brueghel*.

The Corn Harvest

Summer!
the painting is organized
about a young

reaper enjoying his
noonday rest
completely

relaxed
from his morning labors
sprawled

in fact sleeping
unbuttoned
on his back

the women
have brought him his lunch
perhaps

a spot of wine
they gather gossiping
under a tree

whose shade
carelessly
he does not share the

resting
center of
their workaday world   (9)

The beginning suggests something of what is to happen in the poem. The third word, "painting," is a noun that used to be a verb form, here followed by a passive construction that bespeaks the determinations of an active will. The time word "Summer" with which the poem opens is more or less answered by the space terms and spatial focus of the conclusion: "the / resting / center of / their workaday world." The lines between are taken up with a striking interplay between process and state, involving nouns rooted in verbs ("reaper," "rest" [from OE *restan*: to rest]) and verb forms bespeaking a change from action to condition: the present participles "sleeping," "gossiping," and "resting," the past participles "relaxed," "sprawled," and "unbuttoned." This sense of stopped process is, in fact, implicit in the first word of the poem, "summer" being the make-do name we give to a more or less arbitrary cross section of the flow of time. Even the suggestion of ongoing activity in "gossiping" is undercut by the presumably end-stopped action in "they gather." In this intransitive use of "gather" we have a finite, determinate action that by its nature cannot proceed indefinitely. The tension here between action and the cessation of action is characteristic of Williams, and it links up with other tensions in the poem, specifically in lineation and stanza structure. The jagged and arbitrary line endings perform the simultaneous functions of keeping the narrative line moving and impeding its flow (if only by visual suggestion), and the peculiarities of stanzaic structure have a similar effect: the stanzas are marked by a kind of floating short line—now the first line in a stanza, now the third, sometimes the second—so that the stanza is a visual fact and almost (but not quite) a metrical one. (The stanzas can also be seen as employing a floating long line, which is sometimes the first, sometimes the second, sometimes the third line in the stanza, but the effect is the same. The poem both does and does not have stanzas.)

Even within the participle forms lies a hidden tension. The force of the passive construction "is organized" is quite different from that of the participles "relaxed" and "sprawled": in one phrase, the painting is the passive recipient of the painter's intention; the others convey what the reaper himself is doing for himself. It will turn out to be important to the poem that he is designated the "resting" but not the "passive" center of the women's workaday world.

Like a Buckminster Fuller tensegrity sphere, the poem seems a self-sustaining system of internal tensions reproducing nothing more concrete than a sense of what it is like to scrutinize Brueghel's painting. In being a poem about another work of art, a second-level discourse about another fiction, "The Corn Harvest" in fact offers itself to at least one false reading. It can be seen not only as nonreferential but as self-reflexive, an internally consistent balancing of the concept "sprawl" against the paradoxical companion concept "organized." In such a reading the various verb forms can be taken as action canceled and as functioning to keep the poem outside any category of pragmatic discourse: no verb here points anywhere save into the painted scene. Even the finite transitive "have brought" has indirect and direct objects that are part of the fiction merely. The women's other finite verb, "gather," is self-reflexivity itself, and "share" is directed at another direct object within the fiction and is negated: the young reaper does not share. His function is to be a center, but a center of an absence—the "workaday world" of those women who never existed. Time, furthermore, is stopped in the poem; as Bergson might point out, "Summer" and "young" are both falsifying cross sections snipped from the continuing flow of true being. In any case, the gradual shift in the middle of the poem from focus on time to focus on space is Williams's ingenious attempt to capture in the temporal art of verse the spatiality of painting; he has performed the difficult feat of divorcing discourse from the time-bound, referential state in which he found it. As he once said, "The word must be put down for itself . . . aware— civilized" (*Imaginations* 102).

All this speculation is perhaps tempting, but it falsifies Williams's whole poetic and this poem in particular. For one thing, "Summer" at the beginning and "their workaday world" at the end of the poem are not just abstract words for time and space; they are both humanized. "Summer!," a homely Anglo-Saxon word, is punctuated so as to bear an obvious human relevance or human emotional investment, and there is something in the phrase "their workaday world" that needs reflection: its status as cliché.

The phrase shares this status with a number of phrases in the poem—a remarkably large number for so short a poem. The young reaper is enjoying "his / noonday rest," relaxed from "his morning labors"; the women have perhaps brought "a spot of wine" for him, the center of "their workaday world." The pedestrian tone of these terms testifies to their human use and in part to their history. They are commonplace, and in that very characteristic they reveal their powerful relevance to human life: they are the common coin of workaday experience, and to use them as they are used here is to exploit their humanity. They are, then, Williams's version of one of the characteristics that give Brueghel's painting so much appeal and impact.

The poem, like the poet, in every way prizes life and proclaims the ability of art to touch it; that the experience here should be mediated by attention to a second work of art is simple testimony to the concrete vitality of art in general—art and its human witness. In the figure of the women, the hypothesis that they "have brought him his lunch," and the observation that "they gather gossiping under a tree," we have a rudimentary narrative line that constitutes the poem's commitment to concrete, event-bound life (the whole static left side of Brueghel's painting is left out of Williams's account, of course).

The term *event-bound* is important. We know from Williams's theoretical writing that to his mind, words are energy centers that articulate the facts of the world as the items of human experience they quintessentially are. We know how powerfully Williams was impressed by Whitehead's *Science and the Modern World*. One interesting remark in the book appears in the lecture on relativity: "An event," says Whitehead, "is the grasping into unity of a pattern of aspects" (119). And words are one way of expressing the grasping into unity that emerges as pattern. Indeed, the inadequacy of nonpoetic language for Williams lies on the one hand in its failure to preserve the substantial unity of act or thing and name ("When we name it, life exists" [*Imaginations* 115]) and on the other hand in its conferral of a specious existence on abstractions masquerading as real things. For the adequate artist, the materials of art are the embodiment of imaginative volition. "Brueghel the painter," Williams says in "Hunters in the Snow," "concerned with it all has *chosen* a winter-struck bush for *his* foreground . . ." (*Pictures* 5), and the text under consideration here opens on a frank assertion of the same theme: "the painting is organized. . . ." The construction here looks like an impersonal passive, but it is not, as the other poems in the sequence (and especially the one that precedes "The Corn Harvest") make clear.

A Williams poem is always an act of mind, always a thoughtful looking at a powerfully realized scene or object—this too is illustrated by the poem about Brueghel himself, "Haymaking," the two poles of which are the painter's grasp and the scenes grasped; and the artist's grasp is not just a taking in but a giving out—a giving out of the ordinarily neglected or undetected or unexperienced vitality of the object or scene. The speaker of "The Corn Harvest" begins with an act of superficial looking that centers for a moment on time but that gradually comes to apprehend more and more of the painting and the painted scene.

The poem begins with an implicit wavering of the observing mind between time and space as primary. The nunciatory opening, "Summer!," would not seem particularly probing as a first remark about a painting as painting (though it firmly takes possession of the represented scene as a human consideration). It is a remark more or less on the same level as "Those are apples." But the active mind of the poet, grasping into its own unity this pattern of aspects, moves on to remark, "the painting is organized / about a young / reaper," which is at least partly a spatial view, if we take "about" as meaning "around." But "about" also means "concerning," and already the appeal to space is peculiarly meaning-laden. A stronger temporal focus asserts itself in the reaper's enjoying a noonday rest after his morning labors on this summer day; perhaps we *are* in the presence of an attempt to render the inevitable spatiality of painting into the presumably temporal phenomenon of poetry. The reader of this poem should regard such a suggestion with suspicion, for Williams long since showed himself to be an intently spatial poet. Time for him, even in *In the American Grain* and *Paterson*, has always been merely a mode of existence for his primary reality of place. And so here: the temporal fades and spatiality takes over, as "rest," a more or less abstract notion (an abstract version of "resting") modulates into the concrete, physical "relaxed," which is in turn revised by the gazing and organizing poet into the frankly spatial designation "sprawled." The poem clearly modulates out of its initial focus on time into its primary focus on space. Odd though the observation may seem, space is a more significant component of human relations than time. The child who asks, "When is daddy coming home?," is thinking of spatial, not temporal, reunions. The women in Brueghel's painting have moved through space to perform an important act of nurturing, bringing the reaper his lunch (perhaps, though the painting doesn't really encourage that reading— there are many other reapers); and the powers of human organizing, perhaps, can be credited with amassing the potential flow of liquid into the "spot of wine" the speaker surmises they have brought. Space and speech create a human community as the women "gather gossiping / under a tree." From "sprawled" onward, in fact, the poem finds meaning primarily in spatiality. Williams's organizing act of mind is that very discovery.

The final three lines are complicatedly ironic. In this poem about a painting, written by one of our most visual poets, the chief subject vanishes into concept as the young reaper is characterized as the "resting / center" of the "workaday world" of the people in the painting. "Center" is a complicated pun: the young reaper, putatively administered to by the women, may be the conceptual center of their purposive world, but in terms of real spatial relations Williams has revised the painting: the reaper is off to one side of the eating and drinking women. Nonetheless, as the center of their workaday world he is proof that the language of spatiality is the best conveyor of the significance of life and life relations. Whether the young man is truly the center—moral, spiritual, social—of their workaday world is another question. At any rate, the poem moves from the essentially stopped time of its opening to the value-laden spatial language of its close—a spatial language that has burst the confines of spatiality and become conceptual interpretation of the world of the painting.

Here the various tensions that were mentioned at first as parts of an inviting false reading of the poem regain their relevance. The Bergsonian view of "Summer!" I offered at first is pertinent. A painting of a summer's day is stopped time; it cannot be a painting of any other season's day. Therefore a time poet's reading of the painting would be inappropriate to Brueghel. The more pregnant world of space, on the other hand, contains and can present those potentialities that energize life. This is why the noun "rest" of the second stanza becomes the adjective "resting";

the noun is on the way to being reactualized as the verb from which it seems to have developed, and in any case it bespeaks the energy latent in the resting man. Further, the spatial centrality of the resting man attests to his conceptual centrality (imagine a cadenza with its harmonic resolution in the middle). At the close, having capitalized on its spatiality in this way, the poem returns to energetic tension between verb and noun in the first real adjective since "morning," "workaday"—another noun come from a verb, and moreover, a complex that includes the temporal within itself (work*day*). It is perhaps an inevitable result of English syntax that the last word in the poem should be "world," but it is a happy result, bracketing the poem meaningfully between its opening exclusive time word and its final comprehensive space word.

But the tension between time and space is not sustained; it collapses in favor of space.[2] The tension created by the stanzaic arrangements in the poem are more characteristic of Williams, and they are so expressive of his mind-set that in any given poem, as here, they must be regarded as part of his theme. The nervous ambiguities created by the lineation are material versions of the important tensions between stasis and motion, or for that matter between being and becoming: the women gossip under that tree "whose shade / . . . / he does not share," the "resting / center of / their workaday world." This tensional contrast between reaper and feeder is congruent with a network of others. As resting center, the young reaper embodies a concept that stands in dynamic tension with the physical, concrete women (who are, moreover, the subjects of the only past-tense verb in the poem; all the verbs governed by the reaper are present-tense or participial forms). And yet his very timelessness is only temporary—will he be a reaper in May? Rather a sower, and in motion, so we catch him here at a point of precarious temporal balance.

There is the further tension of male and female. That this is a tension and not just a difference is the result of the mechanical separation created by the stanza forms and by the incipient narrative line of the poem on the one hand and the conceptual unity on the other: in Williams's reading of the painting, the women are there because the man is, and he is, again, intimately theirs, though he lies definitely apart. An additional tension may be concealed here, one between active servant and static master—or is that simply another way of looking at the same thing?

To posit a genuine creative tension between the two artists—for there are two, of course—may be far-fetched, and one might ask how it is to be seen. Williams himself, as a matter of fact, goes to some lengths to keep some such tension before us. Throughout the sequence Williams emphasizes Brueghel's part in what he is doing in the poems: the first poem is about the painter's self-portrait; the second, about Icarus, begins, "According to Brueghel"; the fourth is full of explicit remarks about the manner of painting. A significant part of the energy of the poem arises in this repeated playing off of poet and painter, poetry and painting. Even "The Corn Harvest," again, is declared to be "organized" before Williams gets to it, and the poem presents itself in part as a reverential violation of a preexistent given world, to that extent acting out a theme it never states. What is involved is

Williams's form of detachment, comprising a recognition of the otherness of the other, its integrity, in tension with a feeling of kinship, of love, of connectedness. I emphasize that general level because it is important that the poem not be read as merely about art. The painting functioned for Williams almost as an emblem (in the Renaissance sense) or rather (and also) offered a human or humanlike scene already removed from a pragmatic context, sparing him the need to perform those distancing, revising processes he must go through in other poems. And as with those other poems, the altered context allows the revelation of forces customarily hidden from casual view. What is liberated here, I think, is a vision of certain deep roots of human conciousness, for the poem is at bottom a form of myth.

Sexual myth, for one thing. The center of the workaday world of the gossiping women is the dormant male principle, embodied in the young reaper. (But he embodies it only so far as the feminine principle so regards him; the tension involved is dynamic.) He is, for the speaker, the inactive principle of form in the world of the painting and the poem, enacting on the canvas for Brueghel and in the poem for Williams what the artist, or part of him, enacts in creating the finished work. In a way, then, the poem *is* a poem about art. But art is only a special case of something more general, more nearly universal. The painting more than the poem drives home the consideration that Ceres is female—all the reapers in the picture are male. But even in the poem the situation is unquestionably resonant, and as the momentarily inactive principle of form of his world the sleeping reaper is to be associated with Adonis being served by his priestesses or, better, with Dionysus being served by his worshipers—or even with the drowsing Pluto in his court. Neither painting nor poem makes any bones about death, which is the necessary condition for nurture. The creative tension between destruction and creation and between the terms of many such pairs of opposites always played a large role in Williams's sense of life and in his poetry. I am not suggesting that the poem is an assertion about what life is like but that he has seized upon an image that is true of life, that applies to it at several levels, that names it—or names a fundamental configuration of life that applies to something as specific and temporal as the poet's own womanizing and something as dark and general and timeless as the myth of Dis. The poem becomes, then, a poem about sexual relations, about art, about nurture, about the beastly/godly that underlies the life we live.

The striking number of possessives and possessive relations in the poem—only two of its eight stanzas lack a possessive adjective of one kind or another—might tempt one toward a covert political reading suggesting a displaced consciousness of bourgeois property relations disguised or evaded by the poet's appeal to the timeless level of myth. But the political impulse seems remote, principally because of the way these possessives are distributed. The first four are "his," governed by the reaper; the presumably neuter tree governs the impersonal "whose"; and the women get "their" in the last line. The contrast of masculine and feminine modes of possession is plain enough (the women are communal; the male, singular and egotistic); indeed, the conclusion of the poem comes close to removing the death-tinged, ego-mongering male as the point of focus and replacing him with the nurturing, unity-oriented women, who, after all, have everything social in the poem—gossip, food, wine. But an ineluctable tension unites them to him: they may be the world of which he is merely the center, but he is the center, and each principle needs the other to be what it is. In the end, this interpretation and the nonsexual political reading hang together: as presented, the reaper as reaper is a tension-laden principle of both union and separation, in the ways already outlined; the reaper as man over against the women functions similarly, as the occasion of their gathering and an assertion of masculine separateness and domination; the reaper as an agent of possessive relations is at once a cornerstone of one sort of social order and the cause and principle of social alienation. The creative tensions of the poem exfoliate nearly endlessly, and we have finally not an "overdetermined" work with a putatively definite or determinate meaning, not a text vulnerable to free play founded on the absence of presence or of a center, but a node of energy resonating to a myriad of human concerns.

Notes

[1] This includes, I realize, a vast number of unglamorous utilitarian objects; our culture's reluctance to apply the principle advanced may account in part for the devastating ugliness of so many of our unglamorous utilitarian objects.

[2] Could Williams's emphasis on spatiality account for the superiority of his "The Fall of Icarus" to Auden's rendition of the same painting in "Musée des Beaux Arts"? In that poem, too, Williams is vividly spatial, whereas Auden's less compelling version seems to spend itself ruminating on events simultaneous with Icarus's fall and avails itself of little in the way of spatial consciousness.

Forms of Mimesis and Ideological Rhetoric in Cervantes's *La gitanilla*

FELIX MARTINEZ-BONATI

Many, if not most, forms of criticism in our century have shared some basic phenomenological attitudes, regardless of whether they have been directly influenced by the philosophy of Edmund Husserl and his followers. The predominant intellectual bent since the early decades has been to favor accurate perception and description of the object as the fundamental way of gaining knowledge of its nature and grasping its sense. This has meant turning away from genetic explanations, which were suddenly seen as imperceptive, precipitous reductions of the object's particularity to preestablished and rather summary, all-encompassing conceptions of cultural life. Thus, the shift was, in a sense, nonhistoricist and nondeterministic, but it was not really antihistoriological, as its critics are still saying today. Rather, the idea was and is to postpone the historical account of sources and forces until the object of our interest has become thoroughly known as it presents itself to us within the forms of reading that—both traditionally and critically—are established as relevant and that determine literary perception and objectivity. If we wish to explain something as the product of certain natural or historical circumstances (which, incidentally, most literary critics know only summarily), let us first find out what this something really is. To this end, let us first see what it looks like, how it is constructed, what its actual effect is on our own life. Things, Husserl thought, carry their essence and their sense within themselves. Back, then, to the things themselves! Reflexive awareness of the world as it is given to us and description of the phenomena therein became imperative.

The procedures of the New Criticism, which are the most characteristic of this century's literary studies, clearly correspond to the general intellectual mode to which I am alluding. But recent deconstructivist criticism is also, at its best, predominantly descriptive—indeed, so minutely applied to the thingness of the text that it can be seen as a maximization of phenomenological attitudes. Any description of that which is consciously experienced within a structured operation of objectification can be called "phenomenological" *sensu lato*.

Within this general methodologically immanentist and descriptive current, there are, of course, phenomenological approaches in a stricter sense. Husserl's efforts to ensure the possibility of objectivity theoretically and methodically (which determine a large part of his writings) led to his influential version of transcendental idealism. According to this view, objectivity is engendered by acts of consciousness, and the essence of any phenomenon can best be grasped in the constitutive intentions of the transcendental subject. Description consequently becomes reflexive; the originating center of sense and world structure is to be found in the pure ego. The founder of phenomenology was interested in the a priori constitution of the intersubjective experience of the world. Phenomenologically trained students of literature began by examining the structure of the literary work in general (Roman Ingarden's studies exemplify this trend) and went on to describe the fictional worlds of literature as imaginative projections of an individual mind. (Of this group, Georges Poulet is the best known in the English-speaking community.) This reflexive description of the constitutive structures of fictional objects, of the laws that erect and sustain imaginary worlds, has been phenomenological criticism in the narrow, classic sense of the term, and the closest to Husserl's own thought. We have a lucid account of this criticism in Magliola's *Phenomenology and Literature.*

In recent years, the depreciation of the notion of a personal subject (a consequence of revived Marxist, Nietzschean, Freudian, and Saussurean views) has undermined a method so intimately bound to the idea of a spontaneous, self-aware, and originally creative ego. The source of objectivity appears to be no longer consciousness but collective cultural structures that the individual subject cannot control or even be entirely aware of. Literature is seen as a field of textual movements not unified by the conscious center of an objectified intentionality.

The phenomenological approach endures, however, if in a less doctrinal form, mainly in studies of literary reception (whose representative scholar is Wolfgang Iser). The text may or may not be intentionally organized, but the reading of literature certainly is a structured activity that produces an object of aesthetic experience. This object—the literary work—is given to consciousness and can be described from the viewpoint of the activity of the reader, thus revealing the rules and modes of literary experience. Therein the sense and essence of the work are given and can be circumscribed. The priority of the given continues to be the ultimate distinguishing principle of phenomenology (what Husserl stated to be "the principle of all principles" [§24]). No object of experience can be denied within the limits in which it is given; its lived sense and nature cannot be nullified insofar as they are phenomenal items. Whether it is the product of a standard, traditional reading or of innovative textual operations, something occurs in the reader's mind that is meaningful and deserves careful observation and reflexive description—before we try to explain it as a deceptive facade or as an effect of heterogeneous forces.

As methods of interpretation, then, the approaches that are the opposite of and complementary to phenomenology are reductive and genetic—for example, the psychoanalytic and sociohistorical approaches, along with those structuralist and deconstructivist studies that use the assumption of unconscious meanings. Although many phenomenological elements appear in these contemporary kinds of exegesis (mistakenly seen as incompatible with the descriptive one), a proper phenomeno-logical approach must operate on the principle that the reflexive intuition of the subject is the final form of truth. Thus phenomenology does not exclude ideological, psychological, and rhetorical criticism, insofar as such interpretations can become evident for the reader of the pertinent text. What it does exclude, in my opinion, is an interpretation whose elements cannot be found in any literary reading of the text in question or whose sense does not fit into those readings. Of course, whether a certain element or sense is part of or akin to a literary experience is debatable, but such a debate will take place on the basis of experienced evidence—that is, on phenomenological grounds.

In the following pages, I intend to show rhetorical and ideological meanings through a descriptive examination of the literarily experienced work. This represents merely the beginning of an interpretation, offered here as a sample of a sort of phenomenological analysis that could certainly be pursued to greater depth and with a higher degree of accuracy.

Freud postulated a functional affinity between fictional literature and both dreaming and daydreaming, while explaining the latter processes as manifestations of basic forces and conflicts of the psyche. He and many of his followers regarded literature and art as nearly primordial mental activities, deeply rooted in human nature. Pointing to Freudian insights, Lionel Trilling has written that the father of psychoanalysis "establishes the *naturalness* of artistic thought" and that he "did more for our understanding of art than any other writer since Aristotle" (156).

But are these functions—the imaginary satisfaction of conscious desire (usually aimed at in daydreaming) and the blind handling of the unconscious in unsuspected dreamlike symbolism—the only, or even the major, anthropological raisons d'être of poetic imagination? We should not forget that literature shares another equally fundamental psychic function with everyday life: simply imagining what may happen or may have happened, or imagining what we think has not happened but ought to. The anticipatory vision of the concretely possible, the probable, and the necessary, the strategic consideration of possible events, as well as the tentative filling of gaps in experience or memory, are operations of this kind. Often we ponder whether persons we know may have done this or that—can we imagine them doing such a thing? Is it "like them"? We may also wonder whether we can imagine any person doing a certain thing—say, living a rich and healthy life during years of total isolation.

Testing the latent possibilities in an individual we know by trying to imagine him or her doing this or that, trying out our views of what is possible for a particular class of beings by concretely imagining an event according to a certain general assumption (which is not part of the definition of that class)—these activities are different from dreaming and daydreaming but not less ordinary or necessary. Furthermore, they are diametrically opposed to dreaming, since they correspond to a most intense and reality-bound form of wakefulness. In this way, we probe the boundaries of complex universal notions and also the consistency of the implications of assumed singular events.

Literary fiction essays a stylized image of life in a counterplay of coincidence with and contrast to our ordinary notions of reality. At the same time, it mobilizes our sympathies and aversions vis-à-vis fictional value carriers, and, as a consequence, it may help persuade the reader that certain forms of life are desirable. Imagination can be tendentious and can produce ideological exempla. Of course, this is the connection between art and human life that Plato and Aristotle (Trilling's reference to the latter being not without point) and the poetological tradition, not exclusively, but primarily, have asserted: that is, art taken at its face value as an indirect form of knowledge, the sounding of universals through the imagination of fictive individuals—mimesis. Not a symptom, a disguised operation, a false consciousness.

What vision of life does a given work present? What ethos does it promote? These questions are not less legitimate than those concerning hidden, unconscious meanings of imaginary transactions and the archetypal structures of the reader's quest. Fictional discourses, entities, and worlds are the given in straight literary experience. The oldest, never-ending task of criticism is to describe them and explain their perceived effect. What I intend to suggest here is the possibility of sharpening the focus of these old questions by means of some logical distinctions.

Mimesis is the game of the imaginable. From a logical point of view, the structure of this game can be understood formally as a confrontation of (almost always tacitly) assumed general laws and imagined singular events, or of universal and singular propositions. Thus the story of a man living alone on an island for years will constantly bring into play our general assumptions about human life and solitary existence. Propositions like "After almost a year of dwelling on the island he began to feel a profound and steady happiness" will connect with assumptions such as "Human life flourishes only in human society." Of course, formulating general assumptions like this one not only grossly simplifies them but falsely suggests that our views about life are held in our minds' store near to conceptualization and ready to be appropriately worded. Our most basic general knowledge of life is unformulable; we vaguely hint at it in maxims and definitions but never adequately make it explicit. Nonetheless, that elusive total knowledge is the repository activated in the game of the imaginable, the sensorium that determines whether a work of fiction has or does not have what Henry James calls "the odor of [reality]" (664).

But the game of the imaginable also includes pieces of fiction that definitely do not have the quality of realism. In such cases we can consider their formal structure as a confrontation between the reality-dissenting laws implied by their fictional events and the unstated laws of our sense of reality: it is the game of fantasy, in the stronger meaning of the word—the imagining of worlds dissimilar to our own (among them, the dreamed worlds of romance, which are akin to the adventures of daydreaming).

The general laws implied by singular fictional events will establish a certain kind of imaginary world, an order of pseudoreality, a region of imagination. In varying degrees and shades, this imaginary world will either fuse with our sense of reality (in which case we speak of a "realistic" work of fiction) or depart from it, as a fantastic order of things. The narrator of a story may or may not explicitly formulate

some general laws of its world, and these formulations may or may not be consistent
with the implications of the events it contains. Thus we may have a game in which
three sets of general laws are involved: (1) the expectations pertaining to our sense
of reality, (2) the general laws formulated by the narrator, and (3) the general
implications of the narrated events (which may be in part anticipated by the reader
if the work in question belongs to a conventional genre). The rules of literary fiction
favor the third group of laws as the strongest within the imaginary experience. By
contrast, the test of what is imagined in ordinary life, of course, gives priority, not
to the fictional world but to our own. This fact indicates that it is not unfounded
to relate some literary fictions to the operation of daydreaming. Daydreaming,
however, typically presupposes the conscious desirability of the imagined events for
the subject, a feature that is not a part of all literary fiction, not even of all fantastic
or romantic fiction. As for dreams proper, the sense of reality hardly pertains to
their game.

Let us now examine some aspects of the world and the ethos of Cervantes's *La
gitanilla*. This is how it begins:

> Parece que los gitanos y gitanas solamente nacieron en el mundo para ser ladrones;
> nacen de padres ladrones, críanse con ladrones, estudian para ladrones, y, finalmente,
> salen con ser ladrones corrientes y molientes a todo ruedo, y la gana de hurtar y
> el hurtar son en ellos como accidentes inseparables, que no se quitan sino con la
> muerte. Una, pues, de esta nación, gitana vieja, que podía ser jubilada en la ciencia
> de Caco, crió una muchacha en nombre de nieta suya, a quien puso nombre Preciosa,
> y a quien enseñó todas sus gitanerías, y modos de embelecos, y trazas de hurtar.
> Salió la tal Preciosa la más única bailadora que se hallaba en todo el gitanismo, y
> la más hermosa y discreta que pudiera hallarse, no entre los gitanos, sino entre
> cuantas hermosas y discretas pudiera pregonar la fama. Ni los soles, ni los aires,
> ni todas las inclemencias del cielo, a quien más que otras gentes están sujetos los
> gitanos, pudieron deslustrar su rostro ni curtir las manos; y lo que es más, que la
> crianza tosca en que se criaba no descubría en ella sino ser nacida de mayores prendas
> que de gitana, porque era en extremo cortés y bien razonada. Y, con todo esto,
> era algo desenvuelta; pero no de modo que descubriese algún género de deshones-
> tidad; antes con ser aguda, era tan honesta, que en su presencia no osaba alguna
> gitana, vieja ni moza, cantar cantares lascivos ni decir palabras no buenas. Y,
> finalmente, la abuela conoció el tesoro que en la nieta tenía, y así, determinó el
> águila vieja sacar a volar su aguilucho y enseñarle a vivir por sus uñas. (3–5)

The Gipsy Maid

It would seem that gipsies, men and women alike, came into the world for the
sole purpose of thieving. They are born of thieving parents, are reared among
thieves, study to be thieves, and end up as polished and perfect thieves, in whom
the impulse to steal and stealing are one and the same thing, extinguished only
by death. One of this race, an old woman, a past-mistress of the art of thievery,
raised a girl she said was her granddaughter, upon whom she bestowed the name
of "Preciosa," and to whom she taught all her gipsy tricks, deceits, and light-
fingered arts. This Preciosa turned out to be the most unique dancer to be found

in all gipsydom, and the most beautiful and circumspect not only among the gipsies, but among all the beautiful and circumspect women in fame's annals. Neither sun nor wind, nor all the inclemencies of the heavens, to which gipsies are exposed more than others, could darken her face or tan her hands; and, what is even stranger, for all her rough upbringing, she seemed to have been born with finer qualities than a gipsy girl, for she was most courteous and well-spoken. Yet, withal, she was sprightly of manners, but in no wise over-bold; on the contrary, she was so virtuous that in her presence, no gipsy, matron or maid, ventured to sing lewd songs or say an unseemly word. The grandmother realized the treasure she had in such a granddaughter, and so the old eagle made up her mind to put her eaglet to the wing and teach her to live by her talons.   (Onís 91)

The first sentence of this text is a universal judgment stated by the narrator. It is amplified by the subsequent sentences up to the word "death." As a topical view of an ethnic minority, this judgment evokes a host of universals pertaining to the reader's view of the real world, although it expresses simply that gypsies are thieves by blood and by upbringing. The repetitions and the emphasis of this narrator's assertion impart to it a light, humorous tone; such is the temper modifying the real-life knowledge (congruous with the narrator's generalization) of gypsy ways possessed by the implied reader. The serious condemnation contained in everyday assumptions is weakened, deactivated, for the part played by this story's reader should include some (small) measure of sympathy for gypsies. Thus there is a prompt deviation from a thoroughly realistic presentation, as an element of comic idealization is introduced from the beginning. Nevertheless, the social group fictionalized in this way is placed at the bottom of the scale of esteem thus inaugurated in the narrative.

The narrator's generalization and the corresponding real-life assumptions keep the variable consonant-dissonant relation perceptible in the first sentence alive throughout the narrative. Even the apologetic description of gypsy life pronounced (later in the story) by one of the tribe's elders is internally dissociated by his topical-mythical eulogy of that life and self-incriminating outpouring of thievish lore; his voice is possessed alternately by the rhetoric of primitive freedom and contentment (the sympathetic coloration) and by the forthright expression of the anticipated criminal character. The conflict between sympathy and contempt toward the gypsies is never resolved in this narrative, although the contemptuous note is far stronger. Despite the disparaging tone, the imaginative evocation of gypsies is always touched here by a sense of unreality.

The second period (the third one in the English translation) introduces individuals and begins the descriptive-narrative discourse proper. This change of logical level is marked by the otherwise unmotivated conjunction "pues" (actually, a metanarrative sign—that is, a sign referring not to the things narrated but to the narrative discourse itself—understandably not included in the English translation). The general implications of the first singularizing sentences (the characterization of the old *gitana*) confirm the negative yet humorous view of gypsies. Immediately, however, a second individual is presented: the protagonist (as the reader will at this point presume). She is implicitly understood as both belonging to and not belonging to this group of people on the fringe of society. The pertinent general expectations are only partly satisfied by Preciosa's personal qualities. The title of the novella calls her categorically "gitanilla," but from the start this appellative is restricted, and it is first suggestively, later positively, limited to her upbringing. The fictional narrator, by the way, follows the development and the resolution of the enigma of Preciosa's birth from the point of view of everybody who knows her (including herself) except the old gypsy woman. Instead of hiding the truth about her identity, the narrator may seem not to know it until the end. What Cervantes, at any stage of his writing, "knew" is, of course, an entirely different matter, and one of mere conjecture.

The suggested eccentricity of Preciosa among gypsies allows for her disrupting the positions in the narrative's scale of esteem. She is an apprentice thief, but she is superlatively beautiful and intelligent; furthermore, her body triumphs over some laws of nature, connoting a supernatural favor bestowed on her. This first obvious break with verisimilitude serves to reinforce the nonrealistic frame of expectations that will permit wonderful coincidences and idealized improbable gestures later in the course and resolution of events.

The shifts in position of the protagonist's emotional appeal between the top and the bottom of the scale of esteem are, in this first paragraph, truly vertiginous. From among a contemptible group that, in the expectations of the reader, connotes criminality, uncleanliness, and lasciviousness (Preciosa's absolute "honestidad" is repeatedly affirmed as if to counter this unstated suspicion, and later in the text her "limpieza" is emphatically praised), she ascends in one sentence to a stature of supreme charm, intelligence, and beauty and in the next, to supernatural privilege. In the following sentence she descends to the impropriety of "desenvoltura" and then reemerges as perfectly "honesta" and resolutely virtuous. "Finally" (also a metanarrative word that is absent from the above translation), she returns to the status of rapacious apprentice thief. These variations in levels of esteem open up to the reader the broad range of possible peripeteias associated with the protagonist.

The counterpoint of universals or themes—the common notion of what it is to be a gypsy, the modified notion (the narrator's view of it), and the implied notion arising from the concrete qualities and actions of the gypsy or quasi-gypsy characters—is also, as we see, a counterpoint of value carriers and of the reader's emotional assessments. The configuration and movement of emotional and evaluative responses in the course of reading constitute the text's rhetorical structure (using the term *rhetoric* in the classic sense of the discourse of persuasion). The logical structure of the work is closely bound to its rhetorical structure, simply because the universals of our worldview (and consequently the modified versions of them in the imaginative game) are seldom if ever purely theoretical constructs and often clearly belong either to the likable or to the negative field of experiences.

The rhetorical configuration of this novella is grounded (not unconventionally) on bearers of the qualities of moral virtue, physical beauty, and optimum procreative age. The archetypical comic outcome is therefore marriage. Marriage and the series of tests and qualifications leading up to it are the central theme of the action. The main trial for the protagonist couple is to live virtuously as gypsies in the midst of gypsies. The closeness of the positive heroes to the gypsy community confers on the latter a shade of sympathy (in keeping with the humorous touch that modifies its commonplace appreciation from the outset), but at the same time, their difference and ultimate departure confirm the abjectness of the gypsy nation. The gypsies are ultimately seen as a people fallen from grace, the somber and seductive opposite of the good life. Is this ethnocentric, "ideological" worldview the core of the logical-rhetorical structure of *La gitanilla*? With some qualifications, yes, it is. Indeed, the obvious course of the action satisfies a sympathetic attachment of the reader to both Preciosa and Andrés. They are the positive value carriers; they are in moral danger (Preciosa is "un poco desenvuelta," and Andrés must feign criminal behavior) living on the wrong side of the law; and they are liberated and optimally reintegrated into God-pleasing society where they find a place in the sun. Their salvation is due in large part to their own merit, and their virtue is a property of their blood and high birth. Thus, the individual peripeteia and anagorisis exalt their race and class and, conversely, are exalted by these consecrating social ideals. This rhetorical structure seems to obey the formula of romance combined with ideology; certainly, it is a version of the Horatian concepts *prodesse* and *delectare*. The elementary appeal of the romance's plot favorably colors the ideological implications. Is Cervantes (somewhat cynically perhaps) merely satisfying the expectations of his public? Is this a case in which the game of the imaginable consists of quasi daydreaming an individual adventure that concludes in happiness while at the same time surreptitiously confirming the anthropological assumptions of a society? Indeed, the romance story of Preciosa and Andrés is in the foreground of the narrative. Cervantes displays Preciosa's acknowledged charm and unacknowledged suffering (resulting from her innocently being in a condition unworthy of her) as well as Andrés's physical and moral qualities and pangs of jealousy, so that the reader may participate vicariously in an adventure that includes debasement, trial, and triumph. However, because this story is so openly a romance, its ideology carries little weight. It does not aim at confirming views of life, as a Zola would expect a naturalistic novel to do. Thus its numerous and strong ideological inconsistencies are not shocking. Not only some of the generalizations voiced by the narrator (such as his statement that in the court "todo se compra y todo se vende" [6] 'all things are bought and sold' [Onís 92]), but also the general implications of the narrated events present Spanish society as notably corrupt at all levels, including the aristocracy. The gypsies, who are outlaws, have laws of their own that are repugnant to the dominant sense of right and wrong but that are observed with scrupulous propriety, in contrast to the sometimes arbitrary behavior of the social powers. The romantic transfiguration of the commonplace image favors, as a group, only the gypsies, while Spanish society at large is portrayed in a more severe and realistic light. At the end, a metonymic reconciliation of the two nations emerges with generous gestures of the old gypsy woman and Preciosa's progenitors. The old *gitana* who, at the beginning, was said to have raised Preciosa merely "under the name of a granddaughter of hers" (as "a girl she said was her granddaughter," reads de Onís's translation), will finally stay at the side of "her granddaughter Preciosa" (161). This concluding twist of the story exaggerates the romance character of the happy ending to the point of self-irony. Here we can sense Cervantes's smile: "As you are aware from the beginning, this is only a fantasy," he seems to be saying, thus modulating the generic irony of self-conscious literary activity.

In this way, the romantic, daydreamlike element is interwoven with some threads of realistic imaginings. The great values and myths of historic society are evoked in a key of apparent unseriousness that allows for both their apotheosis and their ironization.

We have summarily traced the movement through the text of a basic assumption of the implied reader: the value of the implied reader's own nation as opposed to that of an alien minority. The narrative activates this view, along with other general notions, by embodying it in the peripeteias of the characters. The normally unreflected cultural tenet is put into play, indirectly exposed and ironized, although not really discredited. Nor is it forcefully reasserted, because the fictional world erected with this story is marked as nonrealistic, both through positive idealization and caricature.

Needless to say, the development of this ideological notion in the story can be examined in more detail. Also, other cultural beliefs—sex roles, age stereotypes, and so on—can be taken as threads of the story's mimetic play. But even if we could exhaustively treat the several major themes of the story, its universal implications, we would only have analyzed the mimetic-rhetorical dimension of a piece of fiction. There are other essential and describable aspects of literary experience outside the scope of the concepts that I have used (and I will not submit that they all necessarily can be bound together under a single unifying meaning). One example of other dimensions of meaning, already hinted at in passing, is the reader's quest for an enjoyment less abstract than the indirect exposure of universal presuppositions: the private vicarious adventure of happiness experienced through the imaginary actions of the protagonists—that is, the game of individuality. (This structure, however, is clearly linked, as we have seen, to the ideological rhetoric.)

The compound of this novella is heterogeneous both because of its variations in tone and because at least two laws of stylization are operative (idealizing romance and caricaturizing satire). These characteristics of the novella are clearly detectable in the first paragraph, with its extremes of morally debased and high-standing human beings and the mockery and praise in the voice of the narrator. Gypsy life is presented according to both principles of stylization alternately. There is, doubtless, some irregularity in the style and vision of this work. However, by means of this departure from consistent generic and stylistic patterns, Cervantes exposes—as he also does in other works of his—the conventionality of literature without ceasing to use it. But for this very reason the ideological-mimetic implications of his tale—as I have repeatedly indicated above—are touched by the shadow of unreality and skepsis. The metanarrative expressions in the initial paragraph quoted—which I pointed out—are among the signs of the intense self-reflexivity of this discourse, a discourse that promotes the awareness of its elaborated quality, of its literariness, and thus counters its own mimetic transparency. *Exemplary Novels* is the title Cervantes gave to his collection of novellas. We can see how complex the question of their exemplarity sometimes is.

We can guess that, as a general principle, the rhetorical and ideological force will be attenuated and in some cases even neutralized by the self-reflexive and the openly fantastic aspects of the literary work. The more the text marks its own fictionality, the less imperative becomes the worldview that it presents. But it also seems true that persuasion, by its very nature, demands an effective use of fictional images that must involve a biased selection of aspects of the actual world and positive and negative stylizations—and, therefore, breaks in objectivity and verisimilitude. Thus, not only is rhetoric necessarily in conflict with literariness, but, within the space of literature, it is self-destructive, inasmuch as it divests the picture of the convictive force of the image of reality, precisely in order to give that picture the desired tendency. Rhetoric is in conflict here with realistic mimesis and the illusion of reality—and, therefore, with itself. The more tendentious, the more clearly fictional; the more clearly fictional, the less effectively tendentious. Literariness (that is, fictionality) subverts rhetoricalness.

Note

[1] The reader interested in further examination of *La gitanilla* regarding some of the points touched here is especially referred to Selig, El Saffar, Lerner, Avalle-Arce, and Forcione.

The Making of a Style

Borges's *Universal History of Infamy*

Stylistics and Poetics: A Note on Method

Stylistics was first conceived as a field of study within linguistics. Bally, who coined the term and laid the foundations of the new discipline, refused to deal with literature. Since those pioneering days, it has evolved into a solid and complex method for the study of literary texts, and it has avoided stagnation by assimilating the lessons of its own mistakes and by turning its problems into factors for growth. Seymour Chatman best summarized the present state of the field when he observed:

> Modern literary stylistics has in recent years developed methods of analyzing texts and characterizing literary language and forms that is disciplined, without losing a refreshing diversity: there is the Russian Formalist-Jakobsonian school, the French *structuralists*, influenced by the Russians, the Czechs, and Hjelmeslevian linguistics, the British school, in the tradition of J. R. Firth, the American School with its debt to the New Criticism and to Bloomfieldian and Chomskian linguistics and more recently to linguistic philosophy, the inheritors of the Continental and particularly the Spitzerian stylistic tradition, and so on. (ix)

One has only to go through the volume Chatman edited—*Literary Style: A Symposium*—along with an earlier and equally valuable collection edited by Thomas A. Sebeok—*Style in Language*—to become aware of the multiplicity of directions found within the same approach. Far from being obstructive, this diversity has proven to be most fertile and enriching. "Disagreement," said Jakobson in "Linguistics and Poetics," "generally proves to be more productive than agreement; disagreement discloses antinomies and tensions within the field discussed and calls for novel exploration" (350). The bibliography on stylistics has grown to colossal proportions, and this theoretical storehouse, though of uneven value, represents a sound basis for the growth, performance, and consolidation of a viable discipline. I'll try to summarize some areas of disagreement confronting the method and what I consider its most effective direction.

At the center of the controversy stands the old question of what constitutes a mark of style. Even today, Spitzer's first formulation—following Bally's—continues to be a point of departure that one accepts, rejects, or modifies: style as deviation from a norm. Those who accept this definition question its ambiguity. What is the norm? Is it language in general? Or is it the language of a given period, genre, author, or text? Michael Riffaterre, the most energetic defender of the concept of deviance, has underlined A. G. Juilland's view that

> if we are to see style in the deviation from the norm, we will have to limit style to what is left after eliminating every normal element, but the answer is that we cannot then account for the fact that this very material we now reject may play a stylistic role when seen in other relationships.

Riffaterre then adds:

> To this use of the norm I see an objection which is more fundamental than those just mentioned, namely not so much that the linguistic norm is virtually unobtainable, but that it is irrelevant. It is irrelevant because the readers base their judgements (and the authors their devices) not on an ideal norm, but on their individual concepts of what is the accepted norm.   ("Criteria" 168)

To overcome this inadequacy, he suggests replacing the notion of "norm" by that of "pattern," since in every text there is a different norm. Riffaterre calls this variable norm "context," and he offers the following definition of style:

> The hypothesis that context plays the role of the norm and that style is created by a deviation from it is a fruitful one. . . . The stylistic context is a linguistic *pattern suddenly broken by an element which was unpredictable*, and the contrast resulting from this interference is the stylistic stimulus. The stylistic value of the contrast lies in the relationship it establishes between the two clashing elements; no effect would occur without their association in a sequence. A consequence of the principle of contrast is that it enables us to draw the line easily between a personal style and a literary language: literary language needs no contrast; it is in fact a predictable pattern, whose linguistic elements receive no stylistic value from merely belonging to the language; should the same element appear in a context where no such conventional words are expected, they will be stylistic devices.   (169, 171)

The notion of context as norm has been nevertheless either contested or disregarded. Todorov has proposed giving up the idea of deviance altogether:

> To characterize poetic language as a deviation from the norm is tautological: any homogeneous discourse will prove deviant, since the "norm" will be the agglomerate of all discourses and thus will not have the characteristics of any among them. It is unclear why we should speak of a norm; ordinary language is the meeting-place of a thousand norms and thus "normless" in the truest sense.   ("Place" 31)

Pressed to comment on Riffaterre's notion of a contextual norm, Todorov replied:

> The norm as context does not cover all possible stylistic effects. There are some cases when the norm is not given in the context and we do not always perceive

the particular stylistic feature as a contrast. Further, many linguistic elements while not deviations are a part of style; on the other hand, there are many deviations in texts which are not stylistically interesting. (41)

The principle of deviance from a norm (regardless of whether the norm is determined inside or outside the text under analysis) has been further challenged by M. A. K. Halliday. Where Todorov talks about "style as coherence," relating it to other elements of the text—a thematic motif, for example—bringing together thematics and stylistics so that one confirms the other, Halliday emphasizes the place of semantics in the study of style. He accepts as a truism that the text and not some supersentence is the relevant unit for stylistic studies, but he sees theme rather than deviance as the basis for style analysis: "It is not the theme in isolation but the total theme-rheme which contributes to the texture of the discourse" (336). Furthermore, Halliday underlines the necessity to relate any pattern or prominence of style to the meaning of the text as a whole:

> This relationship is a functional one: if a particular feature of the language contributes, by its prominence, to the total meaning of the work, it does so by virtue of and through the medium of its own value in the language—through the linguistic function from which its meaning is derived. (339)

Since this functional style still depends on the notion of "prominence," which reinstates the concept of deviance (some feature of the language of a text "stands out in some way" [339]), Halliday makes clear that the "departure" view puts too high a value on oddness and suggests that normal forms are of no interest in the study of style, a view René Wellek earlier cautioned us about:

> The danger of linguistic stylistics is its focus on deviations from, and distortions of, the linguistic norm. We get a kind of counter-grammar, a science of discards. Normal stylistics is abandoned to the grammarian, and deviational stylistics is reserved for the student of literature. But often the most commonplace, the most normal, linguistic elements are the constituents of literary structure. (qtd. in Halliday 340)

A. McIntosh offers a similar reservation: "Quite often the impact of an entire work may be enormous, yet word by word, phrase by phrase, clause by clause, sentence by sentence, there may seem nothing very unusual or arresting, in grammar or in vocabulary" (qtd. in Halliday 341). Halliday concludes:

> Deviation is of very limited interest in stylistics. It may be more helpful to look at a given instance of prominence in one way rather than in another, sometimes as departure from a norm and sometimes as the attainment of a norm, either way, whether the prominence is said to consist in law-breaking or in law-making, we are dealing with a type of phenomenon that is expressible in quantitative terms. . . . And thus if style cannot be reduced to counting, this is because it cannot be reduced to a simple question of prominence: an adequate characterization of an author's style is much more than an inventory of linguistic highlights. (341–44)

If quantity cannot account for stylistic prominence or, rather, if prominence alone cannot explain a given style, what can? What should take the place of a broken norm as the criterion for style analysis? Halliday answers with Richard Ohmann's words:

> Since there are innumerable kinds of deviance, we should expect that the ones elected by a poem or poet spring from particular semantic impulses, particular ways of looking at experience. . . . Syntax need not be deviant in order to serve a vision of things. . . . *The vision provides the motivation for their prominence*, it makes them relevant, however ordinary they may be. . . . The prominence, in other words, is often due to the vision. (345; emphasis added)

Style is no longer perceived in isolation but as an integral part of the textual whole in which all components cohere and contribute to the realization of its theme. This understanding of stylistics is concerned with language in relation to other levels of meaning that a work may have.

> It is not a matter of a semantic choice and a syntactic choice, one weakening or cutting across the other, but rather of a combined and cumulative effect, one reinforcing the other: an interaction, not of meaning and form, but of two levels of meaning, both of which find expression in form, and through the same syntactic features. (Halliday 347)

Deviance from the norm as the criterion for style analysis has thus been replaced by the particular vision governing the production of a text. This vision appears embodied in a theme or motif or, in more general terms, at the semantic level of the work, and it is also expressed through other components integrated in that text. Style is measured by its role and participation in the realization of that vision and not merely by its linguistic deviance from a norm. This new criterion enables the analyst to account for elements of style that may be normative—and therefore stylistically innocuous—and yet relevant in the performance of a stylistic function. We have come full circle to the concept of style postulated earlier by the Russian formalists, who emphasized the close correlation between stylistics and thematics in literary studies. V. V. Vinogradov insisted once and again on the "internal unity of literary composition" (81) and on the systematic nature of a text in which style is but one wheel more joining the others in the conveyance of literary messages. For this reason he underlined "the functional and immanent study of a style" (82), meaning style in its rapport to a given literary vision as well as to other textual elements. It has been pointed out that in Boris Eikhenbaum's study "How Gogol's *Overcoat* Is Made," "the consideration of the rhythm of the sentences finds an immediate echo in the analysis of themes" (Todorov, *Poetics* 242). In a later work devoted to the Russian poet Anna Akhmatova, Eikhenbaum studied the frequency of oxymoronic constructions in her poetry, and he arrived at the conclusion that this figure of style becomes also the dominant principle governing every level of her work: subject, composition, and of course language:

> Akhmatova's heroine, who unites in herself the entire sequence of events, scenes, or sensations, is an oxymoron incarnate; the lyrical narrative whose center she

> occupies moves by antithesis, paradoxes, it avoids psychological formulations. . . .
> The moving and the sublime occur alongside the terrifying; simplicity is juxtaposed
> to complexity; sincerity to cunning and coquetry; kindness to anger; monastic
> humility to passion and jealousy.   (qtd. in Todorov, *Poetics* 242–43)

Commenting on his own book on Akhmatova, Eikhenbaum said in his account of
the "formal method" that there he dealt, among other questions, with "the relation
of poetic diction to semantics" ("Theory" 129).

One of the most distinguished members of the Russian formalist school, Roman
Jakobson, has integrated stylistics to what he calls "poetics": the study of the verbal
structure of a text through its different functions—referential, metalingual, phatic,
and poetic proper. Like his fellow formalists, Jakobson sees style as intrinsically
connected with meaning: "Poetry is not the only area where sound symbolism makes
itself felt, but it is a province where the internal nexus between sound and meaning
changes from latent into patent and manifests itself most palpably and intensely"
("Linguistics" 373). He has shown this nexus at work in several analyses of poetry,
most memorably in his study of Fernando Pessoa's "Ulysses," where he demonstrates
that the use of oxymoron is not only a major stylistic device (in spite of its frequency
and its condition of "pattern" within the poem) but also the underlying principle
controlling the configuration of the poem at its various levels. Compositionally, the
text presents a mirror symmetry in which one half parallels and opposes the other.
In terms of outlook or vision, the poem echoes the paradoxical nature of oxymoron
and formulates that vision in its first verse: "O mytho é o nada que é tudo." All
the other elements of the poem—rhyme, rhythm, verbs, nouns, syllables, gender—
participate in the same conflictive clash that characterizes oxymoron. Each of them
adds new tension toward the realization of theme, and their integration into a verbal
system is responsible for the efficacy of the text. Style reacts not to a norm but to
a vision embodied in a theme, and it is measured no longer as deviance but as
coherence.

Jakobson has also illustrated this interplay between style, structure, and meaning
in his classic *Fundamentals of Language*, where he showed how two figures of style—
metaphor and metonymy—become also the structuring principle of poetry and prose:
"The principle of similarity underlies poetry. Prose, on the contrary, is forwarded
essentially by contiguity. Thus, for poetry, metaphor, and for prose, metonymy is
the line of least resistance" (81–82).

From this summary, one may conclude that the changes in the way style analysis
is understood have been addressed to integrating style with other elements of the
text. The concept of deviance from the norm (even when that norm was established
in the text itself as context or pattern) was based on the assumption that literary
style must be described in relation to the linguistic code; style was thus perceived
as an exclusively linguistic phenomenon. The Russian formalists and the followers
of Jakobson see style as poetic function interacting with other functions; consequently, they described it in relation to the literary code. Part of the confusion
stems from the fact that literature uses the code of another system, that of language;
in Hjelmslevian terms, "literature is a semiotic system whose means of expression

is another semiotic system—language." The theory of signs has taught us that language as a system whose units include the two constitutive elements of any sign— "expression" and "contents," signifier and signified—enters the literary code to become the expression of a new content: the semantics of language yields to a new semantics, that of the literary code. It is therefore evident that style in literature can be measured or described not by the first code but by the second; it concerns not the semantics of language but that of literature (vision, theme). Oxymoron, for example, has stylistic relevance not as a deviation from a norm but by its implications and functions in the configuration of a literary vision within the text.

In the following analysis, I try to show that the use of oxymora in Jorge Luis Borges's early narratives responds to his literary vision of infamy as a travestied form of heroism. This parodic approach to his theme engages style as well as other elements of the literary code. Since infamy as theme or motif is not new in Borges's fiction, I begin by defining the peculiar treatment of that theme in the collection under examination, A Universal History of Infamy. I find that the burlesque approach to his theme is expressed, stylistically, through the use of oxymoron, hypallage, and litotes and that the fact that these stories are summaries of books by other authors has its stylistic counterpart in the use of metonymy, which, like Borges's adopted narrative strategy, condenses the whole in one of its attributes. Finally, for the purpose of my analysis, I choose from a multiplicity of stylistic devices those that— following the Russian formalists' concept of "the dominant"—"specify the work and guarantee the integrity of the structure" (Jakobson, "Dominant" 751).

Borges's *Universal History of Infamy*

It would be an overstatement to say that A *Universal History of Infamy*, published in 1935, contained, even in an embryonic state, the mature fiction of the author of *Ficciones* (1944) and *The Aleph* (1949). The truth is, though, that the early collection prefigures the later Borges. One can safely approach those stories through the notion of the precursor as understood by Borges himself in his memorable— and by now axiomatic—essay "Kafka and His Precursors." In each of the texts included in the collection of infamy "Borges's idiosyncrasy is present in greater or lesser degree, but if Borges had not written *Ficciones* we would not perceive it; that is to say, it wouldn't exist."[1] And if it is true that "each writer *creates* his precursors," it is equally true—I suggest—that his later work "modifies our conception" of his earlier work (*Other Inquisitions* 113) The pieces that compose this first collection anticipate *Ficciones*, but our reading of *Ficciones* refines and changes perceptibly our reading of his first narrative endeavors. To go back to the Borges of 1935 after the successive Borgeses of 1944 (*Ficciones*), 1949 (*El Aleph*), 1960 (*Dreamtigers*), 1970 (*Doctor Brodie's Report*), and 1975 (*The Book of Sand*) is to recognize his voice when that voice was still a sort of sketch or first draft, to read him as he couldn't have been read when those "exercises of narrative prose" (*Universal History* 13) appeared almost fifty years ago. This is the type of reading we are about to undertake.

Infamy as Theme

The first and most evident trait underlying this type of reading occurs at the level of theme. Infamy as a subject does not disappear in Borges's subsequent collections. It is present in various degrees in several of his later stories. "Emma Zumz" is the story of a self-inflicted rape and a vindictive murder to avenge an infamous injustice. The spy Yu Tsun, in "The Garden of Forking Paths," kills the venerable sinologist who solved the enigma of his ancestor just to signal to his chief in Berlin the needed information about the new British artillery park. "The Shape of the Sword" is the story of an informer or, rather, of the mark of his infamy. So is "Three Versions of Judas," where we are told that "God became man up to the point of infamy" (*Labyrinths* 99). Other forms of infamy are recorded in "The Lottery in Babylon," "The Approach to al-Mu'tasim" (which the narrator describes as a "kind of contest of infamies" [*Ficciones* 40]), "Theme of the Traitor and the Hero," "The Secret Miracle," "The Theologians," "Deutsches Requiem," "Ibn Hakkn al-Bokari, Dead in His Labyrinth," "The Dead Man," "The Waiting," and "The Man in the Threshold." This gallery of spies, traitors, murderers, kidnappers, informers, rapists, killers, torturers, thieves, stranglers, despoilers of corpses, and so on suffices to prove that Borges's fascination with infamy transcends his *Universal History* and pervades his later collections. But "variegated infamy," as he refers to it in one story, enters *Ficciones* and *The Aleph* in a way different from that of the early collection. The subject seems to be the same, but the tone and the manner are not. Borges approached infamy in the first collection as a kind of fine art reminiscent of De Quincey's definition of "murder in fiction," that is to say, devoid of value judgment or ethical implications.

As the detective story purports to be an intellectual operation—an exercise of the intelligence without any moralistic connotations—the story of infamy in Borges's first collection seeks to amuse and astonish. If detective fiction appeals to the intellect and the imagination, these exercises with infamy are intended to entertain by suspending our beliefs in good and evil, by turning despicable acts into laughable fits, by drawing a caricature out of civil horror and abhorrence. Hence the words of the prologue: "The man who forged this book was utterly unhappy but entertained himself writing it; I hope that a fraction of that pleasure may reach the reader" (*Historia* 10–11; trans. mine).

The approach to infamy in the later collections is different. By mixing justice, heroism, holiness, shame, ideals, faith, and, in short, virtue with infamy, Borges restates Plotinus's old notion: "Everything is everywhere, anything is all things, the sun is all the stars and the sun" (*Enneads* 5.8.4; qtd. in Borges, *Other Inquisitions* 73). "The world," says the narrator of "The Immortal," "is a system of precise compensations" (*Labyrinths* 115). To explain further:

> In an infinite period of time, all things happen to all men. . . . Just as in games of chance the odd and even numbers tend toward equilibrium, so also wit and folly cancel out and correct each other. . . . I know of those who have done evil so that in future centuries good would result. (114)

This pantheistic understanding of good and evil permeating his later fiction presents striking similarities with the Kabbalistic notion of the "breaking of the Vessels" as formulated by Isaac Luria. These Vessels contain the divine light or cosmic seed from which the visible world resulted. But the shells (*Kelipot*) of those Vessels carried in them the forces of evil that existed already before their break. When the Vessels broke, comparable to the breakthrough of birth, the divine light diffused together with the powers of evil released from the scattered fragments. "In this way the good elements of the divine order came to be mixed with the vicious ones" (Scholem 268). This Kabbalistic understanding of the coexistence of good and evil, of virtue and infamy, is echoed in Borges's short prose piece "*Paradiso, XXXI, 108,*" where Diodorus Siculus tells the story of "a god, broken and scattered abroad. . . . We lost His features, as we may lose a magic number, as one loses an image in a kaleidoscope, forever" (43).

Borges's keen interest in infamy is present in the later stories but without the tongue-in-cheek characteristic of the first collection. The letter is present, but the spirit has changed. Infamy is no longer a show of sheer burlesque, but one more character in a much broader fictional drama.

In Search of a Style

But the stories of infamy are important in Borges's development as a writer, less as theme than as form. It is in this latter account that *Universal History* represents a real breakthrough. When Borges wrote the stories of infamy, he definitely left behind the contorted baroque style of his *ultraist* (avant-garde) years. As early as 1927, in his book *El idioma de los argentinos*, he harshly criticized "the ornaments, lavishness and pretended wealth" of the Spanish language as forms of fraud, and he saw in "its perfect synonymity and its profuse verbal parade" a dead language, a display of ghosts and mummies. In that same essay, he proposed a goal that was the very opposite of that showy, expressionless, and affected style: "Total invisibility and total effectiveness" (158). In the prologue to the second edition of the stories of infamy of 1954, he renewed that attack, now free of the controversial circumstances of 1927 and also free of his own youthful insecurities: "I should define as baroque that style which borders on its own caricature. . . . Baroque is the final stage of any given art, when it parades and squanders its own means of expression." And regarding his own tales of infamy, he added: "The very title of these pages flaunts their baroque character" (11). The prose of *Universal History*, however, is far from suffering from that baroque ill of his youth. In those "falsified and distorted" stories, as he calls them, Borges found his voice, the style of the mature writer. Amado Alonso was the first to record that change, in a note published the same year the book appeared:

> This book surpasses the previous ones, by the same author, in its prose. It is a masterful prose in a strictly literary sense and not by its sumptuous tricks of pluperfect and its ostentatious language. . . . The ideas find always a rigorous form and words are addressed to their target. Economy and condensation. Borges achieves

here a style of high quality. I mean a true style, and not an impeccable grammar and a profuse vocabulary: a style which is not a rhetorical exercise. Words and sentences are pregnant with meaning. His youthful phraseology and vocabulary which used to bestow to his prose a bumpy and squeaky course, have almost completely disappeared. (345)

Alonso also pointed out, in that early note, several features of that prose: "its precision and conciseness," "its careful perfection and exactness," and, as a summary, "its accomplished stylistic level." Those stylistic features he noticed in the early collection of 1935 would become the attributes of Borges's later prose.

Let us now examine those attributes in *Universal History*, from the perspective elicited by his later prose. Some of them are readily visible to the alert eye; others require a more meticulous analysis. I will just mention the first ones, but I'll elaborate on the second type. Here is a list of narrative devices and stylistic traits from the early prose of *Universal History* that also appear in the later prose of *Ficciones* and *The Aleph*:

1. The story as a rereading and a summary of another story, either an imaginary text or an actual one or both. The list of sources given at the end of the collection on infamy attests to this practice, which Borges formulated in 1951 in his essay on Bernard Shaw: "One literature differs from another not so much because of the text as of the manner in which it is read" (*Other Inquisitions* 173).
2. An ostensible preference for the use of adjectives, anaphora, and enumerations.
3. The return to the lost or unused etymological meaning of some words ("conmovido palacio" refers to the Latin *commoveo* [79]; "nos ilustró la condición de Rosendo" points to *illustrare* 'to clarify' [96]).
4. The narrator's commentaries on his own text or metatexts (37, 73–74).
5. A declaration of sources at the beginning of the story (53).
6. The frequent use of parenthetical commentary in the middle of a sentence with various functions.
7. Transposition of neutral verbs into transitive verbs and vice versa (18).
8. Bivalent adjectives of a physical and abstract nature modifying the same noun.
9. A series of nominal phrases governed by the same verb.
10. Use of rhetorical notions to describe a character.
11. The frame story as a frequent narrative technique.

I will now examine in greater detail a few dominant stylistic features that stand out in *Universal History*.

Metaphor

I begin with metaphor because of its paradoxical absence in the prose of *Universal History*. For an author who during his ultraist years defined metaphor as an "essential element," who admired and greeted the eighteenth-century baroque author Torres

Villarroel as "a brother" of the writers of his generation and celebrated him for this love for metaphor, the absence of metaphor in the prose of 1935 is perplexing, to say the least. His early books of essays and poetry are plagued by metaphor and simile. This overabundance of images in his early writings was responsible, to a great extent, for the mannerist and downright euphuistic style of *Inquisitions*, *El tamano de mi esperanza*, and the first volumes of poetry. By 1935, Borges contracted all the linguistic ills he had criticized in his essay of 1927. He reasoned, like Averroes: "The only persons incapable of sin are those who have already committed it and repented" (*Labyrinths* 153). He didn't have to prove any more—as he put it later—that "he knew many rare words and could combine them in a startling and showy way" ("Encuentro" 14). By 1935, he was able to purge from his prose the metaphorical excesses of his youth. When images appear in the tales of infamy, they have the same restraint and classic finality as those sparingly present in his later prose. This one, for instance, from "Kotsuké no Suké": "Una *nube* de arqueros y de esgrimistas custodiaba su palanquín" (76), so tempered that it disappears in the English translation as "A *crowd* of archers and swordsmen" (*Universal History* 71), but Borges must have liked the image since it recurs in "The Circular Ruins" as "*nubes* de alumnos taciturnos" (60), translated as "*clouds* of silent students" (*Labyrinths* 146). The metaphor pointed, of course, to the motley and in-motion quality of the crowd.

With few exceptions, the prose of *Universal History* avoids figures of similarity. The absence of such figures strongly contrasts with the heavy use of metonymy and synecdoche. Borges's preference for contiguity is of one piece with his marked penchant for brevity and synopsis in the sense that, just as a summary is an effort toward conciseness and focalization, so is metonymy. Saying "casas de farol colorado" 'houses showing red lanterns' (54) is a way of describing the bordellos through one of their many aspects, but it is also a form of summarizing in one attribute the totality of the object. The choice of one attribute over others is not and cannot be accidental: it seeks to condense the whole in the part that best suits the purposes and effectiveness of the story; this is precisely the strategy Borges adopts in his stories of infamy and those that followed, when he chooses to offer a summary of the books indicated at the end of the volume as the sources of his narratives.

Other instances of metonymy reappear in the stories of *Universal History*. Thus the metonymic construction "The man who would become known to *terror and glory* as Billy the Kid" (61) is fairly common in the later stories. (In my book on Borges's prose I examined the use of metonymy in those stories [237–68].) The metonymy "un alcohol pendenciero" ("quarreling alcohol") from the same story on Billy the Kid reappears in the story "The Dead Man." Here Borges did what he pointed out regarding the word for "threat" in Old English, which meant "crowd" but was used to mean a crowd's effect, "the threatening crowd." In both translations, the figure has vanished: in the story of infamy, it is rendered as "men drink a liquor that warms them for a fight" (63); in "The Dead Man," "beben un alcohol pendenciero" becomes "the men fall into quarreling over their liquor" (98). Finally, the metonymy that so dazzled Amado Alonso in "Street-Corner Man": "Later there were blows at the door, *and a big voice called"* ("Al rato llamaron a la puerta con autoridad, *un golpe y una voz"* [97]); "He looked exactly like his voice" ("El hombre era parecido a la voz" [97]) is repeated in "Funes the Memorious": "His voice was speaking in Latin; his voice was articulating a speech" (*Labyrinths* 62). And, once again, slightly modified, in "Emma Zunz": "The face looked at her with amazement and anger, the mouth of the face swore at her in Spanish and Yiddish" (*Labyrinths* 136).

Oxymoron

Another figure of style frequently used in his later prose and abundant in the stories of infamy is oxymoron. The title of the collection offers a first example. Borges must have felt the epigrammatic twist in linking "infamy" to "universal history," since he commented in the prologue of 1954 that "the very title of these pages flaunts their baroque character." It is hyperbolically baroque, but the paradoxical nature of the link, which opposes a negative element to a positive one, generates the same tension and incongruity that crisscross the entire collection. Notice that, with one exception, all the stories of the first part have similarly oxymoronic titles: "The Dread Redeemer," "The Implausible Impostor," "The Lady Pirate," "The Purveyor of Iniquities," "The Disinterested Killer," "The Uncivil Master of Etiquette." These titles anticipate the adopted treatment: not the reproving or moralistic side of infamy but its splendidly humorous and parodic vein. One single instance encapsulates this approach. In "The Purveyor of Iniquities," we are told about heroes who are "insignificant or splendid" (56), that is, men who achieve their heroic stature through their insignificance. The world of these heroes is not epic but infamous; as the same text puts it: "Heroes from police files, heroes reeking of tobacco, smoke and alcohol . . ., heroes afflicted with shameful diseases, tooth decay, respiratory or kidney problems" (56). These infamous heroes owe their reality less to their crimes than to the travestying account that records those crimes. The frequent use of oxymora in this prose comes, therefore, as no surprise.

In a natural way, as if style were already dictated by the adopted narrative strategy, Borges speaks of "the *guilty and magnificent* existence of the *nefarious redeemer* Lazarus Morell" (20), of "the incomparable villain" (20), of "bestial hopes" (21), of "white-haired scoundrels and successful murderers" (22). A bullet, a knife, or a blow is a means *"to free* the runaway slave from sight, hearing, touch, day, infamy, time, his benefactors, pity, the air, dogs, the world, hope, sweat and himself" (25). The tone is clearly sardonic, bordering on caricature. In the first eight stories of infamy, the number of oxymora climbs to forty.[2] In addition, there are three paragraphs whose organization is also oxymoronic. Their number alone indicates the dominant presence of an artifice that expresses at the level of style what the story does at the level of theme or narrative vision.

Hypallage

Like oxymoron, hypallage is frequently used in the stories of infamy. Hypallage, or "exchange," is a change in the relation of words whereby a word, instead of agreeing with the word it logically qualifies, is made to agree grammatically with another word. The normative sentence "Bartolomé de las Casas, taking great pity on the *laborious Indians* who were languishing in the hells of Antillean gold mines" (19) becomes the first sentence of the collection's first story: "Bartolomé de las Casas, taking great pity on the Indians who were languishing in the *laborious hells* of the Antillean gold mines" (19). The logical relation—in semantic terms—is "laborious Indians" and not "laborious hells," but while the first is stylistically neutral, the second carries an expressive intention absent in the first: the emphasis is now on the hells to which the Indians are condemned. Notice that "hells" is here a metaphor for the "Kingdom of Heavens" the Indians were promised. But, in addition to that merely stylistic function, hypallage, like oxymoron, defines Borges's approach to the theme of infamy—an approach not in logical terms, in which case we would be facing a moral issue, but in imaginative terms that are the only ones literature cares for: that is, grammatical terms.

In another place, Borges defines literature as a "syntactic fact" ("Elementos" 161). He has also said that all literature is made up of tricks or artifices. Here those imaginative terms lie less in the events proper than in the tone or rather in the intonation with which those old stories are retold. The stories are about infamy, but the tone of the narrative is nonchalant and parodic, since they deal with infamous people disguised as heroes. Hence the epic overtones and gestures the narration often assumes, making us laugh because it is a heroism of carnival, a festival of masks, inversions, and displacements. There are twenty-seven examples of hypallage in the first eight stories of infamy. Some of them are literally repeated in his later prose. The "imperious cigar" (*Labyrinths* 77) of Inspector Treviranus in "Death and the Compass" had been "the thoughtful cigars" (27) smoked by Lazarus Morell. The "numerous bed" (translated as "populous couch" [*Labyrinths* 24]) that Ts'ui Pên renounced in order to compose *The Garden of Forking Paths* has its forerunner in the "numerous bed" (now translated as "the plural bed" [*Labyrinths* 63]) that Brigham Young did not renounce in the story on Billy the Kid. The "happy war" in "Deutsches Requiem" (translated as "successful war" [*Labyrinths* 145]) and the "balazo anhelado" or "desired shot" (translated as "a long-desired bullet" [*Labyrinths* 75]) that entered the breast of the traitor and hero derived from "the happy detonation" (translated as "lucky blast" [64]) that converts Bill Harrigan into Billy the Kid.[3]

These three elements of style (metonymy, oxymoron, and hypallage) appear in the stories of infamy as well as in the later ones. They constitute active ingredients in the texture and functions of Borges's prose. There is, however, a difference in the proportion: they are considerably more frequent—as their counting indicates— in the first ones. The new themes and motifs of the later stories have also resulted in a change in the ludicrous tone and intent characteristic of the early stories, and the sly style that reinforced the grotesque quality of the themes has also suffered a readjustment. The proclivity toward caricature in the early prose has yielded to a more balanced style: the number of those three figures—and particularly of the last two (oxymoron and hypallage)—is now much lower, and for a good reason. In the stories of infamy, those figures contributed to the same dislocations advanced by the themes: infamous heroes. The stories of *Ficciones* and *The Aleph*, however, are addressed to those "games with time and infinity" that require from the same devices different functions.[4] Despite these differences, the early and the later styles share some distinguishing marks of Borges's best prose. In addition to a deliberate effort to overcome the baroque style of his early writings and the use of those three stylistic devices, the prose of a *Universal History of Infamy* anticipates a few pearls that are repeated—verbatim or nearly so—in the subsequent collections. Here are a few memorable samples:

1.   "The Shape of the Sword" opens with the sentence "A rancorous scar crossed his face" (*Labyrinths* 67). Almost the same is said about Kira Kôtsuké: "A scar crossed his forehead" (translated as "His forehead still bore a scar" [74]). The narrator of the first story says further on: "With that half moon I *rubricated* [translated as "carved" or "sealed"] on his face forever a half moon of blood" (71); the narrator of the story of infamy uses the same images: "De la Torre drew his sword and aimed a blow at the master's head. Kôtsuké ran away, his forehead *rubricated* [translated as "barely marked"] with a faint thread of blood" (70).

2.   The declaration of the heresiarchs from Uqbar recalled by Bioy in "Tlön, Uqbar, Orbis Tertius"—"Mirrors and fatherhood are abominable because they multiply and extend the universe" (*Labyrinths* 4)—appears for the first time in the cosmogony of "The Masked Dyer": "The world we live in is a mistake, a clumsy parody. Mirrors and fatherhood are abominable because they multiply and confirm it" (84).

3.   Otálora in "The Dead Man" thinks that "just as the men of certain countries worship and feel the call of the sea, we yearn for the boundless plains that ring under the horse's hooves" (*Aleph* 95); Billy the Kid, too, in his flight west, feels that "the nearness of the elementary earth quickens the heart like the nearness of the sea" (63).

4.   Like Tadeo Isidoro Cruz, who one night "saw his own face" and "understood that the other man was himself" (*Aleph* 83, 85), Yakub, in "The Mirror of Ink," was able to see that face (the Man with Mask) in the mirror of ink "and understood it was his own" (128).

5.   Finally, it should be noticed that the magic lantern, or "Fanusi Jiyal," in "The Mirror of Ink" is a preview of the epiphany glimpsed through the iridescent sphere called the "Aleph" in the story so entitled.

Litotes

Since the stories of infamy are parodic in nature and intent, they employ two devices peculiar to caricature: exaggeration by augmentation and exaggeration by diminution, or overstatement and understatement. In rhetoric, those two devices are called hyperbole and litotes. Because Borges's approach to infamy is not based on moralistic principles, it preserves an imaginative distance aimed at producing irony and at times sarcasm that at the level of style results in hyperbole at the positive pole and litotes at the negative one. Examples of the first from *Universal History*:

1.   "Morell contemplated a *continental response,*—a response in *which crime would be exalted to the point of redemption and History*" (27).

2. "Over *this whole country*, another image—that of Billy the Kid, the hard rider firm on his horse, the young man of the harsh pistol shots that *bewildered the desert* sending out *invisible bullets which (like magic) kill at a distance*" (61).

3. Of the Mexican Belisario Villagrán, from the same story, it is said that "*he was overfilled with a gargantuan sombrero*" (translated as "endowed with an immense sombrero" from "abunda en un desaforado sombrero"). But in the previous sentence, the narrator explains, "Someone has come in—a burly Mexican, with *the face of an old Indian woman*" (64).

The hyperbolic description of the Mexican's hat contrasts with the description of his inoffensive face. Hyperbole next to litotes acts like the obverse and the reverse of the same operation: to exaggerate by inflating or by deflating. In both cases, the effect is irony, but while in the first it borders on humor and laughter, in the second the irony is more subtle and at the same time caustic, since the face of an old Indian woman is the face of a killer.

To describe the pirates' excesses and wretchedness in "The Lady Pirate," the narrator says with a beguiling poker face: "Their object is not benevolent; they are not and never were the true friends of the seafarer" (45), after which a violent tirade of hyperboles describes the same activity. To describe the bloody cruelty of the Emperor Kia-king in the same story, he tells us: "Never forget that clemency is an attribute of the Emperor" (46). Other examples:

1. "For each troublemaker *he calmed down*," for "he killed" ("he quelled" is a better translation but loses the artifice [54]).

2. Monk Eastman's gangs of murderers are referred to as "recreative societies" (translated as "sporting clubs" [57]).

3. The encounter between two groups of gangsters that left "four corpses, seven critically wounded men and one dead pigeon" (56) is later alluded to as "the indiscreet battle of Rivington Street" (57).

4. The recalcitrant racism of Billy the Kid is referred to as "the pride of being white" (62).

5. Billy the Kid's enthusiasm for cowboy melodramas is described in the sentence "he was not indifferent to cowboy plays" (62).

6. Suké's refusal to perform hara-kiri is presented as "Suké refused to suppress himself as a gentleman" (translated as "Suké refused to perform hara-kiri" [56]).

7. Kyoto, the ancient capital of the empire, the heart of Japanese culture and the center of her history, is described as "a city unmatched in all the empire for its autumn colors" (72).

8. Hakim the Masked's unquenchable sexuality, which "114 blind women did their best to satisfy," is referred to as "the needs of his divine body" (83).

It is quite possible that Borges's taste for this figure stems from his fondness for Anglo-Saxon. Litotes appears in *Beowulf* and Old English poetry with such frequency that together with kennings, or *kenningar*, it became a distinguishing mark of that literature. Borges wrote his essay "The Kenningar" in 1932 and included it in *Historia de la eternidad* (1936). It is evident that his stories of infamy, written and published during those years, are contaminated, as far as the prose is concerned, by those verbal games used and abused by kennings. In the story "The Widow Ching Lady Pirate," the subchapter "The Dragon and the Fox" mentions "shiftless flocks of airy dragons" that "rose each evening from the ships of the imperial squadron and came gently to rest on the enemy decks and surrounding waters" (47). We are told nothing about those "airy dragons" except that they were constructions of paper and strips of reeds and that when their number increased the Widow Pirate surrendered. But in the catalog of *kenningar*, compiled by Borges himself, the dragon is the kenning for sword and for spear. The same text refers to blood as "reddish water," a variant of the kenning "sword's water," and describes the clouds as "yellow dragons." In the last section of the same story, it is said that "from that day, ships regained peace. The four seas and the innumerable rivers became safe and happy *roads*" (48). Two kennings for the sea are "road of the sails" and "the whale's road."

In his essay on *kenningar*, included in *Historia de la eternidad*, Borges defined them as "deceiving and languishing exercises." They are often defined as implied similes in circumlocution for nouns not named. He has also said that "the dead *ultraist* whose ghost still haunts him delights in these verbal games" (64, 66). In the stories of infamy, he has left a testimony of that pleasure through the evocation of a few kennings and the convoluted manner that underlies litotes, thus conveying at the level of style the same playful and parodic approach adopted at the level of vision.

Coda and Conclusion

The style of the code of rules drawn up by the Widow Ching, in "The Lady Pirate," is described as "laconic and straightforward, utterly lacking in the faded flowers of rhetoric that lend a rather absurd loftiness to the style of Chinese officialdom" (44). It is the style that Borges himself was striving to find and that he had, to a certain extent, achieved in the stories of infamy. The reference to the "faded flowers of rhetoric" is a clear allusion to the fierce battle he waged against the baroque excess of his time and against his own early abuses of that mannerist style. Remnants of those abuses appear scattered in this first collection—the portrait of Monk Eastman, for example:

> Era un hombre ruinoso y monumental. El pescuezo era corto, como de toro, el pecho inexpugnable, los brazos peleadores y largos, la nariz rota, la cara aunque historiada de cicatrices menos importante que el cuerpo, las piernas chuecas como jinete o de marinero. Podía prescindir de camisa como también de saco, pero no de una galerita rabona sobre la cíclopea cabeza. (57)

> He was a battered, colossal man. He had a short bull neck; a barrel chest; long, scrappy arms; a broken nose; a face, although plentifully scarred, less striking than his frame; and legs bowed like a cowboy's or a sailor's. He could usually be found without a shirt or coat, but not without a derby hat several sizes too small perched on his bullet-shaped head. (54)

Other examples of this overloaded style: "A hunchbacked house by the water" (66) (translated as "a waterfront dive" [62]); criminals "pullulate" over their victim (67) (translated as "swarm him" [62]); "Mitford's account leaves out the continuous distractions of local color" (69); "El incivil maestro de ceremonias le dijo que, en verdad, era incorregible, y que sólo un patán era capaz de frangollar un nudo tan torpe" (75) (translated as "The rude master of etiquette told him that, in truth, he was unteachable and that only a boor could tie a knot so clumsily" [70]).

Yet these few excesses stem more from the excessive nature of the subjects than from an unruly or merely self-indulgent style. The proof that this is indeed so is given in the translated pieces included in the last section of the same volume under the title "Etcetera." Here is a prose that in its straightforwardness and exactness, its tightness and conciseness, reminds us very much—and strangely—of the "invisible" prose style of his last two collections: *Doctor Brodie's Report* (1970) and *The Book of Sand* (1975).

A Universal History of Infamy not only represents Borges's first attempt at writing fiction but also anticipates some of the major stylistic features that will typify his later prose. The changes in ratio and frequency of those stylistic devices, from this early collection to the later ones, respond to changes in theme and narrative vision: caricature yields to metaphysical ponderings, laughter to intellectual ruminations. What the stories of infamy tell us at the level of theme, these figures—metonomy, oxymoron, and litotes—perform at the level of style. The story as the summary of another story defines the modus operandi of metonymy; plot is organized as hyperbole or litotes; characterization is oxymoronic. Thus, theme and style are just different manifestations of the same literary vision; poetic diction and semantics have been closely intertwined.

Notes

[1] I have paraphrased the passage in which Borges concludes his survey of Kafka's precursors: "Kafka's idiosyncrasy, in greater or lesser degree, is present in each of these writings, but if Kafka had not written we would not perceive it; that is to say, it would not exist" (*Other Inquisitions* 113).

[2] In addition to the quoted examples, I have found the following ones: "Algunos cometían la ingratitud de enfermarse y morir" (20); "coraje borracho" (7); "una respuesta donde lo criminal se exaltaba hasta la redención y la historia" (27); "miseria insípida" (31); "color rosa tiznado," "Era persona de una sosegada idiotez," "su confusa jovialidad," "pudoroso temor" (32); "insensata ingeniosidad," "inmejorable ignorancia," "Sabía también que todas las similitudes logradas no harían otra cosa que destacar ciertas diferencias inevitables" (35); "plácido fantasma" (37); "Desprovistos de lágrimas y de soledad, pero no de codicia" (38); "[Bogle cruzó] las decorosas calles de Londres [en las que los cascos de un vehículo] le partieron el cráneo" (39); "Para ejercer con dignidad la profesión de pirata" (41); "La golosina fue fatal" (43); "la metódica aventura," "una majestad más bien irrisoria" (44); "y

convidan a su víctima a la ruina, a la mutiliación o a la muerte" (47); "fiestas espantosas" (48); "ineptitud gigantesca," "asesinos precoces" (54); "era un hombre ruinoso y monumental"; "el epiceno Capone" (57); "terneras degolladas con rectitud" (56); "los honorarios del malevo: 25 dólares un balazo en una pierna, 25 una puñalada" (58); "la errónea seguridad" (60); "los dos ilustres malevos," "mujeres de frágil peinado monumental" (61); "un gato, desconocedor feliz de la muerte" (63); "el hombre que para el terror y la gloria sería Billy the Kid" (66); "Ve a los hombres *tremendos, felices, odiosamente sabios*" (69; emphasis added); "de esa feliz detonación [que mata a un hombre]" (70); "el hombre más temido (y quizá más nadie y más solo)," "practicó ese lujo, el coraje" (71); "incivil maestro de ceremonias" (73); "espías incorruptibles" (76); "esa pesadilla tan lúcida," "la razón ignominiosa de esas lealtades" (78); "El asco es la virtud fundamental," "Dos disciplinas: la abstinencia y el desenfreno" (90); "basura venerable" (91).

³ In addition to the quoted examples, the following appear in the same collection: "río de aguas mulatas" (18); "miedos africanos," "el sórdido Jordán," "cultura impaciente" (for "cultivos de los blancos impacientes"), "el desierto confuso" (20); "efusiones sagradas" (for "efusiones pronunciadas en el lugar sagrado") (22); "calles decorosas de Londres" (for "calles de vida decorosa") (38); "Ciento veinte mujeres que solicitaron el *confuso amparo*" (for "ciento veinte mujeres confundidas"), "las miserables lágrimas" (for "lágrimas de las mujeres miserables"), "Lo cierto es que organizó una segunda expedición *terrible*" becomes "Lo cierto es que organizó una segunda, *terrible* en estandartes, en marineros, en soldados, en pertrechos de guerra, en provisiones, en augures y astrólogos"; "pesada muchedumbre de naves" (for "las naves con esa muchedumbre") (48); "cubiertas enemigas" ("cubiertas de los barcos enemigos") (49); "felices caminos" ("caminos de viajeros felices") (50); "dos compadritos en *seria* ropa negra" ("dos compadritos serios en ropa negra") (53); "el brutal garrote" ("el garrote del malevo brutal") (58); "la brutal convicción" ("la convicción de los brutales protagonistas"), "el estrépito insensato de cien revólveres" ("el estrépito de cien revólveres disparados por los insensatos protagonistas"), "el combate obsceno o espectral" ("el combate que tiene lugar a esa hora asociada con la obscenidad o los espectros") (60); "su vigilante nube de pistoleros" ("su nube de vigilantes pistoleros") (61); "a la menor impuntualidad del telón" ("la impuntualidad de los que levantaban el telón") (67); "el muerto lujoso" ("el muerto vestido lujosamente") (69); "Aprendió el arte vagabundo de los troperos" ("Aprendió el arte de los troperos vagabundos") (71).

⁴ I have studied those functions in *La prosa narrativa de Jorge Luis Borges*. See the subchapters devoted to metonymy (239–68), oxymoron (223–33), and hypallage (215–23).

Bashō

EARL MINER

My interest lies in cognitive literary theory, an interest shared, in some fashion, with every other reader and critic who presumes that what one remembers is alone what one can discuss. But the majority of critics today seem to wish to talk about other matters. My author is Matsuo Bashō (1644–94), the poet best loved by his own people and the Japanese poet most familiar in the West. My suggestions will be that he has not been known in the West as he would have wished to be known and that when we attend to the discrepancies we are able to know some new things about literature. Of course, to talk of Bashō does not permit me to presume what another person writing in this book can presume: familiarity in terms and assumptions, knowledge of a certain canon of works. I fear that my approach will have to be less direct, lengthier, and more explanatory. Although the faults of what I write are not attributable to length, I can assure every reader that I wish it were not necessary to identify, explain, and exemplify what seems so familiar or obvious on Japanese grounds.[1]

Bashō's greatest prose work, *The Narrow Road through the Provinces* (*Oku no hosomichi*), offers an account of the first six months of a foot journey that began in 1689 and lasted more than two and a half years. The prose is studded with various kinds of verse: fifty opening stanzas (hokku) by Bashō, others by his traveling companion, Iwanami Sora (1650–1711), and quotations or echoes of other poems in Chinese and Japanese.[2] Works like *The Narrow Road* are variously classified by the Japanese, the usual term being "travel literature" (*kikōbun*), although Bashō used the term "diaries of the road" (*michi no nikki*).[3] A prose work dealing with but part of a journey, studded with partial poems and allusions, seems to offer an unstable intertextual unit by recent Western standards. But the Japanese have never assumed the work anything but integral: to intersperse partial or whole lyric poetic units in prose narrative writings is altogether common in Chinese as well as Japanese literature, and to employ allusion is less remarkable in many respects than to claim originality. Above all, there was no convention of realism or mimesis for Bashō to undo, no conflict between fact and fiction.

A bit later, in the spring of 1690, Bashō drafted "A Record of the Unreal Hermitage" ("Genjūan no ki"). This "Record" is like *The Narrow Road* in that it tells of his thoughts at a moment in his long journey. Toward the end of this essay, he writes:

> Reflecting on myself over these months and years, I recall that I once envied those holding official positions and that I once thought of becoming a priest. But I drift to uncertain end like a cloud borne by the wind, devoting myself to poetry about this flower or that bird. For although it turns out that I have neither capacity nor talent, this one subject preoccupies me.[4]

A clear implication is that in these writings we should take these literary accounts to be factual, not fictional at all. *The Narrow Road* has been treated by Japanese in the same terms, as a work at once factual and literary. We are fortunate in the recovery of Sora's entirely factual, literal diary for most of the trip, a definitely nonliterary account. He covers details treated by Bashō except for the final portions, since Sora fell ill and had to hurry on to obtain medical assistance. Comparison of the two accounts has shown that Bashō adjusts a few details, describes one or two things that had not been done, and invents a meeting with two prostitutes near the Ichiburi Barrier. With these exceptions, all well known, the literary diary by Bashō and the nonliterary diary by Sora agree.

What Westerners need to understand is that neither account is fictional (except for that meeting with the prostitutes), that Bashō's is considered literary, and that Sora's is not. The first major issue for us to face is, then, what (if not fiction) determines literary status? There is no need to quote Sora's diary, which nobody would think literary. The need is rather to establish the literary quality of Bashō's account. The opening will establish this quality, even if there is no fiction.

> The months and days are the wayfarers of the centuries, and as yet another year comes round, it, too, turns traveler. Sailors whose lives float away as they labor on boats, horsemen who encounter old age as they draw the horse around once more by the bit, they also spend their days in travel and make their home in wayfaring. Over the centuries many famous men have met death on the way; and I, too, though I do not know what year it began, have long yielded to the wind like a loosened cloud and, unable to give up my wandering desires, have taken my way along the coast. Last autumn, as I cleaned the old cobwebs from my dilapidated house by the riverside, I found that the year had suddenly drawn to its close. As the sky of the new year filled with the haze of spring, I thought of going beyond the Shirakawa Barrier, and so possessed was I by some peripatetic urge that I thought I had an invitation from the god of travelers himself and so became unable to settle down to anything. (*Narrow Road* 157)

Let us set beside this nonfictional prose poem on time a typical lower-keyed episode in which Bashō tells of his and Sora's seeking the village of Iizuka:

> We crossed the river at Tsukinowa Ford and emerged in a post town called Se no Ue. Three and a half miles farther on, just to the left of the hills, there is a site recalling Vice-Governor Satō. Having heard that the hamlet of Iizuka was in the vicinity of Sabano, we walked on inquiring everywhere. For all our questions, we

came at last to a hill called Maruyama, the site of the vice governor's palace. When people told us of the grand gate that had stood at the foot of the hill, the image of the past led me to tears. At an old temple nearby there remain the graves of the whole Satō household, and standing between those of the two brave young wives, I wiped my eyes. They may have been women, but they had left a name for bravery to the world. There is a famous Chinese monument that made all visitors weep, but we need not seek so far for such a stone. Upon entering the temple to ask for tea, we were told that the sword of Yoshitsune and the pannier of Benkei were kept there as treasures.

> The pannier and sword:
> use them to decorate the Boys' Festival
> along with carp streamers.

That happened on the first of the Fifth Month. (167)

Sora's diary confirms everything but one detail: he explicitly says that they did not enter the temple (and so could not have had tea there). The divagation from fact is minimal, one of the few in *The Narrow Road*, and scarcely seems worthy of comment: what does it matter? The nonfact gives as much a sense of factuality (with whatever artistic heightening) as do the probatively factual details in an account at once literary and verifiable—if verifiability is what we are after, which seems most unlikely, even though we anticipate factuality.

Two other passages of humble nature deserve setting side by side. The first is what follows immediately after the opening given in the quotation before last:

> I mended my underpants, re-corded my rain hat, and took three bits of moxa cautery. I could not put from my mind how lovely the moon must be at Matsushima. I disposed of my property and moved to Sampū's house. (157)

The contrast between this passage and what precedes is remarkable, but the one quotation is no more or less factual than the other. The complementary passage again follows one of factual prose poetry, and again it offers a deflationary sequel as the two travelers arrive at Shitomae and take lodgings at Sakaeda:

> We looked for a moment upon the road to the north, where it ran obscurely off toward Nambu, and went our way, stopping that night at Iwade. We had decided to pass by Ogurozaki and Mizunoojima, following a route past Narugo Hot Springs to the Barrier of Shitomae, then crossing the mountains to Dewa Province. Because there are so few travelers on this route, the barrier guards treated us with great suspicion, and we were let through only after much delay. We struggled up a steep mountain trail and, finding that the day had grown dark, stumbled into the house of a provincial border guard and asked to be let lodging for the night. A fierce rainstorm howled for three days, keeping us in those worthless lodgings in the mountains.
>
> > Fleas and lice,
> > and the sound of horses pissing
> > disturb my pillow. (177–78)[5]

The place-name can be read homophonously as "In Front of Pissing," much as the hokku puts it, using however "pari" instead of "shito" for what the horses do. The place-name is made to accord all too well with the misery experienced, through a wordplay that is at once artistic and nonfictional.

As these examples show, the problems posed by *The Narrow Road* are fundamentally theoretical and cognitive ones. What is literature? What are its grounds? What are we knowing when we are reading Bashō's account that we are not knowing while reading Sora's nonartistic one or an extreme fiction like the travels of Spenser's Red Crosse Knight or Bunyan's Christian? The venerable, honorable Western belief in mimesis is the first casualty to be identified in this encounter with Bashō.[6] Mimesis differs from more recent Western semiotic systems in its assumption that the "real" or "noumenal" world is knowable and representable on a systematic, large scale instead of requiring discrete units of signs. East Asian poetics also assumes the world to be knowable (even if in its illusory character, as Buddhists held), but the East Asian systems are nonmimetic in not presuming, with Western theories of artistic ontology, that gap between (Plato's) forms and imitations, between (Aristotle's) reality and the representation of its universals, or between signifier and signified in modern Western semiotics. I pass over many other Western semiological conceptions but point out that East Asian poetics is neither mimetic nor antimimetic but simply nonmimetic. This general subject requires further discussion, but for the moment, it suffices to say that Bashō's writing about time and travel or mending his underwear is simply taken as what he thought and did. If in an otherwise factual section he reports entering a temple and drinking tea and if it can be shown that he did not, the proper response is surprise and interest, not concern with any difference between signifier and signified. This is not to deny that semiotically fed appetites can treat Bashō's writing semiotically or that the Japanese and Chinese can read Spenser's *Amoretti* as a reliable account of the poet's wooing of Elizabeth Boyle. But the explanation given does entail different ways of regarding literature. The Japanese classify some diaries as one species of literature (*nikki bungaku*) but assume that other diaries may not be literary at all.[7] Neither Bashō nor Sora is considered more representational or mimetic than the other. But one was taken to assume a literary presentation and the other a nonliterary, with appropriate symptoms, as they might be termed, establishing the distinction.

The presence of so many poetic units in *The Narrow Road*—and of a prose style to accommodate them—testifies to Bashō's assumption that he was writing literature, as opposed to what he wrote in his letters or spoke in various remarks about poetry recorded by his followers. Here again, however, we discover that the difference for Bashō is not between written and spoken expression, as it is variously for Socrates, Saint Paul, Saussure, and Derrida. His conversation might involve "quotation"— or rather, inclusion—of poetic units. Yet there is no debate such as we find in the West over a privileged status for spoken or for written expression. Socrates or Saussure might argue for the priority of spoken expression, and Derrida for the priority of written. It is all one to Bashō and his predecessors (including Murasaki Shikibu in her *Diary*). On the last day of the Third Month (mid-April by our calculations), Bashō reports spending a night in a place in the foothills of Mount Nikkō. How much irony is meant in the passage may be open to question, but the factuality has not been disproved:

> The owner of the inn approached us. "People call me Buddha Gozaemon," he said. "I am honest in all my dealings—people will tell you as much—so spend a night of your travels in my little inn." Had the Buddha appeared, then, as an expedient in this corrupt world of ours to save one like myself, a mendicant or pilgrim in the habit of an itinerant priest? (159)

Not long thereafter, Bashō records his writing on a similar Buddhist topic.

> I jotted down the matter that follows.

The character for "chestnut" is made up of "west" written above "tree." It therefore suggests the Western Paradise and recalls that during his lifetime the Bodhisattva Gyōgi made up his staffs or pillars from this wood.

> To which I added,

> > It is a common flower
> > that the worldly think not worth note
> > chestnut at the hermit's eaves. (166)

Both the prose writing and the poem are in obvious contrast with Gozaemon's speech, yet they are taken to be equally factual, and neither has a privileged status.

Bashō's problem as a writer was not in sorting privileged from nonprivileged forms of expression but in getting others to extend privilege to him. In normative terms, his art was too "low." Bashō was altogether aware that his haikai art included much that was far less pure or exalted than the material treated by the *waka* and *renga* poets.[8] He insisted that his art was genuine, however, and in the mainstream of Japanese art. He spoke of true art, implicitly entering a claim for his own, in terms of the continuing native tradition:

> [It] is all one in nature, whether in Saigyō's waka, in Sōgi's renga, in Sesshū's painting, or in Rikyū's tea ceremonial. Moreover, in matters of art one follows the creative principle and accompanies the four seasons of the year. It is impossible to speak of looking without looking for cherry blossoms, of longing without longing for the moon. Those who keep no image of flowers are like barbarians, and those whose hearts are not stirred by flowers are no better than beasts. One must expel such barbarity; one must leave the beasts and join humankind, constantly pursuing or returning to the creative principle.[9]

What then is the special province of haikai? Bashō treats that topic in a carefully schematic passage:

> There are three elements in haikai. Its *feeling* can be called loneliness. That plays with refined dishes but contents itself with humble fare. Its *total effect* can be called elegance. That lives in figured silks and embroidered brocades but does not forget

a person clad in woven straw. Its *language* can be called aesthetic madness. Language
resides in untruth and ought to comport with truth. These three elements do not
elevate a humble person to heights. They put an exalted person in a low place.

(qtd. in Miner, *Poetry* 112; emphasis added)

Bashō uses versions of the three most hallowed words in Japanese poetics. His *nasake*
or "feeling" is a version of *kokoro* (mind, heart, or spirit). His "total effect" is the
traditional *sugata*. His "language" or *gengo* replaces the *kotoba* or words, images,
subjects, expression of traditional poetics. The use of the traditional language in
modified form images the import of the whole remark.

Bashō's aim clearly entailed maintaining the seriousness and grandeur of the past
within the realities of his own life. In 1688 he visited Suma, a place rich in
associations. It had been a place of exile for the radiant hero of *The Tale of Genji*
and before that for Ariwara Yukihira (818–93), who had ended a poem to a friend
in the capital: "If anyone should ask of me, / Tell him that I suffer so" (*Kokinshū*,
18: 962). Bashō could only have had these figures in his mind, but he refers to the
doomed romantic figure of Taira Atsumori (1169–84), whose dates show he died a
lad, while in armor during a period tantamount to civil war. Mentioning Atsumori,
he wrote to his boyhood friend Ensui (1640–1704): "The loss on that day and the
pain of this—I shall never forget you among thoughts of life and death, the sub-
servience of the weak to the powerful, mutability, and swift time" (qtd. in Miner,
Poetry 115). "Times change, and we"—and our art—"with them." The issue was
one of honoring both past and present, and the burden of the present was such that
a new art was called for, an art true to tradition and yet one that would not falsify
present experience.

As Bashō and Sora trod on toward the north along the Pacific coast of Japan,
they came at last to Hiraizumi, where Japan's greatest chivalric figure, Minamoto
Yoshitsune (1159–89), met his end. A great general in the wars that had claimed
young Atsumori, Yoshitsune took refuge from his vengeful brother Yoritomo (history
and legend are impossible to sort out by now) at the Hiraizumi fortress of three or
four generations of a family (including Fujiwara Yasuhira and Hidehira, mentioned
by Bashō), only to be betrayed and have to take his own life. Bashō's eloquence
does not fail him:

> The splendors of the three generations of Hiraizumi now make up the briefest of
> dreams, and of the grand façade there are only faint remains stretching out for two
> and a half miles. Hidehira's castle is now leveled to overgrown fields, and of all
> the splendors of his past, only Mount Kinkei retains its form. Climbing up to the
> high ramparts of what had been Yoshitsune's stronghold, one can see below the
> Kitakami River flowing in a wide stream from the south. The Koromo River pours
> past the site of loyal Izumi Saburō's castle, then beneath these ramparts, and at
> last into the Kitakami. The old relics of others like Yasuhira are to be found
> separated to the west at Koromo Barrier, which controlled the southern approach
> and probably was meant to protect the area against incursions by the northern
> tribesmen. Yoshitsune and his brave adherents took refuge in this citadel, but the
> most famous names claim the world only a little while, and now the level grass
> covers their traces. What Tu Fu wrote came to my mind—

The country crumbles, but mountains and rivers endure;
A late spring visits the castle, replacing it with green grasses . . .

and sitting down on my pilgrim's hat I wept over the ruins of time.

The summer grasses;
the high bravery of men-at-arms,
the vestiges of dream.   (*Narrow Road* 176–77)

Passages like these are unforgettable. They and the miseries of lodging at Sakaeda with horses pissing nearby are equally integral to Bashō's art. By admitting the latter, Bashō forfeited the esteem of his contemporaries, whose blindness seems almost willful to us today. Yet his is really an unstable art that comprehends such a variety of seemingly disparate experiences, such discordant worlds. In all this, he makes an implicit claim to a fuller reality. There may be those who would deconstruct Bashō precisely because of the varied elements he considered real and whole. Such critics have their rights, but those rights are not ratified by centuries of Japanese readers. For if no one subject, neither prose nor verse, speech nor narrative is privileged in *The Narrow Road*, in another sense the integrated totality does have the privilege of being assumed to be real. (We shall get to the integration of *The Narrow Road* in aesthetic terms; the present argument turns on the experiential and on assumptions about reality.) Without that belief in variegated wholeness, Bashō's art is impossible. It is also true that the harmonizing of such discordant elements into literary concord did not survive Bashō. On his death, the members of his school went their more or less separate and certainly lesser ways.

Bashō defined himself in many explicit as well as implicit ways. Above all he defined himself as a poet of linked poetry, of sequences written with two or three or four other poets in alternation. These sequences now require our attention for the differences they reveal between Eastern and Western conceptions of self and art. Linked poetry is a rules-governed poetry that would have given even Thomas Rymer pause. For Bashō's favored sequence of thirty-six stanzas, two sheets of paper were used: the front of the first and the back of the second held six stanzas each; the back of the first and the front of the second, twelve stanzas each. Each side (except, almost invariably, the back of the second sheet) was required to have a moon stanza, and each sheet was to have a flower stanza (i.e., a stanza using the word *hana* 'flower'; a named flower such as iris did not count). Stanzas were classified as being devoted to one of the four seasons or as miscellaneous. In addition to these major topics there were various subtopics (love, travel, etc.), with elaborate rules for continuance and discontinuance governing all topics and subtopics.

Two other canons require emphasis. One is stanzaic connection. A given stanza was rated by degree of formal impressiveness, which need not have all that much to do with abstractly considered quality, and above all by closeness ("heaviness" was Bashō's designation) or distance ("lightness") of connection. Of the two, the art of stanzaic connection—especially variance—was crucial. The second canon of vital importance involved the rhythm of the whole. The front of the first sheet (stanzas

1–6) was taken to be an introduction more or less calm and stately. The next twenty-four stanzas (7–30, the back of the first sheet and the front of the second) made up an agitated development or breaking section, and the last six (31–36, the back of the second sheet) constituted a fast close. Terms like "fast" are of course metaphorical, and long study is required to understand them, lengthy and detailed accounts to explain them.[10]

One further feature of linked poetry requires explanation, since it seems so different from our literary expectations. Each stanza except the first has an added stanza with which it must be joined, since the two constitute a poetic integer. The added stanza may well change the meaning of the predecessor by drastically altering the situation (the most frequent and indeed the regular alteration) or by changing the status of the persons involved—their sex, number, social station, or age. Moreover—and this cannot be stressed enough—no stanza relates semantically to any other (whether by echo, parallel, or "spatial form") except its predecessor and its successor. If stanzas 7 and 26 deal with travel in an autumn dusk, there is no connection between them, no recall.

To enumerate the canons and the assumptions so briefly no doubt causes dizziness. An example or two will make matters clearer. A good illustration of the art of linked poetry can be found in a run of stanzas from a sequence Bashō composed with two of his closest poetic disciples, Mukai Kyorai (1651–1704) and Nozawa Bonchō (d. 1714), and another, lesser-known poet, Nakamura Fumikuni (dates uncertain). In the early winter of 1690 the four poets sat in Kyoto to compose *Even the Kite's Feathers*, a sequence of thirty-six stanzas. The first two lines given here are stanza 22, composed by Bashō. Since the stanzas are 22–30, they complete the agitated development section.

<blockquote>
All the wood thrushes that he heard
have finished their summer songs
23   wasted to the bones
he still cannot summon strength
    to rise from his bed
Fumikuni
</blockquote>

<blockquote>
Wasted to the bones
she cannot summon strength
    to rise from her bed
24   her visitor finds the place is cramped
and borrows carriage space next door
Bonchō
</blockquote>

<blockquote>
He used to find my place so cramped
he borrowed carriage space next door
25   his neglect is heartless
if only he would come again to see me
    through my mock-orange hedge
Bashō
</blockquote>

His neglect was heartless
but he went again to visit her
through the mock-orange hedge
26 now is the time of lovers' parting
and she helps him put on his sword
Kyorai

At the time of lovers' parting
she helped him put on his sword
27 left all restless
with her comb she worried her hair
messing its lines
Bonchō

In a restless state
with his comb he worries his hair
messing its lines
28 summoning determination
to hazard his life in battle
Fumikuni

He summoned determination
to hazard his life in battle
29 in the chill blue sky
the yet remaining moon dissolves
in the light of dawn
Kyorai

In the chill blue sky
the yet remaining moon dissolves
in the light of dawn
30 as autumn comes to Biwa Lake
and to Mount Hira with first frost
Bashō (Miner, Poetry 291–93)

The agitation will be evident. It must be observed that the subtopic of love enters, because Bashō felt it particularly important in this section of a sequence. Stanza 26 is not a love stanza, but by connection with 25 it continues that sense of longing or yearning, of loved without being loved in return, that is the essence of Japanese poetic versions of love. To make the selection clearer, I will add commentary that designates—in order—the formal impressiveness of a stanza, its heaviness or lightness of connection with its predecessor, its topic and subtopic, and various motifs. These matters are never constant, and dynamic variation is the rule— as a counterpart to the assumption that no stanza relates to any other than its predecessor (and therefore its successor).

23 *Ground. Light. Miscellaneous.*
The sudden shift tells us that another stage in the development (ha) section has begun. In itself, this is wholly undistinguished, even prosaic. But for a sequence, Fumikuni's mastery is like that other kind shown by him in 15.

24   *Ground-Design. Light. Miscellaneous. Love. Products. Residences.*
The language is plain and does not justify a Love classification, which is presumed
by the allusion (honzetsu) to *The Tale of Genji*, where in "Yūgao" the visit to a
sick old woman leads to Genji's liaison with Yūgao. The recollection raises the
impressiveness of the stanza and perhaps suggests Court as a classification.

25   *Ground-Design. Heavy. Miscellaneous. Love. Persons. Cultivation.*
A clear-cut love stanza, this is haikai in language but timeless in conception: the
betrayed woman waiting, the lover who might come through the hedge, as Narihira
and countless literary lovers did after him. Some see an echo of "Ukifune" in *The
Tale of Genji*. The "k" alliteration is striking. Love appears two-thirds through the
sequence.

26   *Design-Ground. Heavy-Light. Miscellaneous. Military. Products.*
Lovers part in the morning. Kyorai alters the aura of court nobility in the preceding
to a more contemporary scene, as the woman hands the sword to her lover, who
had slipped in through the hedge of 25. It is not clear whether the "ima ya" of
farewell is imagined to be said/thought by the woman alone.

27   *Ground-Design. Heavy-Light. Miscellaneous. Products.*
Left by her lover, who will probably be long in returning, the woman feels great
agitation. The stanza could hardly stand apart but is a splendid contribution to
the sequence, both for its connection with 26 and the possibilities it leaves open.

28   *Ground. Light. Miscellaneous. Military.*
Fumikuni achieves a major change: in sex of the speaker and of the situation
justifying agitation. . . .

29   *Design. Light. Autumn. Night. Radiance.*
In a major departure—even greater in some ways than 23—Kyorai introduces
Autumn after six miscellaneous stanzas and gives the third moon stanza in its
approved position. His successor is put on his mettle. The moon fades into a lovely
morning sky.

30   *Design. Heavy-Light. Autumn. Peaks. Waters.*
Bashō specifies the location of the scene in 29—some few miles from Kyoto, enough
for imagination to play—one of the eight famous views of Lake Biwa. The joining
of noun-elements by no particles recalls waka poetry in one of the styles of the
Shinkokinshū, the eighth royal collection (beginning of 13th century). The development (ha) section has led up to two design poems. Frost is a falling thing in
renga.   (Miner, *Poetry* 292–94)

Another illustration will be useful, since it features a different group dynamism,
that of Bashō sitting in the circle of six haikai poets in 1684. *In the Month of Frosts*
involved five poets besides Bashō; their names will be given with their stanzas but
their dates will be omitted. The following stanzas (6–14) include the last stanza of
the formal introduction and the initial run of the agitated development section
(Yasui composed stanza 6). Once again we have a love stanza (12) typical of the
lengthy development section. This time the translations will be interspersed with
the commentary.

The young lad who will serve sake
has gone out to cut some asters
7   it was in the autumn
their lordships relaxed in travel
    with impromptu renga
Bashō

7   *Ground-Design. Heavy-Light. Miscellaneous. Travel.*
The honorific (gorenga) suggests courtiers or military aristocrats. Some peaceful
moment in the war-torn age of the renga master Sōgi (1421–1502) is perhaps
meant. "Aki no koro" suggests some general time in autumn, as if the travel took
enough time not to be identified as early or late in the season.

    It was in the autumn
    their lordships relaxed in travel
8   with informal renga
    at last the clearing sky reveals
    the temple has a Fuji view
    Kakei

8   *Design-Ground. Heavy. Miscellaneous. Buddhism. Peaks.*
With 7, this suggests that the travelers turned to renga because bad weather kept
them from other occupations. Both stanzas share an auspicious character. Only the
diction, especially the "yōyaku," prevents this from being a Design stanza. The
introduction (jo) seems actually to end here.

At last the clearing sky reveals
the temple has a Fuji view
9   this is solitude
the sound of a camellia flower
    dropping to the ground
Tokoku

9   *Design. Heavy-Light. Spring. Cultivation.*
Now the mountain temple of 6 seems emptied of visitors, peopled only by monks
in meditation. Only such stillness would allow one to hear the soft sound. One of
a number of outstanding and varied stanzas by Tokoku, who excels in this sequence.

    This is solitude
    the sound of a camellia flower
    dropping to the ground
10   light shimmers above the tea
    dyeing the breeze with its fragrance
    Jūgo

10   *Design-Ground. Light. Spring. Cultivation. Day. Radiance.*
The considerable verbal magic of the stanza conceals problems of interpretation.
Ceremonial tea (the tea assumed by the commentators) has no such fragrance. Either
the fragrance of the tea here is the result of its being heated in leaf for curing or
the synaesthetic imagery is a product of Jūgo's fancy.

Light shimmers above the tea
dyeing the breeze with its fragrance
11   chasing the pheasants
there are some five thirty women
    wearing men's court caps
Yasui

11 *Ground-Design. Light-Heavy. Persons. Birds. Clothes.*
Editors cite a number of occasions, including one on which Kiso Yoshinaka (1154–
84) had women act out roles normally performed by men. The "go sanjū" ("five
thirty") is a puzzler. It may mean "fifty or thirty," "what first seemed five and
then seemed thirty," "thirty-five" in unusual syntax—or, as it is taken here, a
haikai witticism such as Yasui favors in this sequence.

    Chasing the pheasants
there are some five thirty women
    wearing men's court caps
12 light in clothes and love the women
see Kiso modeled in the garden
Uritsu

12 *Design-Ground. Light-Heavy. Summer. Love. Persons. Residences.*
Uritsu seems to regard 11 as an allusion to Yoshinaka. The garden must be extensive
to model the mountainous Kiso area.

Light in clothes and love the women
see Kiso modeled in the garden
13   summer is deep
in wealth of mountain roses
    looking like cherries
Kakei

13 *Design-Ground. Heavy-Light. Summer. Trees.*
The scene is well advanced in time and blossoms. Since we have (two) Named
Flowers (na no hana), this is not a Flower stanza (hana no ku). In general, this
stanza closely emulates renga diction.

    Summer is deep
in wealth of mountain roses
    looking like cherries
14 and I am collecting waka
for the *Flax-Reaping Collection*
Bashō

14 *Design-Ground. Light. Miscellaneous.*
In keeping with the agitation of the development (ha) section, Bashō reintroduces
people after the natural scenery of 13. Flax was cut in summer, but since that
plant is only in the anthology's title, this stanza is Miscellaneous. In good haikai
fashion, this stanza poses an activity and a (merely suggested) plant, elements at
variance from Kakei's grand scene.   (Miner and Odagiri 66–69)

Before turning to the theoretical implications of linked poetry, we ought to consider the one sustained section of *The Narrow Road* that Bashō made up, the episode on the two prostitutes encountered at the Ichiburi Barrier.

> Today we passed the most trying part of our north-country journey, going through dangerous places with such horrible names as Deserting-Parents—Abandoned-Children, Excluded Dog, and Rejected Horse. I was so tired that I searched out a pillow and lay down as soon as I could. Two young women were talking, however, in the next room but one, toward the front of the building. Mingled with their voices was that of an old man, and from what was said I understood that the women were from Niigata in Echigo Province, and that they were prostitutes. They were on their way to worship at the Ise Shrine, and the man had come to see them as far as this barrier at Ichiburi. He would go back to Niigata tomorrow, while they were writing letters and giving him various broken messages to carry back.
>
> The conversation floated to me. "We are as they say waves falling upon the beach, coming to ruin on the shore, expecting no better end than 'fisherwomen' like us ever have. People treat us with disgust, and we fall lower and lower. Each night we are pledged to love a different man. To have to endure such a shameful life, what terrible things must we have done in a previous existence?"
>
> I fell to sleep with their words in my ears, and just as we were setting out the next morning, the two women came up to us weeping.
>
> "We don't know what route to take," they said, "and so we are terribly worried about our trip. Our anxiety has made us miserable about what lies ahead, and we wonder, may we follow you—at a distance far enough so we would not embarrass you? Your clothes show that you are priests, and that means you will have pity. The boundless grace of the Buddha can be bestowed even on such as we, so please help our souls to enter his Way." They continued in tears as they spoke.
>
> "I regret it very much," I told them, "but we are not so much traveling anywhere as stopping here and there for periods of time. It would really be better for you if you accompanied ordinary travelers. The favor of the gods should enable you to get to Ise without trouble." With that we set out on our way, but the great pity of their situation troubled me for some time.

> Prostitutes and priest
> slept under a roof lent a beauty
> by bush clover and moon.

I spoke out the verses to Sora, who set them down in his diary. (187–88)[11]

Bashō provides this episode three fourths of the way through *The Narrow Road*, in a place comparable to the run of stanzas in *Even the Kite's Feathers*. As recent Japanese critics have pointed out, *The Narrow Road* is organized on the introduction–development–fast close design of a linked-poetry sequence. In other words, the episode corresponds to a run of love stanzas in the development section. Given their priestly or semipriestly status, Bashō and Sora were not likely to be involved in amatory experience. It was necessary, therefore, in this instance, to provide a fictional episode (along with the factual record of the places visited) in order to satisfy Bashō's design of *The Narrow Road* on the basis of a linked-poetry sequence. Once we understand the ordering principle, the fiction takes on an artistic status akin to that of the factual material elsewhere. The episode is no less "real," given the design, than anything else is. The encounter is what *ought* to have happened at that stage in the account.

Both in *The Narrow Road* and in the haikai sequences, there are certain theoretical issues involved for us that even Bashō could not have been aware of. One is the status of author and audience. Our problem involves a contradiction in recent Western criticism between the Romantic conception of the expressive author and the poststructuralist conception of a text empowered as a subjective agent: the text is now said to do what formerly the author (or reader) was thought to do—be, think, and act. Holding to neither the Romantic nor the textualist claims, I prefer to consider the actualities of linked poetry.

If four poets are writing a thirty-six-stanza sequence, they will agree ahead of time that each will write nine and, probably, that the order of composing will shift in the second half of the work. The real or nominal host will compose the first stanza, which will be the only one required to take note of the season, time of day, or other circumstances of the occasion of the meeting. The real or nominal guest will compose the second, and a gifted poet the thirty-fifth, which is the "seat" (*za*) for the second flower stanza. Because he traveled so much, Bashō often composed second stanzas as the guest, but sometimes he would use an opening stanza more than once, until he felt its potential for development had been realized. Social formality, literary aim, and sociology governed the writing of linked poetry.

Linked poetry reminds us strikingly of what we usually overlook: the first audience or "reader" of a work is none other than the creating poet. Milton would compose about forty lines of *Paradise Lost* in his head for dictation, and Dr. Johnson a whole *Rambler* essay. The mental revisions necessary show that no text exists, save that which is always necessary for literature to exist—some physical coding. In the two examples just given, the text is physically encoded in memory engrams of the brain, where it reposes physiologically until the next encoding, Milton's recitation to an amanuensis, and then by ink to paper. In linked poetry, not only does each poet constitute the initial audience, but as turns to write come and go, one who is a poet in one round turns audience until another round to compose. Yet to be a revolving author is to be an author steadily *in potentu*, since one must constantly understand what one's fellow poets are up to, realizing that it is time for a light stanza, that a third autumn stanza is required to bridge the front and the back of the first sheet, or that a shift to spring will make the second flower stanza easier to write. With so many canonical expectations, half the fun lay in manipulating them. In the summer of 1690, Bonchō wrote the following opening stanza for *Throughout the Town*:

> Throughout the town
> above the welter of smelly things
> the summer moon.   (Miner, *Poetry* 301)

The place for the first moon is the fifth stanza, not the first. And a summer rather than an autumn moon is odd as a first stanza, just as the smells of fish products and fertilizer in the heat hold little ordinary poetic appeal. Yet by ancient poetic tradition, night is the proper poetic time for summer. Bonchō's first stanza sets the terms in which the sequence will go—at least as far as that is possible given three gifted poets (Bashō and Kyorai are the other two). The opening of the back of the first sheet will further show how these poets work. (The sixth stanza is by Kyorai.)

> He is an odd one to carry on
> swaggering with an enormous sword
> 7   he quakes in fright
> from a frog croaking in the weeds
>   as twilight thickens
> *Bonchō*

> She jumps with fright
> at the frog's croaking in the weeds
>   as twilight thickens
> 8   so in search of butterburr shoots
> her shaking hand puts out the lamp
> *Bashō*

> While hunting butterburr shoots
> I shook the lamp and put it out
> 9   my waking to the Way
> came long ago at that season
>   of budding flowers
> *Kyorai*

> His waking to the Way
> came long ago at that season
>   of budding flowers
> 10   now at Nanao Bay in Noto
> the winter cold is hard to bear
> *Bonchō*   (Miner, *Poetry* 303)

Bonchō's seventh stanza shows that the bullyboy Kyorai introduces is really a coward; it is a fine comic addition. Bashō alters to a more elegant situation: there are courtly associations to the picking of young shoots and an air of romance to doing it at night with a lantern, even if the comedy is also retained as the shake of the hand extinguishes the burning wick. Kyorai makes the incident the first stage of the person's enlightenment: the Buddha uses expedients such as these little accidents to illumine our darkened minds. We have now had three stanzas involving causation in one guise or another. Bonchō decides on good grounds that it is time to shift, adding a stanza of considerable lightness and no sense of causation. He shifts the topic from spring to winter. A shift to summer would have implied some continuance. By turning instead to winter, Bonchō suggests a gap in time, just as his use of a place-name suggests a change in location. Solely in connection with stanza 9, Bonchō suggests that the person is now some older monk nearing the end of his life while recalling the glories of the time when he first became devout. There are continuances as well: a winter stanza is still a seasonal stanza, not a miscellaneous

one; the sense of time is maintained, as is the seriousness Kyorai had introduced.
What will follow this? It is Bashō's turn. We observe that he shifts to a miscellaneous
stanza, grasps at once what Bonchō is up to, and, recalling that Noto was famous
for its fish, writes a stanza of heavier connection:

> At Nanao Bay in Noto
> the winter cold is hard to bear
> 11   all that I can do
> is suck upon the bones of fish
> and think of old age.
> *Bashō*   (304)

As these examples and this discussion will have made clear enough, linked verse
was written by poets who were both collective author and first audience. In spite
of—but to some extent because of—the complex rules, the composition by alternating poets increases a sense of the unexpected or random—different poets and
people are involved. Yet we may contrast with the examples given here those in
Renga, an attempt by four Western poets of different nationalities to write a linked
sequence in a Paris basement.[12] One of their stated aims was to do away with the
Romantic notion of the expressive poet mentioned above. Of course they do not
succeed. The Japanese poets, on the other hand, show that they know how to
combine, giving up a real degree of individual independence in order to function
as a creative group.

For centuries the most important publication of Japanese poetry had been in
collections (see Bashō's stanza above on the fictional *Flax-Reaping Collection*), and
the ordering of the collections was neither by chronology nor by poetic canon but
by topic, as in a linked-poetry sequence. If a poet had twenty-five poems in a
collection, it was highly unlikely that any more than two of them would appear in
succession; more probably, they would be scattered throughout the usual twenty
scrolls. The poetic topic and the created collection (meant to be read as one reads
a linked-poetry sequence and in fact an ancestor of linked poetry) held priority over
authorship as a critical principle. That is why the honor of compiling a royal
collection was even greater than that of having poems included in it: it gave an
individual or individuals the opportunity to order poems they thought important
in ways of their own devising. Naturally, the compilers would include poems they
had written; after all, their poetic abilities had been a major ground for their being
given royal commission to compile. But it is altogether in accord with the way
individuals function in Japanese society—more as members of some group than as
individuals in the sense Westerners are likely to assume—that the Japanese should
make of linked poetry what no other people has done: a distinct and great art. (The
Chinese had tried, but the cardinal Chinese poetic principle, "state your intention,"
did not lead to truly integrated sequences by Japanese standards.)

Just as we must revise our sense of what authorship may mean, so must we revise
what is said of texts. When Bonchō, Bashō, and Kyorai were composing *Throughout
the Town*, some friend no doubt wrote down the stanzas recited in turn, and no

doubt that bystander or scribe could show one of the poets what was written. But for the most part, the text of what had been written and what was just now being composed was part of the short-term memory of all three poets. However less assertive as individuals they were than are Western poets, their texts were merely encodings of their knowledge (whether in the human cerebral cortex or on paper), and it was their knowledge as poets–initial readers that constituted the existence of the work or the poem. Later, when this sequence was incorporated in *The Monkey's Straw Raincoat Collection* (*Sarumino Shū*), it became widely available to other readers than those first ones. [13]

The status of the author raises other issues, especially the complex of matters characterizable as "point of view." Point of view is not a term made much of today, but it does relate to something important: texts do not speak themselves, whatever some people may say. A poem has a created speaker or a narrator, a semblance of a thinking human subject, a stylized version more or less like the author. With *The Narrow Road* one would be crazy to assume great unlikeness between author and narrator; with linked poetry, we can only assume a group authorship. Even with that assumption there are many problems. The identity of the person assumed and the distance from the authorial group shift constantly in a way that is so easy and so radical as even to be unpresentable in English. We last saw Bashō's work as a stanza added to one by Bonchō. The translation goes: "all that I can do / is suck upon the bones of fish / and think of old age." Now the word "I" is not in the Japanese, but the word "one" or "you" or "they" is also not meant. Even in *The Narrow Road* Bashō uses a word for "I" (*yo*) only a couple of times. Something must be said about the Japanese language and how it is handled.

The four parts of speech in Japanese (nouns, adjectives, verbs, and particles) include personal nouns instead of pronouns. There are numerous personal nouns for "I" and "you," and levels of honorific and deference in word choice as well as in auxiliaries and inflections can indicate person when it is not specified by a personal noun. Japanese has topics as well as subjects, and either or both may be a personal noun in a given sentence. In practice, however, personal nouns are avoided, particularly in poetry. In the translation of *Throughout the Town*, the following pronouns are used the number of times indicated: third person, five times; first person, twice. (The figures involve repetitions of stanzas as new stanzas are added, often requiring a shift in pronoun.) In none of these instances is there a personal noun in the Japanese. There is none at all in the entire sequence. Often the identity is simply not clear, but English demands some choice.

The dispersal of authorship in a group writing linked poetry has as its counterpart a far weaker sense of point of view. It is clear that there are fluctuations, but it is often not clear from whom to whom the fluctuation occurs. Instead, what comes strikingly to occupy a great importance is what may be termed point of attention. Any of the examples given would do, but let us take a fresh one, from a duo, *Poetry Is What I Sell*, written by Bashō with the irrepressible Enomoto Kikaku (1661–1707). Bashō writes stanza 24, and the capital letters designate Japanese treated as if it were Chinese.

EVIL DEMONS' powers are used
on a cape by the wild sea
25   with your iron bow
o brave good man come forth to help
in this warring world.
Kikaku

with your iron bow
o brave good man come forth to help
in this warring world
26   a tiger there within her breast
she pregnant with a son at dawn
Bashō

A noble tiger in her dream
she pregnant with a son at dawn
27   the mountain is cold
THREE MEN WITH A TIGER in bed
as high winds blow
Kikaku

The mountain is cold
THREE MEN WITH A TIGER in bed
as high winds blow
28   the priest's charcoal fire gone out
a finger serves him as a wick
Bashō

The banked charcoal fire gone out
her finger sets alight a lamp
29   the queen of low birth
wishes to sleep late each morning
and shuts out the moonlight
Kikaku   (Miner and Odagiri 57–59)

In that phantasmagoria, seemingly anything can happen, and the shift of point of attention is constant in a double sense: we are constantly being shifted from one to another surprising object of attention, and there is always a point of attention. Here the focus is largely on a succession of roles. In other sequences, or passages, natural scenery offers an equally important point of attention:

Sleeping at noon
the body of the blue heron
poised in nobility
where the waters trickle trickle
the rushes sway in utter peace.   (Miner, *Poetry* 333)[14]

Our attention shifts from a view of a lovely bird in the stasis of Buddhist enlightenment to the sound of waters and the sight of slowly moving plants. The lesser importance of point of view and the lesser lexical presence of personal nouns are complemented by the greater importance of point of attention and nonauthorial, nonnarrator elements. In a sense this feature of haikai was better grasped by the eighteenth-century master, Yosa Buson (1716–83), whose poetry (especially his opening stanzas) exploits the importance of point of attention more fully than does the poetry of Bashō. On the other hand, Bashō uses the point of attention to focus what is essentially human and reflective of his own interests. His blue heron offers what he and others aspired to. Bonchō recognizes as much, creating the perfect scene for the bird, and with a movement that suggests the bird will awaken, whether as we may awaken from that dream which is the sense of the vanity of the real to yet a higher sense, or as, from a moment's enlightenment, we awake into old illusion. The subjective counterpoise is what Japanese appreciate in Bashō, just as masters like James, Joyce, Mann, Borges, and Beckett may use the Western concern with point of view to increase irony and threaten the authority of the subjective point of view. Whatever the emphasis in a given language or culture, it should be clear that point of attention is as important as point of view and that the interplay between them is crucial for much subtle directing of our responses.

One last issue involves genre, by which is meant here drama, narrative, and lyric, along with their attributive possibilities (a dramatic lyric: a poem dominantly lyric but with dramatic features), the cogeneric (lyric narrative), and even the counter-generic (narrative vs. drama), all being possibilities in single works. Bashō's work, as we have been seeing it, is as definitely rich in lyric as it is weak in drama, in spite of his composing with others in a single ring (or triangle). The issue is whether or not this writing also deserves to be termed narrative. Plot is often dismissed today as a concept, and it is seldom defined by users of the word. But if a plot is a continuance of personages, times, and places with temporal and motivational causalities and other successions, and if plot is necessary to narrative, then linked poetry is not narrative. Linked poetry is continuous from stanza to stanza, but the lack of any connectedness in the whole rules out plot except on small scale and on radically discontinuous terms.

Is *The Narrow Road* a narrative? Readers of a translation would be likely to conclude that it is. Certainly it is more continuous than linked-poetry sequences. But much of what seems essential—first-person narration—is an illusion necessitated by the English language. In it as well as in the linked sequences, the point of attention is crucial: it is by what he sees that we discover the poet, the speaker, or the narrator. Moreover, the continuousness of *The Narrow Road* reflects the travel-diary form: a certain route at a certain time dictates the sequence. Thus *The Narrow Road* is far more continuous than linked poetry, at least in appearance, but less continuous than we think or than we expect a novel to be. As we have seen, the episode of the two prostitutes at Ichiburi is made up as the counterpart of a run of love stanzas, and the whole work is given dynamic variation, as a linked-poetry sequence would be, and also the very rhythm of introduction–agitated development–fast close that a linked sequence would have. In any event, the causal and contingent features of plot continuance are all but entirely lacking. If linked sequences have only momentary plots, so *The Narrow Road* has but the weakest and faintest of plots.

If plot is not necessary to narrative, as I believe it is not, then the question becomes what is? This issue is too large to be dealt with even perfunctorily here. It involves conceptions such as literary units and integers, beginnings and endings, continuousness and discontinuousness—and, in a word, that sequentiality which is more important to literature than is plot. Given the minimal plot of *The Narrow Road* and the momentary plot elements of the linked sequences, it can at least be seen that this kind of writing (which predates in *renga* versions the Columbian discovery of the new world) will have much to show us by example. This is another way of saying that, yes, Bashō is a great poet and prose writer, but that we are wise not to consider that he is great on terms completely familiar to us. In fact, the differences in the terms of artistic presumption and practice are what reveal most to us. They extend the realm of our literary experience, they offer alternatives to what we presume to be universal norms, and they test the conclusions of Europe-generated literary theory. That is true not only of Bashō within Japanese literature, or of Japanese literature alone. Until we know much more than we do about a number of lengthy literary traditions, we are going to have to be chary in our pronouncements, limiting their reference to the evidence from which they are derived until they are proven to hold elsewhere. There seem to be, in each of us, intellectual Siamese twins of opposed persuasion, one holding to language universals and the other to the Sapir-Whorf relativist position. Put another way, I (like everyone else) find it easy to use relativism to see the inadequacies in the ideas of others and universalism to give application to what I deem true. In that respect, at least, I am in the critical mainstream.

> Poetry is what I sell
> flowers not my debts concern me
> so I drink all the time
> as sun sets on the SPRINGTIME LAKE
> AND PLEASURE HAS BROUGHT HOME OUR POEM. [15]

Notes

[1] The standard study of Bashō in English is that by Makoto Ueda, *Matsuo Bashō*. The most generous portion of translation of his prose is Nobuyuki Yuasa, *Bashō: The Narrow Road to the Deep North and Other Travel Sketches*. I shall be using my own translations. Japanese give the surname first (but Ueda and Yuasa do so second, following English practice). Poets are usually known by their pen names or styles. "Bashō" is only the most familiar of several.

[2] Opening stanzas (hokku) were composed on principles that will be touched on subsequently. The second stanza added its 7-7-syllable distich to the 5-7-5 of the opening. Thereafter stanzas were added alternating the stanza forms till a desired number—36 in Bashō's favorite kind—were written. For details on these matters and on studies in English and Japanese, see my *Japanese Linked Poetry*.

[3] The phrase is taken from *The Traveler's Book-Satchel* (*Oi no kobumi*) and the translation from my *Japanese Poetic Diaries* (42), from which translations of *The Narrow Road* will be taken.

[4] Miner and Odagiri 312. As the next quotation, from *The Narrow Road*, will show, his cloud image in this passage had been anticipated by a similar image in the opening of *The Narrow Road*.

⁵ This follows directly after the Hiraizumi episode, quoted in part earlier.

⁶ I have found to my surprise that many who espouse Saussurian semiotics and modern theories of related kinds yet bridle at the thought of a whole nonmimetic tradition. For discussion of the nonmimetic nature of Chinese poetics, see Liu. For a bridling against Liu's account, see Touponce. Touponce admits, however, that he is not a "sinologue," and he does not cite any Chinese term equivalent to "mimesis." My own cognitive presumptions are most readily available in English in two articles published in *Critical Inquiry*: "That Literature is a Kind of Knowledge" and "On the Genesis and Development of Literary Systems."

⁷ Richard Bowring compares an account of the birth of a royal son in *The Diary of Murasaki Shikibu* (*Murasaki shikibu nikki*) with a contemporary account of the same event by a man, wittily asking if the different literary status accorded the one is due to its female authorship (168). But the wit is dependent on reading Bowring's *translations* of works, one originally written in the vernacular, another in Chinese prose, and he fails to make the Japanese distinctions based on style and certain subjective matters between Bashō's literary diary and Sora's nonliterary one. The Japanese have not collapsed all styles and all else into a single *écriture*.

⁸ *Waka*—the poetry of the court and others in the same style—and *renga* use purely Japanese diction, excluding all the Sinified expressions that had come into speech and writing. Bashō and other serious haikai writers sought to enlarge—and inevitably to "lower"—the world of poetry, much as Defoe, Richardson, and Fielding enlarged and depreciated the heroic world of Milton, Dryden, and certain prose romances.

⁹ Qtd. in Miner, *Poetry* 117–18. Saigyō (1118–90) is the favorite *waka* poet of many Japanese, as of Bashō. Sōgi (1421–1502) is the greatest of *renga* masters, just as Sesshū (1419–1506) and Sen no Rikyū (also known as Sōeki; 1420–1501) excel in their arts.

¹⁰ For a detailed account in English, see my *Japanese Linked Poetry*, chs. 3–6, and the figures on pp. 163–67.

¹¹ The evidence of Sora's *Diary* shows that this episode (after its opening) simply did not occur.

¹² Paz et al. Claude Roy's preface makes clear the poets' understanding—and the limits of their understanding—of linked poetry. It is particularly interesting that they sought to avoid the romantic expressive "I" of the poet (and found it impossible to do so) and that they invoked the example of surrealist writers.

¹³ That collection is, however, itself a new aesthetic whole carefully constructed by Kyorai and Bonchō with supervision by Bashō; see the introduction in Miner and Odagiri.

¹⁴ These are stanzas 33 and 34 from *At the Tub of Ashes*, 33 by Bashō and 34 by Bonchō.

¹⁵ The concluding stanzas of *Poetry Is What I Sell*, Miner and Odagiri 63. I have altered our translation by changing the plural to singular pronouns in the first three lines.

Baudelaire's
Beleaguered Prose Poems

ROBERT GREER COHN

Epistemological criticism is defined by four cardinal points: (1) an absolutely free epistemological theory; (2) an equally profound belief in meaning in the world and its authentic texts; (3) a comparable respect for the normative (sanity, history, conventions, classical forms); and (4) a concern for clarity and elegance of presentation. It will be noted that these four points constitute a "tetrapolarity," in the terms of the theory itself.

"Polypolar epistemology" can be defined as a relation of multiple dimensions, each a polarity—such as the Cartesian cross—but absolutely (in the pure phase of thought) free and flexible. All four (or six, etc.) poles—and the point of origin as microcosm, together with the macrototality encompassing it all—and the two (or more) dimensions are fully interchangeable; they "jump around" underneath.

As you move into normal, logical thought, through operational distinctions between the dimensions—vertical versus horizontal, holistic versus fragmentary, metaphoric versus metonymic, and so on—you get linear patterns such as the separation of space and time, of beginning and end, of form and matter, spirit and body, up and down, as well as the irreversibility of time and incest prohibition. All these allow *sense* (etymologically from the word for "direction" as is French *sens*), ordinary meaning. The philosophical move toward sophisticated freedom is made through powers of paradox, going beyond the usual binary paradox to "paradox squared" (tetrapolarity) and so on (polypolarity). This *dimensional* thinking is parallel to that in music, where tones are related through division (or multiplication) of strings.

As tetrapolarity moves into becoming, a new concept, "antisynthesis," must be added to Hegel's dialectical triad. This entity has to do with such phenomena as backward movement in time (hypothesized of electrons by Feynman et al.), Nietzsche's "Eternal Return," Kierkegaard's "absolute paradox," Mallarmé's deconstructive "n'abolira le hasard," various "setbacks," and so on. An application of this theory to a study of Baudelaire's prose poems now follows (other expositions and applications appear in my books in the list of works cited).

In the familiar preface to his *Petits poèmes en prose*, Baudelaire states as his aim the

> miracle d'une prose poétique, musicale sans rythme et sans rime, assez souple et
> assez heurtée pour s'adapter aux mouvements lyriques de l'âme, aux ondulations

de la rêverie, aux soubresauts de la conscience. . . . C'est surtout de la fréquentation des villes énormes, c'est du croisement de leurs innombrables rapports que naît cet idéal obsédant.

miracle of a poetic prose, musical without rhythm and without rhyme, sufficiently supple and jerky to be adaptable to the lyrical movements of the psyche, the undulations of revery, the jumps of consciousness. . . . It is especially from the frequentation of enormous cities, from the crossing of their innumerable relations, that this obsessive ideal is born.   (281)[1]

This passage puts well what he in fact brings off in the best of the prose poems—for example, "Les veuves." The metaphoric depth of poetry—the "musicale" or the "mouvements lyriques de l'âme"—does combine in a vibrant fusion, "miraculously," with the metonymy of the "heurté" aspect, the jumbled variety of reality in a big city (and the prosaic or analytic rhythms implied in "conscience"). The ruggedness of texture is represented in "Les veuves" by the "rides profondes et *nombreuses*" and the "*innombrables* légendes de l'amour trompé, du dévouement méconnu, des efforts non récompensés, de la faim et du froid humblement, silencieusement supportés" (297; emphasis added). I emphasize the plural aspect here—number—in connection with metonymy, although in these passages the fusion is already there. Similarly, Walter Benjamin brought out the "heurté"—rugged or jerky—quality by alluding to stumbled-on cobblestones set unevenly in the Parisian streets ("On Some Motifs"). One feels a certain parallel between the wrinkles and the dirt-separated cobblestones, together suggesting the flavor, in realistic poetry, of the city, in this general horizontal direction.

In "A Poetry-Prose Cross" I demonstrate that the meeting or crossing of the epistemological dimensions underlying Jakobson's terms tends to effectuate a certain imagery: windows (e.g., *croisées*) are scattered generously throughout the similar pieces of Bertrand and Mallarmé as well—as in "Les fenêtres," "Le mauvais vitrier," the framed picture one feels in "L'invitation au voyage," or the carrefour in the park of "Le fou et la Vénus" or "Les veuves." Baudelaire, in his preface, speaks of the "villes" and the "*croisement de leurs innombrables rapports*" (281; emphasis added). And in many of the poems, the number four dominates: for example, "L'étranger," where the tetrapolarity of the rejected family is followed by a series of four refused entities (friends, country, gold, and a routine sort of beauty). Significantly for our thesis, there is at the end a quintessential affirmation—the above-it-all clouds—parallel to the Kierkegaardian leap from the midst of a tetrapolar dilemma (in "The Absolute Paradox").

This tilt or resolution, offsetting any "antisynthetic" (fourth term deconstructing a Hegelian synthesis) movement, is what leaves almost all the prose poems with a positive tone, a bias for art, contrary to the opinions of many critics of today. In "Le *confiteor* de l'artiste" the little shivering sail at the center of such a crossroads stands for this vibrant zero-infinite quintessence, provisionally, and foretells the suggested reconciliation and victory of art at the end. Many other pieces have this tetradic pattern: in "Les dons des fées" there are two series: "Les Dons, les Facultés, les bons Hasards, les Circonstances invincibles" and "les Jours, les Heures, les Minutes, les Secondes" (the number is doubled into eight in the series of "Fées, Gnomes, Salamandres, Sylphides, Sylphes, Nixes, Ondins, Ondines" [309]). In "Les vocations" there are "quatre enfants" who discuss their desires. The "quatre hommes" of "Portraits de Maîtresses" are "ni vieux, ni jeunes, ni beaux ni laids."

T.S. Eliot was of course right: through this ("squared") chiasmus structure Baudelaire does raise the sordid and helter-skelter city to poetry of the "first intensity" (341).

He follows an old lady through the streets with the sort of fascinated devotion one recalls in Poe's *Man of the Crowd* (or for that matter the stubborn efforts of Proust to fathom, or be, the flower in front of which, according to Hahn, he sat for hours). The same happens in "Les fenêtres." At other times, he merely casts a "curious" glance over a motley crowd at an outdoors concert. But again the (vertical) figure of the noble "vieille" emerges right out of the "foule" or relatively indifferent (horizontal) ground, and the feeling of crossing, of organic fusion or exchange as in poetic-realistic impressionist painting—perhaps a crowd scene of Manet or Renoir or Pissarro—is strong.

He wondered why the old lady couldn't pay for an admission to the concert and merely hung on the outskirts with a little boy she held by the hand. He guessed it was because she wanted to keep her modest means to pay for some little gift to the child, maybe a toy. And he ends thus: "Et elle sera rentrée à pied, méditant et rêvant, seule, toujours seule; car l'enfant est turbulent, égoïste, sans douceur et sans patience . . ." 'And she will have likely gone home on foot, meditating and dreaming, alone, always alone; for children are turbulent, egotistical, without sweetness and without patience . . .' (299). His fascination with the "vieille" likely has something to do with a typical theme of pity on the part of men, the same kind that goes into the extreme pathos of "sacrificial women" such as in *La bohème*, *Madame Butterfly*, *La traviata* (both the operas, of course, and the texts behind them). I have spoken elsewhere of the "Madame Butterfly sympathy" for the deserted woman in Rimbaud's "Mémoire" (*Poetry of Rimbaud* 19). It is a poignant old theme indeed. Baudelaire's Andromaque in "Le cygne" is, to be sure, much younger, but the sorrowing identification is similar; competent critics have seen the ghost of widowed Caroline behind her.

Baudelaire's extreme attachment to his mother needs no documentation. It may be harder to accept that she is connected with the "vieille" here and in other poems of Baudelaire, but his emotions—such as charity—did tend to such extremes. He did not readily respond to just any other but, naturally for a genius, when he did go out, he tended to go far, toward *ruines, ma famille,* or toward outcasts, *les éclopés de la vie.* The feeling for the old woman would embody both a special pity—such as Flaubert's for Félicité—and a sort of sacrificial evening of scores with the mother who had betrayed him by marrying a stranger. Something like this happens, it has been remarked, in Camus's *L'étranger.*

In a memorable passage of the *Journaux intimes,* Baudelaire describes a scene in which he weeps together with Jeanne Duval (undoubtedly it is she) in an instant of something like total sympathy (1202). These moments are rare for anyone and perhaps especially for one who like Baudelaire felt and expressed such separateness from the opposite sex (along with the moments of reconciliation, which, however, were apt not to be so much total sympathy as rather self-indulgent enjoyment, as has often been observed—not that they were not sincerely heterosexual, despite a current corrosive view). But the point is he does make it in this trice to a profoundly moving "intersubjectivity" or "encounter" with the other, as Martin Buber and Gabriel Marcel would put it, and this is the personal "miracle" of which the prose poems such as "Les veuves" are the artistic equivalent.

This high instant of presence, of overriding tone, is what he unequivocally set his sights on in the collection and what he achieved in a few wonderful cases and approximated in others. And this, I submit, totally invalidates the deconstructive approaches to these masterpieces in various pieces of recent criticism. To be sure, these eager studies bring much talent to bear, but unfortunately they display even more a compulsive ingenuity that shoots right past the true targets in a mechanical trajectory. Whereas a mature critic knows when to change directions—a few examples are usually sufficient to establish a point, whereupon an imaginative mind wants to move on and round out a complex investigation—these *modernes* get stuck in their scheme and establish an elaborate new kind of pedantry.

One reason for this, I suspect, is that they tend to read Baudelaire with hindsight, through a Mallarméan perspective. Now, my regard for that perspective is second to none and I have devoted most of my energy to it, but at some point in my work on this unsurpassable poet I realized a sort of danger of automatism in the wide-open epistemology where paradox, as I noted in *L'œuvre de Mallarmé*, "invades all forms of thought" (63, n. 30). Indeed, in explicating the *Coup de dés*, or *Igitur* or most of the *Poésies* (and *Divagations*, passim) one had almost constantly to observe that rule; no one, not even Kierkegaard or Nietzsche, is more ironic and inexhaustible than Mallarmé in this respect, and the critic is forced to extreme mobility and ironic awareness. But Baudelaire is not at all at that level, even in his most mature work, though he does move up to it intermittently.

In this way, an exaggeration of Baudelaire's epistemological complexity, as well as the one-sided emphasis on negation—even in the *Petits poèmes en prose* where indeed a "cold wind" of aging, sickness, and disenchantment blows intermittently, as opposed to the plenitude of tone that he still reaches, at times perhaps unprecedentedly (as fine readers like Soupault and Jouve have felt [61, 137])—these newer critics miss the mark by a wide margin, as I now will try to demonstrate on a text they have particularly misused, "Le *confiteor* de l'artiste."

> Grand délice que celui de noyer son regard dans l'immensité du ciel et de la mer! Solitude, silence, incomparable chasteté de l'azur! une petite voile frissonante à l'horizon, et qui, par sa petitesse et son isolement, imite mon irrémédiable existence, mélodie monotone de la houle, toutes ces choses pensent par moi, ou je pense par elles (car dans la grandeur de la rêverie, le *moi* se perd vite!); elles pensent, dis-je mais musicalement et pittoresquement, sans arguties, sans syllogismes, sans déductions.

A sheer delight it is to drown one's look in the immensity of the sky and the sea! Solitude, silence, incomparable chastity of the azure! a little sail shivering at the horizon and which, by its tininess and isolation, imitates my irremediable existence, monotonous melody of the sea-swell, all those things think through me, or I think through them (for in the greatness of revery the self is quickly lost); they think, I say, but musically and pictorially, without quibbling, without syllogisms, without deductions. (284)

This is the metaphoric dimension the preface alluded to, with the "musicalement" echoing the "musicale" there (music and visual art are more openly and fluidly metaphoric than literature is and characterize more and more nineteenth-century aesthetics, as we all know). There is a dialectical tension between the plenitude of "délice" and "isolement" versus "irremédiable existence," corresponding to the "fleurs" and "mal" of the collection in verse, but here as there (in this deep dimension) is a resolving tone leaning to the positive, aesthetic joy. It is the same with any serious music, that final tilt despite *lacrimae rerum*: beauty as high culture usually knows it.

But the mood is interrupted by a suffering that is equally familiar, as often following such extremes of delight. And then Baudelaire ends the piece with an ambiguous remark: "L'étude du beau est un duel où l'artiste crie de frayeur avant d'être vaincu."

Barbara Johnson, in her *Défigurations du langage poétique*, sees this as a deconstructive conclusion. Is she right? I do not think so. Nor is it, despite the ambiguity, the sort of undecidable (paradox, irony) that the deconstructionists always regard as the high point of art and find everywhere *comme par hasard*. No, the moment of suffering does not at all, on the one hand, finally negate the strong note of artistic aliveness in the first and determining section—it is much longer, more impressive, sustained, felt, than the few lines devoted to the reaction, which really ends when he apostrophizes "Nature, enchanteresse sans pitié . . ." and so on to the end, for nature in this context is tantamount to the supreme principle of beauty he still believes in. She is a "rivale toujours victorieuse." There is no hint of irony here but rather a pathetic appeal to an awesome mistress-muse and to life itself, inevitably redolent of his own mother, as are those many poems hymning the power of the feminine ("La beauté," "La géante"). And the ambiguity of the end tilts, once again, toward a quintessential resolution that affirms faith in art. For even if the artist cries with fright and is "vaincu," what can that mean except that he is overcome by beauty itself as a man is in the throes of love with life-affirming and procreative or creative effect?

No amount of ingenuity will ever persuade me of anything else in Baudelaire's intention and achievement here. This prose poem is not as typical of the genre at its best as is "Les veuves": rather than a metonymic going out into a city, there is a somewhat didactic excursion into suffering and negation, which does deconstruct the poetic flight but only for a moment. Thus the horizontal is reabsorbed, resolvingly, into the vertical-horizontal synthesis of the genre finally, just as the city's negation and ugliness is caught up in the overall tone of "Les veuves" through a savory complexity of wrinkled, elegiac sweetness and compassion, perhaps like a fine old wine, or an intimate winterscape by Pissarro or Monet. In "Le *confiteor* de l'artiste" the clearly impressionist effect is different, to be sure, rather like a breezy and light-brimming Monet oceanscape at first, with a menacing cloud later dimming it all, but with the light promising to break out again for another go at artistic awareness. Contrary to the critics in question, there is no hint of pulling down his previous poetry, in disenchanted, bitterly ironic old age, even though this "cold wind" does blow through other prose poems, such as "Perte d'auréole" and "Chacun sa chimère." And the collection holds a number of dark-toned, grimly realistic pieces, but there is nothing programmatic about them, no collective effect of burning what he had adored. The grim pieces are merely bad-tempered vignettes, parallel to some sombre poems in *Les fleurs du mal*, such as "Une charogne" or "Le squelette laboureur": that they are in prose and hence more realistic proves nothing at all about a subversive intent. They are really not very interesting and are hardly to be dwelt on except for tendentious purposes. One feels sure that Baudelaire thought little of them and that his apologetic remarks in the preface may well refer to them in particular. He was getting old and ailing, and he did tend to knock off works hastily to fill in a collection—for the *Fleurs du mal* as well, it is known.

"Le galant tireur" is wrily cynical rather than grim: a man shoots the head of a doll off replacing a desire to kill his wife and so informs her in a twisted bit of gallantry. Hardly worth stopping at except for the incredible ingenuity that Jeffrey Mehlman ("Baudelaire with Freud") and Johnson apply to it. Johnson makes an immense lot of the phrase *"tuer* le Temps." Over a long series of pages, she charts its supposed infolding, *en abyme,* ironies. All that adds nothing; Baudelaire is merely referring as he often does to Time (often capitalized for that usage: in "L'horloge," "La chambre double," etc.) as a monster that kills us in the end; here too he calls it "ce monstre-là." The italicizing of "tuer" does no more than point up the overtone of the setting, the shooting gallery where dolls are "killed." Of course, paradoxes (such as the Freudian-Lacanian one of cultural *Aufhebung*—the nothing-something of the phallus resulting from the castration threat in the oedipal crisis) underlie this as they do all language, all signifiers. And, yes, there is even a Mallarméan meta-ambiguity in the relation of (vertical) figural and (horizontal) literal, parallel to our contemporary awareness of the deeper relation of metaphor and metonymy, and going back to Mallarmé's polydimensional ironies as in "Il y a et il n'y a pas de hasard" (and "Artifice que la réalité") or forward to Derrida's *clôture.* But either it is an unconscious, subjacent complexity or, if Baudelaire was aware of it, it has to do with a free play of syntax fairly characteristic of his verse poems, hence hardly a new attitude negating those poems. For example, in "Le cygne" the paradoxical relation of figure and ground, figural and literal, is present in "tout devient allé-gorie," and the play between past and present, poet and city, self and other, is very lively. In "Le voyage" to see desire as an antinomy between the sun and the earth, as a "grand arbre," is to postulate an organic fusion and reversibility like Yeats's "great rooted blossomer . . . how can we tell the dancer from the dance?" These fluidities of thought are scattered throughout Baudelaire's verse poetry from the earliest.

Mehlman, commenting on the same prose text and finding just as much epistemological to-do, concludes not only for the new disabused Baudelaire's superiority over the merely poetic old, but, in a moment of triumph recalling the aging Hegel's he sees *himself* soaring above all artists like the Nietzschean *Übermensch* ("Freud with Pain"). This mood is prolonged in a tendentious reading of "Une mort héroïque," where the critic finds an open-minded superiority in the Prince, over the poor rejected artist Fancioulle. In this, Mehlman turns against his quondam mentor Mauron. But Mauron, in his *Le dernier Baudelaire*, is much closer to the *Stimmung* and the truth of his poet. Psychology doesn't have the mobility of epistemology, but Mauron manages well anyway, mostly because, unlike the newer critics, he had a solid sense of the essential. (Unfortunately, elsewhere, he is carried off wildly by his hobbyhorse of dead-mother imago, particularly in the case of Mallarmé.)

"Une mort héroïque" is complex, and the Prince does represent a challenging entity, deconstructive if you will, prosaic and murderously cool and analytic in the mood of the detective story since Poe. He is the eternal-revenant father authority (like Hamlet's ghostly sire), an ingredient that Baudelaire or any other artist never finally can do without, as goad and dialectical partner.[2] Up to the decisive moment! Then an artist naturally sides with the artist (especially if he is as deeply tragicomic as Fancioulle is—compare the old *saltimbanque*) and with art, just as he did in "Le confiteor de l'artiste" and really everywhere else, even in "Perte d'auréole," where he doffs his halo (as Mallarmé did later, speaking to his friend, Dauphin), yes, but as a strategy familiar in geniuses, perhaps particularly those who are struggling against old age and fate—compare "*Petits* poèmes en prose" (emphasis added) or titles like *Divagations*. But when Baudelaire made a self-deprecatory remark in Belgium and the Belgians took him at his word, the true Baudelaire rose up in resentful wrath and poured contempt on them.

"L'invitation au voyage" is another basically glowing piece, bathed in serene lowland light and middle-class luxurious reality with furniture (and even cooking). Johnson makes much of the use of metonymic devices such as a series of phrases using *comme*, which Baudelaire would never have employed in the poetry in verse. This is true, and these devices do impart a somewhat dry and flattening effect, but not decisively; the understatement is not deconstructive but rather experimentally lyric, and it may indeed raise the poetic presence, just as the enumeration of exiles at the end of the fully poetic "Le cygne" does, including the throwaway last line "et bien d'autres encore." I repeat, that is poetic understatement as effective as Laforgue's or Pound's and just as risky: the proof is that many critics find it plain flat. But to me, caught up in the irresistible mood (much in the poetic is indeed contextual, part of a code if you will) set by that incredibly poignant and stirring poem most of the way, that throwaway enumeration is the gesture of one who has something deeper to say than even his art at its best could convey. Just the opposite of deconstruction in intent. The maneuver provisionally moves that way (a *reculer pour mieux sauter*, or "stoop to conquer") but does not stop there. In other words, the repeated *comme* is parallel to the "innombrable" metonymy of "Les veuves," raised into the poetic miraculously, as pop art with its rows of tomato cans or Marilyn Monroes manages to do at its luckiest, or camp, or Joyce's "Plumtrees Potted Meat" sign on the Dublin streets. The examples from modern art, roughly starting with Nerval and Sainte-Beuve, are endless.[3]

Almost everyone agrees that "Les fenêtres" is a high point of the collection and of the modern tradition generally. The young critics seize on the somewhat disabused final sentence to try to pull the whole thing their way, but they get nowhere. As in the "*Confiteor* de l'artiste," the tone is too well established, and the ending is just a pinprick in the new manner, adding almost dutifully a dry flavor to a moment of sincere sensibility bursting with life, yearning, Parisian, wistful poetic presence at the brim. Rimbaud ends most of his poems in *Illuminations* with the same sort of minor deflation, mostly a strategy for dealing with terminal pomposity.

The same full-circle dialectic applies to the following jaunty remark in Baudelaire's preface: "il n'a ni queue ni tête, puisque tout, au contraire y est à la fois tête et queue, alternativement et réciproquement. . . . Enlevez une vertèbre, et les deux morceaux de cette tortueuse fantaisie se rejoindront sans peine" (282).

Some readers see this passage as a validation of the currently important vogue of the fragment in critical theory, but it is mainly just a light-hearted suggestion to the editor, Houssaye, that "Nous pouvons couper où nous voulons, moi ma rêverie, vous le manuscrit." There is no connecting unity in the collection, but not because that is any artistic *gain*, it is just a fact; the unity is in each poem.

If anything, Baudelaire is being self-deprecatory here; clearly, unlike the modern theorists, he believed in overall harmony and architecture and tried for it when it seemed appropriate, as it did in *Les fleurs du mal*.

One might add that to hypostatize the fragment is just as sterile as its opposite, a pretentious claim to completeness. Mallarmé indicates the richly human middle ground here when he states that obscurity is to be neither courted nor eschewed ("Le mystère dans les lettres," *Œuvres* 385). Along this middle course—not just the clung-to "undecidable"—the artist muddles through toward something as fully present and real as it is remote.

No, totally unlike the subsequent practitioners of the *aléatoire* in composition—Duchamp, Cage, Boulez, Pollock—Baudelaire was incapable of hoping for anything to come of the randomness of this sequence in *Le spleen de Paris*. If prose tempted him, it was not because its looseness, as opposed to poetry's constrictions, was conducive to mere chance but rather because it could lead to an even higher (and subtler) control, as Mallarmé, Proust, and Joyce demonstrated. Prose offered him opportunities of "metaphoric" openness and fluidity parallel to music or visual art in this sense. The critics are following the same will-o'-the-wisp of something for nothing that has led to our contemporary emptiness, such as the childish belief that a drug-induced stupor can produce masterpieces.

Other pieces in the collection are worthy of our attention if only because the skeptical critics avoid them in a telling way. "Chacun sa chimère" is a case in point:

it is skirted as being insufficiently undecidable. There is an indecision or ambiguity in the "condamnés à espérer toujours" of the procession of artist figures (recalling "La Caravane" of Gautier and "Le Guignon" of Mallarmé), but the final image is of Baudelaire himself unambiguously weighed down by this "rat-race" of his species and, more generally, of mankind. *A quoi bon?* No undecidable there, and it doesn't deconstruct anything; rather, it tears down everything—it is just an old Job-like lamentation about existence, anybody's who hopes. It's one big sigh and not very rewarding. (Note that there is no synthesis followed by a deconstructive antisynthesis, but a jump to a negative "quintessence").

"La belle Dorothée" on the other hand is all smiles and sunlight, graceful feminine nature, and totally useless to the contemporary thesis about the *Petits poèmes en prose*. It is accordingly ignored as a sheer embarrassment. I must allow that it is not typical of the genre: it is too relaxed on the reality side, being rather exotic, without much resistance from existence, as is felt to be true of lush tropical nature generically.

The rest of the prose poems offer all sorts of interest but none particularly for our rescue operation. The prose poems are usually well worth saving from the modernist onslaught (including Breton's). Not that all or even many are true masterpieces—some contemporary critics have exaggerated their power altogether. *Les fleurs du mal* is much richer in density of achievement—particularly the *Tableaux parisiens*, which are often close to the prose poems in realistic magic. But one senses too how Baudelaire, tiring and unhappy, played around with this new form, in some resurgence of old ambition—the hoped-for miracle—but often to settle some rankling scores, to try out understatement (not always "taking off"), to write out some minor curious experiences almost journalistically or half journalistically, sketchily, summarily (or too lengthily), with all sorts of tentative expressions playing around his vital core of intensity and vulnerability. One is at last grateful for the successes and even the half-successes: "Les bons chiens," for example, where he speaks characteristically of his "muse citadine," is rambling and overly personal but points in passages to the best the new manner can do.

The critical fads and approaches will slip around him and fade in time: this lucid, suffering, exquisitely sensitive, and indispensable Baudelaire will remain.

Notes

[1] All translations are mine.

[2] This haunting figure is everywhere in great literature: Balzac's Dr. Bianchon; Flaubert's Dr. Larivière; Stendhal's Republican Gautier or Altamira; Proust's father. He is often mediated by a contemporary older boy friend as in *Le grand Meaulnes*, *Tonio Kröger*, or *The Last Pilgrim*.

[3] See my *Modes of Art*, "From Poetic Realism to Pop Art" (144–52).

Petrarch's Song 126

GIUSEPPE MAZZOTTA

This analysis of one of Petrarch's most celebrated *canzoni* can certainly be construed as a parable, if little else, of the way I approach a literary text. How can the method I follow be described? The answer, putting aside the inclination to ignore the question, is that mine is a philological method.

The more orthodox practitioners of philology—those for whom erudite research into the storehouse of tradition is its own reward, or those who professionally investigate the external features, the materiality, of a text (variants, emendations, sources, manuscript tradition, biographical data, etc.)—will in all likelihood object to this definition and feel that my use of the term lacks any scientific rigor. And I would have to agree that my understanding of philology has little to do with what has come to be known, somewhat dismissively, as antiquarianism. It has even less to do with the philological positivism that still lurks, in a variety of sociological and ideological disguises, within historicist approaches to literary texts.

As I practice it, philology is involved, if I may distort Martianus Capella's title, in a troubled love affair with Mercury; that is, philology is primarily the discipline that accounts for the elements making up the historical specificity of any text. As Vico (who also knew how unaccountable the power of the imagination is) puts it, nothing lies outside the archives of philology: textual echoes, sources, etymologies, specialized vocabulary (terms that have specific identifiable frames of reference), topoi, genres, rhetorical and thematic structures—all are in the domain of its concerns. These concerns are scrutinized not as the preestablished apparatus of literary history or as generalized extratextual formulas but as they work within a text, as the text's metaphors. From this viewpoint, the philologist necessarily turns into a scrupulous reader of textual details, the sort of reader New Criticism has nurtured in the last thirty-odd years. This is tantamount to saying that what originally may appear as objective facts are in reality the other side of an interpretive choice, that disguised as philology there is always Mercury, who makes his way hidden and, as he goes, unveils and assesses the textual value of each and every metaphor.

The reluctance to talk about method (which seems to have mixed motives: indifference to the theoretical implications and assumptions of one's practical criticism in the naive belief that practical criticism alone counts; resistance, in the name of some illusory intellectual autonomy, to being pigeon-holed in a fixed area; and even suspicion that a general method, codified a priori, always fails to render the unpredictability and wealth of individual texts) turns out to be the symptom of a genuine critical predicament. It points to the awareness of a split between "objective" philological facts and interpretive values, between the poet and tradition, and, more generally, between the core of a lyric text and the critical understanding of it.

Because of this gap, theoreticians of literature, such as Croce, have yielded to the temptation of dismissing philology altogether as a mere preamble to the purity of aesthetic appreciation or as a science that may well illuminate the mechanics of a literary text but is in no way essential to its interpretation. Although philology is devoid of any power to release the understanding of a text, it still has, I think, an ineliminable role to play in literary analysis: it establishes boundaries for what might otherwise prove the arbitrary, unwarranted vagaries of the critical imagination confronted with the elusive resonances, subtle hints, and clues—the dark secret, beneath a readable literal surface, of any poetic text.

As it happens, few poets have felt, as Petrarch has, the depth of the split between historical knowledge and the language of poetry. To begin with, the question that I ask of Petrarch (and that I would ask, with the proper adjustments, of, say, Dante or Leopardi) is why he writes poetry. What does poetry have to say, what message can it bear that other discourses do not? The question is legitimate because all these poets have written texts of moral philosophy, were translators and, in varying degree, theorists of poetry. For Petrarch, poetry is the privileged language of specular self-reflection, and it is concerned with the crisis of moral knowledge. More than that, poetry to him marks the retrieval of the language of the imagination as the way to probe his unsettled sense of himself and the world.

There is, as a matter of fact, a Petrarchan vision of poetry, which can be gauged by what it excludes: other selves; crude Aristotelean philosophy with its simplified, rational formulas about the truth; the physics of love, peddled by scientific-medical authorities who are largely identified with the Aristoteleans because they assume that the world of desire is contingent on and subject to objective conditions of reality. What it includes is the simple but vast sphere of the imagination, in which everything is implicated and complicated and in which mechanical laws of time, categories of sense, projects appear to be unstable forms. This understanding of the imagination is what Petrarch steadily evokes. Take, for instance, a discursive text such as "The Ascent of Mont Ventoux," a letter he addresses to an Augustinian monk, Dionigi da Borgo San Sepolcro. Like a true philologist, Petrarch begins the account of his mountain climbing by comparing sundry descriptions of mountains in Hellenic myth; he then translates the experience of his ascent into an allegory of the flight of the mind. The allegorical scheme he conjures up does not quite work, but once he reaches the top of the mountain and gazes toward the Alps, the power of the imagination emerges in the shape of memory and longing and new thoughts that seize him.

One would look in vain at a text such as "The Ascent of Mont Ventoux" for Petrarch's sustained thinking on the working of the imagination. The place to look is his poetry—for instance, the *canzone* that follows.

Chiare fresche et dolci acque
ove le belle membra
pose colei che sola a me par donna,
   gentil ramo ove piacque
(con sospir mi rimembra)
6 a lei di fare al bel fianco colonna,
    erba et fior che la gonna
leggiadra ricoverse
co l'angelico seno,
aere sacro sereno
ove Amor co' begli occhi il cor m'aperse:
date udienzia insieme
13 a le dolenti mie parole estreme.

  S' egli è pur mio destino,
é l cielo in ciò s'adopra,
ch' Amor quest'occhi lagrimando chiuda,
   qualche grazia il meschino
corpo fra voi ricopra,
19 e torni l'alma al proprio albergo ignuda;
    la morte fia men cruda
se questa spene porto
a quel dubbioso passo,
ché lo spirito lasso
non poria mai in più riposato porto
né in più tranquilla fossa
26 fuggir la carne travagliata et l'ossa.

  Tempo verrà ancor forse
ch' a l'usato soggiorno
torni la fera bella et mansueta
   et là 'v ella mi scorse
nel benedetto giorno
32 volga la vista disiosa et lieta,
    cercandomi, et—o pieta—
già terra infra le pietre
vedendo, Amor l'inspiri
in guisa che sospiri
si dolcemente che mercé m'impetre
et faccia forza al cielo,
39 asciugandosi gli occhi col bel velo.

  Da' be' rami scendea
(dolce ne la memoria)
una pioggia di fior sovra 'l suo grembo,
   et ella si sedea
umile in tanta gloria,

45 coverta già de l'amoroso nembo;
        qual fior cadea sul lembo,
    qual su le treccie bionde
    ch' oro forbito et perle
    eran quel dì a vederle,
    qual si posava in terra et qual su l'onde,
    qual con un vago errore
52 girando parea dir: "Qui regna Amore."

        Quante volte diss' io
    allor, pien di spavento:
    "Costei per fermo nacque in paradiso!"
        Così carco d'oblio
    il divin portamento
58 e 'l volto e le parole e 'l dolce riso
        m'aveano, et sì diviso
    da l'imagine vera,
    ch' i' dicea sospirando:
    "Qui come venn' io o quando?"
    credendo esser in ciel, non là dov' era.
    Da indi in qua mi piace
65 quest'erba sì ch' altrove non ò pace.

        Se tu avessi ornamenti quant' ài voglia,
    poresti arditamente
68 uscir del bosco et gir infra la gente.

Clear, fresh, sweet waters, where she who alone seems lady to me rested her lovely body,
    gentle branch where it pleased her (with sighing I remember) to make a column for her lovely side,
    grass and flowers that her rich garment covered along with her angelic breast, sacred bright air where Love opened my heart with her lovely eyes: listen all together to my sorrowful dying words.

If it is indeed my destiny and Heaven exerts itself that Love close these eyes while they are still weeping,
    let some grace bury my poor body among you and let my soul return naked to this its own dwelling;
    death will be less harsh if I bear this hope to the fearful pass for my weary spirit could never in a more restful port or a more tranquil grave flee my laboring flesh and my bones.

There will come a time perhaps when to her accustomed sojourn the lovely, gentle wild one will return
    and, seeking me, turn her desirous and happy eyes toward where she saw me on that blessed day,
    and oh the pity! seeing me already dust amid the stones, Love will inspire her to sigh so sweetly that she will win mercy for me and force Heaven, drying her eyes with her lovely veil.

From the lovely branches was descending (sweet in memory) a rain of flowers over her bosom,

and she was sitting humble in such a glory, already covered with the loving cloud;
    this flower was falling on her skirt, this one on her blond braids, which were burnished gold and pearls to see that day; this one was coming to rest on the ground, this one on the water, this one, with a lovely wandering, turning about seemed to say: "Here reigns Love."

    How many times did I say to myself then, full of awe: "She was surely born in Paradise!"
    Her divine bearing and her face and her words and her sweet smile had so laden me with forgetfulness
    and so divided me from the true image, that I was sighing: "How did I come here and when?" thinking I was in Heaven, not there where I was. From then on this grass has pleased me so that elsewhere I have no peace.

    If you had as many beauties as you have desire, you could boldly leave the wood and go among people.[1]

There is a certain amount of arbitrariness in isolating for a critical analysis one poem from the *Rerum vulgarium fragmenta* as if it were a self-sufficient unit, absolutely autonomous from the poetic sequence. The arbitrariness is the more evident in the present case of song 126, which is explicitly in antithetical and yet complementary position to 125, its "sister song." In 125 the poet quests for Laura in an uncharted, desolate landscape that yields no signs of her presence. Song 126 begins with the poet returning to the same landscape where the preceding poem ends. The landscape is the enchanted bower of Vaucluse and is the space of the original encounter between lover and Laura. The spot, by a transparent extension of the etymology of the real place, is a *hortus conclusus*, and in 126 it is imaginatively transfigured into a paradise (line 55). This reversal of mood from the *planctus* of 125 to the hymn of 126 is not unusual in the *Rime sparse*. Another case in point is the pair of sonnets, 61 and 62. Sonnet 61 intones a blessing to the privileged time of the encounter—"Benedetto sia 'l giorno e 'l mese et l'anno / e la stagione e 'l tempo et l'ora e 'l punto . . ." (lines 1–2)—in which the polysyndeton gives an illusion of continuity to the antithetical movement of expansion and contraction. The subsequent sonnet, "Padre del Ciel, dopo i perduti giorni . . ." (line 1), is a *miserere*, the poet's lament for the wasted time of his passion.

The symmetrical coupling of contradictory experiences is, in one sense, the emblem of Petrarch's split, the steady play of attraction and repulsion for Laura that has come to be identified as the distinctive trait of his morality and of his voice. In rhetorical terms this oscillation of moods has other implications. The convention of the lyric, for instance, rests on the assumption of immediate and spontaneous emotions, while time is viewed as not a constitutive category of the lyrical expression. The movement between contrasting poles of moods implies, however, that each poem's autonomy is unreal, that the origin of each lyrical experience lies always outside of itself, and that each reverses and implicates others in a steady movement of repetition. From this perspective song 126 is a fragment that reenacts within its formal boundaries the same splits and tensions that exist between it and the adjacent poems in the sequence. But unlike song 125, which overtly tells the impasse of a poet in his quest for a poetic style, 126 seeks to retrieve an original visionary experience.

The poem starts with an extended apostrophe to the waters, bough, grass, flowers, and air of the natural setting where Laura first appeared to the lover's eyes. The language of this opening stanza recalls a spring song, yet it is not a celebration of the general *reverdie* of nature according to the conventions codified by the Provençal troubadours. For the troubadours the description of the landscape tends to be an ironic counter to the abiding winter in the lover's heart or a way of dramatizing the inner renewal of desire. Petrarch's landscape, however, is a particularized, concrete topography: we are near the source of the Sorgue river, where the original vision of Laura occurred. The main burden of the apostrophe, actually, is to localize exactly the spot of the vision, and the insistent adverb, "ove" (2, 4, 11), seeks to define, within the contracted perimeter of the natural enclosure, the marks left behind by Laura's body. The verb "pose" (3), which evokes the body, conveys the impression of a frozen, fixed image, almost a lifeless statue, which is in sharp contrast to the easy, spontaneous flow of the river, to the graceful fall of the flowers on Laura's garment, and in general to the animation of nature that the apostrophe suggests. This contrast in imagery is a hint of a deeper contrast hidden in the stanza.

The opening line with its three adjectives gliding on to the noun at the end (a case of *epitheton ornans* for which Petrarch is justly famous) calls attention to the symbolic interaction of light, touch, and sound, which are blended in the figure of the water. The impression of iridescent light produced by "chiare" is absorbed by the resonance of "dolci," which is a musical attribute. In *De vulgari eloquentia* Dante refers to *dulcedo* as a musical metaphor, the quality of style by which harmony is engendered (2.8.3). Within this context we might remark the appropriateness of the choice of the *canzone*, which technically is a harmonization of words for musical setting. The rhetorical mode adds to the overall impulse to mime the melodious, limpid fluidity of the waters, its seductive euphony, which in the line is heightened, we might add, by the discreet alliteration of "ch-qu." But the poet's is a song of sorrow, and the elegy he promises is markedly out of tune with the musical pattern of the natural order.

This dissonance has an extended thematic counterpart. The lover's retrieval of the place where Laura was seen turns into the awareness of a temporal dislocation. The phrase "con sospir mi rimembra" (5)—given parenthetically (and the parenthesis is a distinctive trait of Petrarch's poetry) as if to suggest the irrelevance, the secondary quality, of the remark—actually discloses that the experience is represented through the haze of memory. Memory is the metaphoric filter through which the past is reclaimed as present and that also accounts for the dematerialization of the landscape: the epithets "angelic breast," "sacred air," "gentle branch" openly spiritualize the substances they qualify. More to our concern, the image of the sigh, which implies simultaneously longing and loss, unveils the resurrections of memory not as the restitution of the past to the present but as a temporal disjunction.

Petrarch, in effect, is giving a special twist to Saint Augustine's classical reflections on the category of time. It is too well known how in the *Confessions*—a text that

Petrarch, as he tells us in "The Ascent of Mont Ventoux," always carried with him—time is experienced as a sequence of self-annihilating moments. This is what is known as fallen time, time in a random and hollow succession of itself, a pure fragmentation whereby no relation can be said to exist between a moment and what precedes or follows it; Saint Augustine crystallizes this condition in the formula "praesens nullum spatium habet" (*Confessions* 11.15). The three dimensions of time—past, present and future—do exist as a sort of timeless time, as memory and expectation in the present, when fallen time is transformed by the *kairos*, the event that redeems and lends significance to the emptiness of *chronos*. Petrarch takes the vision of Laura, which happens on the day of Christ's passion, to be such an occurrence, but in this poem time and space are at odds with each other. The poem's dramatic pivot, in a sense, is to reflect on the discrepancy between the stability of the place and the radical instability of time.

The luminosity conjured up by memory is shadowed in the second stanza. The valedictory strain in the first stanza, triggered by the awareness of the gaps of time, takes over completely as the poet comes to grips with death as the imminent boundary of his own life. The intimation of mortality is marked by a verbal shift from the past of memory (5) to the future tense (20), as well as by the overt reversal in the role of Love. Love, a personification that appears in and gives continuity to the first four stanzas, is evoked first as opening the lover's heart (11) and second as closing his eyes (16). The antithesis between Love's steadiness and the self's subjection to mortality is further played out in this second stanza as a Platonic duality of perishable body (18) and immortal soul (19) or, later, as spirit (23) and flesh (26). The tension between the two terms is commonplace enough throughout Petrarch's poetry (with the apparent valorization of "alma" over the "corpo"), but we must acknowledge the precision of the Neoplatonic vocabulary in these lines. Petrarch, I would suggest, is alluding to and bringing together a number of Platonic motifs that all focus on the myth of the soul's return to the place of its original dwelling. If the phrase "torni l'alma" in the line "e torni l'alma al proprio albergo ignuda" (19) translates what is actually the Platonic topos of the *regressus animae*, the epithet "ignuda" also refers to the Platonic notion of the body as the integument, the cloth that wraps the captive, naked soul and impedes its flight back to its place of origin.[2] Even the reference to "porto" (24) largely belongs to this tradition in that the Platonic metaphor of life as a sea itinerary conventionally ends up in the promise of the bark securely landing in the port of philosophical wisdom. But Petrarch recalls this Neoplatonic paradigm of the soul's redemption only to twist it around: the poet's concern is not the soul's fate alone but also the hope that the body will be buried in the place of his bliss.

The conversion of the love garden into burial ground (a move adumbrated earlier in the *canzone* through the metaphoric equivalence of love and death) yields the figuration of the poet's posthumous existence. There is no tranquillity in the grave. As if struggling against the threat of a possible oblivion—he envisions the dross of his body scattered among the stones—Petrarch evokes the never named figure of Laura, who, as she is looking for him, discovers his tombstone. The oblique hint of the poet's monument, disguised in the language of humility—he says he is "terra" (34)—is not meant to convey the ironic insight into death's triumph over human life and its illusory artifices. The bleakness of such a perception is generally available from later iconographic motifs, such as the inscription "Et in Arcadia ego" (see Panofsky for a study of this motif), or even from Petrarch's own *Trionfi*, which thematize, among other things, how time is subsumed into death. In this *canzone*, however, the tomb is imagined as healing the rift that love has opened up. The shift of perspective in this stanza (whereas in the first stanza the poet is a sort of Actaeon spying on the bathing goddess, now we are told that the tomb is erected there where she first noticed him) signals that his tomb will receive her recognition. It will inspire Laura—who ironically comes to this place for her delight: "soggiorno" (28)—to pity, while her sighs bring together, as if she belonged to the repertory of women of the Sweet New Style, the double perspective of heaven and earth. This harmonization of opposites achieved through Laura's prayer is no deluded flight, as the pathos of her tears or her upward glance might suggest, away from the darker realities of the tomb. The ostensible statement of this third stanza—the tame vision of the future, wherein Laura will come to the place of his burial—hides a more radical threat to the poet. The phrase "tempo verrà" (27) translates a line from Vergil's *Georgics* (1.493), "scilicet et tempus veniet," the context of which is of some moment to Petrarch's text.

Vergil's poem of the earth begins as a call to the labor of the plow, to the knowledge of nature's laws—of the soil, weather changes, and the cycles of the seasons—so that the land may be properly nurtured and be, in its turn, fruitful. The first book, however, climaxes both in the spectacle of the Italian farmlands, which, ravaged by civil war, lie forlorn, and in the prayer to Augustus that he restore peace to the world. The lament over the ruins of the times is preceded by Vergil's visionary celebration of the future golden age when the farmer, once again working the ground with his plow, will bring to light the tools of strife the earth had long concealed: javelins, empty helmets, and the huge bones in dug-up graves ("Grandiaque effossis mirabitur ossa sepulcris" [*Georgics* 1.497]).

There is no doubt that the brunt of the Vergilian passage is to affirm the creative value of the husbandman's toil: it renews the land and brings life where the spears had disseminated death. In this sense the disinterment, which will take place in some utopian future, cannot be said to carry any sinister suggestion that the farmer's work of peace actually causes the undesirable rediscovery of the tools of war and death. Nonetheless, there is an ironic (if more cryptic) undercurrent, which Petrarch shares, in this exalted Vergilian vision. The irony in this picture of a pacified future is made manifest by the verb "mirabitur," which describes the farmer's wondering eye at what will seem to him nothing more than archaeological marvels unearthed by his plow. In effect, the scene anticipates a time when the past will no longer be recognized and acknowledged and the earth will be a reliquary of spent and forgotten passions. It is precisely this threat of oblivion, paradoxically betrayed in a context in which Petrarch is most obstinately intent on remembering and being remembered by the woman who most harshly ignored him, that Petrarch wants to bury.

This hint of radical annihilation is abruptly erased as the poet retrieves in the fourth stanza the original vision of Laura. Futurity gives way to the pleasures of memory, and we are once again in the sparkling bucolic setting that echoes the first stanza. The pastoral scenery certainly obliterates the composite picture of the shadow of mortality, fallow fields, and raging violence that the *Georgics* have superimposed on the piety of Laura's grief. But the setting is further transfigured into the Garden of Eden, where Laura sits enthroned. The oxymoron for her stance, "umile in tanta gloria" (44), revises the earlier one, "la fera bella et mansueta" (29), which primarily attempts to capture her dual essence, her mixture of elusiveness and allurement that in turn is the erotics of the text. But the attributes of humility and glory, which echo Dante's doxology for the Virgin Mary (one obviously thinks of "umile e alta" of *Paradiso* 33.2), collapse all hierarchies, intimate that the poet's visionary experience has abolished all boundaries and distinctions. The vision reverberates with another, less hidden, textual allusion to Dante. The rain of flowers falling on Laura's skirt is clearly patterned on the cloud of flowers within which Beatrice appears to the pilgrim in the Garden of Eden (*Purgatorio* 30.28–33). It is no doubt possible to view this poetic encounter as a variant of an agon (and like most poetic contests this one takes place in a pastoral setting, as if agons and the pastoral are bound together). But the representation of the ecstatic vision, which is patterned on Dante's *second* encounter with Beatrice, seems to be more Petrarch's acknowledgment of his predecessor than a polemical gesture, in which he frequently indulges elsewhere. It is, nonetheless, through this circuitous path that Petrarch reaches the point where the place and the present tense coincide, "Qui regna Amore" (52).

The poet's trancelike experience is rendered through the incantatory repetition of "qual" (46, 47, 50, 51). The anaphora, to be sure, is primarily a technique employed to individualize the random rain of flowers. Thus one flower falls on Laura's skirt, another on her braids, and so on, in a process of individualization that dramatizes Petrarch's desire to impose a clear, purposeful, and distinguishable pattern on the "nembo" (45)—a word that, in effect, describes either an undifferentiated vapor or a uniformly gray luminosity. The anaphora, then, plays a double role in the stanza: it creates, first of all, the impression of a harmonious totality that blends together, for instance, the colors of Laura with the elegant curves, as if it were an airy dance, of the flowers; but it also undoes the plenitude and wholeness of the scene by enumerating the parts that compose it. Seen in this sense, the anaphora can be said to disclose the principle of repetition that sustains the articulation of the *Rime sparse*. The collection is a series of individual poems arranged to form a coherent unity and totality, but the unity always appears to be made of contiguous, adjacent parts that steadily repeat themselves, even while they aspire to mark new imaginative departures.

More to our concern, the poet's ecstatic vision comes forth as a flight from the bondage to time: it is said, more precisely, to charge the poet with forgetfulness, "carco d'oblio" (56). The forgetfulness, in the first place, signals the reversal of the pattern of memory and future that structures the dramatic movement of the *canzone*, but more is at stake than simply another turn in the metaphoric system. For forgetfulness, which is the condition that accompanies the rapture (a kind of *torpor lethargi* that traditionally precedes or follows the *excessus* of the mind), announces the loss of the power to know the difference between the imaginary and the real. But the poet, far from receiving a higher, transcendent vision in the rapture, actually goes through the separation from the world of natural forms and the real Laura, the "imagine vera" (60), as he refers to it. In a poem such as this, in which there is an extraordinary awareness of her physicality—her body is cherished as "le belle membra" (2)—as well as a concern with the destiny of the poet's own body, the loss of Laura as a concrete image is not altogether a positive value. More important, what emerges from the poet's wonder at his paradisiac ecstasy is a radical disorientation, the sense of being somewhere else, of having lost contact with the spot that haunts his imagination: the question Petrarch raises, "Qui come venn' io o quando?" (62), which calls attention to the transfiguration of the landscape, at the same time conveys the lingering consciousness of the wedge that divides the real from the visionary. The fact is that the rapture comes forth through the representation of memory, and Petrarch is undeluded about memory's power to bring back the original event. Hence the statement of acceptance of and pleasure in "quest' erba" (65): the precise locale of the quest is acknowledged as the middle ground of the imagination, as the theater of memory where nostalgia for the past vision and longing for the new one are simultaneously played out.

In the hands of Petrarch, the language of the lyric is not the language of primary vision but its simulacrum, a secondary—prosaic, as it were—search for that original vision or its renewal. Retrospectively we can read the whole *canzone* as a series of searches into emblems of origin that, however close at hand they may be, become unavoidably elusive. The poet's memory, at the beginning, unfolds at the source of the river, but the source remains concealed, and we are allowed to see only the river's flow, a veritable image of self-dislocation. By the initial apostrophe, Petrarch animates nature, but the natural landscape becomes the place of his death; nature may even seem to speak, as one flower "con un vago errore / girando parea dir: 'Qui regna Amore' " (51–52). The voice is illusory, as the "parea" clearly announces and the slightly pleonastic "vago errore," which joins aimlessness and error, confirms. "Vago errore," one might add, is the poem's emblem in that the poem is *gyrovagus*, following a spiral path, rotating its metaphors and confronting its illusory moves. More to our concern, Laura herself, the main source of the poet's voice, appears always veiled, either literally behind her "bel velo" (39) or evoked through metonymies (her garment, voice, face, and side) or covered with the loving cloud. The phantom of Dante is conjured up, but it is a Dante who is echoing another text of his, the *Vita nuova*. In short, all the possible sources of the poet's voices are interrogated, but none can yield the secret of the voice's origin.

We can perhaps grasp, finally, the authorial modesty of the envoi: "Se tu avessi ornamenti quant'ai voglia, / poresti arditamente / uscir del bosco et gir infra la gente" (66–68). The envoi places the poem in a landscape of nature, which is neither the landscape of vision nor that of memory: it acknowledges the failure of the lyric to live up to the poet's idea, but it also seals the poem's unavoidable loneliness.

From this point of view song 126, which begins by being antithetical to its sister song, ends in the same recognition of a voice that can never coincide with a vision, or, to put it differently, of an understanding that can never be at one with its lyrical origin.

The figure of Echo can best describe Petrarch's insight into his own poetry. Echo is the figuration of a desire that can never coincide with its object; it is the nymph whose body has faded away and who only exists in the articulation of sounds that originate outside of itself. To speak of Echo for Petrarch's sense of his own poetic predicament is not arbitrary. The myth of Echo may indeed be the story of some literary criticism and practice, but in song 126 there is an oblique recall of Ovid's account. The image of Laura in the first stanza is a faint echo of Narcissus by the treacherous pool (*Metamorphoses* 3.410–58), the scene when spellbound by his own image, the youth sits on the bank, motionless, with a fixed gaze like a statue's, admiring his "smooth cheeks, ivory neck, lovely face where a rosy flush stained the snowy whiteness of his complexion." With Laura cast as Narcissus—as Petrarch does explicitly in sonnet 45, for instance—the poet becomes Echo, each the insubstantial and forever elusive shadow of the other, and each the double of itself.[3]

Notes

[1] Text and translation are from *Petrarch's Lyric Poems* 244–47. I have also used *Canzoniere*, as well as *Le rime*.

[2] *De regressu animae* is a text by Porphiry; see its fragments in Bidez 25*–44*. For the motif of the port see St. Augustine, *Contra academicos* 3.2.3.

[3] On this, see Giuseppe Mazzotta, "The *Canzoniere* and the Language of the Self."

Whitman's "When Lilacs Last in the Dooryard Bloom'd"

HELEN VENDLER

"When Lilacs Last in the Dooryard Bloom'd" is one of six elegies that Whitman wrote for Lincoln. Two of them were rejected from *Leaves of Grass*;[1] he printed the other four together (1871 Second Issue) under the general title "Memories of President Lincoln." This group title is in fact misleading; there are no "memories" of Lincoln—of his upbringing, character, or actions in office—in the first three printed elegies at all. Only in the last, "This Dust," first published in 1871 (Second Issue), is it said that Lincoln was "gentle, plain, just and resolute" and that under his "cautious hand" the Union was saved (339). The other three poems, all written in 1865, could well have named Lincoln and attributed to him the preservation of the Union, but they do not. The first of the printed elegies, "Hush'd Be the Camps Today," dated the day of Lincoln's burial, was composed early enough to be included in *Drum-Taps* (1865); the other two elegies, "Lilacs" and "O Captain! My Captain!," were included in the 1865 *Sequel to Drum-Taps*. Against "O Captain" and its appeal to public taste, we set the more private "Lilacs." In both "Hush'd Be the Camps" and "O Captain!" Whitman places himself in a subordinate role; in the one he is a soldier whose commander in chief has died, and in the other he is a son and a crew member on the ship of state whose father-captain has been shot to death. However, the end of "Hush'd Be the Camps" presages the writing of "Lilacs," as the humble "soldier" who speaks the poem charges an unnamed poet to "sing in our name, . . . / Sing . . . one verse, / For the heavy hearts of soldiers" (339). We know what the mourning soldier says and what the grieving son-shipmate says, and even, in the 1871 elegy, what the orator-eulogist at the grave says—"This dust was once the man" who saved the Union. But not until we come to "Lilacs" do we learn what the poet says, and how it is that a poet says things, and how his words differ from what a citizen-mourner might say, or an orator, or a eulogist, or a historical chronicler.

When, in "Lilacs," Whitman rises to his own utterance as poet, he takes a commanding position, turning away from the frigid public allegory of the ship of state to what he knew much better—the land. He proposed to make what he called "the large unconscious scenery of my land" conscious at last. The slow progress by rail of Lincoln's coffin from the East Coast to the middle of the continent, from

Washington to Springfield, Illinois, from city to city through the rural expanses of America, gave Whitman a peculiarly congenial pictorial base to his poem, satisfying his appetite for progressive and teleological movement to a goal and his equal appetite for expanding visual panoramas. But if we ask where he gathered the other materials of his poem, we must look beyond the historical narrative of Lincoln's burial journey, into Whitman's own history and the history of some earlier compositions.

In 1840, when he was twenty-one, Whitman had boasted that America, in contrast to Europe, would never know the evil of political assassination:

> . . . Here at length is found
> A wide extending shore,
> Where Freedom's starry gleam,
> Shines with unvarying beam;
>   Not as it did of yore,
> With flickering flash, when CAESAR fell,
> Or haughty GESLER heard his knell
>   or STUART rolled in gore.
>
> Nor let our foes presume
>   That this heart-prized union band,
> Will e'er be severed by the stroke
>   Of a fraternal hand.
>
> ("The Columbian's Song," Brasher 13)

The war between the states and the death of Lincoln refuted these naive words, and "Lilacs" is the elegy for Whitman's own untried hopes and for a fantasized America of pure optimism and progressive harmony. Whitman's own past had to be represented in "Lilacs" so that he could base his own present grief and his future resolves upon it; nothing is more touching in the poem than the reprise in it of Whitman's earlier work.

I want to mention first of all those fragments from the past—fragments, we may say, of Whitman's own past perceptions. Out of the voluminous writings that antedate April 1865, Whitman gathered a few crucial passages; in some fashion they were in his mind while he wrote "Lilacs." The first is a group of fragments called "Debris," which he had published in 1860; he never again reprinted those portions of the group I am about to quote, as though he knew he had used them up in "Lilacs." The first is Whitman's beautiful, humorous, and hopeful presentation of himself as a new messiah, holding the happiest emblems he can find from the world of copious nature—a robin's egg, a branch of gooseberries, a scarlet tomato, and a white pebble from the beach:

> I will take an egg out of the robin's nest in the orchard,
> I will take a branch of gooseberries from the old bush in the garden, and go and
>   preach to the world;
> You shall see I will not meet a single heretic or scorner,
> You shall see how I stump clergymen, and confound them,
> You shall see me showing a scarlet tomato, and a white pebble from the beach.   (607)

This passage undergoes a metamorphosis for "Lilacs":

> . . . From this bush in the dooryard,
> With delicate-color'd blossoms and heart-shaped leaves of rich green,
> A sprig with its flower I break. . . .
>
> Blossoms and branches green to coffins all I bring. . . .
>
> Copious I break, I break the sprigs from the bushes,
> With loaded arms I come, pouring for you,
> For you and the coffins all of you O death.   (329–331)

The young risen god of the egg and gooseberry branch is now a god of a different tonality, perceiving not the annual (the egg, the tomato) but his new emblem, the perennial, the lilac of mourning and heart-shaped tenderness. But above all, and crucially for Whitman, the flower is "the lilac that blooms the first" (331)—first not only temporally, but first in his history of perception. Here Whitman is remembering the autobiography of his perceptual life, "There Was a Child Went Forth" (1855), where the first things mentioned that became part of that child were "the early lilacs" (364). In that verse autobiography, Whitman takes the child from his dooryard (where at his first step outside the house he sees the lilac at the stoop) out to the horizon's edge, but the untried child who sees the lilacs is aware only of their name and color. It is the grieving poet, in a change of perception, who now sees that the leaves are heart-shaped, remarks the delicacy of the lavender color of the blossoms (that lavender which was in dress the color of subdued mourning), and recalls the recurrent stable promise of its bloom—"lilac blooming perennial" (328). The lilies and roses that Whitman adds to his armfuls of lilac represent in their emblematic purity and passion a homage to the language of flowers in literature;[2] but Whitman's heart is not with the cultivated "bouquets of roses" so much as with the domestic sprigs broken from his childhood lilac.

The second borrowing from "Debris" gave Whitman his elegiac "solution" to "Lilacs"—the remarkable image of his walk into the swamp holding by the hand two comrades, whom he enigmatically names the knowledge of death and the thought of death. In "Debris," Whitman envisaged an odd procession by threes in which, in each line, an old man holds two other old men by the hand:

> They are beautiful—the one in the middle of each group holds his companions by
>   the hand,
> As they walk, they give out perfume wherever they walk.   (607)

The deliberately nonerotic companionship implied by a group of three coincides, here, with Whitman's imagining this form of association as the appropriate one for the old; any procession of the young would have to be paired off two by two. In reimagining the trio in "Lilacs" and placing himself between two forms of death, Whitman turns definitively away from that erotic self which had dominated *Children of Adam* and *Calamus* and sets himself in the orbit of age and death. This change from walking with an erotic companion to walking in the company of more than one person comes about only by a loss of love; the last vignette in "Debris" (reused and changed in "As If a Phantom Caressed Me" in the 1892 edition of *Leaves of Grass*) reads:

> I thought I was not alone, walking here by the shore,
> But the one I thought was with me, as now I walk by the shore, [the one I loved
>   that caress'd me][3]
> As I lean and look through the glimmering light—that one has utterly disappeared,
> And those appear that perplex me.   (608)

Those perplexing apparitions, hinted at in 1860 in "Debris," become in "Lilacs" Whitman's death companions.

Other fragments pressed forward in Whitman's mind as he composed. One was his recent question in *Drum-Taps*:

> Must I change my triumphant songs?
> Must I indeed learn to chant the cold dirges of the baffled?
> And sullen hymns of defeat?
>
> ("Year that Trembled and Reel'd Beneath Me" 308)

It was in "Lilacs" that Whitman sought to find a middle ground between triumph and "the mournful voices of the dirges pour'd around the coffin" (330), to find not a sullen hymn of defeat but an acceptable "Burial Hymn" for a man whose life, he was certain, transcended the brutal fact of his death. He wished to find, in the language of perception, an equivalent for transcendence, and he turned to three objects of perception—the star, the flower, and the song of the bird—as ways of exploring that problem of equivalency.

In 1850, Whitman had printed in the *Daily Tribune* a poem about the carnage of the 1848 revolutions abroad; in the 1856 *Leaves of Grass* he had called it "Poem of the Dead Young Men of Europe, the 72d and 73d Years of These States."[4] At that time, the far-off carnage had seemed to him necessitated by the struggle against European decadence—not a phenomenon that could happen in an America where democracy, as he thought, had been achieved. Now, made ill by his sight of the dead young men of America, he remembered his earlier poem, which declared that the "bloody corpses of young men . . . / those hearts pierc'd by the gray lead, / Cold and motionless as they seem live elsewhere with unslaughtered vitality" (267–68). In 1865 he could no longer affirm the unslaughtered vitality of the dead. He remembered too his "Song of the Banner at Daybreak" (1865), written in the elation of the first days of the Civil War: "Over all, (aye! aye!)" sings the poet, "my little and lengthen'd pennant shaped like a sword,"

> Runs swiftly up indicating war and defiance—and now the halyards have rais'd it,
> Side of my banner broad and blue, side of my starry banner,
> Discarding peace over all the sea and land.   (288)

This star-spangled banner, it is true, presages "slaughter, premature death," but the banner, undaunted, announces a new aesthetic that will blend the peaceful with "demons and death"—"Our voice persuasive no more, / Croaking like crows here in the wind" (289). At the beginning of the poem, the poet had used the "Lilacs" word "twine":

> I'll weave the chord and twine in,
> Man's desire and babe's desire, I'll twine them in, I'll put in life,
> I'll put in the bayonet's flashing point, I'll let bullets and slugs whizz. . . .
> I'll pour the verse with streams of blood.   (285)

This facile aesthetic, in which all perceptions can intermingle simply because the perceiving apparatus is itself single, "a kosmos," is sharply rebuked in "Lilacs," where what is twined together must have a symphonic harmony, even if it includes life and death at once. Whitman's later "twining" of lilac and star and bird is a sober recantation of this earlier flashy twining; his hermit thrush is a recantation of the croaking crow; his pouring of dirges and flowers is a recantation of the pouring of streams of blood. The slaughtered young men of 1848 and the intact banner of 1860 reappear, corrected, in "Lilacs." The battle flags now are "pierc'd with missiles . . . and torn and bloody, / And at last but a few shreds left on the staffs" (336), and the young men have now no unslaughtered vitality; the carnage is complete:

> I saw battle-corpses, myriads of them,
> And the white skeletons of young men, I saw them,
> I saw the debris and debris of all the slain soldiers of the war.   (336)

Whitman has resuscitated his earlier title, "Debris," to use not only of the remains of bodies but also of the remains of organic life; the violets of "Lilacs" had been seen "spotting the gray debris" of the woods. From "Song of the Banner at Daybreak" Whitman borrowed also the unrolling scenery of "Lilacs," down to the phrase "measureless light"—but again the perception is corrected, abandoning the original shrill cry of the pennant "Fly in the clouds and winds with me, and play with the measureless light" (285), and adopting a deeper sense of the value and charity of the light: "Lo . . . / the gentle soft-born measureless light" (333). With the correction of various perceptions—of what battle flags are likely to become, of the future of corpses, of the gifts of light—comes a correction of tonality, a modifying depth of reflection, as Whitman reins in his wish to be assertive and boisterous and celebratory—whether of martyrs or war banners or gooseberry branches. At the same time he checks his rebellious "Luciferian" self, which wishes, in defeat, to be baffled, sullen, and vengeful. In the gap between the aggressive perceptions dominated by unmediated visual energies and a defensive optimism, on the one hand, and the balked and despairing perceptions of "thick gloom," on the other, Whitman finds the new tonality of "Lilacs."

Yet another borrowing deserves mention. The "Year of Meteors (1859–60)," as Whitman called it, brought forth a poem by that name in *Drum-Taps*, which recalled a comet that after a moment "departed, dropt in the night, and was gone" (239). The reworking in "Lilacs" addresses the star "where you sad orb, / Concluded, dropt in the night, and was gone" (331). The earlier poem applies the disappearance of the comet to the poet's own envisaged death:

> Year of comets and meteors transient and strange—lo! even here one equally transient and strange!
> As I flit through you hastily, soon to fall and be gone, what is this chant,
> What am I myself but one of your meteors?   (239)

The star that drops in "Lilacs" is tinged by this recollection with thoughts of Whitman's death as well as Lincoln's. (Later, in "O Star of France" [1871], Whitman will say of the "dim smitten star" that it is a symbol "not of France alone" but also a "pale symbol of my soul, its dearest hopes" [396]; we may assume the same of the star of "Lilacs.")

Finally, Whitman borrowed from his unpublished early (pre-1855) poem "Pictures," which represented his own skull as a house in which he keeps pictures:

> In a little house pictures I keep, many pictures hanging suspended—It is not a fixed house,
> It is round—it is but a few inches from one side of it to the other side,
> But behold! it has room enough—in it, hundreds and thousands,—all the varieties.   (642)

In turning his picture house into a tomb in "Lilacs," Whitman himself becomes in effect as one "disembodied, triumphant, dead" (506), transformed into his own memorial gallery as well as the decorator of a tomb for his president. Insofar as he is an artist, he is already as one dead; this realization, articulated more completely elsewhere in *Leaves of Grass*, in part enables the song of the bird in "Lilacs."

I have emphasized these "corrected perceptions" present in "Lilacs" because I believe that the pathos of the poem depends in part on them and on our noticing that Whitman included them as he composed the elegy. But the pathos of the poem also depends on what we might call its "mythology of modern death" (to borrow a phrase from Stevens). Whitman was determined not to invoke, for Lincoln's burial hymn, those Christian consolations that were being relied on in the "dim-lit churches" with their "shuddering organs" and "tolling tolling bells' perpetual clang" (331). Whitman's unusual choice of three recurrent keynotes—lilac and star and bird— has often been remarked, but varying symbolic burdens have been attributed to these objects of perception.[5] It seems to me that Whitman was constrained to his three objects by a wish to represent the three traditional divisions of the universe into the heavens, the earth, and the underworld. A poem was always, for Whitman, both a cosmos and a human body, as the poem "Kosmos" (1860) declares: the poet "out of the theory of the earth and of his or her body, understands by subtle analogies all other theories / The theory of a city, a poem, and of the large politics of these States" (392–93). In "Lilacs" then, the perennial lilac of earth stands between the fateful star above it and the bird singing in the ghostly trees of the swamp, that swamp which with its water and its dim shore, mimics the geography of Hades. The lilac, broken and offered by the elegist, is governed from above by the celestial

star and from below by the unconscious outlet song of life. These are only approx-
imations; but we may also say that fate, free will, and the unconscious are as much
invoked by Whitman's tripartite chord of symbols as are heaven, earth, and Hades.
The archetype of overworld, this world, and underworld is an ancient one in elegy,
and has found both classical and Christian embodiments. Whitman deliberately
makes the overworld represented by his star fateful rather than providential and the
underworld of the bird one of shades rather than demons; in this he is consciously
post-Christian, as he reverts to the Greek myths of fate and the afterlife. He is also
post-Christian in imagining the sort of tomb, or burial house, he will construct for
Lincoln; he models it after those Egyptian tombs frescoed, on the inside, with scenes
of daily life:

> O what shall I hang on the chamber walls?
> And what shall the pictures be that I hang on the walls,
> To adorn the burial-house of him I love?
>
> Pictures of growing spring and farms and homes,
> With the fourth-month eve at sundown, and the gray smoke lucid and bright,
> With floods of the yellow gold of the gorgeous, indolent, sinking sun, burning,
>   expanding the air . .
> And the city at hand with dwellings so dense, and stacks of chimneys,
> And all the scenes of life and the workshops, and the workmen homeward re-
>   turning.   (332–33)

(It was, we recall, an Egyptian tomb that Whitman seemed to wish to construct
for himself, years later, in a final protest against Christian memorial architecture,
whether Gothic chantries or New England slates with skulls and crossbones.) The
only residue of Christian symbolism in "Lilacs" lies in the majestic sight of the
risen wheat— "the yellow-spear'd wheat, every grain from its shroud in the dark-
brown fields uprisen" (330)—but that phrase is so defiantly naturalized by its
placement among violets and apple blossoms that it becomes as much pagan as
Christian. Whitman's idea of an American elegy is one that promises the dead no
afterlife, one that celebrates its rite far from those of the churches, and one that
ends, as this one does, in the Hades of the mind—"There in the fragrant pines and
the cedars dusk and dim" (337).

  This is the place where all the Lincoln poems end. In the first of them, Lincoln
is the dead commander: "They invault the coffin there. . . . / They close the doors
of earth upon him" (339). In "O Captain!" he is "fallen cold and dead"; in the last
of the poems he is "this dust" that "was once the man." Whitman's youthful poems
had made promises of immortality, sometimes bold ones, as in the conventional
resurrection of "Our Future Lot" (1838):

> . . . That sorrowing heart of thine
> Ere long will find a house of rest;
> Thy form, re-purified shall rise,
> In robes of beauty drest.   (Brasher 28)

Sometimes the promises were more cautious, as in "We Shall Rest at Last" (1840). There, wise men say

> That when we leave our land of care,
> We float to a mysterious shore,
> Peaceful, and pure, and fair.   (Brasher 17)

We can judge from Whitman's unremitting wish to end poems in the affirmative the degree of moral strength and aesthetic purity of intention he needed to draw on when he ended "Lilacs" in the shadows.

The "plot" of the elegy is a long resistance on Whitman's part to the experience in the swamp. Finally, he concedes to it, and accepts the brotherhood of the bleeding throat, tallying with his own "outlet song" of death the song of the bird. But before that wordless song can be translated into language by his voice he must undergo an ordeal by silence. He flees forth, with the knowledge of death and the thought of death as companions, entering the triadic social grouping of age, and subjects himself to "the hiding receiving night that talks not" (334). "The night that talks not" is perhaps the strangest of all the strange phrases in the poem. "The hiding receiving night" is formally linked by its participial adjectives to two other forms in the poem: the light "spreading bathing all" (333) and the oceanic "cool-enfolding" "sure-enwinding" death (335). Light, darkness, and the ocean seemed to Whitman the three elemental enveloping mediums that we know—each was capable of taking the whole world in its fluid embrace.[6] Each precludes the others. Light is one facilitating medium, and many things can be seen only through its mercy: "The gentle soft-born measureless light, / The miracle spreading bathing all" (333). But in the night that talks not, in noiseless dreams, all in silence, Whitman is able to see with a sight different from that of his corporeal eye that saw the large unconscious scenery of his land with its lakes and forests. The night, for Whitman, is rarely a time of sleep; rather, it is a time of vigils, of tears, and of insight. In the darkness of the underworld, a different sight is unbound, loosed from the constrictions that paradoxically kept it bound in the upperworld of fulfilled noon: "My sight that was bound in my eyes unclosed, / As to long panoramas of visions" (336).

"And I *saw*" says Whitman. What he sees is that naked vision of the corpse to which all truthful elegists must come. Whitman deflects it briefly by seeing instead the anthropomorphized banners pierced and shredded, torn and bloody, and the staffs all splintered and broken; but he then sees the "battle corpses . . . / And the white skeletons of young men . . . / . . . the debris and debris of all the slain soldiers of the war" (336). It has taken Whitman 180 lines to come in darkness and silence to the heart of his vision. Then, mediating between the spectacularly beautiful sights visible in the medium of daylight and the spectacularly somber visions revealed by the medium of darkness, comes the passage through the medium of water—the carol of the bird, tallied by the voice of Whitman's spirit. Water, for Whitman, is the element of rest, of floating, of buoyancy, of abandon to being without sight or insight; we might say that it was only in the water that he could sleep. The swamp to which he goes is a distinctly watery underworld—he flees "down to the shores of the water, the path by the swamp in the dimness, / To the solemn shadowy cedars and ghostly pines so still" (334).

It is surely the most extraordinary word in the poem, the word "swamp"—doing duty for Hades, for the realm of the ghosts and the shades, and for the domain of the solitary singer. A dark and hidden place of water must here do service for Whitman's more usual turning to the sea, when he needed a final origin and destination.

One source for Whitman's "lovely and soothing death" that "undulates round the world" can be deduced from his earlier version of this passage in "Reconciliation" (1865). It is beautiful, Whitman there says, "That the hands of the sisters Death and Night incessantly softly wash again, and ever again, this soil'd world" (321) —and this passage is a reminiscence of Keats's "Bright Star," in which the North Star sees "the moving waters at their priestlike task / Of pure ablution round earth's human shores." The "soil'd world" of "Reconciliation" was soiled by the hideous spectacles of war that Whitman recorded in *Specimen Days*—the amputations, the gangrene, the typhoid, the gaping wounds, the tuberculosis, the heaps of unburied corpses, the starving prisoners from Andersonville. In the carol of the bird, no soiled earth is mentioned, but from the first note of the carol—the apostrophe to death as "sane" and "sacred"—we sense the implied insanity and profanity that provoke the adjectives Whitman chooses. The same is true of subsequent phrases—"soothing death," "delicate death," "strong deliveress": under these words we deduce an unspoken set of opposites, something exacerbating, something gross, and something forcibly fettering the soul. It is only against these concealed horrors that death reveals itself contrastively to be sane, sacred, soothing, delicate, strong, a deliveress. Against the physical and metaphysical carnage of the war there rises in the aria of the bird a carol not of prophesied affection and victory (as in "Over the Carnage Rose Prophetic a Voice") but rather of ultimate despair of human solutions to violence.

It is, as the poem says, the living who remain and suffer. Only the dead are excused from suffering, insanity, and the gross inflictions of war. With characteristic delicacy, Whitman puts himself in a minor place in the list of survivors: for each dead soldier "the mother suffer'd, / And the wife and child and musing comrade suffer'd" / And the armies that remain'd suffer'd" (336). The thrice-repeated "suffer'd" is paired inextricably with the twice-repeated "remain'd" until the two verbs become synonymous: to remain is to suffer. It is only as the song of the suffering remnant, voiced by the musing comrade, that we can read the central aria of the poem. It lies, with the knowledge and thought of death, under that long black trail which now spoils the sky for the suffering remnant. Whitman has understood that neither the "measureless light" (the medium of bodily perception) nor the night sky sorrowful with the black cloud and drooping star (the medium of wakeful grief in the troubled soul) will do as the medium of song. He does not sing in the day; he does not sing in the night. He sings only in the swamp, and the medium of song is the ocean, with its rhythmic rise and fall, its capacity to float things on its motion, its preverbal whisper, its cleansing force, and its capacity to absorb all that it receives. Unlike the land in "This Compost," the ocean gives nothing back. Soul and body are alike "lost" in it; it annihilates what it receives, returns all to a prenatal nonbeing. Nothing in the ocean is "perennial"; nothing returns like the evening star. Whitman's carol is "floated" as the ocean is "floating": by predicating the same verb of each, Whitman encourages us to see his funeral song as comparable to the ocean and to death in its ability to embrace all being—lilac and star and bird and dead president—and to enfold them in an undulating coolness far from the warmth of life. The flood of the bliss of rhythmic language absorbs and annihilates the living panorama of the unconscious scenery of the land. In the intoxication of apostrophe, Whitman loses all means of perception; he recalls that there are such things as cities and fields, but he sees and hears nothing, absorbed in his hymn of praise.

For Whitman, finally, every passage from the lived to the written is a passage from the solid to the fluid, the ethereal, the aerial, or the vaporous: "I am as one disembodied, triumphant, dead" (506). The liquid carol, as death's outlet, becomes one of those eluding and fleshless realities made of words toward which Whitman was always tending:

> Human thought, poetry or melody, must leave dim escapes and outlets—must possess a certain fluid, aerial character. . . . Poetic style . . . becomes vista, music, half-tints, and even less than half-tints. True, it may be architecture, but again it may be the forest wild-wood, or the best effects thereof, at twilight, the waving oaks and cedars in the wind, and the impalpable odor. (Preface to *Leaves of Grass* 1876, Blodgett and Bradley 788)

It is thus, always, that Whitman's perceptions culminate. They diffuse into the oceanic or the impalpable, as they draw further away from the senses and closer to the pure rhythmic utterance of words forming in air. Of course, if the enfolding impalpable "retrievements" were not grounded in radically fresh perception, they could not move us. And it is equally true that if this great American elegy were not rooted in all the most venerable elegiac traditions (the procession of mourners, the decking of the grave, the confronting of the corpse, the eulogy, the dirge, and the hymn) we would not appreciate Whitman's profound de-Christianizing of the form[7]—his recourse to Egyptian burial customs and Greek mythology, his denial of the customary apotheosis, and his refusal (among all his apostrophes to lilacs, star, bird, and death itself) to address the human subject of the elegy. Lincoln, irremediably dead, can never again be addressed as "you"—in his personal being, he is forever dead and inert, deaf to all voice. To abandon the convention—more moving than any other in elegy—of the address to the one dead, is to risk everything in the service of the true.

Finally, the form of "Lilacs" itself embodies Whitman's deepest feelings. The body of the poem is almost rigidly periodic, with successive heaped-up clauses of suspense finally reaching a human end, those conclusions where the syntactic suspense subsides—"A sprig with its flower I break"; "Night and day journeys a coffin"; "I give you my sprig of lilac"; "you . . . dropt in the night and was gone"; "I knew death"; "I saw they were not as was thought"; "I cease from my song." The periodic "stanzas" of the poem, each long sustained and then dropping to a conclusion, are Whitman's embedded syntactic figure for the temporality of all life and action. But the bird's overarching song is understood to be cotemporal with the whole unfolding, from first to last, of the action of the poem; the poet listens constantly to the bird but cannot tally the chant of the bird with the chant of his soul till he enters the darkness of vision in the swamp. The rhythm of the death carol is not periodic. Rather, like the waves of the ocean or the verses of poetry, it is recursive, recurrent, undulant, self-reflexive, self-perpetuating. While the steady temporal progress of daily life can exist only in a forward direction, there occurs around it and enveloping it, Whitman suggests, another ceaseless rhythm, the perpetual arriving, arriving, of death, in the day, in the night, sooner or later, to all, to each. Suitable to this rhythm are the rhythms of ritual events taken out of the routine linear successions of the hours—serenades, dances, feastings; suitable to the rhythm, too, are geographical expanses beyond the reach of ordinary measurement—the open landscape, the high-spread sky, the myriad fields, the huge night, the ocean shore, the wide prairies. The oceanic current of the immeasurable and the perpetual encircles and bathes, Whitman tells us, the forward-directed current of periodic time. We participate, as we read this poem, so dutifully and bitterly in the prolonged periodic suspense of elegiac time that we feel the expansion into oceanic and cosmic space— and the new recurrent rhythms of the carol—as a grateful release. After moving painfully with the coffin on its journey (even if the landscape is beautiful), after being enveloped by the black cloud, we also find a bliss in being given a rhythm on which to float. Though we recur to the vision of human mortality in the final scene of the skeletons of the battle corpses and though we return to a slow temporal and linear withdrawal with our "retrievements out of the night," we have had as we read the poem not one inner experience but two: one is a funeral journey, one is a floating. We have thus a double sense of life and death alike. In his forsaking of historical specificity (so present in all his prose reflections on Lincoln) and in incorporating elements of earlier poems presaging his own death, Whitman composed not a patriotic exercise but a genuine lyric, as inward and personal as it was occasional and historic and American. If it is true, as I think it is, that "When Lilacs Last in the Dooryard Bloom'd" does not reach that vigor of language which we find in "Song of Myself" or "As I Ebb'd with the Ocean of Life," it remains equally true that even in the fetters of a formal occasion and a formal genre Whitman's voice was not quenched. The slight constraints of a decorum that would honor Lincoln make the piece more stately than other poems more purely lyric, but there is room in it still for Whitman's characteristic gestures—a yearning perception, an intransigent Americanness of borrowed non-Christian mythology, and an eventual dissolution into the impalpability of floating song. We keep these as our retrievements out of the night.

Notes

[1] These two poems, "Unveil Thy Bosom, Faithful Tomb" and "Thou West that gave'st Him to Us" are both "burial poems": the one consigns Lincoln to his grave, while the second bears him to a larger grave, the entire West that bore him.

In the first, Whitman speaks as poet; in the second, as one of a procession of pallbearers or mourners. See Blodgett and Bradley 670. Subsequent quotations of Whitman's verse taken from this edition will be cited by page number only. Early poems will be cited from Brasher's edition.

² He will offer, in his Memorial Day poem of 1888, "While Not the Past Forgetting," an entirely conventional bouquet—"Wreaths of roses and branches of palm" (529).

³ The phrase in brackets was added in 1892.

⁴ In 1850, Whitman had called the poem "Resurgemus." In the Civil War elegies, there is no mention of resurrection.

⁵ Blodgett and Bradley call them, respectively, the poet's love, Lincoln, and the chant of death (328). While this may not be untrue, I believe there is more to be said.

⁶ Whitman's identification of the sea with poetry recurs throughout *Leaves of Grass*; sometimes he emphasizes the law of the tides as the law of meter, sometimes the different moods of the sea, sometimes the tears of its waters, sometimes its whispering or muttering. See the following excerpts:

- In "A Font of Type" he says the font of type is not merely a long primer but rather "ocean waves arousable to fury and to death, / Or sooth'd to ease a sheeny sun and sleep." These waves "slumber" "within the pallid slivers" (509).
- In "Had I the Choice" he says he would gladly barter the meter or wit or choice conceit or perfect rhyme that would enable him to "tally greatest bards" if the sea would transfer to his verse the trick of the undulation of one wave, or leave in his verse the odor of the sea's breath (514).
- When he gazes on a "long scan of waves" he sees "in every crest some undulating light or shade—some retrospect . . . / The long past war, the battles, hospital sights, the wounded and the dead" and thinks of his life as a drop or wave "within God's scheme's ensemble" ("By That Long Scan" [516]).
- The law of the tides, their swell and ebb, is the law that governs "the brain that shapes, the voice that chants this song" ("Then Last of All" [516]).
- He refers to the ocean's "many tears" and sees in it "Some vast heart, like a planet's, chain'd and chafing in those breakers"; he calls it "The first and last confession of the globe, / Outsurging, muttering from thy soul's abysms" ("With Husky-Haughty Lips, O Sea" [518]).

⁷ Though Lincoln died on Good Friday, Whitman refuses any Christian association.

Toward a Midwifery of Thought

Reading Kleist's *Die Marquise von O . . .*

DEBORAH ESCH

I suspect that, as you yourself believe, your mind is in labor with some thought it has conceived. Accept, then, the ministration of a midwife's son, who himself practices his mother's art, and do the best you can to answer the questions I ask. (Plato, *Theateatus* 856)

Das Druckenlassen verhält sich zum Denken wie eine Wochenstube zum ersten Kuss.

Publishing is to thinking as confinement is to the first kiss.

(Friedrich Schlegel, *Athenaeums-Fragmente* 32)

In an essay first published in 1878 under the title "Über die allmähliche Verfertigung der Gedanken beim Reden" ("On the Gradual Fabrication of Thoughts while Speaking"), Kleist concludes a celebration of the virtues of thinking aloud by ironizing the institution of oral examinations in the university, arguing that

es ist so schwer, auf ein menschliches Gemüt zu spielen und ihm seinen eigentümlichen Laut abzulocken, es verstimmt sich so leicht unter ungeschickten Händen, dass selbst der geübteste Menschenkenner, der in der Hebammenkunst der Gedanken, wie Kant sie nennt, auf das Meisterhafteste bewandert wäre, hier noch, wegen der Unbekanntschaft mit seinem Sechswöchner, Missgriffe tun könnte.

so difficult is it to play upon a human mind, to coax from it its proper tone, so easily does it sound out of tune under misguided hands, that here even the most practiced expert, masterfully skilled in what Kant calls the art of the midwifery of thoughts, might nevertheless, out of ignorance of his pupil, miscarry.[1]

The allusion is to the exposition of the systematic methodology of ethical instruction in the second part of *Die Metaphysik der Sitten*, in which Kant, following Socrates in the *Theateatus*, maintains that the function of the teacher is to guide the student's train of thought ("Gedankengang") by means of adroit questioning (what Kleist terms "geschickte Fragen" [810]). Serving as interlocutor in a dialogical exchange, the teacher plays on the pupil's faculty of reason, arousing him to consciousness of his own ability to think, and thereby serves as the midwife of his thoughts ("die

Hebamme seiner Gedanken").[2] Given the consequences for Kleist's own thought of his notorious "Kant crisis," the episode of debilitating doubt precipitated by his reading of "the so-called Kantian philosophy," which seemed to him to subvert any possibility of epistemological or ethical certainty,[3] his reader might assume that there is something critical, for Kleist, about this borrowed *Denkfigur*—a figure that yokes the activity of critical questioning, in which the teacher and the reader engage, with a certain (or uncertain) maieutic practice. Indeed, his better known narrative *Die Marquise von O . . .* thematizes this artful delivery of thought, with results that raise further questions for reading Kleist, and perhaps for reading as such.

Contemporary critics dealt severely with Kleist's novella when it first appeared in the literary journal *Phöbus* in 1808 at the urging of Kleist's friend and coeditor Adam Müller (their publication of Kleist's comedy *Amphitryon*, which bears some thematic resemblance to the story, had already won him the disapproval of Goethe).[4] One reviewer was moved to write that

> Nur die Fabel derselben angeben, heisst schon, sie aus den gesitteten Zirkeln verbannen. Die Marquise ist schwanger geworden, und weiss nicht wie, und von wem. Ist dies ein Süjet, das in einem Journale für die Kunst eine Stelle verdient? Und welche Details erfordert es, die keuschen Ohren durchaus widrig klingen müssen.

> Even to summarize its plot is to banish it from polite circles. The Marquise is pregnant, and does not know how or by whom. Is this a subject that deserves a place in a journal dedicated to art? And the details it necessitates must thoroughly jar on chaste ears.[5]

The most striking detail necessitated by the scandalous plot is what Dorrit Cohn calls "surely the most pregnant graphic sign in German literature" (129)—namely the enigmatic dash (*Gedankenstrich*) that appears in midsentence toward the end of the novella's second paragraph. This turns out to be the only textual marker of the story's pivotal event, a blank whose filling in effectively justifies the narrative that follows. Prior to the dash, the reader is confronted at the text's outset with the advertisement placed in the local newspaper (presumably in an early equivalent of the personals column) by the Marquise von O . . ., a woman of otherwise spotless reputation, who finds herself under the constraint of what she euphemistically terms "unabänderliche Umstände" 'unalterable circumstances.'[6] In this extraordinary want ad, the Marquise requests that the unknown father of her unborn child come forward, for the purpose of legitimating a union of which she avowedly has no recollection. The narrative proceeds to recount in capsule fashion the history of the woman and her family and then returns, as it were, to the scene of the crime. Rendered in rapid-fire succession are the siege of the fortress under her father's command by the invading Russian army, during which the Marquise falls prey to some marauding soldiers, and her rescue from their clutches by the dashing Russian officer, Graf F . . ., who appears like a knight in shining armor (he is in fact a knight of an order of merit, as the reader subsequently learns) and conducts her to apparent safety:

Der Marquise schien er ein Engel des Himmels zu sein. Er stiess noch dem letzten viehischen Mordknecht, der ihren schlanken Leib umfasst hielt, mit dem Griff des Degens ins Gesicht, dass er, mit aus dem Mund vorquellendem Blut, zurücktaumelte; bot dann der Dame, unter einer verbindlichen, französischen Anrede den Arm, und führte sie, die von allen solchen Auftritten sprachlos war, in den anderen, von der Flamme noch nicht ergriffenen, Flügel des Palastes, wo sie auch völlig bewusstlos niedersank. Hier—traf er, da bald darauf ihre erschrockenen Frauen erschienen, Anstalten, einen Arzt zu rufen; versicherte, indem er sich den Hut aufsetzte, dass sie sich bald erholen würde; und kehrte in den Kampf zurück. (659)

To the Marquise he seemed an angel sent from heaven. He smashed the hilt of his sword into the face of one of the murderous brutes, who still had his arms round her slender waist, and the man reeled back with blood pouring from his mouth; he then addressed the lady politely in French, offered her his arm and led her into the other wing of the palace which the flames had not yet reached and where, having already been stricken speechless by her ordeal, she now collapsed in a dead faint. Then—the officer instructed the Marquise's frightened servants, who presently arrived, to send for a doctor; he assured them that she would soon recover, replaced his hat and returned to the fighting. (69–70)

The headlong narrative sequence, with its accentuation of incidental "circumstances," serves initially to distract the reader from the seemingly extraneous, grammatically unmotivated dash that separates the Count's rescue effort from his return to the fray.[7] What subsequently proves to be the most graphic detail, the critical moment in the passage, is left out, effaced and replaced by the eventful dash.

The gesture of omission is already prefigured in the story's title—that is, in the Marquise's name, which, along with the other family names in the narrative, is likewise partially obliterated: it takes the abbreviated form of the letter O (itself an empty cipher, a placeholder, identical in form with the arithmetical zero),[8] with the balance of the name suppressed. The terminology of rhetoric provides the reader with a name for this double gesture, a common designation for the form of the Marquise's proper name and of the nameless act of which she is the object: ellipsis, from the Greek for "to fall short" or "to leave out," denotes such incomplete constructions from which particular letters or words are missing. The rhetorical manuals concur that the elements actually expressed in such a construction generally provide sufficient hints as to what is elided that the reader is not left in the dark. One lexicon goes so far as to supply an affective interpretation of the figure, justifying its use on the grounds that a violent passion speaks more quickly than words can follow it.[9] A later rhetorician maintains that the succinctness of the ellipsis lends its context a certain ardour and force, that it is often employed when passion is the discursive object, and observes further that "the language of passion ought to be as lively, animated, precipitous and impetuous as is passion itself" (Fontanier 307). Kleist's text would seem to serve as an admirable example for such propositions, since what is omitted in the space of the dash is certainly a heated moment, characterized by passion and an exertion of force. It is also noteworthy in this connection that the other name for the figure of ellipsis, for an abbreviated construction in which more is implied than is explicitly expressed, is *praegnans constructio*, or "swollen construction" (see Lausberg 74 and Lanham 40, 79). The first of the textual details confronting Kleist's reader thus does, as his early reviewer contended, prove somewhat jarring.

A further unsettling feature with which the reader of Kleist's story must sooner or later come to terms is the volatile relation between the Marquise and her father, particularly as it is enacted in two successive passages that tend to strain critical decorum. [10] The first recounts the Commandant's outbreak of murderous violence when he discovers that his daughter is pregnant; the companion passage narrates their reconciliation, witnessed in voyeuristic fashion by the mother, in which the father's caresses are compared with those of a lover and described with an explicitness verging on the pornographic. [11] The two scenes are intimately linked, and in the second, the father seems capable of transgressions even graver than the ones he has already committed. While respectable criticism is understandably disconcerted by the latter scene in particular, to account for the uneasiness produced by these passages as one interpreter (speaking for numerous others) does, with the observation that "The erratic development of the Marquise's father . . . illustrates Kleist's view of life as essentially uncertain and replete with tragic potential" (Weiss 539) is to ignore their textual specificity and to beg the serious critical questions they raise.

Finally, analysis of the text has foundered on a third question: the reliability of the Marquise's persistent allegations of her ignorance as to what—or who—befalls her in the space of the dash. In an epigram written as an oblique afterword to the first published version of the story, Kleist gives further credence to the possibility, implicitly raised at several contradictory moments within the narrative itself, that the Marquise was in fact conscious at the time of conception. The epigram cites a parent, sex unspecified, in the act of censoring the story: "Dieser Roman ist nicht für dich, meine Tochter! In Ohnmacht! Schamlose Posse! Sie hielt, weiss ich, die Augen bloss zu" 'This novel is not for you, my daughter. Unconscious! A likely story! She merely, I'm sure, kept her eyes closed' (*Sämtliche Werke* 1:22). By virtue of this suggestion, borne out in the scene in which the Marquise informs the midwife that "sie habe wissentlich emfangen" 'she had conceived knowingly,' a variant interpretation of the censored moment of the ellipsis is constituted that would depend on her faint being, in effect, a feign. This further question posed by the text—is the Marquise innocent and ignorant, as she elsewhere claims repeatedly? or does she somehow know all along what she ostensibly finds out only when the Count presents himself in response to the want ad?—remains a problem for reading. [12]

Each of the scandalous "details necessitated by such a plot" (to quote once again Kleist's contemporary critic) thus stands in a particular relation to the first—the initial riddle of the dash, which is also the riddle of the initial, the elliptical "O. . . ." The limitations of the prevalent characterological interpretations of the story (whether they foreground the Marquise, her father, or the Count) suggest that this governing riddle and the questions contingent upon it may not be solvable in such terms (which are finally those of a moral system that has little in common with Kant's critical ethics) but may rather be related to a predicament imposed by what the text itself repeatedly calls "unabänderliche Umstände." In the case of Graf

F . . ., for example, the slipup marked by the dash is the only blot on an otherwise immaculate character and career—the intimation is that he is somehow unable to interrupt the "fatal" sequence of events that compound his initial wrongdoing (cf. Fries 1319). A consideration of some of these textual "circumstances," focusing on the language of their articulation, may serve not so much to acquit the guilty party as to account more specifically for the "unalterability" at work in Kleist's story.

The circumstances in question have first of all to be read, and read as a text. As such they are clearly indecipherable to its characters, whose imperviousness to this demand for reading leads to a pervasive irony that consistently exploits the literal and figurative possibilities with which the language of the narrative confronts the reader. The story is arguably structured around such ironic moments,[13] one of which occurs following the Count's first visit to the family to solicit the Marquise's hand. He is on the verge of disobeying orders and forgoing a necessary journey to Naples to try to persuade the Marquise to marry him immediately. The family cannot grasp the urgency of his suit, especially since the prospective bride and groom scarcely know one another; they observe of the Count that "er Damenherzen durch Anlauf, wie Festungen, zu erobern gewohnt scheine" (665) 'he seemed accustomed to taking ladies' hearts, like fortresses, by storm' (79). This mode of double-talk, of "so to speak," is sustained throughout the story, accounting in part for its comic tone (see Moering 231–90), and it seems to allow for a measure of ironic distance that would keep the reader at a safe remove from the plight of Kleist's characters. But a potential implication of the reader in these ironic moments in the text is suggested by the juxtaposition of two passages that delineate more precisely the reader's own predicament, and what may be unalterable about it.

Following the Count's efforts to convince the Marquise to marry him without delay, in which he puts his career in jeopardy by defying express orders, the Marquise's father remains skeptical about his intentions, judging that the Count has "merely been firing a warning salvo" (79) 'es sei ein blosser Schreckschuss' (665) and would surely think twice before taking so decisive a step. In the context of a passage that alludes to the dangerous consequences of an unreflected action, the figurative expression "Schreckschuss" (a shot fired into the air as a warning signal, or a false alarm) seems wholly appropriate. But the reader who traces the textual fate of the figure arrives at the violent episode alluded to earlier, in which the Marquise tries to convince her father of her innocence, without avail:

> Sie warf sich ihm, der ihr den Rücken zugekehrt hatte, eben zu Füssen, und umfasste zitternd seine Kniee, als ein Pistol, das er ergriffen hatte, in dem Augenblick, da er es von der Wand herabriss, losging, und der Schuss schmetternd in die Decke fuhr. Herr meines Lebens! rief die Marquise, erhob sich leichenblass von ihren Knieen, und eilte aus seinen Gemächern wieder hinweg.   (674)

> She had just thrown herself at his feet and tremblingly clasped his knees when a pistol which he had seized went off just as he was snatching it down from the wall, and a shot crashed into the ceiling. "O, God preserve me!" exclaimed the Marquise, rising from her knees as pale as death, and fled from her father's apartment.   (92)

The Commandant here literalizes his own figure for the Count's irresponsible behavior—the warning shot fired into the air—in an explosive scene in which it is
unclear whether his intention is to stop there, or to do worse (after all, he later
explicitly threatens to shoot the man who comes to the door in response to the ad).[14]
This reading of the passage suggests that his oscillation between murderous violence
and incestuous passion may be more a function of the rhetorical structures of the
text than of the precarious psychic makeup of its characters. The "unalterability"
that is ascribed to the sequence of events would not be one of "fate" understood in
any conventional sense but would rather be a function of certain operations of
language when it demands to be read as a text.[15] The reader of these figures is asked
to take them either literally or figuratively—as the Marquise's mother observes when
confronted with the alternatives of the doctor's diagnosis of the pregnancy being
either a mistake or a groundless defamation of her daughter: "Und gleichwohl muss
es doch notwendig eins oder das andere gewesen sein" (671) 'And yet of course it
must necessarily have been one or the other' (88). But this model of binary opposition—of either-or, of literal versus figurative—does not do critical justice to the
text, suggesting that it may be not "one or the other," but both, perhaps, or neither.
What emerges unmistakably is that reading as it is allegorized in the text—involving
the possibility of taking (or mistaking) the literal for the figurative (as in the example
of the Count's taking ladies' hearts, like fortresses, by storm) and the figurative for
the literal (as in the Commandant's warning shot into the air)—is, whatever else
it may be, inevitable.

This sense of the inexorable is reinforced by the precipitate temporality of the
narrative, exemplified initially in the telegraphic account of the siege of the fortress
and later when the wedding occurs on the morning after the Count presents himself
as the father of the unborn child. The narrative makes this haste a theme at several
points: speculation about the motive for the Count's "post-haste wooing" ("Kurierpferden gehenden Bewerbung") of the Marquise immediately follows a passage
punctuated with ellipses and interruptions, with words like "hurried" ("eilte") and
"great rapidity" ("Eilfertigheit"), in which the Count impatiently asks what time
it is and dispatches his servant in a speeding carriage (666). What is perhaps most
indicative in the passage of the "unalterable circumstances" that structure the story
is the figure of "post-haste wooing," which is more pronounced in the original:
"Kurierpferden gehenden Bewerbung," literally, a courtship going like courier horses,
like the pony express. This figure follows directly a reference to the receipt of letters
by the Count and the hasty departure of the horse-drawn carriage bearing messages
to be delivered in Naples:

> Und die Briefe Ihres Herrn Onkels? rief der Adjutant, sich aus der Tür hervor-
> beugend. Treffen mich, erwidert der Graf, in M . . . Fahr zu, sagte der Adjutant,
> und rollte mit dem Wagen dahin. (666)

> "And your uncle's letters?" called the adjutant, leaning out of the carriage door.
> "They will reach me in M . . .," replied the Count. "Drive on," said the adjutant,
> and the carriage sped on its way. (80)

It also precedes by a few pages the moment when Graf F . . ., reassured of the favorable outcome of his suit, reverses his decision to remain with the family and hurries off to catch up with his dispatches:

> Hierauf umarmte der Kommandant ihn auf das herzlichste, der Forstmeister bot ihm sogleich seinen eigenen Reisewagen an, ein Jäger flog auf die Post, Kurierpferde auf Prämien zu bestellen, und Freude war bei dieser Abreise, wie noch niemals bei einem Empfang. (669)

> At this the Commandant heartily embraced him, the Marquise's brother at once offered him his own travelling carriage, a groom was dispatched in haste to the post station to order horses at a premium rate, and there was more pleasure at this departure than has ever been shown at a guest's arrival. (84–85)

The concluding word in the passage, "Empfang," is used several times in this sense of "arrival," as when the family debates how the respondent to the ad should be received when he comes to their door ("wie es denn mit dem Empfang der Person gehalten werden solle" [684] 'how the visitor was to be received' [108]). But the same word also denotes conception, becoming pregnant—it appears in this sense, for example, at the moment, already cited, in which the Marquise tells the midwife that she conceived knowingly. Notable once again in this passage in which the Count hastily orders the post-horses is the text's literalization of the figure "post-haste," which is, significantly, a figure for the pressure of time in and on the narrative. Thematically, of course, what exerts this temporal pressure is the fact alluded to in the use of "Empfang" in the passage: the Marquise's pregnancy, which, as the Count knows, will not wait; this accounts for the specificity of his promise to the family: "so versicherte er, . . . er in Zeit von vier bis sechs Wochen unfehlbar wieder in M . . . sein würde" (669) 'he [assured] them . . . he would without fail be back in M . . . within four to six weeks' (85). The two distinct etymologies of the "complex" word *pregnant* thus converge here: *preignant*, from the Latin *premere*, signifying "pressing, compelling, convincing, forcible" (said of an argument, proof, evidence, reason, etc.), and the other sense, from *prae* and *gnascor*, *gnatus*, of being with child.[16] The question then becomes to what extent the narrative of the pregnancy, understood in textual terms, can be read as the temporal residue not so much of an act or event as of a figure, and a swollen figure at that.

At the isolated moment of its occurrence in the narrative, the ellipsis marked by the dash could signify anything or nothing—it has no self-evident referent. Only when the reader of the story is required retrospectively to interpret the construction, in order to make sense of what follows, can the question of significance be settled, if only provisionally. One might argue, though, that the text turns on itself—independently of what the reader may decide to impute to the dash—to stage, as it were, a reading of its own ellipsis; one might claim, in other words, that the subsequent narrative makes its own decision and literalizes the figure of the *praegnans constructio* in the Marquise's unaccountable pregnancy.

While such a scheme of reading seems to work well enough, the text calls for a degree of circumspection on the reader's part, especially since the attempt to interpret the story is inscribed in the text, in sinister fashion, in the Marquise's more desperate efforts to read her situation. This is particularly sobering given that the critical moment of her reading—the discovery of the identity of her child's father—comes not as a reassuring disclosure that sets everything in order but on the contrary as the disconcerting specter of madness. On the day of reckoning, when the Count is announced and enters looking exactly as he did when he came to her rescue, the Marquise reenacts her response at the fateful moment of the dash: she nearly faints from sheer confusion and is (along with her mother) momentarily struck speechless; when she does find words it is to confess that she fears she is losing her mind:[17]

> Die Marquise glaubte vor Verwirrung in die Erde zu sinken . . . und wollte eben in ein Seitenzimmer entfliehn; doch Frau von G . . ., indem sie die Hand derselben ergriff, rief: Julietta—! und wie erstickt von Gedanken, ging ihr die Sprache aus. . . . ich bitte dich, Julietta . . . wen erwarten wir denn—? Die Marquise rief, indem sie sich plötzlich wandte: nun? doch ihn nicht—? und schlug mit einem Blick funkelnd, wie ein Wetterstrahl, auf ihn ein, indessen Blässe des Todes ihr Antlitz überflog. . . . Wen sonst, rief die Obristen mit beklemmter Stimme, wen sonst, wir Sinnberaubten, als ihn—? Die Marquise stand starr über ihm, und sagte: ich werde wahnsinnig werden, meine Mutter! . . . Die Mutter rief: Unglückliche! Was fehlst du? Was ist geschehn, worauf du nicht vorbereitet warst—? . . . Doch diese—: gehn Sie! gehn Sie! gehn Sie! rief sie, indem sie aufstand; auf einen Lasterhaften war ich gefasst, aber auf keinen—Teufel! . . . Die Marquise blickte, mit tötender Wildheit, bald auf den Grafen, bald auf die Mutter ein; ihre Brust flog, ihr Antlitz loderte: eine Furie blickt nicht schrecklicher. (685)

> The Marquise felt she would sink into the ground from sheer confusion; she . . . was about to rush off into a neighboring room, when her mother, seizing her by the hand, exclaimed: "Giulietta—!", and her thoughts seemed to stifle any further words. . . . "Why Giulietta, whom have we been expecting—?" The Marquise, turning suddenly, cried: "Well? You surely cannot mean him—?" She fixed on the Count such a look that it seemed to flash like a thunderbolt, and her face went deathly pale. . . . "Who else?" exclaimed her mother, her voice almost failing. "Who else but him? How stupid we have been—!" The Marquise stood over him, rigidly erect, and said: "Mother, I shall go mad!" . . . Her mother cried: "Poor wretched girl! What is the matter with you? What has happened that can have taken you by surprise—?" . . . But she, standing up, cried: "Go away! Go away! Go away! I was prepared to meet a vicious man, but not—not a devil!" . . . The Marquise stared at them each in turn with annihilating rage; her breast heaved, her face was aflame; no Fury's gaze could be more terrifying. (109–10)[18]

When the father presents himself, what is wanting in the want ad as well as in the ellipsis is ostensibly supplied: the unaccountable, in other words, becomes once more accountable, and the "gebrechliche Einrichtung der Welt" 'the fragile order of the world' (687), which would prohibit conception without a father (with one notable exception, duly noted by the midwife), is restored. But the consequences of this revelation for the order of the narrative is, as attested in the passage, a series of "convulsions" 'konvulsivischen Bewegung' (671), of violent textual contractions. It is as though the initial, isolated ellipsis were disseminated over this passage punctuated by dashes and riddled with incomplete thoughts. The figure in question

becomes no longer a singular and superfluous textual detail that can be compensated
for by way of one logic or another: the relegation of logic to relative impotence has
already taken place, as, for example, when her mother can only reply to the Marquise's
request that a midwife be sent for, despite the fact that she cannot conceivably be
pregnant, with the formulation not merely of a logical paradox,[19] but of a more
radical double bind—the structure of mutual exclusion that is constitutive of Kleis-
tian irony:

> Eine Hebamme! rief Frau von G . . . mit Entwürdigung. Ein reines Bewusstsein,
> und eine Hebamme! Und die Sprache ging ihr aus. (671)

> "A midwife!" exclaimed the Commandant's wife. "A clear conscience, and a mid-
> wife!" And speech failed her. (88)

At the moment when the order of logic threatens to collapse, speech fails the
characters.[20] But the text itself, in spite of its derangement, does not fail. The
ellipsis is extended over the points of a figural line to structure the narrative succession—to structure it, that is, as an allegory of its own figuration. The succession
itself is figured as well, in the Commandant's practical response to the discovery of
the identity of the father: "Möge der Fluch des Himmels von diesen Scheiteln
weichen! rief er: wann gedenken sie zu heiraten?" (686) ' "May the curse of heaven
be averted from your head!" he exclaimed. "When are you intending to get married?" ' (111). More explicitly, it is thematized in the generative chain produced
by the reunion of the Count and the Marquise (who, following her marriage, becomes
the Countess F . . .; the 0 is effaced, converted into a still elliptical appellation
that is a trope of her former name): "Eine ganze Reihe von jungen Russen folgte
jetzt noch dem ersten . . ." (687) 'A whole series of young Russians now followed
the first . . .' (113),[21] recalling Friedrich Schlegel's account of "the irony of irony":
". . . es würde bald eine neue Generation von kleinen Ironien entstehen" ("Unverständlichkeit" 538).

If the response to the want ad and the completion of the ellipsis have the effect,
provisionally, of derailing the discourse, they are also the condition of possibility
of the continuation of the narrative, which can then be read as the temporal or
sequential dissimulation—the allegory—of its own instantaneous and ironic collapse. It is not, despite what some interpreters of the story (including Kleist) have
suggested, the Marquise who dissembles, who feigns rather than faints, who simply
"keeps her eyes closed"—it is, rather, the narrative that bears her name. What that
narrative recounts, then, is the impossibility of *its* reading the ellipsis except by
literalizing it, in a reading that takes the form of the repetition of its unreadable
point of departure on the basis of an irreducible residue—the pregnancy. It is the
effacement of this insight, the striking of this thought—the *Gedankenstrich*—that
makes the temporal succession of the narrative possible as well as inevitable. In
place of the thought, the text delivers the story of the thought, its reinscription in
an allegorical *Gedankengang*. And it is reading that assists at this delivery, that
brings this second story to light through its operation of critical questioning.

Notes

[1] *Werke in einem Band* 813–14. My translation modifies that of Miller (222). Further references to Kleist's works, cited by page number in the text, are to the one-volume Sembdner edition. All translations of *Die Marquise von O . . .* are from Luke and Reeves.

[2] Kant 618. Interestingly, the figure in question—"er ist die Hebamme seiner Gedanken"—which appears parenthetically in Kant's text, is omitted—elided, effaced—in J. W. Semple's standard translation (296). Unlike Kant, Rousseau does not subscribe to the Socratic method, particularly as practiced by women: "J'ai remarqué depuis que cette manière sèche d'interroger les gens pour les connoitre est un tic assez commun chez les femmes qui se piquent d'esprit" 'I have since observed that this dry method of interrogating people in order to know them is a fairly common trick with women who pride themselves on their brains' (*Les confessions*, *Œuvres complètes* 1: 82).

[3] The crisis is documented in Kleist's letters to Wilhelmine von Zenge and Ulrike von Kleist, 22 and 23 March 1801. For a sustained interpretation of Kleist's relation to Kant and to Fichte, see Cassirer. Warminski rereads the Kant crisis as "quite literally a crisis of reading" (76).

[4] For one account of this and other details of Kleist's problematic relation to Goethe, see Mommsen, especially 24–25.

[5] From the review in *Der Freimuthige*, 4–5 March 1808; qtd. in Sembdner, *Lebenspüren* 175.

[6] The word "Umstände", or "circumstances," appears not only in the want ad, but on virtually every page of the text. The phrase "in andere Umstände" (or "in gesegnete Umstände") is a euphemistic idiom for pregnancy.

[7] Because of the syntax, the effect on the reader of the sentence containing the dash is more pronounced in the German than in translation. While "Anstalten treffen" signifies "to make arrangements or provisions," only the conjugated verb form appears in the fateful clause: "Hier — traf er. . . ." "Treffen" itself denotes "to hit or strike (a target); to encounter someone or something; to wound, physically or spiritually; to guess correctly; to designate or characterize." The reader might translate "Hier — traf er" as "Here — he struck," "Here — he encountered," "Here — he wounded," "Here — he designated," with the dash marking the place of the nameless object of the transitive verb "treffen." The dash, like the arithmetical zero, serves as placeholder. Blöcker is among those who question the grammatical motivation of the dash (240). Also questionable is the function of the "Hier," whether understood spatially ("an diesem Ort") or temporally ("in diesem Augenblick"); under these narrative circumstances, it can only indicate a *dis*placement in, and of, the text's signifying system.

[8] The Marquise, of course, has a good deal in common with her predecessor as heroine and victim, Clarissa Harlowe. In Richardson's text, as in Kleist's, the pivotal moment in the narrative—the rape—is elided (with the difference that in

Clarissa it goes unmarked). Clarissa subsequently designates her defiled body as "nothing," and herself as a "cipher" for Lovelace's violent interpretive acts. Terry Eagleton argues persuasively that "this must be taken together with her assertion that 'I am nobody's': a radical refusal of any place within the 'symbolic order,' a rebuffing of all patriarchal claims over her person" (*Rape of Clarissa* 61–62). As the arithmetical zero is heterogeneous to the order of number, to the extent that Clarissa and the Marquise partake of the inscrutability, the opacity, of the cipher, they resist unproblematic incorporation into a semantic system. This hard fact of reading is bound to frustrate even such diligent scholarly attempts to find "the meaning of the O" as that of Huff, who accounts for the elliptical form of the Marquise's name, for example, thus: "By abbreviating personal and place names, Kleist lends the work an ambiance of anonymity in order to support his claim [in a parenthetical note in the table of contents to the first published version of the text] that the story was grounded in reality. This is a common literary convention often used in journalism to avoid giving offence, or, in fiction, to feign reality" (368). But the letter O might be read as well as a figure for the asemantic character of the letter, the unit of discourse that does not, of itself, signify. The unreadability of the letter is thematized in an enigmatic anecdote published by Kleist in the *Berliner Abendblätter* (1810) under the title "Der Griffel Gottes." Jacobs provides a brief but suggestive reading of the anecdote in this connection (47–49).

[9] Bérnard Lamy, *La rhétorique, ou l'art de parler*, qtd. in Genette, *Figures of Literary Discourse* 56. Genette himself provides an illuminating analysis of the place of ellipsis in Stendhalian narrative. Like Kleist, Stendhal calls inordinate attention to seemingly incidental details, such that pivotal events (e.g., the first embrace of Fabrizio and Gina in *La chartreuse de Parme*, the execution of Julien in *Le rouge et le noir*) are virtually eclipsed. "This attention to objects and circumstances—which is accompanied, however, as we know, with great disdain for description—almost always serves to mediate the evocation of important actions or situations by allowing various kinds of material substitutes to speak in their place" (171)—as when, in the crucial passage in Kleist's narrative, the Count "replaces his hat" before returning to battle.

[10] These passages in particular are presumably ripe for a psychoanalytic interpretation. For an attempt at such an account see Hassoun. Fries situates the novella in the context of Freud's "Rätsel der Weiblichkeit."

[11] Comparative studies have elaborated parallels with the scene of reconciliation between Julie (whose name is inscribed in the Marquise's first name, Julietta) and her father in letter 63 of Rousseau's *La nouvelle Héloise*. See for example the important early essay by Schmidt (329–31); see also Wolff 188.

[12] Cohn explores the "problem" of the incompatibilities among variant readings of the status of the Marquise's knowledge. On the same question, see also Ellis and Swales. Investigations into the "sources" of Kleist's story attest to the practically archetypal status of the rape of the unconscious victim: it appears in Montaigne, Cervantes, Lafontaine, and Tieck, as well as in other respectable sources (see Klaar).

[13] The Marquise's initial reaction to her troublesome symptoms provides a further instance. When her mother, in jest, alludes to her giving birth to Phantasus, the Marquise replies in the same spirit: "Morpheus wenigstens, . . . oder einer der Träume aus seinem Gefolge, wurde sein Vater sein." Shortly thereafter, the Count enters, looking "schön, wie ein junger Gott." Both the Marquise and her father (with his scathing remark, "Sie hat es im Schlafe getan") are closer to the truth of the matter than they realize.

[14] Weiss reads the pistol shot as simply "a typical example of his penchant for the sensational and the excessive" (1539). Cf. Thomas Mann: "Das Äusserste— Kleist will es immer, vielmehr, er will das Über-Äusserste" (836).

[15] One subtext of this reading that surfaces here is Benjamin's essay "Schicksal und Charakter."

[16] OED 1272. William Empson includes *pregnant* in his catalog in *The Structure of Complex Words* (321–30).

[17] Paul de Man's articulation, in "The Rhetoric of Temporality," between the structure of irony and that of madness suggests a way to rethink and rewrite the question of the Marquise's consciousness at the moment of conception:

> absolute irony is a consciousness of madness, itself the end of all consciousness; it is a consciousness of a non-consciousness, a reflection on madness from the inside of madness itself. But this reflection is made possible only by the double structure of ironic language. (216)

[18] The Marquise's insistent repetition ("gehn Sie! gehn Sie! gehn Sie!") is an instance of the rhetorical figure known variously as epimone (from the Greek for "tarrying, delay"), perseverentia, and (perhaps most appropriately under the circumstances) love burden. All three terms designate the frequent repetition of a phrase or question. (See Lanham 44).

[19] Müller-Seidel understands this as one paradox among others in the story (angel/devil, pregnant/widow, etc.).

[20] For a thoughtful analysis of this phenomenon in Kleist's oeuvre see Kommerell.

[21] Compare the interpretations of Cohn (139) and Fries (1325).

The Storm in the Eye of the Poem

Baudelaire's "A une passante"

ROSS CHAMBERS

Poststructuralist criticism has taken two main directions. The "deconstructionist" trend has been to challenge assumptions of textual coherence and determinable meaning, while the "contextualist" movement has concerned itself with text as event, its major branch being reader-oriented criticism and *Rezeptionsästhetik*. Without wishing to deny that texts are always actualized by an empirical reader in a specific reading situation, I focus in this paper rather on the textual input into the reader-text relation, being concerned with the construction within the text of an *illocutionary situation*,[1] that is, a set of communicational circumstances capable of giving point to its existence as an *utterance*. It can be shown that many texts employ self-situating devices in order to define themselves as discursive events, which are understandable—or "make sense"—only within particularized illocutionary situations and in light of specific understandings about communication in general and literary communication in particular. This aspect of their *self-reflexivity*, far from producing text as a Jakobsonian *autotelic* phenomenon, defines it as a communicational event by indicating such things as the status of the *emitter* and *receiver*, the nature of *code* and *channel*, and relative focus on *referent* or *message*. (A text may well define itself as autotelic, but unless it does so one may be going against its own indications in assuming that it is.)

I hope this way of speaking of the matter is not misleading. I do not mean to imply that interpreters may not bring to the reading of a text understandings of their own about literary communication. Still less do I wish to suggest (this is a point about which I am cheerfully agnostic) that texts possess objective features—in this case, self-situating ones—that would be analyzable in a way independent of the interpretive categories a given empirical reader may bring to them. If by analysis is meant a context-free procedure undetermined by preexisting interpretive focus, then what follows in this paper is certainly not analysis (my approach to a nineteenth-century poem is informed, for example, by the basics of twentieth-century information theory). But if, on the other hand, analysis is understood as the procedure whereby a text is produced as an object of an interpretation—an activity always already embedded in, and inseparable from, interpretive presuppositions and aims—

then, perhaps, this paper may fairly be taken as illustrating certain analytic procedures. But the two terms *analysis* and *interpretation* are in practice so difficult to distinguish and imply each other so intimately that I will adopt a more neutral term and describe my critical operation here as a *reading* of communicational self-situation in a Baudelaire poem.

How is this reading to be done? Common sense suggests that it is the rare text whose content does not include representations of (virtual or realized) communicational situations and that the understandings about communication that underlie these representations must be related to the understandings presupposed in and by the text itself as an utterance. A central mode of situational self-reflexivity (certainly not the only one) appears to be, then, the production of *embedded* models—what Lucien Dällenbach calls "mise en abyme de l'énonciation" and "mise en abyme du code"—whose identification (and comparison with one another and with the text as a whole) leads, by a series of intricate interpretive procedures, to the construction of an overall model, or set of models (which need not be either simple or fully coherent), as an indicator of communicational self-situation in a reading of the text. That is, in barest outline, the procedure to be followed here.[2]

Baudelaire's "A une passante" is intriguing in that, although the encounter described in the body of the poem is visual and silent—a meeting of glances—the opening line (and sentence) establishes the place of the encounter as full of noise. I want to show that this "place" is not merely decor or descriptive background but that it functions also as an indicator of communicational circumstances relevant both to the meeting with the woman in the poem and to the poem itself. But since the visual encounter itself functions similarly—and in two different ways—as a model for the text, our analysis will need to focus on a number of different situations with a view to determining the relation between them:

1. "I" in the noisy street (line 1)
2. "I" and the woman
   a. the woman as passing figure (2–8)
   b. the exchange of glances (9–14)
3. The poem itself as an utterance, or communicational event

The guiding notions will be, for (1), that of the inevitability for communication of a channel and hence of interference, and for (2) that of the message as (a) code, that is, an order arising from the disorder of the channel, and (b) uncoded content, a glimpse of the chaos at the heart of things, constitutive therefore not only of the channel as such but of an eternal principle of life. The simultaneous relevance of these models for the poem itself will be considered under (3).

A une passante

La rue assourdissante autour de moi hurlait.
Longue, mince, en grand deuil, douleur majestueuse,

Une femme passa, d'une main fastueuse
Soulevant, balançant le feston et l'ourlet;

Agile et noble, avec sa jambe de statue.
Moi je buvais, crispé comme un extravagant,
Dans son œil, ciel livide où germe l'ouragan,
La douceur qui fascine et le plaisir qui tue.

Un éclair . . . puis la nuit!—Fugitive beauté
Dont le regard m'a fait soudainement renaître,
Ne te verrai-je plus que dans l'éternité?

Ailleurs, bien loin d'ici! trop tard! *jamais* peut-être!
Car j'ignore où tu fuis, tu ne sais où je vais,
O toi que j'eusse aimée, ô toi qui le savais!

To a Passer-By

The deafening street howled around me. Tall and slender, in deep mourning and majestic in her grief, a woman went by, with sumptuous hand holding up and swinging scallop and hem; agile and noble, with a leg like that of a statue. I, contorted like a crazy, drank from her eye, a pallid sky where the hurricane germinates, the sweetness that fascinates and the pleasure that kills.

A flash . . . then darkness! Fleeting beauty, whose glance made me reborn, shall I not see you again except in eternity? Elsewhere, very far from here! too late! *never* perhaps! For I do not know where you are fleeing to, and you are unaware where I am going, oh you whom I would have loved, oh you who knew it!

(*Œuvres* 1: 92–93; trans. mine)

1. The Street as Noise (line 1)

Both in common-sense terms and in the contemporary jargon of information theory, *noise* is that which impedes communication. The decor of the poem, the place where its action is set, thus inevitably appears (in a communicational perspective) as the circumstance of disorder within which and against which the message—here the appearance of the woman and the unspoken exchange between her and "I"—will constitute itself as order. But initially, the main consequence of noise in the poem is the isolation of the subject, who is both spatially separate from the street that surrounds him ("autour de moi") and confined within an area of silence by the deafening effect of "la rue assourdissante." We can note parenthetically that the formal structure of the line underscores this isolation of the subject: the *paronomasia* at each extremity of the line ([lary] and [yrlɛ]) strengthens the identification of the street with noise while, grouped around the central caesura, "assourdissante" and "autour de moi" both focus on "I" (as victim of noise and spatial center).

The universe in which the future communicational subject must function is thus defined as one that, favoring isolation, is hostile to communication, at least of a verbal, spoken kind. It makes necessary the type of silent, unspoken communication to which, through their empathetic exchange of glances, "I" and the woman will have recourse. This hostility is conveyed also through a secondary sense of the verb *assourdir* (used of "damping," "muting," or "deadening" sounds)—a sense reinforced here by the vocalic contrast, in connection with [r], or "*tue*" and "h*u*rler" versus "s*our*d." This muting effect on the human subject of a world of noise gives point to "I"'s interpretation (in the tercets) of the exchange with the woman as a rebirth—that is, it seems, as a rediscovery of self through unspoken communication; and the basic contrast we can already perceive between modes of communication in the poem (the difficulty of verbal communication vs. the success of nonverbal communication) suggests that what is at stake may be a tension or conflict between *mediated* messages and *unmediated*, or empathetic, understanding—both, however, in their relation to a world of noise.

For it is worth noticing that it is the noisy street which serves as the channel[3] in which the enlivening encounter takes place: without the street, bringing together the man and the woman with their separate, mutually unknown destinations (13), they could not have met and exchanged meaningful glances. This means that, whatever value is placed on unmediated communication, mediation, with its necessary corollary of noise and disorder, remains logically prior as the necessary condition of their communication. If it is noise that, by contrast, gives unmediated communication its value and significance—almost its miraculous quality—this is because there can be no communicational exchange without a channel, and it is in this channel that noise and disorder reside. The woman, as has already been mentioned, stands for two different ways in which human messages oppose disorder: as mediated, orderly communication (the beauty of her figure) and as unmediated communication (her glance). But in each of them, as we shall see, disorder inevitably lurks.

2a. The Woman as Mediated Message (lines 2–8)

Acted on by the deafening roar of the street, "I" is also the passive recipient ("Moi, je buvais . . .") of a shock (cf. Benjamin, "Motive" 126–31) produced by the woman: between these two active agents—the street and the woman (the channel and the message)—there is consequently a relation, an affinity. But if the woman is to the street as message is to the noisy channel, it is with the woman as mediated message, a figure of poetry as code, that the quatrains are concerned.

For here she is both the impression of rhythmic grace and statuesque nobility produced by her moving form and the liquidity (or formlessness) "I" drinks from her eye: "La douceur qui fascine et le plaisir qui tue." The contrast between plasticity of form and liquidity in the eye is underlined, in successive lines, by the collocation of "avec sa jambe de statue" and "Moi, je buvais"; and it suggests that the woman is an embodiment not of a miraculous unmediated communication but of the mediated message, one in which it makes sense to distinguish between signifier and signified, form and content, vehicle and tenor, code and meaning.[4] So it is not surprising that she should demonstrate some important connections with the street, the noisy place that makes meetings possible.

"Longue, mince . . .": the momentary hint of *anaphora* here (referring back to "la rue") is soon dispelled as the line continues. The woman is not identical with the street; rather, it is as if she is produced by it or out of it. In particular, by her "passing," she realizes the street's potentiality as a space that enables movement from place to place, that is, as a channel of communication and exchange within the city (community)—whereas "I," as a stationary figure, characterizes himself as a "flâneur," an observer marginal to the exchange relations of the city as he is isolated in the world of noise. Movement, in Baudelaire, is inseparable from beauty (see poems like "Le beau navire" or "Avec ses vêtements . . .").[5] Here, the action of walking is, on the one hand, what constitutes the female figure as a realization of the street's potentiality and, on the other, what makes her a figure of rhythmic grace: " . . . d'une main fastueuse / Soulevant, balançant le feston et l'ourlet; / Agile. . . ." But this grace is matched by a type of grandeur ("en grand deuil," "douleur majestueuse," "noble, avec sa jambe de statue") that makes her at the same time a slightly forbidding, or at least awesome, figure. And it is of course her mourning and grief that give her this slightly numinous quality and provide the key to the combination in her of "passing" and grandeur: she is a figure of death, albeit of death in its most beautiful aspect, as it might find aesthetic expression in a work of art ("avec sa jambe de statue"). The deafening noise around "I" has become an aesthetic message, a visual poem of motion incorporating grace, rhythm, nobility, and order (note in particular the implications of control in "balançant")—but it is a message that has death as its signified, and it is death that "I" will confront.

For what he sees at the heart of the message, in the woman's eye ("ciel livide où germe l'ouragan"—the sky pale with lightning that foretells the storm), is disorder; this meteorological manifestation of the disorder at the source ("germe") of the message inevitably relates to and recalls the communicational disorder, or noise, of the street. That such disorder is pleasurable and indeed fascinating when incorporated in beauty is the sense of line 8, but it remains lethal, a "plaisir qui tue" (and the echo of "douleur" in "douceur" as well as the rhyme—at the opening and close of the quatrains—of "rue" and "tue" is certainly significant). Its effect, indeed, can be seen immediately in the spastic reaction of "I," to whom disorder has been communicated in the form of involuntary muscular tension ("crispé") implying loss of verbal (and mental) control (etymologically, "extravagant" means wandering outside of and beyond the limits). This muscular spasm contrasts, of course, with the physical grace and control of the woman ("soulevant, balançant le feston et l'ourlet"), but it has nonetheless been brought on by reception of the "content" of her message, the stormy disorder at its source, in her eye. Contrasting with the street, its channel, as the unspoken (visual) to the noisy and as the orderly to the disorderly, the message has revealed itself to be in profound affinity with the street both by its mediated quality (as orderly message) and by the disorder that is its unspoken content. The suggestion is that to read correctly the meaning of beauty is to receive the fulgurant shock of the chaos against which it works but of which it is also the vehicle.

2b. The Woman as Unmediated Message
(lines 9–14)

"Un éclair . . . puis la nuit!" The word "éclair" captures both the stormy quality of the message and its electrifying impact; but it stresses now something new, which is its momentary character, and it emphasizes what was already implicit in the different tenses of "Une femme passa . . ." and "Moi, je buvais . . ."—that is, that "I" is literally left standing by the passing of the woman. The return to night after the moment of vision and insight would therefore be equivalent to a return to the world of disorder (the noisy street) were it not that the action of the poem now continues within the mind of "I" (whose initial isolation becomes internalized as reflection or absorption) as he reflects on the significance of what has happened. The tercets, then, embody a meditation concerned with interpreting the event recorded in the quatrains, but their focus is no longer the woman's stately and graceful advance but the memory her passing leaves him of the meeting of their eyes.

This meditation introduces a contrast between life (the street in which people move, meet, communicate, and pass on) and a possible world of eternity, beyond death. The rebirth occasioned by the woman's glance is attributed to a vision, mediated fleetingly in the street ("Fugitive beauté") but experienced also, it seems, in such a direct way as to suggest that it will be visible again only in the beyond— that is to say, if eternity should prove an illusion, "*jamais* peut-être," and in any case "Ailleurs, bien loin d'ici, trop tard!" If the storm ("ouragan") constituting the content of the message (quatrains version) represents death and disorder in the world (its initial vowel and following consonant rhyme with the radical syllable—"sourd"— of "assourdissante"), it is perhaps, in a cosmic sense, a source of life that "I" has been granted the privilege of briefly, but directly, glimpsing (tercets version). Disorder, in this latter case, would then be not an accidental and secondary manifestation but something primary and essential, and the manifestations of order we perceive as beauty—that is, our mediated messages—but passing phenomena against this eternal background.

However, all this is hypothetical (note the interrogatory sentence of lines 9–11, the "peut-être" of line 12). What is known at a human level is a certain balance of ignorance and certainty presented in the final couplet. But ignorance, in a trivial sense, of the respective destinations of those we meet in the street signifies (in this context) an ignorance of the final ends just evoked in the discussion of eternity. The street has here become an image of a life through which we pass but whose starting and ending points (its *tenants* and *aboutissants* in the more telling French metaphor relating to streetmaps) are beyond our ken. But in that life there is a certainty, which is that of interpersonal communication—a communication of an unmediated, or empathetic, kind, which has as its content human love. "I" knows that he would have loved the woman, but he knows too that she knew it—that is, in his own eye also something was readable. The communication between them has been a true exchange—not that his desire was necessarily reciprocated by the woman, but that its expression in his eye (consequent on his receipt of the message in hers) was both recognized and acknowledged by her.

So it is the exchange of glances (as opposed to the storm in the woman's eye) that is being interpreted here, and the message now concerns human love more than cosmic vision. The eye that (in the quatrains) represented the signified of a mediated message (the woman) has now become the vehicle of an unmediated message (the exchange of glances) whose content is desire. The tercets seem to imply—since beauty is order and grace in whose "eye" lurks a hurricane and since it is the sight of the hurricane that so affects "I"—that what provokes human desire is vision of the disorder, the storm at the eternal heart of things. (That is why "la douceur qui fascine"—that which arouses desire—is also "le plaisir qui tue"—that which involves us in death. That is why, also, human love, realizable only as desire in the street/ world in which we stand or pass by, can achieve its goal and consummation only somewhere, sometime outside of life, in "eternity.") But the tercets imply also that within life there is a kind of miracle, which is that of unmediated understanding, while suggesting that desire, sparked by the storm in the eye of beauty and visible in turn in the eye of the recipient, is what makes such understanding possible.

3. The Poem

By virtue of the rhetorical structure, also, the tercets introduce a change into the poem. In the quatrains, "I" is addressing the reader and recounting, in narrative mode, an encounter with a woman in the street. Now the woman has become the interlocutor—or more accurately (since she is absent), the object of an apostrophe—and the reader of the poem is in the position of "overhearing" a message addressed in one sense to another figure but, in a different sense, spoken by "I" to himself, in her absence. The poem in these lines is a miming in words of solitary thought, to which the reader is admitted through the operation of an age-old lyric convention. One may even think that this convention encapsulates the generic "communication" situation of literature itself, as a miming of utterance (involving the I-you situation) cut off (like the meditating "I" in the noisy street) from empirical circumstances of communication.

This model of poetic communication can easily—and indeed must, if one is logical—be extended to the whole poem, since the preliminary narrative can have no real point except as it leads up to the questions and reflections in the tercets. This means, then, that we are invited to read the whole poem (and not just the tercets) as if overhearing the meditation of a lonely "I" first going over the events and then reflecting on the significance of his extraordinary encounter with the woman. The empirical reader, in this case, "fills the slot" made vacant by the now absent woman to whom the words are seemingly addressed: in short, we are invited to read thoughts—a feat of empathy comparable to that of the woman herself, who "knew" that "I" might have loved her. The communicational axioms on which the poem rests are consequently that human beings have empathetic understanding for each other—and in particular for the expression of desire—and that they are capable of an unmediated ("unspoken") form of understanding that defeats the noise in the communicational channel (in this case, not just the actual words of the text but all the distance that separates the text from its empirical reader). The reader is thus cast in a role, with respect to the poem, similar to that of the passer-by in the street/world who glimpses in passing the depths of "I"'s being and reads there the intensity of his love.

But the poem is no less clearly a verbal, mediated act of communication, and it figures itself as such through the description of the woman. Rhythmic, graceful, and agile yet noble, majestic, and sumptuous, she figures order and "fugitive beauté," but a beauty in whose "eye" lurks the hurricane and whose glance conveys an ultimately poisonous draught: "la douceur qui fascine et le plaisir qui tue," leaving the recipient "crispé comme un extravagant"—in a state of spastic shock. As an aesthetic phenomenon ("avec sa jambe de statue"), then, she stands for the poem less as an object of immediate understanding than as an active agent of communication, mediating through its graceful and majestic movement a "hurricane" at its source—that is, the cosmic disorder that inspires desire. In this model, then, the reader is invited to fill the slot in the poem represented by "I"—(another "empty" slot in the sense that the *shifter* is by definition asemantic), that is, invited to be the "flâneur" in the street of life with the sensitivity and "disponibilité" to experience the poem as exerting, through the medium of its "fugitive beauté," a fulgurant impact. Baudelaire's mature doctrine (expressed most notably in *Le peintre de la vie moderne*) of the twofold nature of beauty—partly relative and fleeting, associated with fashion (cf. "le feston et l'ourlet"), and partly absolute, unchanging, and eternal—is of course highly relevant here, but we must be prepared to imagine the eternal component of beauty, its absolute, not as something immutable and fixed but as a ceaseless, seething, elemental chaos. (The work of Michel Serres can sensitize us to this.)

These two models both draw on the dramatically successful act of communication described in lines 6–9, at the "turn" between the quatrains and the tercets of the sonnet, the first exploiting human empathy for the expression of desire, the second our ability to read through the mediating signifier to the chaos at its "eye." But what is being communicated here, whether by empathy or by mediation, is a vision of disorder at the formal center of the poem (the hurricane, the "douceur qui fascine," the "plaisir qui tue" and the lightning flash are its manifestations). And in the form of noise, we have said that disorder, as a characteristic of the necessary channel (the street), is logically prior to both empathy and mediated communication. So we must ask ourselves whether the street—of which the woman as message is a kind of emanation—is not itself relevant to the poem's self-situation, to a self-situation that would not now be as an orderly message or as one that miraculously circumvents mediation but as a disorderly communicational act, having an affinity with noise.

The street itself as a model of the poem is indeed a Baudelairean idea (see, for example, "Le soleil"), but especially striking in this poem is the appropriateness of the verb "hurler," used somewhat unexpectedly of a street but characterizing with some precision the type of verbal utterance one might hear from a human subject described as "crispé comme un extravagant"—with all the implications this phrase has of muscular tension, spastic gesticulation, and loss of verbal control. Beneath its grace and nobility, the poem is suggesting, perhaps, the presence of a "hurlement," a howl, a cry; if so, it thus implies for itself a highly dramatic illocutionary situation that identifies the essence of its message in its status as verbal disorder, uncontrolled noise.

So much formal experimentation has taken place in poetry since Baudelaire that it is difficult for contemporary readers to hear the "howl" in these fourteen alexandrine verses that constitute a variant of classical sonnet. Even the poem's own formal experimentation (the deployment of irregular and frequent "coupes," the running on of grammatical structures over the limits of conventional metric structures like line and "strophe"—all the features that have recently led Donald Aynesworth to define it as a "linguistic essay in disjunction, juxtaposition and decomposition" [330]) seems timid by today's standards, although it was certainly not always so. But it is important to understand that the poem is not concerned with *mimetic* effects: it is not imitating or simulating a cry; rather, it is describing its illocutionary situation as that of a cry and inviting us to read it on that understanding. It becomes a cry through self-situation rather than through "objective" characteristics that might be thought in some sense crylike. Perhaps indeed the howl in the poem is a silent one—the voiceless cry of one whose throat is "crispé," a cry we are invited to hear in the unmediated and empathetic way that "I" visually perceives the storm in the woman's eye.

There is a point of some philosophical significance here. The nature of a communicational act is determined not by its objective characteristics, if such there be, but by contextual understandings (self-situation in the present case, illocutionary agreements in so-called ordinary circumstances). There is also a philosophical conundrum, since although we have just concluded that contextual understandings are primary, much literature (including "A une passante") suggests that the illocutionary context can be, and is, a function of text itself. Conceivably, this literary model could be extended to nonliterary cases to show that the determining context is itself produced by discourse. In short, there is a strong case for collapsing the admittedly convenient distinction between "text" and "context" and for seeking another approach to the study of communicational acts.

Meanwhile, however, I want to conclude with an observation that is more narrowly aesthetic in its concerns, relating to what Roland Barthes has taught us to call the "polyphony" of literary texts (*Critique*). A reason why "A une passante" cannot afford to have formal features overly reminiscent of an actual howl (the street as model) is that its characteristics must also be consistent with a reading of the poem as a phenomenon of rhythm, flexibility, movement, and grace (the woman as model) as well as with a reading as an overheard lonely meditation (the "I" of the tercets as model). If I were writing in literary-historical mode, I would wish to show how the central (mediated) model links and allows the coexistence of a model relating to age-old lyric convention and a model highly suggestive of a modern poetics of noise. In the present context, however, my point is that it is the simultaneous validity of these different illocutionary situations (perhaps also of others: I make no claim to an exhaustive analysis) that defines the complex illocutionary situation the poem is producing for itself. And I would suggest further that this ability to situate itself in terms of several simultaneously relevant communicational models constitutes not just the poem's complexity but genuinely its "polyphony"—its speaking in many voices—as literature.[6]

Notes

[1] See the glossary for an explanation of certain technical terms.

[2] Major insights into the linguistics of utterance are to be found in J. L. Austin, *How to Do Things with Words*, and Benveniste. For a discussion of linguistic functions, see also Jakobson, "Linguistics and Poetics." Pratt attempts to develop a theory of literature as utterance.

On self-reflexivity, Dällenbach is fundamental. In my book *Story and Situation*, the theory on which the present paper is based is developed with respect to narrative; on poetry, see also my "Parole et poésie."

For awareness of the communicational significance of "noise" in literary texts, see Michel Serres; for a convenient introduction to Serres's work, see Harari and Bell.

The seminal commentary on "A une passante" is Benjamin, "Motive," esp. 126–31. See also Goebel, Knapp-Tepperberg, Versluys, Oehler, Aynesworth, Stamelman, and my "Pour une poétique."

[3] Another street poem in the same section of *Les fleurs du mal*, "Les sept vieillards" (*Œuvres* 87–88), refers to Parisian streets as "les canaux étroits du colosse puissant": as with "noise," Baudelaire's metaphor coincides (partly) with the metaphor underlying the modern technical term.

[4] Strictly speaking, the woman is not a situational *mise en abyme* so much as a figural one: she stands for a certain conception of poetic discourse rather than for a communicational situation as such. But figuring poetry as code (a set of understandings implying communicational agreements), she presupposes also a situation of communication.

[5] The oft-quoted line from "La beauté," (*Œuvres* 21), "Je hais le mouvement qui déplace les lignes," has to be read as referring to the kind of movement that disturbs line, not to movement in general.

[6] I am grateful to the Humanities Research Centre of the Australian National University (Canberra) for the opportunity to write this paper during my tenure as a visiting fellow (May–July 1982).

Glossary

Anaphora   reference back (to a preceding sentence or line) as opposed to reference forward, or **cataphora**. Also: head rhyme (as opposed to end rhyme).

Autotelic   having no purpose except in itself.

Channel   see **Illocutionary situation**.

Code   see **Illocutionary situation**.

Embedding   a structural phenomenon whereby a unit of discourse surrounds and is divided by another segment, contained within the first. **Mise en abyme** refers to **embedding**, in which there is a relation of similarity (a "mirroring") between embedded and embedding discourse. In **mise en abyme de l'énonciation**, the relation concerns the act of production, or **utterance**, of the discourse; in **mise en abyme du code**, it concerns the conventions that enable communication to occur.

Emitter   see **Illocutionary situation**.

Illocutionary situation   those circumstantial elements that affect the meaning or determine the point of a piece of discourse considered as an event, or act—that is, as an **utterance**. These include the status and relation of the **emitter** and **receiver** of the message, the **channel** (or medium of communication) and the **code** (or agreed conventions on which the communication depends), the relation of **message** (the discourse as a particular realization of the **code**) to **referent** (or context—what the message is "about").

   Illocutionary contrasts, on the one hand, with **locutionary** (implying a communicational relation as opposed to the mere production of an **utterance**) and, on the other, with **perlocutionary** (which refers to the effects or consequences an **utterance** may have).

Mediation   those elements of the **illocutionary situation** that enable a message to pass between **emitter** and **receiver**, here specifically the **code**. Strictly speaking, an **unmediated message** would be one that did not need either a **channel** or a **code** to produce a successful communicational event, but in the Baudelaire text the **channel** is given as an indispensable prerequisite for communication.

Message   see **Illocutionary situation**.

Mimesis   imitation in discourse of aspects of the world (human speech and action, material reality, etc.).

Mise en abyme   see **Embedding**.

Noise   interference to communication caused by the **channel**.

Paronomasia   a near pun (perceived relation between two linguistic items having a number of phonemes in common).

Receiver   see **Illocutionary situation**.

Referent   see **Illocutionary situation**.

Self-reflexivity   the characteristic of discourse that comments on itself (or can be interpreted as so doing).

Shifter   a word whose semantic content is determined by the circumstances of its utterance (e.g., "here," "I," "tomorrow").

Utterance   the act of producing discourse.

When Is a Primitive like an Orb?

J. HILLIS MILLER

My strategies of textual analysis in this reading will more or less speak for themselves. Their provenance will be obvious. This essay was originally conceived as a part of *The Linguistic Moment* (Princeton: Princeton UP, 1985). Here, as in that book, I am concerned with moments in poems when the medium of poetry becomes an issue. I am especially interested here in the way the line between conceptual and figurative terms becomes blurred in Wallace Stevens's late poem "A Primitive like an Orb."[1] The latent figures in abstract terms are extracted and exposed, while overt figures become, in their turn, the only way in which certain "abstract" insights can be expressed. This interchange is related to the way both abstractions and figures here are catachreses, "improper" terms for an evasive center, "the essential poem at the centre of things" that can never be named directly. My interest in the latter gives my strategy of textual analysis here an extralinguistic, even an ontological or metaphysical, orientation. This orientation is demanded by the poem. I think such a bias is in general in one way or another demanded by works of literature, though it is extremely easy to misunderstand what is meant or called for by this demand.

"Like" Yeats's "Nineteen Hundred and Nineteen," Stevens's "A Primitive like an Orb" presents a serial arrangement of images organized in a circular "as" or "is" structure around an absent center. This center can only be named evasively. Why? This taboo against literal naming and the effort to break this taboo make up, one may say, the chief topic of the poem, the place or commonplace around which the poem rotates. "A Primitive like an Orb" has twelve numbered eight-line stanzas in blank verse. These are almost like the digits arranged around the face of a clock. Within the sequence of the twelve, there are sharp grammatical or thematic breaks after each quarter, or group of three. After each quarter the poem begins again with a new syntactical pattern and a new set of images bound together by "as" or "is." Each new set displaces the one before. If the images are linked by their implicit and problematic equivalence, the motive energy that makes each inadequate and makes each need to be replaced by another is their even more problematic relation of likeness to the absent center. This is figured by the unnamed sun. "Sun" is the one word that may not be uttered or written within this poem. If a "primitive" is "like" an "orb," this is because both primitive and orb are "like" the ꜱᴜɴ. A primitive is like an orb. An orb is like a primitive. Neither of these words is the normal "literal" name for what it refers to by a displacement both in its use and in the syntactical slippage of the "like" that follows or precedes it. The sun, that "close, parental magnitude, / At the centre on the horizon, concentrum, grave / And prodigious person, patron of origins" (86–88), emerges gradually in the course of the poem as the apparent literal referent of the chain-linked series of figures making up the poem. But the sun is of course in its turn only a figure for the true "literal" theme of the poem, which is named in the first line: "the essential poem at the centre of things." This obscure phrase is immediately followed by an even more obscure phrase in apposition: "The arias that spiritual fiddlings make" (2). If a primitive is like an orb, the essential poem at the center of things, whatever that means, is like the arias that spiritual fiddlings make, whatever *that* means. The poem moves from enigma to enigma, like a long-legged fly skating on water. It moves in phrases, each of which must be interrogated in detail for its depth of figurative, syntactic, and semantic play.

Saying, for example, as the title does, "a primitive like an orb" differs greatly from saying, "the primitive like the orb," or "the primitive like an orb," or "a primitive like the orb." In Stevens's phrase both primitive and orb are no more than examples of indefinitely large categories of primitives and of orbs, not the original primitive or the original orb. Each of the two words, moreover, opens up within itself an unexpected complexity. An orb may be a solid substance, the fiery paternal orb of the sun, or it may be a hollow 0, a zero, the nothing named at the end of the poem as "the giant of nothingness" (95). This recalls the equation made by Paul Claudel of egg, seed, open mouth, zero—"oeuf, semence, bouche ouverte, zéro" (Claudel and Gide 91). Moreover, an "orb" may be at the center or it may be the circuit around the center, the orbit or trajectory. One example would be the course of that sun which in this poem is a "concentrum" "at the centre on the horizon" (87). Another example would be the circuit of the horizon itself, that vanishing point in the distance all around the spectator. The word "primitive," on the other hand, is something that in one way or another comes first. A primitive fathers forth a sequence of generations modeled on the father but varying it, making the primitive gradually more complex. A primitive is a "patron of origins" (88). The word "primitive" has technical meanings in linguistics, in algebra, and in anthropology. A primitive is a radical or root word from which ever more complex words have been derived through time. A primitive is an algebraic equation that is the source of a series of increasingly complex derived equations. A primitive is an aboriginal human being who is not yet quite human, containing only virtually, in undeveloped embryo, all the burden of civilized culture.

Both a primitive and an orb have simultaneously temporal and spatial dimensions. It might be more accurate to say that each is a spatial image for time. Each falsifies time, since time cannot be mapped as a space. At the same time, each gives the reader access to time, an intuition or sense of temporality that is impossible without spatial images. Both space and time, in this contradictory inherence of one in the other, rotate around the absent center or expand from it or orbit with it, according to the incoherent implications of the images of orb and primitive. Speech, time, and space come together around the eclipsed sun, the essential poem at the center of things. Of this the poet says that "It is and it / Is not and, therefore, is" (13–14). As soon as it is glimpsed through being named in one of the riddling figures that make up the notes or spiritual fiddlings of Stevens's poem, it vanishes in the revelation, once more, of the inadequacy of any name for the poem at the center. The force of the intuition that something is there lies not in its unveiling but in the recognition that any naming, after a moment, covers it over, according to a general law of apocalyptic language: "In the instant of speech, / The breadth of an accelerando moves, / Captives the being, widens—and was there" (14–16). In the next stanza this instant of speech opens "a space grown wide" and reveals "the inevitable blue / Of secluded thunder" (21–22). This blue is an empty sky that nevertheless hides a lightning storm, over the horizon, blinding light occluded. This hidden light is then defined as "an illusion, as it was, / Oh as, always too heavy for the sense / To seize, the obscurest as, the distant was . . ." (22–24). The "is" that is not becomes when it is named or sensed instantly "was" and therefore another simile or another metaphorical equivalent, "as" adding itself to the constantly proliferating chain structure of displacements making up the poem.

To get the reader within the play of language in "A Primitive like an Orb" I shall juxtapose to it a passage from Jacques Derrida's *De la grammatologie*:

> Is it not necessary to think through [*méditer*] this heliocentric concept of speech? As well as the resemblance of the logos to the sun (to the good or to the death that one cannot look at face to face), to the king or to the father (the good or the intelligible sun are compared to the father in the *Republic*, 508 c)? What must writing be in order to threaten this analogical system in its vulnerable and secret center? What must it be in order to signify the *eclipse* of what is *good* and of the *father*? Should one not stop considering writing as the eclipse that comes to surprise and obscure the glory of the word [*la gloire du verbe*]? And if there is some necessity of eclipse, should not the relationship of shadow and light, of writing and speech, itself appear in a different way?   (139)[2]

Derrida's language moves from one to another of a set of terms that are implicitly equivalent, each a substitute for the last, a "resemblance" of it, in a series of transformations in which no term is the first or the pivot around which the others turn or the end at which they may stop. The logos equals the sun equals the good equals the death that cannot be looked at in the face equals the king equals the father equals mind equals speech. In this analogical sequence no term is the beginning or the end, because each is only another term. By the fact that it is only a term, a word, it is not *the* word. It is only a derived image in a potentially endless sequence of images, each of which always refers to another image, an so on indefinitely. Each term for that which is the source of terms is a metaphor drawn from that realm which is supposed to have derived from that which it is a term for. Sun, father, king, light, and so on are supposed to be metaphors for the one, the logos, pale material copies of it, analogies or symbols, as one speaks of the Creation as the speech of God—"news of God," in Gerard Manley Hopkins's phrase. The metaphor drawn from what is condemned as secondary is the most appropriate term for that from which it is supposed to be derived. Derrida's argument is that the condemnation of writing works to obscure this fact. It works to keep the analogical system intact by hiding the similarity between writing and speech. Both equally create that from which they claim to be derived, but the autonomy, repeatability, and detachment from any living voice of writing make this so much more evident that it appears to eclipse the sun, to uncover the blackness at the vulnerable and secret center of this whole analogical system.

A similar set of equivalences may be seen operating throughout "A Primitive like an Orb," though the force of the word "similar" must be taken anasemically[3] here too, ana-analogically. Similarity or analogy inevitably implies some central logos in the name of which the examples are analogous, speak with similar voices, but the existence and nature of that central logos are just what is most in question here. In any case, "Primitive like an Orb," like Stevens's work as a whole, is—as much as Plato's dialogues—heliocentric. Stevens's pervasive use of the figure, or concept, or literal objective fact (it is all three) of the trajectory of the sun, its rising, its majestic march across the sky, its setting, is one more example of the heliotropic unity of the occidental repertoire of tropes. Our metaphorology is a photology, since all metaphors are modes of illustration or of bringing to light, even though this light may be spurious or artificial, a lamp and not the sun. This is, to say it again, in each case just the question. Is the light original or is it human-made, a case of poiēsis? Stevens's "A Primitive like an Orb" seemingly chooses the first possibility. The poem presents a theory of poetry as revelation of the giant on the horizon, the poem at the center of things that preexists any lesser poem, is its source, its begetter, and yet exists only in the lesser poems. "A Primitive like an Orb" proceeds from one to another of the following images in their metaphorical circulation: center, poem, speech, good, food, light, gold, void (by way of the pun in "gorging" [3,5]), air, melody, space, time, music, being, primitive, the primitive as aboriginal man, as primitive word, as radical, as primitive formula from which others are derived, as illustration, as source of form, as egg, as seed, as both center and sphere, concentrum and orbit, as world, as husband, as desire, as will, as joy, as self, as father ("The essential poem begets the others" [47]), as circle ("ring" [56]), as whole, as vis, as principle, as primitive source, as nature, as "repose," as magnet or source of magnetic field, as giant, as fire, as following as well as origin, as angel, as power or source of power, as fate ("prodigious"[88]: Latin prōdigiōsus, from prō- digium 'omen,' 'portent'), as matrix, as abstraction embodied, as illustration, as skeleton, as the total of paintings, prophecies, poems, and love letters, as change.

"A Primitive like an Orb" proceeds through the problematic equivalences affirmed among this astonishing diversity of terms. These equivalences are established by the fundamental syntactical principle of this poem: phrases in apposition. Phrases in apposition, however, are similes without the words "as" or "like." "Like" and "as" appear in the title and in the lines about "the obscurest as." These locutions call attention to metaphor and simile as fundamental instruments of poetic thinking. Metaphor or simile asserts an equivalence between things that are nevertheless not identical. A similar form is taken by sentences that say, "A is B." The series of phrases in apposition is perhaps the dominant form, however, because such a series is held together by the absence or the effacement of the "is" that is nevertheless implied as the basis of their equivalence. That "is" is the "being" that is momentarily captivated, that which is and is not and so is. This potentially endless series of false equivalences, one "obscurest as" after another, rotates by way of the substitution of each new figurative term for the last around the absent center of the nonexistent literal word for which all these terms are figures.

The "obscurest as" organizes the whole poem. Stanzas 7 through 9, for example, the third quadrant of the poem, are one long sentence of phrases in apposition, each replacing the last, only to be instantly replaced in its turn by a new phrase that picks up a bit of debris from the annihilation of the phrase before, the whole turning on a single verb, the little word "is" in the first line. I cite the whole of this extraordinary sentence, so the reader may see here on the page how Stevens feels his way from formulation to formulation, discarding each but trying then another variation of it. The reader should also note the syntactical complexity of the sentence, not only its dependence on the open serial sequence of phrases in apposition and its reliance on the "a" and "an" of the title, as well as on the "the" in its difference from "a" or "an," but also its shifting from one grammatical pattern to another by way of a constant play of "and"s, "or"s, and "of"s. Stevens's work is surely to be defined, in Roman Jakobson's phrase, as an admirable exploitation of the latent "poetry of grammar" ("Poetry"; see also Hammond). It is also an example of what might be called the poetry of punctuation, a poetry of the comma or the absence of the comma (as at the end of stanza 7 here), and of the indefinite postponing of the period. Here is the sentence:

VII

The central poem is the poem of the whole,
The poem of the composition of the whole,
The composition of blue sea and of green,
Of blue light and of green, as lesser poems,
And the miraculous multiplex of lesser poems,
Not merely into a whole, but a poem of
The whole, the essential compact of the parts,
The roundness that pulls tight the final ring

VIII

And that which in an altitude would soar,
A vis, a principle or, it may be,
The meditation of a principle,
Or else an inherent order active to be

Itself, a nature to its natives all
Beneficence, a repose, utmost repose,
The muscles of a magnet aptly felt,
A giant, on the horizon, glistening,

IX

And in bright excellence adorned, crested
With every prodigal, familiar fire,
And unfamiliar escapades: whirroos
And scintillant sizzlings such as children like,
Vested in the serious folds of majesty,
Moving around and behind, a following,
A source of trumpeting seraphs in the eye,
A source of pleasant outbursts on the ear.   (49–72)

"*The* poem of *the* composition of *the* whole" is not quite the same thing as "*the* poem of *the* whole," though their grammatical juxtaposition suggests that the two phrases must or might be two ways to say the same thing. "A poem of a whole" would be something else again, something partial and contingent as against the absolute and exclusive, the distinguished, the right real thing at last. The repetition of the phrase "of the whole" makes the "of" stand out. "Of" in what sense, the reader asks, "of" as "about," or "from," or "participating in"? Is it a poem about the whole, or a poem coming from the whole, or a poem sharing the whole, a "tenacious particle" (92) of it? Does the "of" have the same sense in "composition of blue sea and of green" as in "composition of the whole"? The "of" would seem to go in a different direction in each case, coming from (or going toward) totality in one case ("composition of the whole") and coming from (or going toward) the multiplicity of nature in the other ("composition of blue sea and of green"). The reader must grope his way so from phrase to phrase and from line to line, testing or tasting each on his mental palate to see what is uniquely released by each in its slight difference from the one before.

The stanzas are, moreover, the reader can see, a manifestation of what they talk about. They are a miraculous multiplex of lesser poems. Each phrase is a little burst of aphoristic revelation moving toward an uncovering of the whole or toward an expression of the whole. Or is it more properly "*the* uncovering the whole, *the* expression of the whole"? Stevens's "the's" are insistent here, at least in the first stanza, though "*the* poem of the whole" in line 1 becomes "a poem of / The whole" in lines 6 and 7. Is the "composition" in question the unveiling of a wholeness already there, the already made composition of the whole, or is the composition of the whole a poetic act of making, or putting parts together in one place to make a whole, as in courses in freshman composition? To put this another way, does the "of" in "poem of the whole," placed ostentatiously in the open at the end of a line ("Not merely into a whole, but a poem of / The whole"), have a constative or a performative force? Is such a poem descriptive of a whole already there, or is it the making of a whole not there before the composition of certain words in a certain order? Or is it the revelation of composition (the already there) through composition (the act of making)?

In any case, the constant slight variation of syntactical and lexical patterns not only makes the basic grammatical armatures of thoughtful discourse stand out ("the A of the B," for example). Such variation also releases so-called abstract words like "whole," "composition," and "poem" from their engagement in the flow or curriculum of argument and makes each stand out alone, free of syntax, as a naked power of signification in relation to that absent and unnamed center, or poem at the center, or central poem. This is particularly evident in the second of the two stanzas quoted above, stanza 8. There is a syntactic slippage between stanza 7 and stanza 8, indicated by the absence of a comma at the end of stanza 7. The wholeness of composition of the central poem, what the poet calls "the essential compact of the parts," which I take it means not just that they are compacted or pressed in together but that they have, as it were, an agreement to belong together and to stay together, is said to be an encircling roundness or outer ring, like a final barrel hoop, or rather it is a force that pulls that outer ring tight and holds the whole together. This roundness or compact, that which makes the whole a whole, at the same time "pulls tight" something, a pervasive energy of unification, which otherwise would fly off ("in an altitude would soar").

The poet experiments with various names for this energy in stanza 8. He moves by way of the "or" from one to another and tests each word for its validity, for the insight it releases. Each new formulation replaces the one before but does not disqualify it, as the poet moves toward the most explicit revelation of the ꟷꟷ as such, though it is still veiled in a personification: "a giant, on the horizon, glistening." The reader is invited to test out the difference between saying it is a "vis" and saying it is a "principle," or between saying it is a "principle" and saying it is "the meditation of a principle" (which may mean the principle meditates or, more likely, that we think of the principle), or between saying it is an "inherent order" and saying it is a "nature to its natives / All beneficence," or between saying it is "repose" and saying it is "utmost repose," or between saying it is repose of either sort, and saying it is the lack of repose defined by the muscular pull of a magnet. Once again the poem performs what it names. It is the meditation of a principle of unity by way of the rotational naming of that principle by various names, "moving around and behind" it, as it moves too, in a slow circling dance of language around the orbiting primitive.

Stanzas through 9 and the poem as a whole resist paraphrase or interpretative commentary, since their implicit double assumption is, first, that no phrase or name or figure is an adequate label for the primitive and, second, that each inadequate phrase or name or figure has its own unique virtue, unveiling and unavailing at once. Each phrase reveals a certain glimpse of the primitive in the moment of its vanishing, as though the words themselves were the eclipse of the sun. To say it otherwise in attempted paraphrase or commentary—mine here, for example—is to say something different, something perhaps with its own virtue. The poem itself demonstrates this through its testing of slight variations on a given formulation, "utmost repose," for example, as against "repose." Interpreters might conceivably add to the poem, add more phrases to the phrases in apposition, but they cannot elucidate it in the sense of bringing some obscure meaning further out in the open by naming it correctly or literally at last. It is this shared linguistic predicament, not some vague right to be "poetic" or "creative," that is meant, or should be meant, when it is said that criticism is a form of literature.

The poem then at the end of stanza 8 moves by way of that latent personification in "muscles of a magnet" to the major prosopopoeia of the sun on the horizon as a glistening giant "vested in the serious folds of majesty" but at the same time adorned in prodigally frivolous fireworks, "whirroos / And scintillant sizzlings such as children like." These serious folds move "around and behind," or is it the giant himself who turns on his axis or moves into invisibility when he sets and appears to move around and behind the rotating earth? The grammar of apposition makes it impossible to be sure which it is, just as it is impossible to tell whether the sun on the horizon is rising or setting. This makes him both origin ("source") and end ("a following"), alpha and omega. The brilliant revelation or shining forth of his rising or setting is a synesthesia of both sound and sight, "son et lumière," light so bright it is perceived as sound. The sun on the horizon is origin of "trumpeting seraphs in the eye" and at the same time of "pleasant outbursts on the ear," just as in the great sunrising scene at the opening of part 2 of Goethe's *Faust*, "a stupendous clangor proclaims the approach of the sun" ("Ungeheures Getöse verkündet das Herannahen der Sonne" [stage direction after line 4665]), and the sun rises "ears bedazing, eyes beglaring" ("Auge blinzt und Ohr erstaunet" [line 4673]).[4]

I have said that the personification of the sun as a giant emerges at the endpoint of the sequence in the long sentence making up stanzas 7 through 9. The relation of prosopopoeia, catachresis, and apostrophe is complex. Here there is no apostrophe. Stevens does not speak to the sun, though in "Chocorua to Its Neighbor," a poem of 1943 that in many ways anticipates "A Primitive like an Orb," the mountain speaks to a neighbor mountain so that the reader overhears speech intended for another, one half of a dialogue between mountains. In "A Primitive like an Orb," Stevens speaks "about" the sun, in more than one sense of that word. The poem is spoken to an audience of thoughtful men and women who share with him (a "him" almost wholly lacking identifiable personality) the revelation effected by the meditative voices of the poem as it shifts from register to register: "But it is, dear sirs, / A difficult apperception, this gorging good . . ." (4–5). It would be a long work to identify and discriminate the mélange of voices, poems, and levels of diction here. Their multiplicity is not consistent with the model of a single speaker addressing univocal speech to a single audience. The lexical material of which this mixture is made includes abstract terms like "composition," "whole," "compact"; explicit figures of speech like that of the "final ring" or that of the magnet or that comparing the sun to a firework of whirroos and scintillant sizzlings such as children like; and finally, the emergent personification, "an abstraction given head" (81), of the sun or central poem as "A giant on the horizon, given arms, / A massive body

and long legs, stretched out" (82–83). "A Primitive like an Orb" has been anticipated in this figure by the extraordinary personification of the starlit night as "more
than muscular shoulders, arms and chest" in "Chocorua to Its Neighbor": "Upon
my top he breathed the pointed dark. / He was not a man yet he was nothing else"
(24, 36–37). "Chocorua to Its Neighbor" joins "A Primitive like an Orb" and "The
Owl in the Sarcophagus" in presenting one of Stevens's great prosopopoeias in poems
about the act of prosopopoeia.

Nietzsche, in "On Truth and Lies in a Nonmoral Sense," includes "anthropomorphisms" along with metaphors and metonymies among the mobile army of
catachreses by which humanity first names the "mysterious X" of the world, uncovering it and covering it over again in one linguistic act (83, 84). It may be
personification is the most important or most fundamental of these catachreses: that
giant person we always meet mirrored in the landscape at the other end of our
wrestle to name the world and so confront it as it is. The giant, it may be, is no
more than our own face and body reflected in the mirror of the world, constructed
bit by bit out of our inveterate habit of calling landscape features "faces," "heads,"
"necks," or "legs," as in "body of water," "face of the mountain," "headland of a
shore," and so on. Or it may be that there really is some monster humanlike creature
at the end of that last corridor wound into the center of the labyrinth, that "centre
on the horizon" (87). In any case, for Stevens too there is, in this poem and in
many others of his late masterworks, the confrontation of a person at the farthest
reaches of the imagination's naming power. As Stevens says here, "It is a giant,
always, that evolves / To be in scale" (73–74). This says both that size, "bulging"
(32) mass, and overwhelming "parental magnitude" (86) are always characteristics
of the central poem and that the central poem always has a human form. If the edge
or extreme of sensation, where the light of sense goes out—as for example when
we try to look the sun in the face or in the eye—is a place of synesthesia, the place
of an exchange among the senses, so that the blaze of the sun is heard as trumpeting
seraphs, the reaching of that place is also the moment of the manifestation of a
person, an angel or a giant. This is true whatever Stevens may say in "Notes toward
a Supreme Fiction" about abolishing Phoebus Apollo and seeing the sun "in the
idea of it," washed clean of any metaphor or mythological personification: "How
clean the sun when seen in its idea, / Washed in the remotest cleanliness of the
heaven / That has expelled us and our images" (*Poems* 381). However resolutely the
basic prosopopoeias by which we name the world and so see it are effaced, they
always return again, for example as a giant face and body in the sun, as in that
sunrising scene in Goethe's *Faust*, "Granite portals groan and clatter, / Wheels of
Phoebus roll and spatter" ("Felsenthore knarren rasselnd, / Phöbus Räder rollen
prasselnd" [lines 4669–70]), or as in Turner's *The Angel Standing in the Sun* or in
his *Ulysses and Polyphemus*, with its outline of Apollo, horses, chariot and all, faintly
discernible within the blazing orb of the sun, or as in the giant that evolves in that
long sentence of stanzas 7 to 9 of Stevens's poem.

What is distinctive about Stevens's tracing of that evolutionary return here is the
way he shows the prosopopoeia coming back again not initially or primarily by way

of the remaining personifying catachreses in common language ("eye of the sun") but by way of the kinesthetic movement within abstract words like "composition," "compact," "beneficence," or "repose." The etymological metaphors may seem to be safely dead within such words, but Stevens matches Walter Pater in being acutely sensitive to the "elementary particles" in seemingly abstract words, in feeling "the incident, the colour, the physical elements or particles in words like *absorb, consider, extract*" (Pater, "Style" 20). Those physical elements or particles are not things but acts or movements, as in the act of drawing in the "tract" of "extract" and the movement outward of "ex," or as in the act of placing together in "com-position," or of placing back on itself in "re-pose," or in the act of joining together in "com-pact," with an echo from one word to another of the "com-," or the "pos-." The play on "pos-" had been prepared already in the description in the first stanza of the central poem as "disposed and re-disposed / By such slight genii in such pale air" (7–8). Stevens appears to feel these so-called abstract words as subliminal muscular movement in his own body, kinesthetic acts that respond to or project similar movements into the world outside. The giant on the horizon, glistening, emerges gradually through these obscure bodily acts initiated by the play of abstractions, combined and recombined from phrase to phrase, until finally that inherent order or principle of bringing parts together into a whole, both act and rest, vis and repose, is felt as "the muscles of a magnet." Out of those muscles, inner and outer at once, at once metaphor of a metaphor ("muscles of a magnet"), abstraction, and catachresis as prosopopoeia, the massive giant evolves and takes shape out there in the sun on the horizon.

Among the abstractions is, in stanza 11, the word "abstraction" itself and three accompanying words: "definition," "illustration," and "labelled." These together give Stevens's own analysis of the rhetorical strategy whereby the distinctions between abstract words, metaphors, and personifications break down in the recognition that all are examples of that overlapping area where catachresis and prosopopoeia, in spite of their different orientations, come together in their mutual interference one with the other. Catachresis goes toward revelation, toward shining forth, as of the sun rising or setting in the blaze of its glory. Prosopopoeia goes toward death and occultation, toward invisibility, as the sun is that death which cannot be looked in the face. Prosopopoeia goes toward ode and elegy, as, most evidently, in Stevens's "The Owl in the Sarcophagus." Prosopopoeia is the invocation of the absent, invisible, or entombed, as of the sun when it is below the horizon, has set, or is not yet risen, for example in that extraordinary embodiment of the disembodied, already mentioned, the personification of starlight in "Chocorua to Its Neighbor": "The feeling of him was the feel of day, / And of a day as yet unseen. . . . / He was a shell of dark blue glass, or ice, / Or air collected in a deep essay, / . . . Blue's last transparence as it turned to black" (16–17, 21, 22, 25).

Catachresis that is also prosopopoeia, as so many are, like "muscles" in "muscles of a magnet" here, is at the intersection or crossroads of these two contradictory orientations, where appearance and disappearance come together, at the center on the horizon. That atopical place is also where the lexical distinctions between abstraction, metaphor, and personification break down. Stevens's abstractions are also metaphors, and they are also latent personifications. As the word "abstraction" itself etymologically says, the giant is drawn out and refined or embodied from the abstractions, abs-tracted from them: "Here, then, is an abstraction given head, / A giant on the horizon, given arms, / A massive body and long legs" (81–83). This personification, as the poet exactly puts it, is "A definition with an illustration, not / Too exactly labelled" (84–85). The definition is, it may be, the initial abstraction and its permutations ("The central poem is the poem of the whole," and so on). The illustration is the figuration by catachresis that emerges from the abstractions as a bringing to light (as the word "illustration" etymologically means). The labeling is the final bringing together of these fleeting embodiments as the personification of the central poem as a giant. But all three of these forms of language are at once definition, or a giving boundaries and outline, illustration or bringing to light, and labeling or definitive illustrative naming. All these distinctions, though they are necessary if there is to be poetry or commentary on the poetry, fail or vanish at that center of blinding light, the black hole that must not be too exactly labeled or the terms for it lose all validity. They lose even that fleeting, flickering, or flicking validity of alluding by indirection which Stevens celebrates, and they become the reduced and ludicrously inadequate fixity Stevens's speaker has ridiculed a moment before: "As in a signed photograph on a mantelpiece" (76). Such motionless figures are an abjectly self-referential parody of the definition with an illustration, not too exactly labeled. The giant on the horizon can be given no proper name and does not speak or give himself one, as I do when I sign my own photograph. I have said that Stevens's use, here and in many other poems, of the sun's trajectory as basic abstraction, trope, and figure of personified narrative journey aligns him with Western poetic tradition from the Greeks on down. Stevens also joins himself to a tradition going back at least to Aristotle in making the sun a chief example of catachresis. If a proper or literal name depends on the full visibility, out in the sunlight, of what is named, the sun, in Stevens's phrase "must bear no name" (*Poems* 381), or cannot properly be named, since it is invisible during that part of its orbit when it is hidden or entombed below the horizon. The word "sun" is as much a catachresis as are all the circumlocutions making up Stevens's poem. It is neither through accident nor through arbitrary choice by the poet that the "giant of nothingness," the central poem, the primitive like an orb, turns out to be the sun, nor is it a mere poet's joke that the word is forbidden in this poem.

Even so, the reader of "A Primitive like an Orb," this reader at least, seeks to identify that evasive center, to put a proper name to it, in order to still and to control the dizzying movement from figure to figure that makes up the linguistic texture of the poem. Three possible candidates come to mind for the extralinguistic reference that might, if it were identified, solve the enigma and appease the mind's dissatisfaction as it moves from image to image in this poem and tries to figure out what the poem is "about." (1) The poem may obliquely name some physical referent, some scene or object in the external world that the poem imitates or represents. Once this objective referent is identified, readers then have something to hold to as they make their way through the poem. Such a reading would see the poem as in one way or another a mimetic picture. (2) The poem, on the other hand, may represent some psychic state, for example the mind of the poet, which could be imagined to exist without the poem and which the poem expresses or copies. This would be a familiar theory of poetry as the expression or imitation of psychic states. (3) The poem, finally, may obliquely name some transcendent or spiritual center: God, the idea of the one, being, the "light apart, up-hill" (48) to which the poem refers in stanza 6. This third possibility would be a notion of mimesis like that of Plato, for whom the scale of imitations is governed ultimately by prototypes in the realm of ideas.

These are three versions of a definition of poetry as imitation. "A Primitive like an Orb" systematically baffles all three possible explanations. The poem copies no coherent scene or single definable object. It proceeds rather through a bewildering proliferation of mixed metaphors, each canceling out the one before. There are fragments and bits of scenes all superimposed incoherently: music, cast-iron life and works, essential gold hidden in some treasure crypt, a picnic scene in the woods, a lightning storm in the distance, and so on. Only when the poem reaches finally the giant on the horizon do readers seem to have something definite to think about, but by this time they know that the giant is only another metaphor, not what the poem is "about." The giant too is only another "illustration," a bringing to light by means of an example. The giant is another picture or emblem, that is, something that refers once more to something beyond itself. All the terms in the poem are names for that central invisible and unnamable primitive, the large that all the illustrations are smalls of (85–86), the father poem of which all actual poems are children. The essential poem, as the poem says, begets the others.

As for the second possibility, though it may be comforting to readers to imagine that they are gaining access to the "mind of Stevens" as they read the poem, nevertheless there is no self in the poem, no personal psyche expressing itself to which the words in the poem can easily be referred. The austerity and impersonality of Stevens's poetic voices and their constant shifts of tone are notorious. The notion that poetry is a man speaking to men does not get the interpreter far with "A Primitive like an Orb," nor with such companion poems as "Chocorua to Its Neigh-bor" or "The Owl in the Sarcophagus." This means not that Stevens's poems are without passionate intensity but that psychological categories or categories of self-hood are of little use in their exegesis. To reduce the poem to an expression of Stevens's "selfhood" or "consciousness" would be to turn it into that "signed pho-tograph on the mantelpiece" (76) which the poem so scorns. It is a mean-minded and futile attempt by "virtue" to cut the giant on the horizon down to size, to "[snip] / Both size and solitude or [think] it does" (74–75).

It would seem, then, that the third possibility must be the answer. All the terms in the poem refer to that evasive spiritual reality, what Stevens elsewhere calls "mere being" (*Opus* 117). This reality is the shy paramour whom all his poems court, or rather the totality of what may be perceived is the theater of a courtship by the giant on the horizon of nature and the mind as the spouses of that giant. This marriage is admirably named in lines 39–46 of the poem:

> . . . It is
> As if the central poem became the world,
>
> VI
>
> And the world the central poem, each one the mate
> Of the other, as if summer was a spouse,
> Espoused each morning, each long afternoon. . . .

Even this third possibility, however, the possibility that the poem is a performative act of revelation, that the words of the poem bring something hidden into the open, is put in question by the poem's linguistic strategy. There is a systematic ambiguity in the images of "A Primitive like an Orb" that makes it like that hermetic egg of which Yeats speaks that continually turns itself inside out without breaking its shell. The ambiguity lies in the uncertainty, in spite of the claim that "the essential poem begets the others," about which is father of which. Is the particular poem only a pale copy of the essential poem, or is it actually part of it, as another phrase in the poem affirms? In the successful poem the central poem becomes the world, which becomes in turn her spouse, "her mirror and her look" (44), the particular poem. The essential poem is both outside the particular poem as the center on the horizon, and at the same time it is the total of all "letters, prophecies, perceptions, clods / Of color" (94–95), therefore incarnated in each creative act. These inscriptions or embodiments are both pale imitations of the central poem, its division, fragmentation, and dispersal, and at the same time they are what constitutes it, in both senses of the word. Taken all together they are the central poem, and at the same time they generate it as the vanishing point they all indicate in the failure of each to be more than part of that whole, a synecdoche of it. This paradox is expressed in another way in "The Man with the Blue Guitar" and in the commentary on that poem in Stevens's letters to Renato Poggioli. The imagination must be a son of the kind able to defeat his father and be that father's "true part," his sex. The son will take the place of the father, not destroy him, but become him. The filial imagination must overcome the distance between the lion in the lute and the lion in the stone until they merge and become one.

As soon as this process of merger is complete, it fails. It fails because poet or reader is left with only a faint simulacrum, an image or an illustration in the pejorative sense, a dead husk, a copy—a "second," in Stevens's terminology. This husk must be destroyed, since it instantly loses all authenticity. As soon as it is proffered it has already become something that was, "an illusion, as it was," like "a signed photograph on the mantelpiece." It is for this reason that the definition with an illustration must not be too exactly labeled. Each definition with an illustration must be immediately rejected as soon as it is presented and must be replaced by the next, in that proliferating series of phrases in apposition which makes up so much of this poem. In its vanishing each image reveals itself as a new name for the void. The giant is "the giant of nothingness" (95), however much he is given attributes of bulging masculine substance and muscular solidity. Only as each image reveals itself to be a copy, another mimetic illustration, can it be adequate to that of which it is an illustration, because both the illustration (the act of bringing to light) and that which it illustrates (the giant) are "ever changing, living in change" (96). The image must partake of the nature of that of which it is an image. Its fictive, hollow, evanescent quality is essential to its adequacy. Since the patron of origins himself (itself?) lives in time and change, he (it?) can only be adequately expressed in temporal images—that is, in images that are and are not and therefore are. The light of this central primitive is not a light apart, uphill. Stevens as much as Yeats rejects a universe of Platonic emanations descending from some early spiritual warmth. Stevens too chooses the whirlpool over the waterfall. He chooses the labyrinth of immanence over any hierarchy depending from the transcendent One.

Stevens, like Yeats or William Carlos Williams, makes strong claims for the power of poetry. These claims in each case remain indeterminate. Is it creation or is it discovery, this invention of the poem? Does the illustration illustrate a light that preexists it, the father fire that begets all the little fires? Or are the little fires parts, particles, of the father fire and therefore essential to it, so that only in a poem does the light come into the open? Or are the little fires in fact identical with the father fire, so that the father fire exists in, and is generated by, only the intercourse of images, the child becoming father to his father? "A Primitive like an Orb" is caught, like all Stevens's mature poems, in the space between these three positions. Each position is the mirage of the others. Each generates the others. Each is impossible without the others. Stevens is not confused or willfully contradictory. He is caught in an inevitable oscillation within language and within the experiences language both imitates and creates, in another version of the same oscillation. It is impossible to have creation without discovery, or discovery, illustration, without creation, without the joy of language when it is the human being who speaks it out of desire. There is no invention (in the sense of discovery) without invention (in the sense of creation). Until the lover, the believer, and the poet speak there is no essential poem. The essential poem exists only in lesser poems. Nevertheless, the essential poem then seems always to have been there all along and to bind together all the lesser poems. It makes them whole or creates out of them the poem of the whole—that is, something that moves, like time, always toward the whole, toward an end it can never reach.

The answer to my initial question about Stevens's poem, "Why can the sun not be named directly here?," is now clear enough. It is as clear as such things can be, as clear as looking the sun in the eye. The word "sun" exists, and the sun is named indirectly in manifold ways in the poem. To reduce the sun to its seeming proper name, however, would mislead the reader into thinking that the "subject" or the "object" of the poem, its controlling head meaning, is the literal, physical sun, whereas the sun, named in riddling condensations and displacements in the poem, is only one in a chain of such dislocations naming "the essential poem at the centre of things." This essential poem in its turn, as the word "poem" indicates, is something made in the illustrations of it. Poiēsis means "making." The central poem proceeds from those illustrations, though it also exceeds and precedes any illustration.

At the center of the maze or whirlpool of words that makes up Stevens's "A Primitive like an Orb" is an unknown X that cannot be named except in figure. Those names are therefore not figurative substitutions for a literal word labeling an object open to seeing or to theory. They are tropes of something that is neither a word, nor a thought, nor a thing, nor a force—but is not nothing either. It is, in Stevens's precise phrase, "the giant of nothingness," something that is and is not and therefore is. This "giant" is word, thought, thing, force, person, all at once, all and none. It therefore obliterates or disqualifies the oppositions needed to make a comprehensible topology of the figures and concepts in the poem. The poem cannot quite be thought through clearly, though, as my discussion shows, there is much to be said in commentary on it. Nevertheless, the progress of the commentary gradually deprives the interpreter of the clear distinctions between subjective, objective, and linguistic, literal and figurative, on which explication has traditionally depended for its clarities. The interpreter is left with a paradoxical space at once interior and exterior, objective and linguistic, a space of elements organized as rotating rings around a center that cannot be named or identified as such and that is, moreover, not at the center at all but "eccentric," out beyond the periphery, like a thunderstorm over the horizon. "A Primitive like an Orb," in short, "[resists] the intelligence almost successfully," as Stevens says poetry must do (*Opus* 171).

Notes

[1] *Collected Poems* 440–43. Citations from this poem will henceforth be identified by line numbers only. Other citations from Stevens are identified by page numbers in *Poems* and *Opus Posthumous*.

[2] I have used, with slight alteration, the translation by Gayatri Chakravorty Spivak (91–92).

[3] For this word see Abraham, and see Derrida's discussion of Abraham's use of this word ("Fors" 7–82, esp. 11). For an English translation of this essay see Barbara Johnson, "Fors."

[4] For the translation, see the Norton Critical Edition (119); for the German text, see the Hamburger Ausgabe (147,148).

"Anecdote for Fathers"

The Scene of Interpretation in Freud and Wordsworth

CYNTHIA CHASE

Freud might be viewed as continuing a meditation on language reinaugurated by the early Romantics. Freudian theory is not remote from the Romantics' conjectural histories of language or from poetry described by Wordsworth as "the history and science of feelings" (*Poetical Works* 2:513). And psychoanalysis brings together epistemological and pedagogical questions as they converge too in the writings of Rousseau and Wordsworth. The didactic character of Wordsworth's prefaces and Freud's *Introductory Lectures* and the elaborated pedagogic theory of *Emile* are only the most conspicuous marks of all three writers' persistent concern with the possibility of teaching: with the mutual impact of the conditions of interpretation and persuasion and the conditions of meaning. Freud, like Rousseau, was led to question the value of education as such; he wrote,

> education must inhibit, forbid, and suppress and this is abundantly seen in all periods of history. But we have learnt from analysis that precisely this suppression of instincts involves the risk of neurotic illness. . . . A moment's reflection tells us that hitherto education has fulfilled its task very badly and done children great damage.[1]

But if Freud at times addressed the question of children's education directly, he more persistently confronted it implicitly, in his practice as an analyst and a writer. Not only must his patients be interpreted, but his readers, as well as his patients, must in some sense be taught—be changed, be persuaded, and persuaded about the very nature of persuasion: the nature of interpretation, the significance of negation, forgetting, and narration. The critique of pedagogy is a key dimension of a distinctive pedagogic practice, and it lies at the crux of reflections—common to Romantic and psychoanalytic writing—on the conditions of existence in language.

The critique of practices of interpretation and persuasion that is crucial to Romantic thinking about language gets elaborated with special concision and complexity in Wordsworth's "Anecdote for Fathers," the ninth poem in the first edition of *Lyrical Ballads*. Wordsworth's poem can be interpreted together with a comparably early and inaugural text of Freud's, his interpretation of his dream about his treatment of the patient he calls Irma, in the second chapter of *The Interpretation of Dreams.* Indeed Wordsworth's "Anecdote" may be read as addressing the "father" of psychoanalysis among other fathers, including those who perform the paternal function of teaching language and ethics. The anecdote shows how that function fails. What critical or pedagogical project survives the failure becomes a lasting question in Wordsworth's poem—and the problem that Freud's writing both confronts and provokes.

"Anecdote for Fathers" stages a scene between an adult questioner and a recalcitrant child. Wordsworth gave it the monitory ironical subtitle, "Showing How the Practice of Lying May Be Taught." Their dialogue is the kind of scenario that inspired the satiric glee of Lewis Carroll and Max Beerbohm, showing "Mr. Wordsworth at Cross-Purposes in the Lake District" (Macdonald 289–92), like the repeated questioning of the old leech gatherer in "Resolution and Independence." Wordsworth casts the first-person narrator of the anecdote as an enlightened parent, in conventional terms a concerned and sensitive father; the dialogue shows how such a father makes an egocentric and subtly tyrannical interlocutor. Among other things, this poem is an attack on an educational theory influenced by Hartley's doctrine of the association of ideas, as it was reflected in a project of Thomas Wedgwood and William Godwin's with which Wordsworth had been briefly involved. Wedgwood aimed to foster "Genius" and to render it more productive by a pedagogical method designed to encourage and to systematize children's processes of association. "From earliest infancy," Wedgwood wrote to Godwin in 1797, "children should be questioned about recent and remote impressions; or otherwise induced to repeat all their parts. From this would result a habit of keenest observation and most retentive memory" (Erdman 431). Wedgwood's notion of children "induced to repeat all their parts" holds up as an educational ideal the very development that Wordsworth evokes with pity and irony in the seventh stanza of the Intimations Ode: "the little Actor cons another part." Wedgwood also suggested that a child should be confined to a nursery furnished with a few hard bright objects rather than be submitted to the multitude of chaotic impressions out of doors. Wordsworth's probable dismay at this plan may have intensified his sense of the inadequacy of the doctrine of associationism. The critique of the "progressive" pedagogy influenced by associationist doctrines lies close to Wordsworth's affirmation of the radical autonomy of the imagination, notably in book 5 of the 1805 *Prelude* (where the attack on child prodigies and overzealous educators, "Sages who in their prescience would control / All accidents" [380–81], joins the dream of apocalyptic deluge and the commemoration of the Winander boy). In "Anecdote for Fathers" the sort of questioning envisioned by Wedgwood is staged as a dialogue that culminates in the child's proffering a kind of "caricature of adult reasoning" (Glen 242):[2]

> "Now tell me, had you rather be,"
> I said, and took him by the arm,
> "On Kilve's smooth shore, by the green sea,
> Or here at Liswyn farm?"

> In careless mood he looked at me,
> While still I held him by the arm,
> And said, "At Kilve I'd rather be
> Than here at Liswyn farm."
>
> "Now, little Edward, say why so:
> My little Edward, tell me why."—
> "I cannot tell, I do not know."—
> "Why, this is strange," said I;
>
> "For, here are woods, hills smooth and warm:
> There surely must some reason be
> Why you would change sweet Liswyn farm
> For Kilve by the green sea."
>
> At this, my boy hung down his head,
> He blushed with shame, nor made reply;
> And three times to the child I said,
> "Why, Edward, tell me why?"
>
> His head he raised—there was in sight,
> It caught his eye, he saw it plain—
> Upon the house-top, glittering bright,
> A broad and gilded vane.
>
> Then did the boy his tongue unlock,
> And eased his mind with this reply:
> "At Kilve there was no weather-cock:
> And that's the reason why."   (*Poems* 1: 314)

The scene displays how asking for truth—an ostensibly liberal or liberating use of language common to psychoanalysis and to liberal pedagogical practice—becomes, in effect, the compulsion to produce a lie or a fiction. Such is the effect of the father's intervention, as the teacher of language and ethics. When that instruction goes awry, the father shifts his ground to praise another scene of instruction, what the child teaches:

> O dearest, dearest boy! my heart
> For better lore would seldom yearn,
> Could I but teach the hundredth part
> Of what from thee I learn.

This is the gesture of the great self-critical pedagogues from Rousseau—who wrote, "Si j'ai fait quelque progrès dans la connoissance du cœur humain c'est le plaisir que j'avois à voir et à observer les enfans qui m'a valu cette connoissance" (*Œuvres* 1:1078)—to Freud, who claimed to learn from patients and from children the universal operations of the mind, or, as Wordsworth put it in his Preface to *Lyrical Ballads,* to reveal "the primary laws of our nature." When the one who is supposed to know and to teach learns all he knows from the one who does not know and needs to learn, the sort of knowledge that arises—between these two and in the possession of neither—is difficult to pass on. For what the child teaches the father is that what the father teaches is to lie. The poem's closing lines imply that to teach even "the hundredth part" of this knowledge is impossible and that the one who has learned it will continue to "yearn" for "better lore" than this deconstructed teaching. It will be possible to spell out in some detail how Freud and other analysts lapse into trying to produce a more positive and teachable lore than the resistance of interpretation.

Wordsworth's subtitle seems to promise that his anecdote offers at least a negative knowledge by example: to show "how . . . lying may be taught" implies that it *is* taught and that the father's or the teacher's intervention is to blame. Carroll's and Beerbohm's parodies are faithful to the humorous and self-parodic element in Wordsworth's own text, which shows up, through its understated style, a too-aggressive teaching or interrogation that might have been avoided. In one sense, Wordsworth's anecdote is a low-keyed, gentle version of the archetypal tale of the Fall: a child's fall from innocence into self-consciousness and guilt. This fall is a passage from "beauty" (of a nonverbal, sculptural sort) to language—to the painful but touching eloquence not only of the transparently invented "lie" but also of the "blushing" that subtly disfigures the child whom the first stanza describes in these terms:

> I have a boy of five years old;
> His face is fair and fresh to see;
> His limbs are cast in beauty's mould,
> And dearly he loves me.

The anecdote ends with a temptation scene: this child makes up his "reason why" when he is caught by the glitter of the "broad and gilded vane." Merging the figures of the father and the tempter, the poem gives the Fall a new twist. The tale takes its irony and pathos from revealing the child's would-be guide as the tempter who brings on his fall by questioning him "in very idleness"—classically the tempter's opportunity, here the teacher's initial state of mind.

But while the poem permits us to read the anecdote as an account of avoidable error, of a seductive and aggressive teaching style we should avoid, it also (and not only in the final framing stanza) invites a reading whose pedagogical implications are much more dubious. For the anecdote shows the child betraying the adult's expectation and thwarting his hope to be confirmed in his own contentment and in his notion of the child as naturally contented where he is in the present, without "fond regrets" like the adult's for another time and place. In responding with a preference for "Kilve by the green sea" over where he is, Liswyn Farm, the child displays already the condition that education, according to reasoning in *Emile,* should try to mitigate: "Nous n'existons plus où nous sommes, nous n'existons qu'ou nous sommes pas" (98). Rousseau is deploring that a man should be distressed by receiving a letter, whose words situate his existence in another scene. In this respect Wordsworth's child is the father of the man: little Edward responds to the charm of what exists in words ("Kilve by the green sea") rather than in his physical experience. For the educator to regret or to try to defer this responsiveness would be to check what for Wordsworth in the Preface to *Lyrical Ballads* is a crucial attribute of the "Poet": "a disposition to be affected more than other men by absent things as if they were present" (*Poetical Works* 2: 393).

The narrator as well as the child in "Anecdote" shows such a disposition. A reading of the poem focused on the opposition between the adult and the child (seen by Glen, for instance, as the adult's intrusion of conventional comparative thinking on the child's spontaneous responses [241–42]) overlooks the alignments establishing their likeness.

> One morn we strolled on our dry walk,
> Our quiet home all full in view,
> And held such intermitted talk
> As we are wont to do.
>
> My thoughts on former pleasures ran;
> I thought of Kilve's delightful shore,
> Our pleasant home when spring began,
> A long, long year before.
>
> A day it was when I could bear
> Some fond regrets to entertain;
> With so much happiness to spare,
> I could not feel a pain.
>
> The green earth echoed to the feet
> Of lambs that bounded through the glade,
> From shade to sunshine, and as fleet
> From sunshine back to shade.
>
> Birds warbled round me—and each trace
> Of inward sadness had its charm;
> Kilve, thought I, was a favoured place,
> And so is Liswyn farm.
>
> My boy beside me tripped, so slim
> And graceful in his rustic dress!
> And, as we talked, I questioned him,
> In very idleness.   (lines 5–28)

The "idleness" of the adult meets the "careless mood" of the child, but the opening stanzas suggest the charged and precarious nature of that "idleness." The fourth stanza suggests that, for the speaker, the state of mind in which "regrets" are not too much to "bear" is a rare one, as if only an unusual excess of present happiness can make him feel momentarily invulnerable to a "pain" of loss always ready to reappear. Confidence in the easy contiguity between inside and outside belongs to this mood: "Birds warbled round me—and each trace / Of inward sadness had its charm." The difference between "inward" and "outward" features is marked, like the difference between "shade" and "sunshine," but its significance is attenuated. In this atmosphere the speaker can suppose that regrets for the joys of the past can be coated with the pleasures of the present.

This mood should be compared with a turn in Wordsworth's Intimations Ode.

> Now, while the birds thus sing a joyous song,
>   And while the young lambs bound
>   As to the tabor's sound,
> To me alone there came a thought of grief;
> A timely utterance gave that thought relief,
>   And I again am strong. (*Poems* 1: 524; lines 19–24)

The "thought of grief" is the loss of the child's imaginative power, a loss indifferent to places: "But yet I know, where e'er I go, / That there hath past away a glory from the earth" (lines 17–18).

The Intimations Ode singles out an elegiac moment in which the speaker's vulnerability to loss emerges in a "thought of grief," which then finds relief in "utterance." That vulnerability to loss is suspended for the speaker in "Anecdote," who can afford to entertain "fond regrets" and can find charm in "inward sadness." Comparison with the ode shows how "Anecdote for Fathers" invites two somewhat different readings of the significance of the father's questioning. One reading dwells on hints that the father's questioning of the child about his preference for one or the other equally "favoured" spot is in fact profoundly motivated, impelled by an only tentatively suspended anxiety about imaginative loss; the other registers the indications that this questioning is initially truly whimsical, putting into play a sequence of rhetorical gestures with a momentum of their own. On the one hand, "Anecdote" can be read as representing a state in which the peril of imaginative loss is simply suspended; on the other, as putting into question and indeed invalidating the elegiac plot, the story of loss and compensation, displacing it with a plot in which the discontinuity that checks the father's would-be movement from learning to teaching has afflicted the child from the start, as the motivelessness of his desire for another scene, for what exists in words. The speaker of "Anecdote," unlike the speaker of the ode, encounters not "a thought of grief" but something more ambiguously remediable: surprise and bafflement at the impossibility of grasping the origin of articulate desire.

The opening stanzas of the poem represent a release from the pressure of that anxiety for continuity between the adult's and the child's imagination powerfully condensed in the epigraph to the Intimations Ode:

> The Child is Father of the Man;
> And I could wish my days to be
> Bound each to each in natural piety.

In the abortive dialogue that follows, in the "Anecdote," this wish and conviction change meaning. For the child to be the father of the man turns out not to ensure

but to challenge the possibility of continuity—from learning to teaching and from
inward feeling to rationalized expression. For what the child and the father have in
common is not only imagination or a feeling for "absent things" but a feeling for
words. Taken aback when little Edward asserts that he would rather be where he
was in the past, the father gets agitated when the child can come up with no motive
for this preference. Their intermitted talk then becomes an interrogation, in which
the father's questioning is as witlessly persistent as the child's hapless resistance.
The father clings to his repeated "Why?" with a blind attachment like the child's
for "Kilve by the green sea."

One casualty of a shift from the plot of the ode to the plot of the "Anecdote" is
trust in the nature of the "relief" afforded by a "timely utterance." The father seeks,
in his initial "Why?," a key to the child's heart, the inner "reason" for his preference;
the child needs rather a key to "unlock" his "tongue," to set going the mechanism
of speech, and it is for the sake of that function that he produces his "reason." The
child's desire for what exists in words—for "Kilve by the green sea," in the father's
phrase—edges into a desire for words as such, as a release from silence, from the
agonized muteness of finding no reason for the desire for what exists in words.
"Utterance" brings "relief," here as in the moment evoked by the speaker in the
Intimations Ode, but it gives relief by putting an end to a silence under interrogation
rather than by giving form to an inward thought (or by allowing release from "a
thought of grief"): the "thought" ("At Kilve there was no weather-cock") is merely
the occasion for finding relief in speech. The scene shows us a "reason" or motive
that is not the first and inmost cause of speech but its belated and delusory effect.

The need for a "reason" is then not simply imposed on the child by the adult's
bullying. And this complication of the opposition between the father and the child
is consistent with another dimension of the text. "Anecdote for Fathers" asks to be
read not simply as a representation of a particular scene or dialogue; its fictional
and figurative character solicits an allegorical reading as well. Like the anecdote's
illustration of the child's feeling for words, this reading distinguishes the poem
from a monitory tale of a fall. Rather, the poem represents a rhetorical process in
which "father" and "child" personify moments in that process that are bound to be
generated in any speaking subject.

"Anecdote for Fathers" represents a sequence of rhetorical operations. One of the
first is the possibility of substitution, of exchanging one place for another. Its
importance is emphasized by Wordsworth's replacement of a line in the first version,
"The young lambs ran a pretty race" (Wordsworth and Coleridge 61), with this
added stanza:

> The green earth echoed to the feet
> Of lambs that bounded through the glade,
> From shade to sunshine, and as fleet
> From sunshine back to shade.

This stanza represents the natural as just the repeatedly canceled and repeated
movement from one position to another. All begins from the fact that it is possible

to be located at one site rather than another—to substitute one site of meaning, one word or sign, for another one. The possibility of substitution is followed by the substitution itself or by what we call, in the terms of the story this sequence makes up, the "desire" to change one site for another. The desire arises without a motive, prior to the motive that is thereafter posited as its cause. The quest for "motive" is one product of an inevitable rhetorical operation veiling the primacy of rhetoric: the motivation—the rationalization and naturalization—of the substitution of one site of meaning for another. "Anecdote for Fathers" displays the arbitrary character of the rhetorical operations of substitution and its motivation. But the poem implies that the move from substitution to motivation is inevitable as well as forced or arbitrary. In this text the Child is indeed the Father, not just the victim, of the Man. The Child substituting one site of meaning for another is the Father of the Child-Father finding reason for the substitution.

The Father as the name not for an actual person or a social role but for a rhetorical function, a figure father rather than a father figure, recurs with the "rereading of Freud" proclaimed by Lacan but dating in fact from what is traditionally held to be the foundation of Freudian theory: Freud's switch, in 1897, from his seduction theory to the theory of unconscious fantasy ("Extracts from the Fliess Papers," SE 1: 259; "On the History of the Psychoanalytic Movement," SE 14: 17–18). In interpreting the stories of parental seduction elicited from hysteric patients in his talking cure, Freud came to recognize an effect akin to what Wordsworth's anecdote illustrates: that asking one's interlocutor to reproduce a process of association may compel him or her to produce a lie or a fiction. Freud had first inferred that his patients' symptoms derived from their repression of ideas and feelings aroused when they were victims of a scene of seduction, typically by a father or a governess. He was led to abandon this belief—until then the very ground of his therapeutic method—for the less compelling, more puzzling conviction that his patients' accounts of such scenes did not report real occurrences but rather represented an unconscious fantasy of seduction, which had to be read in inverted form, as an expression of the child's own active desire. Freud reheard, reread, his patients' discourse in such a way that he ceased to hear in it anecdotes bearing a predictable negative knowledge concerning avoidable aggressive interventions by adults, in a story of a fall or a loss. He heard instead a barely transmissible teaching concerning the primacy of fantasies in the unconscious. The father, in the patient's discourse, was a figure in a fantasy of seduction that replaced another fantasy, the child's oedipal fantasy of possessing the mother or the father. The child's Oedipus complex positions the father as possessor of the desired object. The father's position in the oedipal fantasy—and the father's role in censoring it—makes the Father a figure for the rhetorical function that consists in the production of figures for desire, in the impossibility of maintaining unmediated satisfaction.

Freud's "rereading" of his patients' discourse follows the same trajectory as the rereading invited by Wordsworth's "Anecdote": roughly, from a literal or reconstructive to a rhetorical reading, and from the indictment of an adult's intrusion on the natural ease or the autonomous world of the child to the revelation of a child spontaneously engaged in a distinctively human, nonnatural activity: "Imagination," "infantile sexuality," or fantasy—sexual desire and the desire for words. The second reading does not cancel out the first, and indeed the lasting critical interplay between these two moments or movements may be what Wordsworth's and Freud's texts most significantly share. Loss and compensation remain an essential organizing structure in Wordsworth's poetry and prose, and the critique of particular rhetorical practices remains a salient theme. Freud's writings, too, from *The Interpretation of Dreams* to the Wolfman and *Totem and Taboo,* persist in making inferences linked with Freud's first, literal reading of his patients' stories of seduction. Freud continued to assert the prevalence and significance of scences of seduction actually experienced in childhood. He finally conceived in those terms the universal experience of maternal care, which must be charged with sexual meanings since the mother is herself a sexual being. Freud also continued to look out for some specific instigation for the child's fantasy—a "primal scene," typically the sight of the parents' intercourse ("From the History of an Infantile Neurosis," *SE* 17: 36–39). The reference to a scene of seduction endures in Freud's writing not simply because Freud continued to seek for some "ground of reality" for the child's fantasy but because the concept of trauma, central to the seduction theory, is crucial to the Freudian discovery of conflict between consciousness and the unconscious: it implies the violent, contingent, unmasterable character of the individual's accession to language and to sexuality. Freud's theorizing never succumbs to the risk involved in revival of the seduction theory as such, defined by Laplanche and Pontalis as "that of reopening the door to the pre-analytical view of the child as sexually innocent until perverted by adult sexuality" (407); that myth of the child, Freud rejected.

But with the shift to the theory of unconscious fantasy, Freud makes another myth his own. The Oedipus myth comes to function as a narrative figure, explaining how the father figure is experienced and how the figure father is constituted. Freud's appropriation of the Oedipus myth opens his theory to criticism on several grounds. Psychologists aware of the high incidence of child abuse have criticized the notion of the Oedipus complex as a theory that makes the child the seducer rather than the victim of seduction and defines a position for the Father that lets a great many particular fathers off the hook. Freud's abandonment of the seduction theory has been seen as allying him with the seducer, the adult, whom his first theory inculpated and whom his second one dismisses (for the most fully documented and most strident presentation of this critique, see Masson). For like a rhetorical reading of Wordsworth's poem, Freudian theory shifts the blame away from an actual adult aggressor to agencies that cannot meaningfully be blamed at all: the drive to differentiate or substitute and the imperative to construct a scene or an origin. Or like Wordsworth's subtitle read tone-deaf, Freudian theory can appear to blame the victim, presenting the patients' utterance as lies and fictions, showing how fantasies are adduced as reasons for their suffering by those with a motive in being ill, according to the formula Freud persisted in invoking to distinguish neurotic from physical sickness. Freud held on to the idea of a motive behind his patients' dreams and symptoms, though it might consist fundamentally in nothing other than the elaboration of a fantasy. Rather like the interrogator of "little Edward," Freud undertook to investigate his patients' wishes and motives; in some cases, as in the "Fragment of an Analysis of a Case of Hysteria," the case of Dora, his questions and conclusions can sound like moves in a judicial investigation.

A more analytical (less intuitive) version of this critique is worth pursuing, not least because it concerns the interpretive move that Romantic writing—as well as psychoanalysis—encourages. What, then, are the personal and the social or cultural interests served by Freud's conception of the oedipal child? Julia Kristeva stresses that the discovery of the Oedipus complex occurred during the self-analysis Freud undertook in the wake of his father's death and the end of his own fathering of children, in 1897; it was this conjunction that "led him to that telescoping of father and child resulting in none other than Oedipus." Freud's Oedipus is an "image of the child-parent, the seducing child, a child always already older, born into the world with compound drives, erogenous zone, and genital desires" (275). Kristeva proposes reading Freud's discovery of the Oedipus complex as "the discourse of mourning for his father's death": she asks, "could the discovery of the Oedipus complex . . . have been produced through an inverted Oedipus complex?" (276). But in a more interesting move, Kristeva suggests that Freud's father's actual death in 1897 was not a decisive factor. Could the conception of the Oedipus complex, she asks, be "the negative of the guilt experienced by the son who is forced by the signifier to take his father's place" (274)? More than the fact of death, it is the rules of language—the inheritance of the proper name—that force the son to replace the father. The Oedipus complex is invented, the Oedipus myth is appropriated, in response to the effect of a linguistic law. The Oedipus myth serves as a narrative figure to explain effects of the proper name: to explain and account for the guilt entailed by the subject's accession to language through the name of the father.

And the conception of the oedipal child has not only a delusive explanatory function but also an oppressive legitimating function. It makes the father's role of prohibiting desires appear essential and inevitable. What Kristeva attacks, finally, is the way the Oedipus theory works as a rationalization and naturalization of the effects of a linguistic imperative: the way it leads one to infer, from the key function of the Name of the Father, the necessity that father figures and actual fathers should play a dominant social and symbolic role. That Freudian theory can serve this ideological purpose is certain (it has),[3] but to assume that it must do so is not only to ignore the differences among its various receptions (including, in Lacanian theory, that strict dissevering of the role of the signifier from social roles that informs Kristeva's own critique) but also to overlook the heterogeneity of the founding Freudian texts. It would be necessary to gauge, instead, the stresses among the various ways Freud's writing addresses its readers; to attend (first of all) to the various projects that invest and inform *The Interpretation of Dreams*, including Freud's self-analysis, the announcement of a theory of the unconscious, the display of an interpretive method, the didactic presentation of the principles of dreams' construction, and the founding of a new discipline. The interaction among these dimensions of Freud's text will be at least as complex as the double operation of Wordsworth's poem.

An attempt to measure the heterogeneous operations of Freud's writing might well begin with "The Method of Interpreting Dreams: An Analysis of a Specimen Dream," chapter 2 of *The Interpretation of Dreams*. Like the chapters that follow, it is a hybrid text, personal and theoretical at the same time (see Warner, ch. 2). Freud chooses as his "specimen dream"—and as the first dream he presents in detail to his readers—the first dream he ever "submitted to a detailed interpretation" (*SE* 4: 106n). The analysis of the dream of Irma's injection, as it has come to be called, was probably the first time that Freud systematically applied free association to every element of the manifest dream. It led him to the discovery that his dream fulfilled a wish—that he be innocent of responsibility for his patients' suffering—and thereby gave him the crucial insight that he presents as the lesson of this chapter: that a dream has a motive, a wish, and that its content is the fulfillment of a wish.

The analysis of the Irma dream, as much as the relinquishment of the seduction theory two years later, could be held to mark Freud's becoming the "father" of psychoanalysis. Freud is the first to accord it some such historic significance. He singles out this dream in a letter of 12 June 1900 to Wilhelm Fliess, his close confidant in the years Freud was moving from a physiological and neurological to a psychological model of the mind, while he was writing *The Interpretation of Dreams*. Freud wrote to Fliess from Bellevue, the house where he had dreamed the Irma dream,

> Do you suppose that someday a marble tablet will be placed on the house, inscribed with these words?—

> | In this house, on July 24th, 1895 |
> | The Secret of Dreams was Revealed |
> | to Dr. Sigm. Freud |

(*SE* 4: 121n)

Freud's high estimate of this dream finds its place in his intense relationship with Fliess, which had amounted to the state of passionate admiration and dependency that Freud would later call the "transference"; it was especially intense in the years prior to the culmination of Freud's self-analysis, and it was virtually at an end by the summer of 1900, after the publication of Freud's book in the fall of 1899. One way in which the Irma dream, its analysis, and Freud's judgment of the significance of that analysis must be read is as moments in the culmination of Freud's transference onto Fliess. This is a remarkable necessity in the interpretation of an inaugural theoretical text. The Irma-dream analysis takes on exemplary status as the effort in which the two chief factors in a psychoanalysis—free association and transference— come fully into play for the first time. The text of the "specimen dream" interpretation reflects their conflict. But in this it participates in another struggle than the difficulties of a self-analysis addressed to Freud's first reader (Fliess): it addresses, above all, Freud's future readers, who are solicited with particular urgency by this text Freud chooses to place at the beginning of the work he consistently claimed to be his masterpiece.

Freud's readers are presented with a recognizable pedagogical strategy: the author describes his method of interpretation, gives an example, and draws a conclusion about the material he has analyzed. At the same time, the contents of the example—the dream and Freud's associations to it—vividly expose the failures of various therapeutic practices. The Irma-dream analysis shares this structure and some significant themes with Wordsworth's "Anecdote for Fathers." The dream, like the poem, shows the dreamer, the speaker, addressing a recalcitrant interlocutor. Like little Edward, Irma has trouble opening her mouth when she is being examined. The text of the dream is as follows:

> A large hall—numerous guests, whom we were receiving.—Among them was Irma. I at once took her on one side, as though to answer her letter and to reproach her for not having accepted my "solution" yet. I said to her: "If you still get pains, it's really only your fault." She replied: "If you only knew what pains I've got now in my throat and stomach and abdomen—it's choking me"—I was alarmed and looked at her. She looked pale and puffy. I thought to myself that after all I must be missing some organic trouble. I took her to the window and looked down her throat, and she showed signs of recalcitrance, like women with artificial dentures. I thought to myself that there was really no need for her to do that.—She then opened her mouth properly and on the right I found a big white patch; at another place I saw extensive whitish grey scabs upon some remarkable structures which were evidently modelled on the turbinal bones of the nose.—I at once called in Dr. M., and he repeated the examination and confirmed it. . . . Dr. M. looked quite different from usual; he was very pale, he walked with a limp and his chin was clean-shaven. . . . My friend Otto was now standing beside her as well, and my friend Leopold was percussing her through her bodice and saying: "She has a dull area low down on the left." He also indicated that a portion of the skin on the left shoulder was infiltrated. (I noticed this, much as he did, in spite of her dress.) . . . M. said: "There's no doubt it's an infection, but no matter; dysentery will supervene and the toxin will be eliminated." . . . We were directly aware, too, of the origin of the infection. Not long before, when she was feeling unwell, my friend Otto had given her a preparation of propyl, propyls . . . propionic acid . . . trimethylamin (and I saw before me the formula for this printed in heavy type). . . . Injections of that sort ought not to be made so thoughtlessly. . . . And probably the syringe had not been clean. (*SE* 4: 107)

Freud's "preamble" explains that Irma was a patient and a family friend whom his treatment had cured of her anxiety but not of somatic symptoms (gastric pains); he attributed this to her not accepting his "solution" of her case. At the same time he worried that he might have missed some organic cause, and his concern was heightened on the evening of the dream by the note of reproach he detected in the news of Irma brought to him by a friend ("Otto"). As Freud's analysis goes on to explain, he thereupon had a dream that proposed various diagnoses of Irma's trouble (an organic illness; a toxic effect; the consequence of an injection, by "Otto," with a dirty syringe), all of which acquitted Freud of his responsibility. That acquittal, he concludes, was the dream's meaning: its motive.

But the identification of meaning with motive, laid down at the end of chapter 2, is undermined or complicated by the critique of his therapeutic method with

Irma that Freud brings in his associations with the dream text's opening sentences. Getting at "the reason why," to borrow Wordsworth's terms, was Freud's chief therapeutic aim in these early analyses:

> It was my view at the time (though I have since recognized it as a wrong one) that my task was fulfilled when I had informed a patient of the hidden meaning of his symptoms: I considered that I was not responsible for whether he accepted the solution or not—though this was what success depended on.   (SE 4: 108)

For Irma to resist accepting Freud's solution was for her to resist, like little Edward, identifying a motive behind the symptoms the analyst interprets as expressions of a desire. The mode of that resistance becomes not just the obstacle but the very condition of the analysis. "Success depended," Freud declares, on how the solution passes between the analyst and the patient, not on the analyst's arrival at the hidden content of the patient's signs. What passes between the patient and the analyst is not simply discourse but what Freud would later call the transference, which he had overlooked, he tells us, in Irma's case. He had overlooked how he figured as the father in intervening to insist that she open up and reveal the truth. "I owe it to this mistake," Freud goes on, "which I have now fortunately corrected, that my life was made easier at a time when, in spite of all my inevitable ignorance, I was expected to produce therapeutic successes" (108). This comment approaches the tone of Wordsworth's ironical subtitle: Freud's text is "Showing How Hysterical Symptoms May Be Maintained." The force of Freud's remark lies in the recurrence of the word "solution," for in the dream, the issue of Irma's acceptance of a verbal "solution" gives way to the issue of her "injection" with a chemical solution ("a preparation of . . . trimethylamin"). To insist on someone's swallowing a verbal solution, to inject a motive, Freud's text thereby implies, may be as fruitless and intrusive a practice as to treat this sort of patient with syringes and surgical implements instead of words.

   This is not the only way in which the Irma dream and its analysis, read together, exceed the lesson on which chapter 2 closes. The interpretation of this dream is the first step in a chapter-by-chapter argument to persuade the reader that (to quote the formula Freud completes at the end of chapter 4) "a dream is a (disguised) fulfillment of a (suppressed or repressed) wish" (160). But the Irma dream makes a peculiar first step for this argument. For the meaning of this dream, according to Freud, is his wish to be relieved of doubts about his professional conscientiousness: not a repressed but a conscious wish, the subject of his reflections and his writing (a record of the case of Irma) on the evening of the dream. The oddity of the use of this dream for Freud's ostensible argument—as Lacan argues—suggests that the dream is strategically placed to carry another kind of lesson (Le moi 182). The dream and its interpretation together are a "word" of Freud's ("une parole"): a message and a promise, proffered not just in the context of the chapter's immediate argument but in the act of undertaking the fundamental project of disclosing the Unconscious. How does this dream disclose the nature of the Unconscious?

Not simply as the analyst passes from the "manifest content" of the dream to the repressed wish buried in the "latent dream thoughts." Freud warns against a misreading of his distinction between "manifest" and "latent" in a footnote of 1925: some analysts

> seek to find the essence of dreams in their latent content and in so doing they overlook the distinction between the dream-thoughts and the dream-work. At bottom, dreams are nothing other than a particular *form* of thinking, made possible by the conditions of the state of sleep. It is the *dream-work* which creates that form, and it alone is the essence of dreaming—the explanation of its peculiar nature.
>
> (*SE* 5: 506–07n)

The dreamwork (the subject of *The Interpretation*'s penultimate chapter) is the process by which thoughts are transformed into the images of the dream (chiefly by "condensation" and "displacement"). The Unconscious, then—the unconscious "form of thinking" that is "the essence of dreaming"—will be disclosed not in "a latent content *beneath* the manifest" but in "a latent organization *of* the manifest."[4] Lacan dwells on the way the dream presents a series of threes: three women—for Irma evokes two others, one whom Freud thinks would make a more compliant patient, the other his wife; three doctors—Otto, Leopold, and Dr. M.; and finally three groups of three in the formula for trimethylamin. This repetition of a number, says Lacan, is a hallmark of unconscious thought.[5] But the successive modes of representation in the dream are significant as well. The first scene in the dream is a realistic representation of a plausible exchange between Freud and Irma. The second scene assembles three fellow doctors who propose absurd and contradictory diagnoses; the genre, Lacan observes, is farce (*Le moi* 187). The final image of the dream leaves both these modes behind: it is the formula for trimethylamin, "printed in heavy type."

Freud's associations link trimethylamin with sexuality and thereby with his aim of curing nervous illness—and his aim, suggests Lacan, of discovering the meaning of dreams and the nature of the Unconscious. The culmination of the Irma dream in the written formula for trimethylamin signifies that the meaning of the dream is Freud's quest for the meaning of the dream. And it signifies, further, that the sole "solution" to this problem is the word, as such:

> Tel un oracle, la formule ne donne aucune reponse à quoi que ce soit. Mais la façon même dont elle s'énonce, son caractère énigmatique, hermétique, est bien la réponse à la question du sens du rêve. On peut la calquer sur la formule islamique—Il n'y a d'autre Dieu que Dieu. Il n'y a d'autre mot, d'autre solution à votre problème, que le mot. (*Le moi* 190)

It is not far from here to the dictum often cited, since the "Discours de Rome" ("Fonction et champ de la parole et du langage dans la psychanalyse"), as a summary of Lacanian theory: that "The Unconscious is structured like a language." For the hieroglyphic language of the dream signifies by means of the basic operations, "condensation" and "displacement"—metaphor and metonymy, Lacan will say, like Jakobson[6]—that organize spoken or written words. That the word is crucial is the meaning beyond which the word of the dream must not be forced.

This commentary resembles the epigraph from Eusebius that Wordsworth added to "Anecdote for Fathers": "Retine vim istam, falsa enim dicam, si coges" 'Restrain your violence, for I shall speak false if you force me' (*Poems* 1: 313), supposed to be a warning from the oracle. The oracle, in Wordsworth's scheme, is the child. Lacan links it with the Law of the Father, in the shape of the formula for monotheism that shares the dream word's self-referential syntactical structure. With this Freud's parole—the "specimen dream"—becomes a message concerning how it must (not) be read.

How to read the dream may be said to turn on how to read the word "trimethylamin." In particular, the form of Freud's associations to "trimethylamin" calls for attention. For at a certain point this passage dramatically reenacts rather than reports Freud's train of thought. This occurs where the passage refers for the second time (not by name) to Fliess.

> I began to guess why the formula for trimethylamin had been so prominent in the dream. So many important subjects converged upon that one word. Trimethylamin was an allusion not only to the immensely powerful factor of sexuality, but also to a person whose agreement I recalled with satisfaction whenever I felt isolated in my opinions. Surely this friend who played so large a part in my life must appear again elsewhere in these trains of thought. Yes. For he had a special knowledge of the consequences of affections of the nose and its accessory cavities; and he had drawn scientific attention to some very remarkable connections between the turbinal bones and the female organs of sex. (Cf. the three curly structures in Irma's throat.) I had had Irma examined by him to see whether her gastric pains might be of nasal origin. (*SE* 4: 117)

The strikingly odd inquiry mentioned in the last sentence provokes something more than a rhetorical reading. It leads to "day residues"—"preconscious" material for the dream—originating in the events of previous weeks as well as on the dream day 24 July. For the mention of this inquiry links Freud's treatment of Irma to his treatment of another patient, named Emma, whom Freud had also had examined by Fliess, who becomes a major topic of Freud's letters to Fliess in March and April 1895. Emma's treatment had involved more than a metaphorical "injection" with a "solution." Fliess, an ear, nose, and throat man, believed he had discovered analogies between the structures of the nose and the female sex organs that involved the nose in various somatic and psychological disorders. Freud shared these views so far as to have Fliess operate, twice, on his own nose (Kuper and Stone 1228) and to have him come to Vienna to operate on Emma's. The results were dismaying: she got worse; the wound failed to heal and developed a fetid odor; and another colleague's further treatment, in which Emma suffered severe hemorrhaging, revealed that Fliess had in fact left in her nose a piece of gauze nearly a yard long.

The resemblances between the dream and the Emma episode are obvious: the worry that a patient's disorder might be organic or toxic rather than hysterical; the attention fixed on the patient's nose and mouth (the "curly structures" in Irma's throat "evidently modelled on the turbinal bones of the nose" [*SE* 4: 107]); the danger that the patient might die because of a doctor's error; and the inculpation of Fliess in the disorder's diagnosis. These concerns emerge in letters in which Freud reaffirms his trust in Fliess, revealing in the process how far it has been jeopardized. Max Schur, the commentator who brings these letters to light as "Some Additional 'Day Residues' of 'the Specimen Dream' of Psychoanalysis," stresses that the Irma dream, like the Emma episode, took place when Freud could not yet afford to dissolve his transference (70). Schur proposes that Freud's motive in dreaming the Irma dream was to exculpate not simply himself but also Fliess and that this motive remained unknown to him, repressed, both when he analyzed the dream and when he published his book. If in criticizing his therapeutic method with Irma, Freud is recognizing the significance of his patient's transference, he is nevertheless still incapable of recognizing the effects of his own.

Certainly the letter of 8 March 1895, describing the discovery of the gauze and Emma's hemorrhage, reveals strikingly Freud's investment in his relation to Fliess.

> So we had done her an injustice. She was not abnormal at all, but a piece of iodoform gauze had gotten torn off when you removed the rest, and stayed in for 14 days . . . . The fact that this mishap should have happened to you, how you would react to it when you learned about it . . .—all this came over me simultaneously. . . . I was not sufficiently clear-headed to think of blaming R. at that moment. . . . Now that I have assimilated all this, nothing remains but sincere compassion for my "child of sorrow" [*Schmerzenskind*]. . . . Of course no one blames you in any way, nor do I know why they should. . . . Rest assured that I felt no need to restore my trust in you. I only want to add that I hesitated for a day to tell you all about it, and that then I began to be ashamed, and here is the letter. (qtd. in Schur 58)

"Here is the letter": an offering to Fliess, with testimony that it cost a considerable psychic effort. Schur is obviously right to treat Freud's letter as a symptomatic action. But the question remains whether the reenactment of his train of thought in *The Interpretation of Dreams* should be read in the same way. The way in which the passage on trimethylamin dramatizes the movement toward conviction gives it a certain resemblance to the movement toward reassurance in Freud's letter of 8 March. The assurance in the *Interpretation* text, however, concerns something different: "Surely this friend who played so large a part in my life must appear again elsewhere in these trains of thought. Yes."

The question answered with that "Yes" is whether the pertinence of Freud's first associations regarding trimethylamin—which point to Fliess—is confirmed by the appearance of Fliess elsewhere in the dream thoughts as well. The motif of "this friend" does reappear, in association with the "turbinal bones," confirming the pertinence of the preceding associations, which are these:

> What was it, then, to which my attention was directed in this way by trimethylamin? It was to a conversation with another friend who had for many years been familiar with all my writings during the period of their gestation, just as I had

been with his. He had at that time confided to me ideas on the subject of the chemistry of the sexual processes, and had mentioned among other things that he believed that one of the products of sexual metabolism was trimethylamin. Thus this substance led me to sexuality, the factor to which I attributed the greatest importance in the origin of the nervous disorders which it was my aim to cure.

(*SE* 4: 116)

Questioning what trimethylamin represents, Freud reads first not for its referent but for its context. He focuses on the fact that it came up in a conversation between himself and his friend. Trimethylamin represents, in the first instance, a knowledge created as it passes between two people. Implicit in this passage in Freud's text is an insight into the peculiar status of psychoanalysis as a transferential knowledge, arising between two people and possessed by neither.

The mode of analysis generating that insight is an attention not simply to the contents of the dream thoughts but to the organization of the manifest features of the dream:

> *Trimethylamin.* I saw the chemical formula of this substance in my dream, which bears witness to a great effort on the part of my memory. Moreover the formula was printed in heavy type, as though there had been a desire to lay emphasis on some part of the context as being of quite special importance. . . . And how strangely, I thought to myself, a dream like this is put together! . . . I began to guess why the formula for trimethylamin had been so prominent in the dream.
>
> (*SE* 4: 116)

These sentences focus attention on the dreamwork. The final chapters of *The Interpretation of Dreams* describe and theorize the necessity for that "form of thinking," "the essence of dreaming"; why, for instance, must the "day's residues" ("preconscious material") take part in the formation of a dream? Because of what Freud here calls "the fact of the transference"—the fact that "an unconscious idea is as such quite incapable of entering the preconscious" and "can only exercise any effect there by establishing a connection with an idea which already belongs to the preconscious, by transferring its intensity on to it" (*SE* 5: 562). Transference in this sense is the primary rhetorical operation of substitution evoked in "Anecdote for Fathers" with the "lambs that bounded through the glade, / From shade to sunshine, and as fleet / From sunshine back to shade." Transference as the displacement of feelings and meanings from one person to another (the second sense in which the word will appear in Freud's writing) derives—in what sense, in what way, remains a crucial question—from transference as the displacement of feelings and meanings from one idea or site to another.

In this context it is possible to appreciate the remarkable construction of the text on "Trimethylamin." The very gesture by which Freud focuses on the dreamwork or transference in the first sense also focuses on *his* transference. And not only the analysis but the "specimen dream" itself is constructed according to a logic that makes transference, in its double sense, the crucial factor. First of all the image of the throat, with its "remarkable curly structures," enforces the connection between

Emma's nose (with its "turbinal bones") and Irma's throat, site of the organ of speech: the connection between the site of Fliess's surgical intervention and the site of Freud's verbal intervention. Further on in the dream it will be a matter of an "injection" of trimethylamin; trimethylamin appears in the dream first as a chemical substance, then as a printed formula. Solution, injection, and formula represent the forms in which curative knowledge may pass between doctor and patient. The variation from one form to another actually organizes the dream's manifest content; the solution, the injection, and the formula appear in phases of the dream distinguished not just by their different content but by their different modes of expression. The structuring of the dream by the shifts from one of these forms to another stresses further what the content of each one concerns: the importance not of the substance of the knowledge but of the way it passes between two representations or two persons.

This distinction reappears in the analysis of what the formula for trimethylamin signifies. Trimethylamin is "a product of sexual metabolism" (nothing other, in fact, as Lacan discloses with intently theoretic glee, than a product of the decomposition of sperm [*Le moi* 190]). "Thus this *substance* led me to sexuality," Freud writes, "the *factor* to which I attributed the greatest importance." The distinction here follows the distinction in the dream itself between the injection of trimethylamin and the formula for it. Sexuality is to be understood not as a physical essence such as the biochemical substance *referred* to by the term trimethylamin but as an essential *factor* in mental life that operates in the manner of the written formula that performs a structuring role in the dream and its analysis. That structuring role is transference in its primary sense—the displacement of intensity from unconscious ideas onto preconscious ones, which must occur because of the factor Freud will elsewhere call repression. This process of displacement is the fundamental signifying process, the substitution that is the condition for all effects of signification. It appeared in Wordsworth's text as the sheer possibility of movement from one site to another that is the condition for all further rhetorical moves. It both makes particular significations possible and subverts their significance. Psychoanalysis will make its students recognize their own preferences, like little Edward's, as essentially secondary and contingent effects of an impulse to substitute one site or sign for another. In the dream, sexuality and transference are represented by the same culminating image; in its analysis, they are juxtaposed in the same sentence: "Trimethylamin was an allusion not only to the immensely powerful factor of sexuality, but also to a person whose agreement I recalled with satisfaction whenever I felt isolated in my opinions." This cannot be read as simply a reiteration of Fliess's authority for Freud; it should be read as an identification of sexuality with transference. For the wording of the earlier sentence—"This substance led me to . . . the factor"—describes exactly how Freud diverged from Fliess, concluding that sexuality was not a metabolic substance but a factor in mental life.

The allusions to Fliess's biological notions in "The Analysis of a Specimen Dream" can be read in the same way as the allusions to Wedgwood's pedagogical notions in "Anecdote for Fathers" or book 5 of *The Prelude:* as testimony on how a great original thinker and writer emerges from dependency on another's ideas and authority. (Behind Fliess is the authority of Helmholtz and Brücke—the physiological determinism in which Freud was trained; behind Wedgwood is the doctrine of Hartley, and ultimately the associationism of Hume and Locke.) Such a view (Erdman's view of Wordsworth, Schur's of Freud) is accurate enough in its own terms, and it helps one appreciate the salience of certain motifs—for instance, that of the mute or suffering child, who appears not only in "little Edward" (and in the Winander boy) but also in the Emma of Freud's letters, where he writes, " . . . nothing remains but sincere compassion for my *Schmerzenskind*." The expression is odd in its immediate context, insofar as *Schmerzenskind* (like "child of sorrow") means not only a suffering child but a child born of suffering. This aligns Freud's letter about Emma with his dream about Irma, whose "pains in the abdomen" recall those of his wife—who was pregnant at the time of the dream (as Freud's analysis does not mention) with his daughter Anna. As his wife shall bear a child, so Freud shall bear a theory. Freud's true *Schmerzenskind*, then, is his theory of the child. But one would also have to point not only to how this puts Emma's sufferings in the background, of course, but to how the Irma dream fantasizes the termination of a pregnancy. The "pains" due to an "injection" have caused an "infection," but "the toxin will be eliminated." What will be eliminated, one might read, with Kristeva, is the idea of a child genuinely other than the adult or the Child-Father: a child lodged in the mother's body, formed through the process of gestation prior to any social, symbolic, or linguistic contract, formed through the pregnancy of the woman's body, which must be ignored by psychoanalysis because it lies at the limits of nature-as-culture.

Thus even to read Freud's letter to the letter takes on beyond a celebration of the dream achieved to give the world a theory (or a work). How must we interpret, now, Freud's stated judgment of the specimen dream's purpose: his exculpation? The analysis of the latent organization of the dream reveals that it accomplishes an exculpation much more far-reaching than the displacement of responsibility for the suffering of Freud's patient. It is comparable to the effect of a rhetorical reading of "Anecdote for Fathers," in which the poem represents a sequence of inevitable rhetorical operations only allegorically identifiable with the Father or the Child. Lacan's reading dwells on the successive scenes' culmination in a written form. The dream represents "the spectral decomposition of the function of the ego" (*Le moi* 197), as the recognizable and responsible self in the first scene gives way before the vision of the curves and patches in the throat and as the crowd of colleagues (the three doctors' diagnosis) gives way to the impersonal formula that imposes order and meaning. Lacan argues (against Erikson's view that the dream exemplifies a "regression in the service of the ego" [35, n.8]) that the Irma dream reveals the true status of the ego: it is no more than the sum of its identifications, or (to put this in terms suggested by the "trimethylamin" analysis) an effect of "transferences."

What masters the function of speech, the rule of the word made manifest in the culminating image of the written formula, is not the ego, not a self possessed of motives and reasons, but a subject possessed by the desire of language. Wordsworth's "little Edward" is a figure for such a subject. He is animated not by a motive for preferring Kilve to Liswyn Farm but by a wish for words. A word, a formula, comes to the rescue at the close of Wordsworth's anecdote as at the close of Freud's dream, breaking the impasse of the identification and conflict among imaginary selves. The child's eventual response to the father's questioning has the same opaque finality as "trimethylamin" in the Irma dream. It is no more a reasonable explanation for his stated preference than an injection with trimethylamin is a reasonable explanation for the infiltrated patches and scabs on Irma's shoulder and in her throat. But as "trimethylamin" evokes sexuality and transference, the "weather-cock," the "broad and gilded vane," evokes key problems in Wordsworth's text: the pertinence of the story of a fall or a temptation and the dynamics of the desire for words. For a weathercock makes visible the invisible motions of the wind, identified in biblical imagery with the Spirit and the Word of God and associated in an image in book 5 of the 1805 *Prelude* with the power of language: "Visionary power / Attends upon the motions of the winds / Embodied in the mystery of words" (lines 619-21). The "glittering" gilded vane recalls the golden calf worshipped by the Israelites impatient for Moses's return with a written law from an invisible God. It is the visibility of this sign ("It caught his eye, he saw it plain") that makes it tempting; it offers release from the pressure of attention to inner or invisible signs. A weather vane ordinarily functions to make visible the direction of the wind; when it points southward, for example, it indicates that the wind blows from the south. A weathercock is an index, part of what it indicates. An index, instead of designating an object, participates in the object or phenomenon it signals. But this is not how the weathercock functions in the child's reply in "Anecdote for Fathers." For little Edward, the weathercock makes visible not the direction of the wind but the difference between two places. It is not an index but a sign strictly speaking: an arbitrary signifier, a mere mark of difference between one site and another. And it is this that has the power to "unlock" little Edward's "tongue." The child's "lie" tells truly what impels and empowers him to speak: not a wish or a reason, but a signifier.

The weathercock and trimethylamin are figures of the same kind: each can be singled out for the way it is significant precisely not as the index it might be but rather in its minimal role as signifier. This distinction defines a key term in the theory of Lacan: the phallus, which is not, like the penis, an indexical sign (indicating a state of sexual arousal) but rather a signifier (like the weathercock for little Edward), the "privileged" (visible) sign for an invisible difference—the difference between two places, the difference between masculine and feminine. This sign takes its power from its absence. The way "no weather-cock" serves as "the reason why" the child would rather be at the other place is the way castration, according to Lacan, serves as the "reason" for desire (*Ecrits* 281–91). What is *not* at work is a spontaneous response to a natural biological function.[7]

Both Freud's text and Wordsworth's, then, both the Irma dream and the anecdote of little Edward, close on an image of the sign's power of insistence. If trimethylamin is not, in the first analysis, just any old chemical substance but a product of the decomposition of sperm, in the last analysis—in Freud's dream analysis—it is significant not as the substance that it can be but as the written formula it is at the conclusion of the dream, signifying the signifying process at work in sexuality and in transference.

Freud's double use of the word "transference" requires some strategic discriminations. Freud called the illusion generated in the analytic relationship by the same name he had used for the primary process of representation. On the one hand, the term means the primary process of displacement or substitution without which no representation, no conscious thought, could take place. On the other hand, it means a defensive secondary process designed to prevent the disclosure of the first. Transference in the first sense—the unconscious and unmasterable nature of the condition of representation—implies the radical innocence of the subject that Freud recognizes as the end that animates the Irma dream (cf. Lacan, *Le moi* 201–04). With the appearance of the written formula the fundamental conditions of language, the rules of the Unconscious, emerge as the determining factor in the production of acts or texts. The subject is radically innocent insofar as the subject of motives and purposes ceases to exist.

To assert the endemic and primary character of transference in the first sense has roughly the same implications as to ascribe such a status to the related term metaphor (*meta-phorein* 'to carry across'), as *The Interpretation of Dreams* does (Lacan argues) in identifying "condensation" and "displacement" as the constitutive conditions of thought. But Freud's text, like Wordsworth's, suggests that transference in the second sense is unavoidable as well. Freud considered the transference the preeminent form of resistance to the analytic cure, insofar as the analysis sought to repair the patient's memory of forgotten (repressed) events; for the patient to develop a transference was for him or her to repeat rather than remember prior events or relationships. Yet it was found that the analytic encounter invariably provoked such a transference: the analysand's discourse ineluctably came to function as blind action rather than as recognition, took on a performative dimension that conflicted rather than coincided with its cognitive one.

The fundamental problem here is the way transference in the second sense comes into play to obscure the workings of transference in the first sense. This happens not only in the patient's exchanges with the analyst, where the patient's transference onto the analyst becomes a form of resistance to the fundamental transferential process revealed in free association. It also happens in the act of reading[8]—for example in Lacan's interpretation of Freud's dream. What we find at the culminating moment of that interpretation is Lacan's transference onto Freud. Here Lacan is responding to an imperative in Freud's text. Freud had written:

> And now I must ask the reader to make my interests his own for quite a while, and to plunge, along with me, into the minutest details of my life; for a transference of this kind is peremptorily demanded by our interest in the hidden meaning of dreams. (105–06)

Lacan interprets the Irma dream as a "word" addressed not to Fliess and not only to Freud's contemporary readers but to his future readers: "C'est déjà pour la communauté des psychologues, des anthropologues, qu'il rêve. Quand il interprète ce rêve, c'est à nous qu'il s'adresse." Lacan's reading of the Irma dream concludes with a passage in which he speaks in Freud's voice:

> Je suis celui qui veut être pardonné d'avoir osé commencer à guérir ces malades, que jusqu'à présent on ne voulait pas comprendre et qu'on s'interdisait de guérir. Je suis celui qui veut être pardonné de cela. Je suis celui qui veut n'en être pas coupable, car c'est toujours être coupable que de transgresser une limite jusque-là imposée à l'activité humaine. Je veux n'être pas cela. A la place de moi, il y a tous les autres. Je ne suis là que le représentant de ce vaste, vague mouvement qui est la recherche de la vérité où, moi, je m'efface. Je ne suis plus rien. Mon ambition a été plus grande que moi. La séringue était sale sans doute. Et justement dans la mesure où j'ai voulu être, moi, le créateur, je ne suis pas le créateur. Le créateur est quelqu'un de plus grand que moi. C'est mon inconscient, c'est cette parole qui parle en moi, au-delà de moi.
>   Voilà le sens de ce rêve.[9]

Submerging his voice in Freud's, merging Freud's voice with his own, Lacan demonstrates the pathos and rhetorical power of a statement at odds with its performance. There is a peculiar tension and complicity between the performative and constative dimensions of this discourse, the very *profession* of psychoanalysis. The judgment that psychoanalysis is the creation of radically impersonal forces (insofar as it is a creation, not a failure) gets stated in an intensely personal form: confessional self-naming.

Lacan derives his statement from an analysis of the formal structure of the dream text and above all of the formula for trimethylamin, an array of letters branching out in threes; yet his analysis culminates in a passage of direct discourse spoken in the name of Freud. The rigorous extravagance of Lacan's interpretation reveals what is at stake in such a reading. It freezes a potentially endless chain of tropological transformations into a single signifier—a proper name. For the word "trimethylamin" gives place to the name "Freud," figured as a speaking voice. The *parole* of "Freud" bodied forth in Lacan's reading is the personification of a proper name.

This is in fact what the father asks from little Edward, too, whose eventual reply gives a token characterization of "Kilve," as well as the motivation of his first response that is required to make it possible to personify Edward himself. What becomes apparent in both these texts is the violent, arbitrary character of this eminently familiar move—which is a shift from movement among a number of terms or tropes to the movement to a single sign set apart in fact by its untranslatable signifier (a "proper" name) but evoking instead the prerequisite for being a person, appearing to have a voice.[10] The shift from transference in the first sense to transference in the second (reflected in the analytic encounter in the conflict between transference and free association) is thus a shift from trope to anthropomorphism, and these texts suggest it to be at once inevitable and unwarranted—more concisely, forced.

It turns out that the very gesture supposed to bring Freud's meaning, his *vouloir dire*, before the reader, is the gesture that achieves its occultation. The project of teaching Freud is ruined from the start, though *Le Séminaire* (sessions, volumes) goes on and on—and though Lacan's teaching, at least, is as effective, his readings as telling, as any that could be composed. But Lacan's powerful reading has a consequence like the father's initiative in Wordsworth's anecdote, where the query designed to "bring out" the child makes him mute. As Lacan gives rein to his transference onto Freud, the nature of his utterance contradicts the meaning of his statement, effacing the meaning he would lend Freud's text.

The effect of such a transference is to monumentalize a text. So the effect of a transferential encounter, of a transference between a text and a reader, is not (as in this text's earlier formula) a knowledge arising between two people. It rather produces an effect like the sheer repetition of a proper name. With Lacan's reading, it is as if the entire meaning of *The Interpretation of Dreams* were reduced to the minimal oracular inscription Freud had imagined at the start in his letter to Fliess: "In this House . . . The Secret of Dreams was Revealed to Dr. Sigm. Freud." Speaking in the voice of Freud turns into a reiteration of a proper name, or the transformation of Freud's text into an inscription on a monument. The very effort to give voice to a text empties it of referential and figurative content, of any substance for our understanding.

Is there a comparable effect in Wordsworth's poem, which presents itself (Wordsworth claimed) in the voice of "a man speaking to men" (*Prose Works* 1: 138) or as the anecdote of a father speaking to fathers? There is in fact a verbal repetition, stressing the illusion of the poet speaking or voicing the poem, that works to gravely disrupt any claim of meaning. This may be why Wordsworth left this line out of the poem when he revised it. Stanza 4 originally read:

> A day it was when I could bear
> To think, and think, and think again;
> With so much happiness to spare
> I could not feel a pain.

Wordsworth argued against Coleridge, in a note to another of the lyrical ballads, that "repetition and tautology are beauties of the highest kind" (*Poetical Works* 2: 513). But he removed *this* repetition from his poem, replacing it with the version we read: "A day it was when I could bear / Some fond regrets to entertain." The revised line makes it much easier to understand what this state of mind is about: "fond regrets" is easy to associate with the allusion in the preceding stanza to "Our pleasant home when spring began / A long, long year before." In the original version, it is only by recurring verbal repetition that this state of mind is linked with the past: in stanza 3, "long . . . long," and then here, "think . . . think . . . think." And the triple repetition of the infinitive "to think" compounds the difficulty of imagining what sort of reflections this line describes. To think again is to reverse a previous judgment, but to think again and again implies repetition rather than reversal or progression. The triple repetition describes a form of thinking that consists in repetition; and repetition is also what this line does.

Hence the activity of thinking becomes indistinguishable from the activity of repeating the words "to think." Thought, this line suggests, occurs not as a dialogic interplay of ideas or voices but as a stutter or a stammer—the stammering repetition of a text. Hegel's *Enzyklopädie* (401–12) defines thought (*Denken*) in similar terms, as the effect of memorization (*Gedächtnis*)—not remembrance, not *Erinnerung,* the making inward of perceptions; not recollection, the reconstructive faculty that Freud had imagined the talking cure would restore; but the "repair" of the memory—as of a machine—which the analysis of the Irma dream registers in the reproduction of the formula for trimethylamin: "I saw the chemical formula for this in the dream, which testifies to a great effort on the part of my memory." So Freud, and he dates it: 24–25 July 1895. So Wordsworth:

> A day it was when I could bear
> To think, and think, and think again.

This line disrupts our understanding gravely enough so that we should perhaps disregard the invitation to regard it as a beauty of the highest kind, and overcome the impulse to reinscribe it as a verse to monumentalize the text of Freud—whose aim, it might be said, was not knowledge, but thinking.

Notes

[1] *Standard Edition* 22: 149; hereafter referred to as *SE*. On Freud as pedagogue and critic of pedagogy, see Felman.

[2] Glen quotes Wedgwood's letter and argues, "It is difficult to believe that this story of a 'lie,' which is merely a pathetic caricature of adult reasoning, does not in part express Wordsworth's imaginative reaction against this rationalistic project" (242).

[3] Psychiatry in the United States has helped legitimize the subordinate position of women by making use of a version of Freudian theory which ignores the discontinuity and the complex mediations between the Unconscious and the rules of language, and social structures and cultural constructs. For a feminist and Lacanian critique of this tendency, see Gallop, ch. 1.

[4] Mehlman 42. Mehlman's essay remains the most powerful and concise account of the theoretical stakes of the Irma dream analysis.

[5] *Le moi* 190: "Ces trois que nous retrouvons toujours, c'est là que, dans le rêve, est l'inconscient—ce qui est en dehors de tous les sujets."

⁶ Jakobson, *Essais* 43–67; in English in Jakobson and Halle, pt. 2, ch 5. 1–4. For a critique of this identification of "condensation" and "displacement" with "metaphor" and "metonymy" see Lyotard, "Le travail de rêve ne pense pas."

⁷ It would distort Wordsworth's text as much as Freud's to interpret little Edward's response in pseudo-Freudian terms as expressing the wish to be with his mother—"by the green sea"—rather than his father. Such an interpretation assumes a natural correlation between the symbol and the biological nature of the sex symbolized. That assumption of a natural symbolism harmonizes with the classic conception of a one-to-one correspondence between the word and the thing which was displaced by Saussure's description of the arbitrary relation between the signifier and the signified.

⁸ On the role of Freud's attachments and identifications in the reading of *Oedipus*, see (among others) Balmary's righteous but ingenious indictment. On the specimen-dream analysis, see—in addition to Jeffrey Mehlman—Schneider 120–58. On transference in the psychoanalytic movement, see Roustang. On Freud's ambiguous identifications with his patients and colleagues and their crucial significance for his theoretical writing, see Hertz's two essays.

⁹ *Le moi* 203:

> I am he who wants to be pardoned for having dared to begin to heal the ill whom until now no one wanted to understand and whom it was forbidden to heal. I am he who wants to be pardoned for that. I am he who wants not to be guilty of that, for it is always guilty to transgress a limit till then imposed upon human activity. I do not want to be that. In place of me, there are all the others. I am there only the representative of this vast, vague movement which is the search for truth where, myself, I efface myself. I am no longer anything. My ambition has been too great for me. The syringe was no doubt dirty. And just insofar as I have wanted to be, myself, the creator, I am not the creator. The creator is someone greater than me. It is my unconscious, it is that word that speaks in me, beyond me.
>
> That is the meaning of this dream.

¹⁰ On the shift from tropes to anthropomorphisms within a text or a reading, or how "the possibility of anthropomorphic (mis)reading is part of the text and part of what is at stake in it," see de Man, "Anthropomorphism."

From *Patria* to *Matria*

Elizabeth Barrett Browning's Risorgimento

SANDRA M. GILBERT

Then Lady Reason . . . said, "Get up, daughter! Without waiting any longer, let us go to the Field of Letters. There the City of Ladies will be founded on a flat and fertile plain. . . ." (Christine de Pizan, *The Book of the City of Ladies* 16)

Our lives are Swiss—
So still—so Cool—
Till some odd afternoon
The Alps neglect their Curtains
And we look farther on!

10 *Italy* stands the other side!
While like a guard between—
The solemn Alps—
The siren Alps
Forever intervene!
  (Emily Dickinson, no. 80)

Our insight into this early, pre-Oedipus phase in the little girl's development comes to us as a surprise, comparable in another field with the discovery of the Minoan-Mycenaean civilization behind that of Greece.
  (Sigmund Freud, "Female Sexuality" 195)

  And now I come, my Italy,
My own hills! Are you 'ware of me, my hills,
How I burn toward you? do you feel to-night
The urgency and yearning of my soul,
As sleeping mothers feel the sucking babe
And smile? *Aurora Leigh* 5.1266–71[1]

When in 1860 Elizabeth Barrett Browning published *Poems before Congress*, a frankly political collection of verses that was the culmination of her long commitment to Italy's arduous struggle for reunification, English critics excoriated her as unfeminine, even insane. "To bless and not to curse is woman's function," wrote one reviewer, "and if Mrs. Browning, in her calmer moments, will but contrast the spirit which has prompted her to such melancholy aberrations with that which animated Florence Nightingale, she can hardly fail to derive a profitable lesson for the future" ("Poetic Aberrations" 494). Interestingly, however, the very first poem in the volume depicts Italy as a friendless, powerless, invalid woman, asking if it is ". . . true,—may it be spoken,—" that she is finally alive

> . . . who has lain so still,
> With a wound in her breast,
> And a flower in her hand,
> And a grave-stone under her head,
>   While every nation at will
> Beside her has dared to stand,
> And flout her with pity and scorn. . . .
>   ("Napoleon III in Italy" 111-18,
>   *Poetical Works* 412)

Creating an ostensibly "unfeminine" political polemic, Barrett Browning consciously or unconsciously seems to adopt the persona of a nurse at the bedside of an imperiled relative, almost as if she *were* a sort of literary-political Florence Nightingale. Putting aside all questions about the inherent femininity or unfemininity of political poetry, I will argue that this English expatriate's visions of *Italia Riunita* had more to do with both her femaleness and her feminism than is usually supposed. In fact, where so magisterial a reader as Henry James believed that Barrett Browning's commitment to "the cause of Italy" represented a letting down of "her inspiration and her poetic pitch" (quoted by Markus, in *Casa Guidi Windows* xvi-xvii), I believe instead that, as Flavia Alaya has also observed, Italy became for a complex of reasons both the embodiment of this woman poet's inspiration and the most vivid strain in her "poetic pitch."[2]

Specifically, I will suggest that through her involvement with the revolutionary struggle for political identity that marked Italy's famous risorgimento, Barrett Browning enacted and reenacted her own personal and artistic struggle for identity, a risorgimento that was, like Italy's, both an insurrection and a resurrection. In addition, I will suggest that, by using metaphors of the healing and making whole of a wounded woman/land to articulate both the reality and fantasy of her own female/poetic revitalization, Barrett Browning figuratively located herself in a re-creative female poetic tradition that descends from Sappho and Christine de Pizan through the Brontës, Christina Rossetti, Margaret Fuller, and Emily Dickinson to Renée Vivien, Charlotte Perkins Gilman, H. D., and Adrienne Rich. Infusing supposedly asexual poetics with the dreams and desires of a distinctively sexual politics, these women imagined nothing less than the transformation of *patria* into *matria* and thus the risorgimento of the lost community of women that Rossetti called the "mother country"—the shadowy land, perhaps, that Freud identified with the mysterious "Minoan-Mycenaean civilization behind that of Greece." In resurrecting the *matria*, moreover, these women fantasized resurrecting and restoring both the *madre*, the forgotten impossible dead mother, and the *matrice*, the originary womb or matrix, the mother-matter whose very memory, says Freud, is "lost in a past so dim . . . so hard to resuscitate that it [seems to have] undergone some specially inexorable repression" ("Female Sexuality" 195).[3]

Not surprisingly, then, Barrett Browning begins her covertly political 1857 *Kunstlerroman, Aurora Leigh,* with a meditation on this lost mother, using imagery that dramatically foreshadows the figure with which the poet opens her overtly political *Poems before Congress.* Gazing at a portrait of her mother that was (significantly) painted after the woman's death, young Aurora sees the maternal image as embodying in turn all the patriarchal myths of femaleness—muse, Psyche, Medusa, Lamia; "Ghost, fiend, and angel, fairy, witch, and sprite" (1.154). But most heart-rendingly she sees her as "Our Lady of the Passion, stabbed with swords / Where the Babe sucked" (1.160–61): the only *maternal* image of the lost mother dissolves into the destroyed woman/country from *Poems before Congress,* "who has lain so still, / With a wound in her breast" while "every nation" has flouted her "with pity and scorn."[4]

Among eighteenth-, nineteenth-, and early twentieth-century English and American writers, tropes of Italy proliferated like flowers in Fiesole, so much so that the country, as its nationalist leaders feared, would seem to have had no reality except as a metaphor. As far back as the sixteenth but especially in the late eighteenth century, English romancers had exploited what Kenneth Churchill calls "the violence-incest-murder-prison paradigm of Gothic Italy" (66). More seriously, from Gibbon to Byron and Shelley to John Ruskin, George Eliot, Henry James, Edith Wharton, and D. H. Lawrence, English-speaking poets and novelists read the sunny, ruin-haunted Italian landscape as a symbolic text, a hieroglyph, or, perhaps more accurately, a palimpsest of Western history, whose warring traces seemed to them to solidify in the stones of Venice and the bones of Rome. Shelley, for instance, reflecting on the ancient city where Keats died seeking health, sees it both as "that high Capital, where kingly Death / Keeps his pale court in beauty and decay" and as "the Paradise, / The grave, the city, and the wilderness" ("Adonais" 55–56, 433–34)—a place whose ruins, building on and contradicting one another, suggest the paradoxical simultaneity of the originary moment (paradise) and the fall from that moment (the grave), the invention of culture (the city) and the supervention of nature (the wilderness). In "St. Mark's Place," Samuel Rogers is less metaphysical, but he too elaborates a vision of Italy as text, asserting that "Not a stone / In the broad pavement, but to him who has / An eye, an ear for the Inanimate World, / Tells of past ages" (301), and George Eliot develops a similar perception when she writes in *Middlemarch* of "the gigantic broken revelations" of Rome (bk. 2, ch. 15). Finally, emphasizing the dialectic between culture and nature that, as Shelley also saw, underlies all such statements, Edith Wharton summarizes the point most simply: Italy, she writes, is "that sophisticated landscape where the face of nature seems moulded by the passions and imaginings of man" (3).

Interestingly, however, as post-Renaissance Italy sank ever further into physical decay and political disarray, lapsing inexorably away from the grandeur that was imperial Rome and the glory that was fourteenth-century Florence, both native and tourist poets increasingly began to depict "her" as a sort of fallen woman. In Byron's famous translation, for example, the seventeenth-century Florentine patriot Vincenzo da Filijaca imagines "Italia" as a helpless naked seductress, while Byron himself writes of Venice as "a sea Cybele" and Rome as the "Lone mother of dead Empires," "The Niobe of nations!" *(Childe Harold's Pilgrimage,* canto 4, sts. 2, 78, 79).[5] Similarly, Ruskin, who sees Venice as "the Paradise of cities," the positive of Shelley's more equivocal Rome, hints that "her" charm lies in her seductive femininity *(Diaries* 1: 183, *Letters* 128), and the expatriate novelist Ouida writes of her adopted city that "in Florence [the past is] like the gold from the sepulchres of the Aetruscan kings that shines on the breast of some fair living woman" *(Pascarel,* quoted in Churchill 163).[6] The trope of Italy or of one of "her" city-states as a living, palpable, and often abandoned woman had become almost ubiquitous by the time Barrett Browning began to write her poems about the risorgimento, and of course it derived from a traditional grammatical convention that tends, at least in most Indo-European languages, to impute metaphorical femaleness to such diverse phenomena as countries, ships, and hurricanes. As applied to Italy, however, this metaphor of gender was often so intensely felt that, most notably for women writers, it frequently evolved from figure to fantasy, from speculation to hallucination. Thus Italy as art object "moulded by the passions and imaginings of man" becomes Italy as Galatea and, worse still, a Galatea seduced and betrayed by her creator,[7] while Italy as destroyed motherland becomes Italy as wounded mother, Madonna of the sorrows whose restored milk and honey might nourish errant children, and especially daughters, of all nations. Ultimately, then, such women writers as Christina Rossetti and Elizabeth Barrett Browning revise and revitalize the dead metaphor of gender that is their literary and linguistic inheritance, using it to transform Italy from a political state to a female state of mind, from a problematic country in Europe to the problem condition of femaleness. Redeeming and redeemed by Italy, they imagine redeeming and being redeemed by themselves.

More specifically, as artists like Rossetti and Barrett Browning (and Emily Dickinson after them) struggle to revive both the dead land of Italy and the dead metaphor of "her" femaleness, they explore five increasingly complex but always interrelated definitions of this lost, fragmented woman-country: (1) Italy as a nurturing mother—a land that feeds, (2) Italy as an impassioned sister—a land that feels, (3) Italy as a home of art—a land that creates, (4) Italy as a magic paradise—a land that transforms or integrates, and (5) Italy as a dead, denied, and denying woman—a land that has been rejected or is rejecting.

Christina Rossetti's ostensibly religious lyric "Mother Country" is the most visionary statement of the first definition, for in it this poet, who was (paradoxically enough) fully Italian only on her father's side, mourns her exclusion from a dreamlike, distinctively female Mediterranean queendom:

> Not mine own country
> But dearer far to me?
> Yet mine own country,

If I may one day see
Its spices and cedars
Its gold and ivory. (245)

Glamorous, rich, and giving, such a maternal paradise is opposed to *this* (implicitly patriarchal) country, in which "All starve together, / All dwarfed and poor" (245), and the metaphorical climates of the two locales strongly suggest that the luxurious mother country is Italy while the impoverished fatherland—"here"—is England. As if to support such an interpretation with matter-of-fact reportage, Elizabeth Barrett Browning writes countless letters from Pisa and Florence, praising the nurturing maternal land to which she has eloped with Robert Browning after her perilous escape from the gloomily patriarchal household at 50 Wimpole Street. Food, in particular, seems almost eerily ubiquitous. Barrett Browning never tires of describing great glowing oranges and luscious bunches of grapes; the Italian landscape itself appears largely edible, the scenery deliciously beautiful. As for "real" meals, they continually materialize at her table as if by magic. In Florence, she reports that "Dinner, 'unordered,' comes through the streets and spreads itself on our table, as hot as if we had smelt cutlets hours before," while more generally, in another letter, she observes that "No little orphan on a house step but seems to inherit naturally his slice of watermelon and bunch of purple grapes" (*Letters* 1: 341, 343).[8]

This land that feeds is also a land that feels. As both a mother country and, again in Rossetti's words, a "sister-land of Paradise" (377), female Italy neither contains nor condones the super-egoistic repressions that characterize patriarchal England. Literary visions of Italy had always emphasized the passion and sensuality of "her" people, but where Renaissance playwrights and Gothic romancers had dramatized the stagey strangeness of violent Italians, women writers like Barrett Browning, Rossetti, and later Dickinson wistfully set the natural emotiveness of this mother country against the icy artifice of the Victorian culture in which they had been brought up. Indeed, from Barrett Browning's Bianca in "Bianca among the Nightingales," who freely expresses her fiery rage at the cold Englishwoman who has stolen her lover away (*Poetical Works* 428–30), to Rossetti's Enrica, who "chill[s]" Englishwomen with "her liberal glow" and "dwarf[s]" them "by her ampler scale" (377–78), the women who represent Italy in women's writing increasingly seem like ennobled versions of *Jane Eyre*'s Bertha Mason Rochester: large, heated, dark, passionate foreigners who are wholly at ease—even at one—with the Vesuvius of female sexual creativity that Dickinson was later to find *un*easily "at home" in her breast (no. 1705).

Together, in fact, such heroines as Barrett Browning's Bianca, her Laura Savio of "Mother and Poet" (*Poetical Works* 446–48), and Rossetti's Enrica seem almost to propose an ontology of female power as it might be if all girls were not, in Rossetti's words, "minted in the selfsame [English] mould" (377). That most of these women are in one way or another associated with a violent uprising against the authoritarian rule of Austria and the patriarchal law of the pope, with Enrica (according to William Michael Rossetti) based on a woman who knew both Mazzini and Garibaldi, further cements their connection with Brontë's rebellious Bertha, but with a Bertha revised and transformed so that she, the alien, is free, and English Jane is trapped. As if to demonstrate this point, Christina Rossetti was "en route" to Italy ("Italy, Io Ti Saluto") when she imagined herself as "an 'immurata' sister" helplessly complaining that

> Men work and think, but women feel,
>   And so (for I'm a woman, I)
>   And so I should be glad to die,
> And cease from impotence of zeal. . . . (380)

For, as Barrett Browning (and Charlotte Brontë) also knew, that "Italian" speech of feeling was only "half familiar" and almost wholly inaccessible to Englishwomen.

What made the inaccessibility of such speech especially poignant for poets like Rossetti and Barrett Browning, besides Italy's role as a feeding, feeling mother-sister, was "her" special status as the home, even the womb, of European art; this mother-sister became a muse whose shapes and sounds seemed to constitute a kind of primal aesthetic language from which no writer should allow herself to be separated. In Florence, Barrett Browning imagines that she is not only in a city that makes art, she is in a city that *is* art, so much so that, as in some Edenic dream, the solid real and the artful unreal merge uncannily: "The river rushes through the midst of its palaces like a crystal arrow, and it is hard to tell . . . whether those churches . . . and people walking, in the water or out of the water, are the real . . . people, and churches" (*Letters* 1: 332). That the art of Florence is almost entirely male—Michelangelo's monuments of unaging intellect, Ghiberti's doors—appears oddly irrelevant, for living in Florence Barrett Browning begins to believe, if only briefly, that she might live in, even inherit, this art; insofar as art is Italy's and Italy might be her lost and reclaimed self, art itself might at last be her own.

In allowing herself such a dream, the author of *Aurora Leigh* was tacitly acknowledging the influence of a foremother she greatly admired, Mme de Staël, whose *Corinne ou l'Italie* was "an immortal book" that, said Barrett Browning, "deserves to be read three score and ten times—that is, once every year in the age of man" (*Elizabeth Barrett* 176). For not only is *Corinne,* in the words of Ellen Moers, "a guidebook to Italy," it is specifically a guidebook to an Italy that is the nurturing *matria* of a "woman of genius," the enchanting *improvisatrice* Corinne, whose brilliant career provided a paradigm of female artistry for countless nineteenth-century literary women on both sides of the Atlantic.[9] Like Aurora Leigh, Staël's poetic heroine is the daughter of an Italian mother and an English father, and, like Barrett Browning herself, she transforms the Italy dominated by relics of such great men as Michelangelo and Ghiberti into a land of free women, a female aesthetic utopia. Corinne herself, writes Staël, is "l'image de notre belle Italie" (bk. 2, ch. 2., p. 50). Triumphing as she improvises on the theme of Italy's glory, dances a dramatic tarantella, and translates *Romeo and Juliet* into "sa langue maternelle" (bk. 7, ch.

2, p. 183), Corinne becomes not only a symbol of redemptive Italy but also a redemptive emblem of the power of symbolization itself, for, observes Staël, "tout étoit langage pour elle" (bk. 6, ch. 1, p. 141). No wonder, then, that Barrett Browning, *Corinne*'s admirer, seems secretly to imagine an Italian heaven of invention whose speech constitutes a different, mystically potent language, a mother tongue: as if to balance Rossetti's remark that "our [English] tongue grew sweeter in [Enrica's] mouth," she writes wistfully of the way in which "the Tuscan musical / Vowels . . . round themselves as if they planned / Eternities of separate sweetness" (*Casa Guidi Windows* 1.1188–90).

Such a sense that even Italian speech encompasses "eternities of . . . sweetness" inevitably translates itself into a larger vision of Italy as earthly paradise, a vision that brings us back to the "green golden strand" of Rossetti's mother country and the vehement *"Italy"* of Dickinson's "Our lives are Swiss—." In this fourth incarnation, however, Italy is not just a nurturing mother country, she is a utopian motherland whose glamour transforms all who cross her borders, empowering women, ennobling men, and—most significantly—annihilating national and sexual differences. Describing the hopeful celebration of Florentine freedom that miraculously took place on the Brownings' first wedding anniversary in 1847, Barrett Browning writes about a jubilant parade: "class after class" took part, and "Then too, came the foreigners, there was a place for them" (*CGW* 66). She notes that "the people were *embracing* for joy" (*CGW* 66) and expressing "the sort of gladness in which women may mingle and be glad too" (*CGW* 67). In this setting, both sexes and all nationalities become part of the newer, higher nationality of Florence, so that expatriation turns, magically, into expatriotism. Less mystically and more amusingly, Virginia Woolf makes a similar point about Italy as utopia in *Flush*, her biography of the Brownings' dog. Arriving in Pisa, this pedigreed spaniel discovers that "though dogs abounded, there were no ranks; all—could it be possible?—were mongrels." At last inhabiting a classless society, he becomes "daily more and more democratic. . . . All dogs were his brothers. He had no need of a chain in this new world" (75, 78–79).

Finally, however, as Rossetti's "Mother Country," "Enrica," and "An 'Immurata' Sister" suggest, women writers from Barrett Browning to Dickinson are forced to admit that the nurturing, utopian, artful, feelingful, female land of Italy is not their own. Bred in what Barrett Browning and, after her, Rossetti call "the rigid North," such writers are forever spiritually if not physically excluded from "the sweet South," forever alienated from Italy's utopian redemption, if only by symbolic windows like those of Casa Guidi, which mark Barrett Browning's estrangement from Florence's moment of regeneration even while they allow the poet to view the spectacle of that rebirth.[10] As the poets make this admission, maternal Italy, guarded by the intervention of the "solemn Alps" and "the bitter sea," lapses back into the negated and negating woman whose image opens both *Poems before Congress* and *Aurora Leigh*. Dead, she is denied and denying: as Aurora leaves for England, her mother country seems "Like one in anger drawing back her skirts / Which suppliants catch at" (1.234–35), and Christina Rossetti, exclaiming "Farewell, land of love,

Italy, / Sister-land of Paradise," summarizes the mingled regret and reproach with which these English daughters respond to the drastic loss such denial enforces:

> Wherefore art thou strange, and not my mother?
> Thou hast stolen my heart and broken it:
> Would that I might call thy sons 'My brother,'
>   Call thy daughters 'Sister sweet':
> Lying in thy lap, not in another,
>   Dying at thy feet.   ("En Route," *Works* 377)

For Rossetti, the despair these lines express becomes a characteristic gesture of resignation; the mother country is not to be found, not in this world at any rate, and so she immures herself in the convent of her soul, for "Why should I seek and never find / That something which I have not had?" (380). For Barrett Browning, however, the struggle to revive and re-approach, rather than reproach, the lost mother country of Italy becomes the narrative project to which she devotes her two major long poems, *Casa Guidi Windows* (1851) and *Aurora Leigh*.

Though explicitly (and successfully) a political poem that meditates on two carefully defined historical occasions, *Casa Guidi Windows* is also a preliminary working through of important psychological materials that had long haunted Barrett Browning; as such, it is a crucial preface to the poet's more frankly confessional *Aurora Leigh*. To be specific: even while Barrett Browning comments in part 1 on the exuberant 1847 demonstration with which the Italian and "foreign" citizens of Florence thanked Duke Leopold II for granting them the right to form a militia, and even while she mourns in part 2 the temporary failure of the risorgimento when in 1849 the Austrians defeated the Italians at Novara, she tells a more covert story—the story of Italy's and her own seduction and betrayal by the brutality, indifference, and greed of patriarchal history. From this betrayal, this fall into the power of powers not her own, Italy/Barrett Browning must regenerate herself, and she can only do this, the poet's metaphors imply, through a strategic deployment of female, especially maternal, energies. By delivering her children both to death (as soldiers) and life (as heirs), she can deliver herself into the community of nations where she belongs.

For Barrett Browning this plot had distinctively personal overtones. "After what broke [her] heart at Torquay"—the drowning of her beloved alter ego, "Bro"—she herself, as she later told her friend Mrs. Martin, had lived for years "on the outside of my own life . . . as completely dead to hope . . . as if I had my face against a grave . . ." (*Letters* 1: 288). Immuring herself in her room at 50 Wimpole Street, she had entrusted her future entirely to the will and whim of her notoriously tyrannical father, so much so that, as she also told Mrs. Martin, employing a strikingly political metaphor, "God knows . . . how utterly I had abdicated myself. . . . Even my poetry . . . was a thing on the outside of me . . . [a] desolate state it was, which I look back now to [as] one would look to one's graveclothes, if one had been clothed in them by mistake during a trance" (*Letters* 1: 288). Clearly, in some sense, the drowning of the younger brother who was Barrett Browning's only real reader in the family and for whose death she blamed herself, caused a self-alienation so deep that, like Emily Brontë's Catherine Earnshaw Linton mourning the absence of *her* male alter ego, Heathcliff, she felt the world turn to "a mighty stranger." Invalid and isolated, she herself became a figure like Italy in part 1 of *Casa Guidi Windows,* who

> Long trammeled with the purple of her youth
> Against her age's ripe activity,
> Sits still upon her tombs, without death's ruth,
> But also without life's brave energy.   (171–74)

Yet just as the Italy of *Casa Guidi Windows,* part 1, trusts "fathers" like Leopold II and Pio Nono to deliver "her" from her living death, Barrett Browning expected her father to care enough to cure her illness; and just as Italy is duped by "her" faith in these patriarchs, Barrett Browning was deceived by her faith in her father, who refused to send her south (significantly, to Italy) for her health, so that she was "wounded to the bottom of my heart—cast off when I was ready to cling to him" (*Letters* 1: 291). But the plot thickens as the poet quickens, for, again, just as in Barrett Browning's own life a risorgimento came both from another younger brother figure—Robert Browning—and from the female deliverance of motherhood, so, in *Casa Guidi Windows,* promises of resurrection are offered wounded Italy both by the hope of a sturdy male leader who will "teach, lead, strike fire into the masses" and by the promise of "young children lifted high on parent souls," children whose innocence, fostered by maternal grace, may unfold "mighty meanings" (2.769, 741).

Given the personal politics embedded in this story, it is no wonder that Barrett Browning prefaces the first edition of *Casa Guidi Windows* with an "advertisement" in which she takes especially intense "shame upon herself that she believed, like a woman, some royal oaths"; that in part 2 she reproaches herself for her "woman's fault / That ever [she] believed [Duke Leopold] was true" (64–65); and that she also asks "what woman or child will count [Pio Nono] true?" (523). It is no wonder, either, that, in aligning herself with the revolutionary cause of Italy, Barrett Browning aligns herself against the strictures and structures of her fatherland, England, whose "close, stifling, corrupt system," like her imprisoning room in Wimpole Street, "gives no air nor scope for healthy . . . organization" (*Letters* 2: 190), a country for which "nothing will do . . . but a good revolution" (*Letters* 2: 193). As magisterial and patriarchal as Edward Moulton Barrett, England has "No help for women, sobbing out of sight / Because men made the laws" and "no tender utterance . . . For poor Italia, baffled by mischance" (*CGW* 2.638–39, 649–51). What is more remarkable in *Casa Guidi Windows,* however, and what more directly foreshadows the Italian dream of *Aurora Leigh* is the way in which Barrett Browning, dreaming behind the mediation of her windows, imagines Italy ultimately redeemed by the voices and visions of mothers and children: part 1 begins, after all, with "a little child . . . who not long had been / By mother's finger steadied on his feet"

(11–12), singing *"O bella libertà, O bella,"* and part 2 ends with the poet's "own young Florentine, not two years old," her "blue-eyed prophet," transforming society with a clear, unmediated gaze not unlike Wordsworth's "eye among the blind." In between these epiphanies, Miriam the prophetess appears, clashing her "cymbals to surprise / The sun" (1.314–16), and Garibaldi's wife outfaces "the whistling shot and hissing waves, / Until she [feels] her little babe unborn / Recoil within her" (2.679–83).

But what is finally perhaps most remarkable and, as Julia Markus points out, "most daring" about *Casa Guidi Windows* is the way in which, as Barrett Browning meditates on the plight of wounded "Italia," the poet finally presents herself, against the weight of all the literary history she dutifully recounts throughout the work, as "the singer of the new day":

> And I, a singer also, from my youth,
> Prefer to sing with those who are awake,
>   With birds, with babes, with men who will not fear
> The baptism of the holy morning dew. . .
>   .   .   .   .
> Than join those old thin voices with my new. . . .   (1.155–62)

Crossing the Anglo-Italian frontier represented by Casa Guidi windows, Barrett Browning gains her strongest voice in Italy and regains, as we shall see, a vision of her strengthened self from and as Italy, for the female artistic triumph that this passage describes points directly to the triumphant risorgimento of the woman poet that *Aurora Leigh* enacts.

As its title indicates, *Aurora Leigh* is a mythic narrative about "the baptism of the holy morning dew" that Barrett Browning proposed to sing in *Casa Guidi Windows*. But before she and her heroine can achieve such a sacrament or become true singers of "the new day" and of the renewed *matria/matrice* that day implies, both must work through precisely the self-division that left "Italia" (in *Casa Guidi Windows*) and Barrett Browning (in Wimpole Street) living "on the outside" of their own lives. Significantly, therefore, the tale of the poet-heroine's risorgimento, which parallels the plot of the poet-author's own insurrection-resurrection, begins with a fragmentation of the self that is both symbolized and precipitated by a shattering of the nuclear family, a shattering that leads to a devastating analysis of that structure. Just as significantly, the story ends with a reconstitution of both self and family that provides a visionary new synthesis of the relationships among men, women, and children.

As if to emphasize the larger political issue involved in these emotional dissolutions and resolutions, the heroine's self and family are defined by two *paysages moralisés*, her mother country of Italy and her fatherland of England, between which (although at one point Aurora claims that "a poet's heart / Can swell to a pair of nationalities, / However ill-lodged in a woman's breast" [6.50–52]) she must ultimately choose.

Both in its theatrical, sometimes hectically melodramatic, plot, then, and in its intensely symbolic settings, *Aurora Leigh* continually reminds us that it is not only a versified *Künstlerroman* which famously aims to specify the interaction between an artist and the particular "full-veined, heaving, double-breasted Age" (5.217) that created her, it is also an "unscrupulously epic" (5.215) allegory of a woman artist's journey from disease toward what Sylvia Plath once called "a country far away as health" ("Tulips," *Ariel* 12).[11]

Not surprisingly, given these geographical and dramatic imperatives, *Aurora Leigh* begins and ends in Italy, the lost redemptive land that must be redeemed in order for both poet-heroine and poet-author to achieve full selfhood. Here, in book 1, Aurora encounters and is symbolically rejected by her dead mother, "a Florentine / Whose rare blue eyes were shut from seeing me / When scarcely I was four years old" (29–31), and here, even as she comes to terms with "a mother-want about the world" (40), her father dies, leaving her suddenly awake "To full life and life's needs" (208–10). While the mother seems irremediably gone, however, the father, "an austere Englishman" (65), is quickly replaced by "A stranger with authority" (224) who tears the child so abruptly from the land which has come to represent her mother that, watching "my Italy, / Drawn backward from the shuddering steamer-deck, / Like one in anger drawing back her skirts" (232–34), she is uncertain whether the mother country has been rejected ("drawn back") or is rejecting ("drawing back").

This violent, neo-Wordsworthian fall into division from the mother and into "my father's England," home of alien language and orphanhood, is followed by a more subtle but equally violent fall into gender. Arriving in patriarchal England at the crucial age of thirteen, Aurora discovers that she is a *girl*, destined to be brought up in "A sort of cage-bird life" (1.305) by a new and different "mother"—her "father's sister," who is her "mother's hater" (1.359–60), for "Italy / Is one thing, England one" (1.626–27); inexorably parted, the two nations are irrevocable emblems of separation. Hence, as many feminist critics have pointed out, the girl is coerced into (at least on the surface) accepting a typical Victorian education in "femininity," reading "a score of books on womanhood / To prove, if women do not think at all, / They may teach thinking" (1.427–29), learning "cross-stitch," and so forth. That she has "relations in the Unseen" and in Nature, which romantically persist and from which she draws "elemental nutriment and heat . . . as a babe sucks surely in the dark" (1.473–75), and that she darkly remembers "My multitudinous mountains, sitting in / The magic circle, with the mutual touch / Electric . . . waiting for / Communion and commission" (1.622–26)—another striking image of the mother's nurturing breasts—are the only signs that somewhere in the shadows of her own psyche her mother country endures, despite the pseudo-oedipal wrenching she has undergone.

As Aurora grows into the fragmentation that seems to be (English) woman's lot, things go from bad to worse. Exiled from the undifferentiated unity of her mother country, the girl discovers that her parents have undergone an even more complicated set of metamorphoses than she at first realized, for not only has her true dead southern mother been replaced by a false and rigid northern stepmother—her "father's sister"—but her true dead father, after being supplanted by "a stranger with authority," has been replaced by a false and rigid northern stepfather, her cousin Romney Leigh, who, upon her father's death, has become the putative head of the family. To be sure, as Aurora's cousin, Romney has the potential for becoming a nurturing peer, an empowering "Bro" rather than a debilitating patriarch. But certainly, when the narrative begins, he is a symbolic father whose self-satisfied right and reason represent the masculine "head" that inexorably strives to humble the feminine "heart."

"I am not very fond of praising men by calling them *manly;* I hate and detest a masculine man," Barrett Browning told one correspondent (*Letters* 1: 134), and clearly by "masculine" she did not mean "virile" but "authoritarian." Yet such (implicitly patriarchal) authoritarianism is exactly what characterizes Romney Leigh at the cousins' first meeting, for his, says Aurora, was "The stranger's touch that took my father's place / Yet dared seem soft" (1.545–46), and she adds "A godlike nature his" (1.553). That Aurora has evidently been destined to marry this man makes the point even more clearly. Drawn away from the natural lore and lure of the mother, she has been surrendered to what Lacan calls the law of the father, inscribed into a patrilineal kinship system where she is to be doubly named by the father, both as daughter-Leigh and as wife-Leigh, just as Elizabeth herself was originally named Elizabeth Barrett Barrett. That Romney refuses to read her poetry, claiming that her book has "witchcraft in it" (2.77), clarifies the point still further. Her work is either "mere" or "magical" "woman's work" (2.234) because she exists "as the complement / Of his sex merely" (2.435–36), an (albeit precious) object of exchange in a network of marital transactions that must by definition deprive her not only of her autonomy but, more importantly, of her desire.

Nevertheless, Aurora insists on continuing to transcribe the texts of her desire, poems whose energy is significantly associated with her inner life, her "relations in the Unseen," and her mother country. At the same time, because she has been exiled in her fatherland, she must inevitably write these works in her father tongue. Inevitably too, therefore, because she is struggling to find a place in traditions created by that masculine (and masculinist) language, she must study her father's books. Creeping through the patriarchal attic "Like some small nimble mouse between the ribs / Of a mastodon" (1.838–39), she finds a room "Piled high with cases in my father's name" (1.835) and "nibbles" fiercely but randomly at what amounts to a paradigmatic library of Western culture. Most inevitably, however, this furtive self-education, which both parallels and subverts her aunt's effort to educate her in "femininity," leads to further self-division. She can and does reject both Romney's offer of marriage and the financial legacy he tries with magisterial generosity to bestow on her, but once she has internalized—nibbled, devoured—the texts that incarnate patriarchal history, she is helplessly implicated in that history, so that even her "own" poetry is tainted, fragmented, impure.

How, then, is Aurora to rectify and clarify both her art and her self? Barrett Browning's "unscrupulous" epic seeks to resolve this crucial issue, and, perhaps paradoxically, the author begins her curative task by examining the ways in which her other major characters are just as fragmented and self-alienated as her heroine. To start, for instance, she shows that, despite (or perhaps because of) his superegoistic calm, Romney too is self-divided. This "head of the family," she quickly suggests, is no more than a "head," abstractly and, as his abortive wedding to Marian Erle will prove, ineffectually espoused to "social theory" (2.410). In fact, he is not just a false father because he has replaced Aurora's "true" father, he is a false father because, as Barrett Browning decided after her long imprisonment in Wimpole Street, all fathers are in some sense false. Indeed, the very idea of fatherhood, with its implications of social hierarchy and psychic fragmentation ("man with the head, woman with the heart" [Tennyson, *The Princess* 5.439]), is dangerously divisive, not only for women but for men. As a brother like her own "Bro," Romney might be able to "read" (and thus symbolically unite with) the texts of female desire that transcribe Aurora's otherness, but as a father he is irremediably blind to them. As a brother, moreover, he might more literally unite himself to the social as well as sexual others from whom his birth and breeding separate him, but as a father or "head," he is, again, hopelessly estranged from most members of the "body" politic.

That Romney craves a union with both social and sexual others is, however, a sign that, like Aurora, he is half consciously struggling toward a psychic reunification which will constitute as much of a risorgimento for him as it will for her. His ill-fated and "mis-conceived" proposal to Aurora suggests his intuition of his own need, even while the fact that she "translates" him "ill" emphasizes the impossibility of communion or communication between them. In addition, his eagerness to go "hand in hand" with her among "the arena-heaps / Of headless bodies" (2.380–81) till, through her "touch," the "formless, nameless trunk of every man / Shall seem to wear a head with hair you know, / And every woman catch your mother's face" (2.388–90) implies that, at least metaphorically, he understands the self-division that afflicts both him and his cousin, even while Aurora's reply that since her mother's death she has not seen "So much love . . . / As answers even to make a marriage with / In this cold land of England" (2.398–400) once again outlines the geography of "mother-want" in which both characters are situated. Similarly, his subsequent plan to "take [a] wife / Directly from the people" (4.368–69) reveals once more his yearning to heal in his own person the wounds of the body politic, even while Aurora's recognition that his scheme is both artificial and divisive, "built up as walls are, brick by brick" (4.353), predicts the project's failure. For Romney, who feels himself "fallen on days" when marriages can be likened to "galley-cou-plings" (4.334), redemption must come not from the outward ceremony of marriage but from an inward metamorphosis that will transform him from (false) father to (true) brother, from (false) "god" to (true) groom.

Despite its misguided formulation, however, Romney's impulse to wed Marian Erle does begin the crucial process of metamorphosis, for this "daughter of the people" (3.806), an "Erle" elf of nature rather than an "earl" of patriarchy, has a history that parallels his and Aurora's history of fragmentation at the same time that she is an essential part of the reunified family/being he and Aurora must become.[12] Ignored and emotionally abandoned by a drunken father who beat her and a bruised mother who tried to prostitute her to a local squire, this "outcast child . . . Learnt early to cry low, and walk alone" (3.874–77). Her proletarian education in alienation offers a darkly parodic version of Aurora's bourgeois education in femininity. Reading the "wicked book" of patriarchal reality (3.952) with the same fervor that inspired Aurora's studies of her father's patriarchal texts, Marian imagines a "skyey father and mother both in one" (3.899) just as Aurora imagines inscribing her desire for her motherland in her father's tongue. Finally, too, the shriek of pain Marian utters when her mother tries to sell her to the squire—"God, free me from my mother . . . / These mothers are too dreadful" (3.1063–64)— echoes and amplifies Aurora's impassioned protest against the "Keeper's voice" (2.561) of the stepmother-aunt, who tells her that she has been "promised" to her cousin Romney: "I must help myself / And am alone from henceforth" (2.807–08). Repudiating the false mothers of patriarchal England, both these literally or figuratively orphaned daughters cry out, each in her own way, the intensity of the "mother-want" that will eventually unite them, along with Romney and with Marian's child, in the motherland of Italy, where each will become a nurturing mother country to the other.

When Marian and Aurora first meet, however, both are stranded in the alienating cityscape of nineteenth-century London, where each lives in an attic that seems to symbolize her isolation from world and self alike. Though Aurora has ostensibly become a successful poet, her ambition continually reminds her of her failure, since it constantly confronts her with fragmented verses whose "heart" is "Just an embryo's heart / Which never yet had beat" (3.247–48), while Marian, though her "heart . . . swelled so big / It seemed to fill her body" (3.1083–85), lives up a "long, steep, narrow stair, 'twixt broken rail / And mildewed wall" (3.791–92). Parts of a scattered self—the one heartless, the other too great-hearted—this pair of doubles must be unified like the distant and dissonant city-states of Italy, and ultimately, of course, the two are brought together by Romney's various though similar desires for them. To begin with, however, they are united by the visits of yet another potential wife of Romney's—Lady Waldemar—to their parallel attics.

Voluptuous and vicious, the figure of Lady Waldemar offers a further comment on nineteenth-century ideals of "femininity." In fact, as we shall see, she is the (false) wife/mother whose love the (false) father must reject if he is to convert himself into a (true) brother. At the same time, though, her beckoning sexuality both initiates and instigates the "plot" proper of *Aurora Leigh,* emblematizing a fall into heterosexual desire with which Aurora and Marian must variously struggle before they can become whole. Almost at once, Aurora perceives this fashionable aristocrat as a male-created, socially defined "lady"—"brilliant stuff, / And out of nature" (3.357–58)—a perception Lady Waldemar's name reinforces with its reminiscences of generations of Danish kings. But even while Aurora defines her as "out of nature" in the sense that she is an antinatural being, a cultural artifact, this "fair fine" lady defines herself as being "out of nature" in the sense that she is *from* nature, nature's emissary. For, confessing that she has "caught" love "in the vulgar way" (3.466),

Lady Waldemar instructs the poet-heroine that "you eat of love, / And do as vile a thing as if you ate / Of garlic" (3.450–52) since "love's coarse, nature's coarse" (3.455). Two books later, when she reappears at a party Aurora attends, the very image of Lady Waldemar's body reiterates her "natural" sexuality. Gorgeously seductive, "the woman looked immortal" (5.618), her bare breasts splitting her "amaranth velvet-bodice down / To the waist, or nearly, with the audacious press / Of full-breathed beauty" (5.622–24).

As emblems of nurturing maternity, breasts have obsessed both author and heroine throughout *Aurora Leigh,* but this is the first time their erotic potential is (quite literally) revealed, and tellingly the revelation is associated with Aurora's growing sense of artistic and sexual isolation: "Must I work in vain, / Without the approbation of a man?" (5.62–63); with her confession of "hunger . . . for man's love" (5.498); and, most strikingly, with her feeling that her "loose long hair [has begun] to burn and creep, / Alive to the very ends, about my knees" (5.1126–27). Furthermore, Lady Waldemar's eroticism is associated with—indeed, causes—Marian's betrayal into sexuality, a betrayal that leads to both a "murder" and a rebirth, while Aurora's mingled fear of and fascination with Lady Waldemar's erotic presence finally drive the poet back to her motherland of Italy, where she is ultimately to be reunited with both Marian and Romney. In fact, what have often been seen as the awkward or melodramatic turns of plot through which Barrett Browning brings these three characters back together in a sort of Florentine paradise are really important dramatic strategies by which the author herself was trying to work out (and out of) the "problem" of female sexuality by first confronting the engendered world as it is and then reengendering and reconstituting it as it should be.

Trusting the duplicitous Lady Waldemar, who "wrapped" the girl in her arms and, ironically enough, let her "dream a moment how it feels / To have a real mother" (6.1001–03), Marian is treacherously brought to France by the servant of this false "mother," placed in a brothel where she is drugged and raped, and thereby sold into sexual slavery—a deed that, as Marian herself notes, was "only what my mother would have done" (7.8–9). At the same time, Aurora—missing her "woodland sister, sweet maid Marian" (5.109), and convinced that Romney is about to marry the "Lamia-woman," Lady Waldemar (7.152)—finally decides to return to the Italy that she has long heard "crying through my life, / [with the] piercing silence of ecstatic graves" (5.1193–94). Not coincidentally, she plans to finance her trip by selling the "residue / Of my father's books" (5.1217–18), a crucial first step in what is to be a definitive renunciation of the power of the fatherland. Her journey to the mother country, however, is impelled as much by desire as by denial, for, in the passage I have used as an epigraph to this essay, she "burns" toward her "own hills" and imagines that they desirously reciprocate her "yearning . . . As sleeping mothers feel the sucking babe / And smile" (5.1268–71). Thus, when en route she encounters the lost Marian in a Paris flower market, she begins the process of reunification that will regenerate both these wounded daughters. For the "fallen" Marian, whose face haunts Aurora like the face of a "dead woman," has become a mother whose assertion of what J. J. Bachofen was later in the century to call "mother right"—"I claim my mother-dues / By law"—proposes an empowering alternative to "the law which now is paramount," the "common" patriarchal "law, by which the poor and weak / Are trodden underfoot by vicious men, /And loathed for ever after by the good" (6.665–69). Becoming such a powerful figure, moreover, she has become a creative authority whose maternal eroticism speeds the two women toward the unfallen garden of female sexuality that they will plant in the richly flowering earth of Florence. There Marian's "unfathered" child will "not miss a . . . father," since he will have "two mothers" (7.124), there Aurora will set Marian like a "saint" and "burn the lights of love" before her pure maternity (7.128), and there, in a revision of her own eroticism, Aurora will exorcise the haunting vision of what she now comes to see as Lady Waldemar's distorted (Lamia-like) sexuality.

For when she returns to her motherland with Marian as her sister/self, Aurora returns transformed. No longer merely an aching outcast daughter crying her inchoate "mother-want," she has become herself, symbolically at least, a mother, since she is one of the "two mothers" of Marian's child. In addition, transformed into a hierophant of "sweet holy Marian" (6.782), she has learned to devote herself to the specifically female theology of the Madonna, the Queen of Heaven whom the Florentine women worship and whose rituals facilitate Aurora's increasing self-knowledge. Finally, she has become a poet, an artist-heroine who can not only weep but word her desire, in a language that through her interaction with Marian she has begun to make into a mother tongue. In fact, as she learns some weeks after her arrival in Florence, people in England have finally begun to "read" her. Her new book, writes her painter friend Vincent Carrington, "Is eloquent as if you were not dumb" (7.553), and his fiancée, who has Aurora's verses "by heart" more than she has her lover's words (7.603), has even insisted on having a portrait painted with "Your last book folded in her dimpled hands / Instead of my brown palette as I wished" (7.607–08).

That Marian's child is "unfathered" contributes in yet another way to the regenerative maternity both women now experience, for, after all, the baby is only figuratively unfathered; literally, he was fathered by some nameless customer in a brothel. To call him "unfathered," therefore, is to stress the likeness of his mother, Marian, not only to the fallen woman Mary Magdalen but also to the blessed Virgin Mary, whose immaculate conception was the sign of a divine annunciation. That Barrett Browning surrounds Marian's maternity with the rhetoric of Mariolatry implies the theological force she wants to impute to this "maiden" mother's female energy. As opposed to the often sentimentally redemptive power ascribed to such Victorian "mothers' boys" as Gaetano (in Browning's *The Ring and the Book*), Leonard (in Mrs. Gaskell's *Ruth*), or Paul Dombey (in Dickens' *Dombey and Son*), Marian's son has an austerely religious significance. Nameless but beautiful, he is hardly ever characterized as a real child might be. Rather, when Marian explains that, in her despair after her rape, "I lived for him, and so he lives, / And so I know, by this time, God lives too" (7.112–13), the ambiguity of her language—does she believe that he is the "God" who "lives" or does his survival mean that "God lives"?— argues that he is in some sense a divine child, a baby god whose sacred birth attests to the divinity of his mother. Thus, even while she revises the story of the annunciation to question the brutality of a male God who uses women merely as vessels for his own ends, Barrett Browning suggests that the female creativity "holy" Marian and reverent Aurora share can transform the most heinous act of male sexual brutality, a rape, into a redemption. At the same time, by demonstrating the self-sufficient strength of Marian and Aurora's mutual maternity, she interrogates the idea that there is anything more than a momentary biological need for fathers or fatherhood.

It is noteworthy, then, that when she returns to Italy Aurora keeps reminding herself that she has returned to the land where her father is buried, the land of her mother's birth and her father's tomb, her "father's house / Without his presence." Though both her parents are buried near Florence, it is, curiously enough, evidence of only her father's disappearance that Aurora seeks and finds; when she revisits "the little mountain-house" where she had lived with him, she discovers that it has been effaced by female fertility symbols—"lingots of ripe Indian corn / In tessellated order and device / Of golden patterns" (7.1124–26)—so that "not a stone of wall" can be seen, and a black-eyed Tuscan girl sits plaiting straws in the doorway, as if forbidding entrance. While Aurora's mother lives on in the Italian motherland, her father is as irretrievably dead as Marian's child's father is nonexistent.

But how are both Aurora and Barrett Browning to deal with the wished-for but unnerving fate of the dead father? Freud famously argued that anxiety about the murder of this mythic figure ultimately constituted a social order in which "his" absent will was internalized as the superego that creates the law (see *Totem,* esp. 915–19). Barrett Browning, however, as if responding in advance to Freud's hypothesis, implicitly suggests that man as father must be exorcised rather than internalized and that, in a risorgimento of matriarchal law, he must be replaced with man as brother or man as son. For, unlike such a precursor as Christine de Pizan (in *City of Ladies*) or such a descendant as Charlotte Perkins Gilman (in *Herland*), Aurora does not envision an all-female paradise. Rather, she longs for a mother country or "sisterland to Paradise" in which women *and* men can live together free of the rigid interventions and interdictions of the father.

Thus, even when she and Marian and Marian's child have been securely established in "a house at Florence on the hill / Of Bellosguardo" (7.515–16), from which, like goddesses surveying past and future, they can see sunrise and sunset, "morn and eve . . . magnified before us" (7.525–26)—a scene that recalls Marian's "skyey father and mother both in one"—Aurora yearns obsessively for Romney. "Like a tune that runs / I' the head" (7.960–61), the erotic longing for her cousin that was first signaled by the appearance of Lady Waldemar has made her, she admits at last, just what Lady Waldemar confessed herself—a "slave to nature" (7.967). In addition, that longing reveals Aurora's radical sense of incompleteness, a feeling of self-division which suggests that, for Barrett Browning as for her heroine, a *matria* without men might become madly and maddeningly maenadic. As she sinks into a sort of sexual fever, Aurora notes that even her beloved Florence "seems to seethe / In this Medæan boil-pot of the sun" (7.901–02) and ruefully confesses that, in the absence of the consort whom she desires because his presence would complete the new configuration of humanity toward which she aspires, even her old "Tuscan pleasures" seem "worn and spoiled" (7.1041).

In endowing a woman named *Aurora Leigh* with such erotic feeling for a cousin whom she wishes to remake in the image of a brother, however, Barrett Browning must at least half consciously have understood that her wish to provide her protagonist with a fraternally understanding and erotically egalitarian lover might oblige her to risk retracing the outlines of the nineteenth century's most notorious brother-sister incest plot: Byron's affair with his half-sister, *Augusta Leigh*. Unlike such "realistically" depicted sister-brother pairs as Tom and Maggie Tulliver in *The Mill on the Floss,* but like Romney and Aurora, Byron and Augusta rarely met until they were young adults, when both couples discovered and resisted similar mutual attractions. To be sure, the socially illicit Byronic duo made a far weaker effort at resistance than Barrett Browning's socially "legitimate" pair of cousins. Nevertheless, what Leslie Marchand says of Byron and Augusta is equally true of Romney and Aurora: "in their formative years they had escaped the rough familiarity of the brother-sister relationship," so that "consanguinity," with all the equality it might imply for peers of the same generation, was "balanced by the charm of strangeness" (1: 396). But Barrett Browning, who as a girl had dreamed of dressing in boy's clothes and running away to be Lord Byron's page, grew up to become, if not as censorious as her friend Carlyle was toward the hero of Missolonghi, at least ambivalent toward him. Even while insisting that her "tendency" was "not to cast off my old loves," she wrote that Byron's poems "discovered not a heart, but the wound of a heart; not humanity, but disease" (for EBB's ambivalent feelings toward Byron, see Taplin 15, 103). In addition, she was close to both the "wronged" Lady Byron's friend Anna Jameson and to Harriet Beecher Stowe, author of *Lady Byron Vindicated,* both of whom would have reminded her of the masculine exploitativeness involved in Byron's sexual exploits.

Simultaneously inspired and exasperated by the Byron story, therefore, Barrett Browning had to rewrite it to gain strength from it. Thus the seductive and antipoetic Augusta Leigh becomes the pure poet Aurora Leigh, and the morally corrupt but sexually devastating and romantically self-dramatizing Byron becomes the morally incorruptible but physically devastated and romantically diffident Romney. Furthermore, the sexual inequities implied by Byron's sordid secret affairs and by Romney's one-time authority as "head" of the Leigh family are eradicated both by Aurora's purity and by her recently achieved matriarchal strength. Newly defined "brother" and "sister" can unite, and even unite erotically, because the Byron episode has been reenacted on a "higher" plane, purged of social disorder and sexual disease.

The humbled Romney's arrival in Florence does, then, complete both the reconfiguration of the family and the regeneration of the motherland that poet-author and poet-heroine have undertaken. Blinded in a fire that recalls yet another famous nineteenth-century plot—the denouement of *Jane Eyre*—this former patriarch seems to have endured the same punishment that Brontë's Bertha dealt Rochester, although in personality Romney is closer to Jane Eyre's austere cousin St. John Rivers than to that heroine's extravagant "master." Significantly, however, Barrett Browning—

who seems vigorously to have repressed her memory of the *Jane Eyre* episode, no doubt so she could more freely revise it[13]—swerved from Brontë in having Romney's injury inflicted not by a mad wife but by a bad father: William Erle, the tramp and poacher who began his career of destructiveness by bruising and abusing his daughter, Marian. Women do not need to destroy the fatherland, Barrett Browning implies by this revision, because it will self-destruct. Again, Barrett Browning swerves from Brontë in allowing her disinherited patriarch to rescue one item from the house of his fathers—a portrait of the lady from whom Aurora inherited her mouth and chin. A woman, she implies by this revision, may be an inheritor. In the end, therefore, as Romney describes "the great charred circle" where his ancestral mansion once stood with its "one stone stair, symbolic of my life, / Ascending, winding, leading up to nought" (8.1034–35), his saving of the picture suggests also that the power of the Leighs has not been destroyed but instead transferred to "a fairy bride from Italy" (9.766), who has now become the true heir and "head" of the family.

That Aurora has successfully become a "head" of the family, the figure both Romney's father, *Vane* Leigh, and Romney himself only vainly strove to be, is made clearest by her blinded cousin's revelation that he has at last really read and recognized her work. Seeing through and because of his blindness, like wounded father figures from Oedipus and Gloucester to Rochester, Romney receives and perceives Aurora's prophetic message—"in this last book, / You showed me something separate from yourself, / Beyond you, and I bore to take it in / And let it draw me" (8.605–08)—and that message, "Presented by your voice and verse the way / To take them clearest" (8.612–13), elevates her to the "dearest light of souls, / Which rul'st for evermore both day and night!" (9.831–32). Finally too, therefore, he has become, as both "Bro" and Robert Browning were for Barrett Browning herself, a "purely" attentive brother-reader who can at last comprehend the revisionary mother tongue in which the woman poet speaks and writes. It is no coincidence, surely, that Barrett Browning has Aurora, who never before associated Romney with the ocean, envision her lost lover as arising from beneath the bitter waters that had engulfed her lost brother and standing before her like a "sea-king" while "the sound of waters" echoes in her ears (8.59–60).[14] Deciphering the texts of Aurora's desire, Romney has accomplished his own transformation into an ex-patriarch who entrusts himself and his sister-bride to the "one central Heart" (9.890) of love that may ultimately unify all humanity by eradicating the hierarchies and inequities of patriarchy. At the same time, emigrating from the rigid north of the Leighs to the warm south ruled by his "Italy of women" (8.358), he has become both an expatriate and an ex-patriot, a dweller in the new *matria* where, in a visionary role reversal, the empowered Aurora will "work for two" and he, her consort and cohort, "for two, shall love" (9.911, 912).

Romney's violent metamorphosis reminds us of Barrett Browning's implicit belief that, as in *Casa Guidi Windows* (where the poet advocates the self-sacrifice of Italian men), only the devastation of the fatherland can enable the risorgimento of the mother country.[15] Both Marian and Aurora too, however, have experienced violent metamorphoses, Marian literally, in the rape she describes as a "murder," and Aurora figuratively, in her passionate struggle to come to terms with the eroticism Lady Waldemar incarnates and with the murderous rage "the Lamia-woman" evokes. Now, though, after all this violence, these characters are brought together in a symbolically reunified family of brother/husband and sister/wife and mother and son. Is Aurora the dawn in which Marian and Romney can be reborn? Is Marian the womb that gives new life to Aurora's and Romney's light? Is Romney the lover who can read their new roles rightly in the "bittersweet" darkness of his visionary blindness? Is Marian's child the redemptive son whose coming signals a new day? There is certainly a temptation to define each member of this prophetic quartet allegorically. But even without stipulating meanings that the epic "unscrupulously" leaves in shadow, it is clear that in its final wholeness this newly holy family integrates what the writer called "Philosophical Thought" with what she called "Poetical Thought" and unifies both with the powerful dyad of mother and child, womb and womb fruit (see "A Thought on Thoughts," *Complete Works* 6: 352–59). Eastering in Italy, moreover, these four redeemed beings begin to make possible the "new day" that their author imagined in, for, and through the country she chose as her *matria*. For among themselves they constitute—to go back to the qualities women writers have sought in Italy—a land that feels, that feeds, that makes art, and that unmakes hierarchies. In mythologizing them as she does, Barrett Browning sets against the exhaustion of belatedness that she thought afflicted contemporary (male) poets "who scorn to touch [our age] with a finger tip" a matriarchal future that she hoped would be sacramentally signaled by "the holy baptism of the morning dew."

In its ecstatic delineation of a female risorgimento, the redemption of Italy that Barrett Browning began to imagine in *Casa Guidi Windows* and fully figured in *Aurora Leigh* was both predictable and precarious. Given the long history of Italy as a literary topos, together with the country's personal association for this woman poet, it is not surprising that that embattled nation would come to incarnate both a mother's desire for *bella libertà* and a daughter's desire to resurrect the lost and wounded mother. Certainly Barrett Browning's American contemporary Margaret Fuller imagined the country in a similar way. "Italy has been glorious to me," she wrote Emerson in 1847, explaining that her expatriate experience had given her "the full benefit of [a] vision" of rebirth "into a state where my young life should not be prematurely taxed." In an 1848 dispatch to the *Tribune*, she added that in Rome "the sun and moon shine as if paradise were already re-established on earth. I go to one of the villas to dream it is so, beneath the pale light of the stars" (quoted in Chevigny 435, 453).

Part of this visionary passion no doubt arose from Fuller's revitalizing and egalitarian romance with Angelo Ossoli, in whom, as one observer put it, she loved "an imagined possibility in the Italian character" much as Aurora, in loving Romney (and Elizabeth Barrett, in loving Robert Browning), loved "an imagined possibility" in the English character.[16] At the same time, however, Fuller's dream of an Italian paradise was not just energized by her hope for a utopian future that the risorgimento might make possible; it was also shaped by her sense that behind Italy's "official" history of popes and patriarchs lay another history, the record of a utopian, and specifically matriarchal, past. Visiting "an Etrurian tomb" in 1847, she noted that "the effect . . . was beyond my expectations; in it were several female figures, very dignified and calm . . . [whose] expression . . . shows that the position of women in these states was noble." Later, passing through Bologna, she remarked that "a woman should love" that city "for there has the spark of intellect in woman been cherished with reverent care," and she made similar points about Milan, as well as, more generally, about the Italian "reverence to the Madonna and innumerable female saints, who, if like St. Teresa, they had intellect as well as piety, became counsellors no less than comforters to the spirit of men" (Chevigny 427–28).[17]

But in particular Fuller's analysis of Etruscan tomb paintings, like the novelist Ouida's apparently casual likening of Florence's past to "gold from the sepulchres of the Aetruscan kings . . . on the breast of some fair living woman," should remind us that as early as the 1840s, in just the years when both Fuller and Barrett Browning were imagining the risorgimento of an Italian *matria,* the Swiss jurist J. J. Bachofen was visiting Etruscan tombs outside Rome, where his discovery of a painting depicting "three mystery eggs" led him to speculate that in "Dionysian religion . . . the supreme law governing the transient world as a *fatum* [is] inherent in feminine matter" and that "the phallic god striving toward the fertilization of matter" stands merely "as a son" to "the maternal womb" (28–29). This speculation, published only two years after *Aurora Leigh* in Bachofen's 1859 *Essay on Mortuary Symbolism,* led in turn to the even more radical hypotheses of his *Mother Right* (1861), in which he presented the first strong argument that matriarchy was the primordial form of social organization.

In visiting, studying, and "reading" Etruscan tombs (as Freud too would do some fifty years and D. H. Lawrence some eighty years later), Bachofen was in one sense "reading" the palimpsest of Italy the way travelers like Shelley, Rogers, and Ruskin did in the archaeological metaphors I quoted earlier. Unlike them, however, and like both Fuller and Barrett Browning, he was "reading" beyond or beneath the patriarchal history Western tourists had always expected to find among the ruins of Rome and the monuments of Florence and interpreting his reading as Freud did his reading of the "Minoan-Mycenaean" age. Thus Bachofen too was preparing at least his female audience to resurrect the old lineaments of a "new, near Day" (*Aurora Leigh* 9.956) just as the newly matriarchal Aurora does at the end of Barrett Browning's epic when, in a revisionary swerve from Shelley and Ruskin, Barrett Browning has her "read" an Italian sunrise for Romney in the language of Apocalypse: "Jasper first . . . And second, sapphire; third, chalcedony; / The rest in order:—last, an amethyst" (9.962–64). Through such revisionary readings, moreover, both writers (along with Fuller) were preparing the way for such a descendant as H. D.: her *Tribute to Freud* ends with a reading of Goethe's "Kennst du das Land," the German poet's vision of Italy as sister land to paradise, a vision that makes the American modernist think of "the *Ca d'Oro,* the Golden House on the Grand Canal in Venice . . . the *domus aurea* of the Laurentian litany" (111). That it was Goethe who sought also to understand the *Ewige Weibliche* and whose injunction to "go down to the Mothers" deeply influenced Bachofen (see *Faust* 2.1.6215–21) would have surely given extra richness to the regenerated Italy of his (and H. D.'s) "Land wo die Zitronen blühn. . . ." Guarded by siren mountains and a bridge of clouds, as Emily Dickinson also believed, the regenerated *matria* of Italy stands "on the other side" of patriarchal history.

Yet both Goethe's poem and H. D.'s *Tribute* end with Mignon's equivocal plea: "o Vater, lass uns ziehn!" For both the female poet and her German precursor, the journey to the magic land can only be accomplished with the guidance of the father. If he permits, the *matria* will be revealed; if not, the Alps and clouds, emblems of despair as well as desire, must, in Dickinson's words, "forever intervene." Similarly, Barrett Browning's visions of female regeneration are subtly qualified, for even while the plots and characters of *Aurora Leigh* and *Casa Guidi Windows* propose matriarchal apocalypses, the poet acknowledges that such consummations, though devoutly wished, require (in this world) male cooperation—Romney's abdication, the sacrifices of Italian men—and (in heaven) the grace of God the Father, who, with masculine wisdom, will build into "blank interstices" (*CGW* 2.776) and "make all new" (*AL* 9.949). By the time she wrote *Poems before Congress,* Barrett Browning's quasi-feminist vision had darkened even further. In just the poem whose image of Italy as an invalid woman echoes and illuminates Aurora's vision of her dead mother as "Our Lady of the Passion, stabbed with swords," the author imagines the redemption of her *matria* by, and only by, the grace of the French ruler Louis Napoleon, whose feats of male military bravery will make him "Emperor/Evermore." And, in fact, Italy's risorgimento was finally achieved only by the maneuvers of traditionally masculine "heroes" like Louis Napoleon, Mazzini, Garibaldi, Victor Emmanuel, Charles Albert, and—most of all—the Machiavellian statesman Cavour. [18] Thus the specifically matriarchal risorgimento of *Aurora Leigh* is ultimately almost as momentary and provisional as the brief hopeful revelation of the "mercy Seat" behind the "Vail" that ends *Casa Guidi Windows.* For inevitably the reality of patriarchal history, with its successes and successions, obliterated Barrett Browning's implicit but impossible dream of a *matria.*

Though Barrett Browning was disturbed by the unfavorable comparison one English reviewer made between her and Florence Nightingale, then, she might have sympathized with the view that unfairly stereotyped "lady with a lamp" expressed in a book the author of *Aurora Leigh* probably never read. As if commenting on the marriage of true minds Barrett Browning's epic envisions at its close, Nightingale argued in *Cassandra* (written in 1852 and privately printed in 1860) that "the true marriage—that noble union, by which a man and woman become together the one perfect being—probably does not exist at present upon earth" (44). Indeed, this woman, whose Christian name—Florence—was intended to honor the very city in which Barrett Browning found a modicum of *bella libertà* and who hoped that the "next Christ" might be, like the redemptive Aurora, a "female Christ," used a specifically Italian metaphor to describe the enchained reality of nineteenth-century woman: "She is like the Archangel Michael as he stands upon Saint Angelo at Rome.

She has an immense provision of wings . . . but when she tries to use them, she is petrified into stone" (50).

Perhaps, given the power and pressure of history, a woman who is "nobody in the somewhere of patriarchy" can only, as Susan Gubar has observed, be "somebody in the nowhere of utopia" (140), for even a land like Italy, with all the metaphorical possibilities that give it strength as a matriarchal topos, is inextricably part of the larger topos of European time. As such, it is a text whose usefulness to women can be countered by masculinist rereadings that redeem it for both the father and the phallus. Even Bachofen, the theorist of matriarchy, was to argue that "mother right" must historically be transformed and transcended by "father right," and sixty years after Barrett Browning imagined Italy as a *matria*, D. H. Lawrence claimed the land as a metaphorical *patria*, asserting that "To the Italian the phallus is the symbol of individual creative immortality, to each man his own Godhead" (44). Even the word *matria*, moreover, which I have used throughout this essay to describe the visionary country sought by women like Fuller, Rossetti, Barrett Browning, and Dickinson, is nonexistent. The real Italian word for "motherland" is *madrepatria*, a word whose literal meaning—"mother-fatherland"—preserves an inexorably patriarchal etymology. In Italian linguistic reality, there is no matriarchal equivalent to patriarchal power: one can only imagine such an antithetical power in the "nowhere" of a newly made vocabulary.

It is no wonder, then, that Barrett Browning appointed Louis Napoleon "Emperor/ Evermore" and that in the last poem she ever wrote, entitled "The North and the South," she came full circle back to Aurora's self-divided beginnings, admitting the dependence of the matriarchal south on the patriarchal language of the rigid north. While the north sighs for the skies of the south "that are softer and higher," the south sighs "For a poet's tongue of baptismal flame, / To call the tree or the flower by its name!" (*Poetical Works* 450).[19] Though she had enacted and examined a vision of female redemption far more radical than any Rossetti had allowed herself to explore, Barrett Browning would have conceded that, along with Rossetti, she was chained like Nightingale's angel to the rock of patriarchal Rome, and, along with Rossetti, she finally had to bid farewell to the Italy both had dreamed might be a sister land to paradise. As Christine de Pizan and Charlotte Perkins Gilman knew, in the world as it is, the City of Ladies can only be built on "the Field of Letters."

Notes

[1] All the quotations from *Aurora Leigh* in this essay come from the edition introduced by Cora Kaplan. All references to *Casa Guidi Windows* are to the edition by Julia Markus.

I am deeply grateful to Elliot Gilbert for critical insights that have been helpful throughout this essay. In addition, I am grateful to Susan Gubar and Dorothy

Mermin for useful comments and suggestions. Finally, I want to thank my mother, Angela Mortola, for inspiring me to think about Italy. This paper is dedicated to her, with love.

[2] In a brilliant essay on the Brownings and Italian politics, Flavia Alaya notes the connections among the regeneration of Aurora Leigh, the reunification of Italy, and EBB's personal sense of rebirth after her flight with Browning from England to Italy. But Alaya's study emphasizes the literary dialectic between two major poets who were, as she puts it, "quite literally political bedfellows," for she shows through a close reading of *The Ring and the Book* how Browning's Pompilia constitutes a revision of both Elizabeth and Italy, so that the husband's complex set of dramatic monologues is in some sense a response to the wife's earlier, apparently more naive and personal epic of a heroine's risorgimento. In addition, through close readings of Barrett Browning's letters and some of her poems, Alaya vigorously defines and defends this woman poet's often misunderstood (and frequently scorned) political stance.

[3] Though Alaya sees Browning/Romney as the "father" of Elizabeth/Aurora's reborn self, an opinion I disagree with, she does also suggest that "a mother-quest played a much more dominant role in [Barrett Browning's] psychic life" than is usually thought (30, n. 18).

[4] For a discussion of Aurora's vision of her mother's portrait, see Gilbert and Gubar 18–20.

[5] Alaya also discusses this pervasive trope of Italy as a tragic woman and the political function of the image in the risorgimento (14–16).

[6] Significantly, Ruskin describes the way the pillars of the porches of San Marco "half-refuse and half yield to the sunshine, Cleopatra-like, 'their bluest veins to kiss' . . ." (*Letters* 128).

[7] For a discussion of woman as Galatea, see Gilbert and Gubar 12–13.

[8] Elsewhere, Barrett Browning remarks that "[we] can dine our favorite way . . . with a miraculous cheapness . . . the prophet Elijah or the lilies of the field took as little thought for their dining, which exactly suits us" (*Letters* 1: 303).

[9] For an extraordinarily useful analysis of *Corinne*'s significance to nineteenth-century women writers, and especially to EBB, see Ellen Moers 173–210. On *Corinne*'s Italy as a "land of women," see Madelyn Gutwirth 208–15 and Ellen Peel, esp. 34–64. I am grateful to Ellen Peel for sharing this material with me.

[10] For "the rigid North," see "Enrica" and *Casa Guidi Windows* 1.1173; it is possible, even likely, that Rossetti borrowed the phrase from Barrett Browning. For "the sweet South," see Rossetti's "Italia, Io Ti Saluto," 378–79.

[11] Until recently, few critics have dealt directly with *Aurora Leigh;* major modern writers on the subject include Virginia Woolf, "*Aurora Leigh*"; Ellen Moers, esp. 201–07; Helen Cooper; Cora Kaplan, introd., *Aurora Leigh;* Barbara Gelpi; Virginia Steinmetz; and Dolores Rosenblum.

¹² The name Marian Erle evokes Goethe's "Erlkönig," the uncanny and elfish forest spirit who is a manifestation of nature rather than of culture.

¹³ See Kaplan 23–24, in *Aurora Leigh*. Dorothy Mermin has pointed out to me the resemblances between Romney Leigh and St. John Rivers, a likeness Taplin also takes up (316–17). Interestingly, as Romney becomes more like Rochester, he also becomes, in a sense, more Byronic; at the same time, however, his kinship to St. John Rivers mutes (and thus makes acceptable) his Byronic qualities.

¹⁴ Immersed in Browning's very name is a wordplay on "Bro's" fate: "Browning" suggests a conflation of "Bro" and "drowning."

¹⁵ See *Casa Guidi Windows* 2.399–405:

> I love no peace which is not fellowship,
>   And which includes not mercy. I would have
> Rather, the raking of the guns across
>   The world, and shrieks against Heaven's architrave;
> Rather the struggle in the slippery fosse
>   Of dying men and horses, and the wave
> Blood-bubbling. . . .

¹⁶Chevigny ascribes this comment to W. H. Hurlbut, who thought Ossoli an "underdeveloped and uninteresting Italian" (see Chevigny 375). In any case, the parallels between Barrett Browning and Fuller are interesting. Although Barrett Browning makes Romney older than Aurora, both Ossoli and Browning were considerably younger than their mates, as though Fuller and Barrett Browning had each half-consciously decided that in a utopian rearrangement of the relationship between the sexes men should be younger than their wives in order symbolically to free women from the bonds of daughterhood. In addition, both Fuller and Barrett Browning, quite late in life and rather unexpectedly, had children in Italy, and the private experience of maternity may well have reinforced their mutual hopes for a public experience of matriarchy.

¹⁷ As Susan Gubar has pointed out to me, the conclusion of George Eliot's *Romola* (1863) imagines a kind of private matriarchy secretly existing behind the patriarchal facade of fifteenth-century Florence.

¹⁸ As Chevigny notes, Fuller's experiences during the risorgimento were marked by similar—and more dramatically personal—ambiguities, for motherhood simultaneously empowered and weakened her. While Ossoli was fighting in Rome, she was in Rieti, absorbed in child care, and "in their letters [during this period] they came near assuming conventional sex roles" (385).

¹⁹ It is interesting that she wrote this poem to honor a literary man, Hans Christian Andersen, who had produced such visions of redemptive (but self-renouncing) femaleness as "The Snow Queen" and "The Mermaid."

Metaphor, Metonymy, and Voice in Zora Neale Hurston's *Their Eyes Were Watching God*

BARBARA JOHNSON

Not so very long ago, metaphor and metonymy burst into prominence as the salt and pepper, the Laurel and Hardy, the Yin and Yang, and often the Scylla and Charybdis of literary theory. Then, just as quickly, this cosmic couple passed out of fashion again. How did such an arcane rhetorical opposition acquire the brief but powerful privilege of dividing and naming the whole of human reality, from Mommy and Daddy or Symptom and Desire all the way to God and Country or Beautiful Lie and Sober Lucidity? (For an excellent discussion of the importance of the metaphor-metonymy distinction, see Ruegg.)

The contemporary sense of the opposition between metaphor and metonymy was first formulated by Roman Jakobson in "Two Aspects of Language and Two Types of Aphasic Disturbances." That article, first published in English in 1956, derives much of its celebrity from the central place accorded by the French structuralists to the 1963 translation of a selection of Jakobson's work, entitled *Essais de linguistique générale*, which included the aphasia study. The words *metaphor* and *metonymy* are not, of course, of twentieth-century coinage: they are classical tropes traditionally defined as the substitution of a figurative expression for a literal or proper one. In metaphor, the substitution is based on resemblance or analogy; in metonymy, it is based on a relation or association other than that of similarity (cause and effect, container and contained, proper name and qualities or works associated with it, place and event or institution, instrument and user, etc.). The use of the name *Camelot* to refer to John Kennedy's Washington is thus an example of metaphor, since it implies an analogy betwen Kennedy's world and King Arthur's, while the use of the word *Watergate* to refer to the scandal that ended Richard Nixon's presidency is a metonymy, since it transfers the name of an arbitrary place of origin onto a whole sequence of subsequent events.

Jakobson's use of the two terms is an extension and polarization of their classical definitions. In studying patterns of aphasia (speech dysfunction), Jakobson found that they fell into two main categories: similarity disorders and contiguity disorders. In the former, grammatical contexture and lateral associations remain while synonymity drops out; in the latter, heaps of word substitutes are kept while grammar and connectedness vanish. Jakobson concludes:

The development of a discourse may take place along two different semantic lines: one topic may lead to another either through their similarity or through their contiguity. The metaphoric way would be the most appropriate term for the first case and the metonymic way for the second, since they find their most condensed expression in metaphor and metonymy respectively. In aphasia one or the other of these two processes is restricted or totally blocked—an effect which makes the study of aphasia particularly illuminating for the linguist. In normal verbal behavior both processes are continually operative, but careful observation will reveal that under the influence of a cultural pattern, personality, and verbal style, preference is given to one of the two processes over the other.

In a well-known psychological test, children are confronted with some noun and told to utter the first verbal response that comes into their heads. In this experiment two opposite linguistic predilections are invariably exhibited: the response is intended either as a substitute for, or as a complement to the stimulus. In the latter case the stimulus and the response together form a proper syntactic construction, most usually a sentence. These two types of reaction have been labeled substitutive and predicative.

To the stimulus *hut* one response was *burnt out*; another, *is a poor little house*. Both reactions are predicative; but the first creates a purely narrative context, while in the second there is a double connection with the subject *hut*: on the one hand, a positional (namely, syntactic) contiguity, and on the other a semantic similarity.

The same stimulus produced the following substitutive reactions: the tautology *hut*; the synonyms *cabin* and *hovel*; the antonym *palace*, and the metaphors *den* and *burrow*. The capacity of two words to replace one another is an instance of positional similarity, and, in addition, all these responses are linked to the stimulus by semantic similarity (or contrast). Metonymical responses to the same stimulus, such as *thatch*, *litter*, or *poverty*, combine and contrast the positional similarity with semantic contiguity.

In manipulating these two kinds of connection (similarity and contiguity) in both their aspects (positional and semantic)—selecting, combining, and ranking them—an individual exhibits his personal style, his verbal predilections and preferences.   (76–77)

Two problems immediately arise that render the opposition between metaphor and metonymy at once more interesting and more problematic than it at first appears. The first is that there are not two poles here, but four: similarity, contiguity, semantic connection, and syntactic connection. A more adequate representation of these oppositions can be schematized as follows:

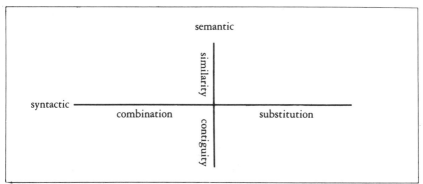

Jakobson's contention that poetry is a syntactic extension of metaphor ("The poetic function projects the principle of equivalence from the axis of selection into the axis of combination" ["Linguistics" 358]), while realist narrative is an extension of metonymy, can be added to the graph as follows:

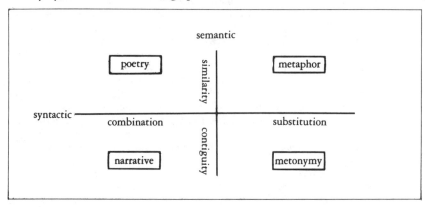

The second problem that arises in any attempt to apply the metaphor-metonymy distinction is that it is often hard to tell the two apart. In Ronsard's poem "Mignonne, allons voir si la rose . . . ," the speaker invites the lady to go for a walk with him (the walk being an example of contiguity) to see a rose that, once beautiful (like the lady), is now withered (as the lady will eventually be): the day must therefore be seized. The metonymic proximity to the flower is designed solely to reveal the metaphoric point of the poem: enjoy life while you still bloom. The tendency of contiguity to become overlaid by similarity and vice versa may be summed up in the proverb "Birds of a feather flock together" ("qui se ressemble s'assemble"). One has only to think of the applicability of this proverb to the composition of neighborhoods in America to realize that the question of the separability of similarity from contiguity may have considerable political implications. The controversy surrounding the expression "legionnaires' disease" provides a more comical example: while the name of the disease derives solely from the contingent fact that its first victims were at an American Legion convention, and is thus a metonymy, the fear that it will take on a metaphoric color—that a belief in some natural connection or similarity may thereby be propagated between legionnaires and the disease—has led representatives of the legionnaires to attempt to have the malady renamed. And finally, in the sentence "The White House denied the charges," one might ask whether the place name is a purely contiguous metonymy for the presidency or whether the whiteness of the house isn't somehow metaphorically connected to the whiteness of its inhabitant.

One final prefatory remark about the metaphor-metonymy distinction: far from being a neutral opposition between equals, these two tropes have always stood in hierarchical relation to each other. From Aristotle to George Lakoff and Mark Johnson, metaphor has always, in the Western tradition, had the privilege of revealing unexpected truth. As Aristotle puts it: "Midway between the unintelligible and the commonplace, it is a metaphor which most produces knowledge" (*Rhetoric*

3.1410). Paul de Man summarizes the preference for metaphor over metonymy by aligning analogy with necessity and contiguity with chance: "The inference of identity and totality that is constitutive of metaphor is lacking in the purely relational metonymic contact: an element of truth is involved in taking Achilles for a lion but none in taking Mr. Ford for a motor car" (*Allegories* 14). De Man then goes on to reveal this "element of truth" as the product of a purely rhetorical—and ultimately metonymical—sleight of hand, thus overturning the traditional hierarchy and deconstructing the very basis for the seductiveness and privilege of metaphor.

I would like now to turn to the work of an author acutely conscious of, and superbly skilled in, the seductiveness and complexity of metaphor as privileged trope and trope of privilege. Zora Neale Hurston, novelist, folklorist, essayist, anthropologist, and Harlem Renaissance personality, cut her teeth on figurative language during the tale-telling or "lying" sessions that took place on a store porch in the all-black town of Eatonville, Florida, where she was born around 1901. She devoted her life to the task of recording, preserving, novelizing, and analyzing the patterns of speech and thought of the rural black South and related cultures. At the same time, she deplored the appropriation, dilution, and commodification of black culture (through spirituals, jazz, etc.) by the predepression white world, and she constantly tried to explain the difference between a reified "art" and a living culture in which the distinctions between spectator and spectacle, rehearsal and performance, experience and representation, are not fixed. "Folklore," she wrote, "is the arts of the people before they find out that there is such a thing as art."

> Folklore does not belong to any special area, time, nor people. It is a world and an ageless thing, so let us look at it from that viewpoint. It is the boiled down juice of human living and when one phase of it passes another begins which shall in turn give way before a successor.
>   Culture is a forced march on the near and the obvious. . . . The intelligent mind uses up a great part of its lifespan trying to awaken its consciousness sufficiently to comprehend that which is plainly there before it. Every generation or so some individual with extra keen perception grasps something of the obvious about us and hitches the human race forward slightly by a new "law." Millions of things had been falling on men for thousands of years before the falling apple hit Newton on the head and he saw the law of gravity. ("Folklore" 41–42)

Through this strategic description of the folkloric heart of scientific law, Hurston dramatizes the predicament not only of the anthropologist but also of the novelist: both are caught between the (metaphorical) urge to universalize or totalize and the knowledge that it is precisely "the near and the obvious" that will never be grasped once and for all but only (metonymically) named and renamed as different things successively strike different heads. I will return to this problem of universality at the end of this essay, but first I would like to take a close look at some of the figurative operations at work in Hurston's best-known novel, *Their Eyes Were Watching God*.

The novel presents, in a combination of first- and third-person narration, the story of Janie Crawford and her three successive husbands. The first, Logan Killicks, is chosen by Janie's grandmother for his sixty acres and as a socially secure harbor for Janie's awakening sexuality. When Janie realizes that love does not automatically follow marriage and that Killicks completely lacks imagination, she decides to run off with ambitious, smart-talking, stylishly dressed Joe Starks, who is headed for a new all-black town where he hopes to become what he calls a "big voice." Later, as mayor and store owner of the town, he proudly raises Janie to a pedestal of property and propriety. Because this involves her submission to his idea of what a mayor's wife should be, Janie soon finds her pedestal to be a straitjacket, particularly when it involves her exclusion—both as speaker and as listener—from the taletelling sessions on the store porch and at the mock funeral of a mule. Little by little, Janie begins to talk back to Joe, finally insulting him so profoundly that, in a sense, he dies of it. Some time later, into Janie's life walks Tea Cake Woods, whose first act is to teach Janie how to play checkers. "Somebody wanted her to play," says the text in free indirect discourse; "Somebody thought it natural for her to play" (146). Thus begins a joyous liberation from the rigidities of status, image, and property—one of the most beautiful and convincing love stories in any literature. In a series of courtship dances, appearances, and disappearances, Tea Cake succeeds in fulfilling Janie's dream of "a bee for her blossom" (161). Tea Cake, unlike Joe and Logan, regards money and work as worth only the amount of play and enjoyment they make possible. He gains and loses money unpredictably until he and Janie begin working side by side picking beans on "the muck" in the Florida everglades. This idyll of pleasure, work, and equality ends dramatically with a hurricane during which Tea Cake, while saving Janie's life, is bitten by a rabid dog. When Tea Cake's subsequent hydrophobia transforms him into a wild and violent animal, Janie is forced to shoot him in self-defense. Acquitted of murder by an all-white jury, Janie returns to Eatonville, where she tells her story to her friend Phoeby Watson.

The passage on which I would like to concentrate both describes and dramatizes, in its figurative structure, a crucial turning point in Janie's relation to Joe and to herself. The passage follows an argument over what Janie has done with a bill of lading, during which Janie shouts, "You sho loves to tell me whut to do, but Ah can't tell you nothin' Ah see!"

> "Dat's 'cause you need tellin'," he rejoined hotly. "It would be pitiful if Ah didn't. Somebody got to think for women and chillun and chickens and cows. I god, they sho don't think none theirselves."
>
> "Ah knows uh few things, and womenfolks thinks sometimes too!"
>
> "Aw naw they don't. They just think they's thinkin'. When Ah see one thing Ah understands ten. You see ten things and don't understand one."
>
> Times and scenes like that put Janie to thinking about the inside state of her marriage. Time came when she fought back with her tongue as best she could, but it didn't do her any good. It just made Joe do more. He wanted her submission and he'd keep on fighting until he felt he had it.
>
> So gradually, she pressed her teeth together and learned how to hush. The spirit of the marriage left the bedroom and took to living in the parlor. It was there to shake hands whenever company came to visit, but it never went back inside the bedroom again. So she put something in there to represent the spirit like a Virgin Mary image in a church. The bed was no longer a daisy-field for her and Joe to play in. It was a place where she went and laid down when she was sleepy and tired.

She wasn't petal-open anymore with him. She was twenty-four and seven years married when she knew. She found that out one day when he slapped her face in the kitchen. It happened over one of those dinners that chasten all women sometimes. They plan and they fix and they do, and then some kitchen-dwelling fiend slips a scrochy, soggy, tasteless mess into their pots and pans. Janie was a good cook, and Joe had looked forward to his dinner as a refuge from other things. So when the bread didn't rise and the fish wasn't quite done at the bone, and the rice was scorched, he slapped Janie until she had a ringing sound in her ears and told her about her brains before he stalked on back to the store.

Janie stood where he left her for unmeasured time and thought. She stood there until something fell off the shelf inside her. Then she went inside there to see what it was. It was her image of Jody tumbled down and shattered. But looking at it she saw that it never was the flesh and blood figure of her dreams. Just something she had grabbed up to drape her dreams over. In a way she turned her back upon the image where it lay and looked further. She had no more blossomy openings dusting pollen over her man, neither any glistening young fruit where the petals used to be. She found that she had a host of thoughts she had never expressed to him, and numerous emotions she had never let Jody know about. Things packed up and put away in parts of her heart where he could never find them. She was saving up feelings for some man she had never seen. She had an inside and an outside now and suddenly she knew how not to mix them. (110–13)

This opposition between an inside and an outside is a standard way of describing the nature of a rhetorical figure. The vehicle, or surface meaning, is seen as enclosing an inner tenor, or figurative meaning. This relation can be pictured somewhat facetiously as a gilded carriage—the vehicle—containing Luciano Pavarotti, the tenor. Within the passage cited from *Their Eyes Were Watching God*, I would like to concentrate on the two paragraphs that begin respectively "So gradually . . ." and "Janie stood where he left her. . . ." In these two paragraphs Hurston plays a number of interesting variations on the inside-outside opposition.

In both paragraphs, a relation is set up between an inner image and outward, domestic space. The parlor, bedroom, and store full of shelves already exist in the narrative space of the novel: they are figures drawn metonymically from the familiar contiguous surroundings. Each of these paragraphs recounts a little narrative of, and within, its own figurative terms. In the first, the inner spirit of the marriage moves outward from the bedroom to the parlor, cutting itself off from its proper place and replacing itself with an image of virginity, the antithesis of marriage. Although Joe is constantly exclaiming, "I god, Janie," he will not be as successful as his namesake in uniting with the Virgin Mary. Indeed, it is his godlike self-image that forces Janie to retreat to virginity. The entire paragraph is an externalization of Janie's feelings onto the outer surroundings in the form of a narrative of movement from private to public space. While the whole of the figure relates metaphorically, analogically, to the marital situation it is designed to express, it reveals the marriage space to be metonymical, a movement through a series of contiguous rooms. It is a narrative not of union but of separation centered on an image not of conjugality but of virginity.

In the second passage, just after the slap, Janie is standing, thinking, until something "fell off the shelf inside her." Janie's "inside" is here represented as a store that she then goes in to inspect. While the former paragraph was an externalization of the inner, here we find an internalization of the outer: Janie's inner self resembles a store. The material for this metaphor is drawn from the narrative world of contiguity: the store is the place where Joe has set himself up as lord, master, and proprietor. But here, Jody's image is broken and reveals itself to have been not a metaphor but only a metonymy of Janie's dream: "Looking at it she saw that it never was the flesh and blood figure of her dreams. Just something she had grabbed up to drape her dreams over."

What we find in juxtaposing these two figural mininarratives is a kind of chiasmus, or crossover, in which the first paragraph presents an externalization of the inner (a metaphorically grounded metonymy), while the second paragraph presents an internalization of the outer (a metonymically grounded metaphor). In both cases, the quotient of the operation is the revelation of a false or discordant image. Janie's image, as Virgin Mary, acquires a new intactness, while Joe's lies shattered on the floor. The reversals operated by the chiasmus map out a reversal of the power relations between Janie and Joe. Henceforth, Janie will grow in power and resistance, while Joe deteriorates both in his body and in his public image.

The moral of these two figural tales is rich with implications: "She had an inside and an outside now and suddenly she knew how not to mix them." On the one hand, this means that she knew how to keep the inside and the outside separate without trying to blend or merge them into one unified identity. On the other, it means that she has stepped irrevocably into the necessity of figurative language, where inside and outside are never the same. It is from this point on in the novel that Janie, paradoxically, begins to speak. And it is by means of a devastating figure—"You look like the change of life"—that she wounds Jody to the quick. Janie's acquisition of the power of voice thus grows not out of her identity but out of her division into inside and outside. Knowing how not to mix them is knowing that articulate language requires the copresence of two distinct poles, not their collapse into oneness.

This, of course, is what Jakobson concludes in his discussion of metaphor and metonymy. For it must be remembered that what is at stake in the maintenance of both sides—metaphor and metonymy, inside and outside—is the very possibility of speaking at all. The reduction of a discourse to oneness, identity—in Janie's case, the reduction of woman to mayor's wife—has as its necessary consequence aphasia, silence, the loss of the ability to speak. "She pressed her teeth together and learned to hush."

What has gone unnoticed in theoretical discussions of Jakobson's article is that behind the metaphor-metonymy distinction lies the more serious distinction between speech and aphasia, between silence and the capacity to articulate one's own voice. To privilege either metaphor or metonymy is thus to run the risk of producing an increasingly aphasic critical discourse. If both, or all four, poles must be operative in order for speech to function fully, then the very notion of an "authentic voice" must be redefined. Far from being an expression of Janie's new wholeness or identity as a character, Janie's increasing ability to speak grows out of her ability not to mix inside with outside, not to pretend that there is no difference, but to assume and articulate the incompatible forces involved in her own division. The sign of an authentic voice is thus not self-identity but self-difference.

The search for wholeness, oneness, universality, and totalization can nevertheless never be put to rest. However rich, healthy, or lucid fragmentation and division may be, narrative seems to have trouble resting content with it, as though a story could not recognize its own end as anything other than a moment of totalization—even when what is totalized is loss. The ending of *Their Eyes Were Watching God* is no exception:

> Of course [Tea Cake] wasn't dead. He could never be dead until she herself had finished feeling and thinking. The kiss of his memory made pictures of love and light against the wall. Here was peace. She pulled in her horizon like a great fish-net. Pulled it from around the waist of the world and draped it over her shoulder. So much of life in its meshes! She called in her soul to come and see. (286)

The horizon, with all of life caught in its meshes, is here pulled into the self as a gesture of total recuperation and peace. It is as though self-division could be healed over at last, but only at the cost of a radical loss of the other.

This hope for some ultimate unity and peace seems to structure the very sense of an ending as such, whether that of a novel or that of a work of literary criticism. At the opposite end of the "canonical" scale, one finds it, for example, in the last chapter of Erich Auerbach's *Mimesis*, perhaps the greatest of modern monuments to the European literary canon. That final chapter—entitled "The Brown Stocking" after the stocking that Virginia Woolf's Mrs. Ramsay is knitting in *To the Light-house*—is a description of certain narrative tendencies in the modern novel: "mul-tipersonal representation of consciousness, time strata, disintegration of the continuity of exterior events, shifting of narrative viewpoint," and so on (482–83).

> Let us begin with a tendency which is particularly striking in our text from Virginia Woolf. She holds to minor, unimpressive, random events: measuring the stocking, a fragment of a conversation with the maid, a telephone call. Great changes, exterior turning points, let alone catastrophes, do not occur. (483)

Auerbach concludes his discussion of the modernists' preoccupation with the minor, the trivial, and the marginal by saying:

> It is precisely the random moment which is comparatively independent of the controversial and unstable orders over which men fight and despair. . . . The more numerous, varied, and simple the people are who appear as subjects of such random moments, the more effectively must what they have in common shine forth. . . . So the complicated process of dissolution which led to fragmentation of the exterior action, to reflection of consciousness, and to stratification of time seems to be tending toward a very simple solution. Perhaps it will be too simple to please those who, despite all its dangers and catastrophes, admire and love our epoch for the sake of its abundance of life and the incomparable historical vantage point which it affords. But they are few in number, and probably they will not live to see much more than the first forewarnings of the approaching unification and simplifica-tion. (488)

Never has the desire to transform fragmentation into unity been expressed so suc-cinctly and authoritatively—indeed, almost prophetically. One cannot help but wonder, though, whether the force of this desire has not been provoked by the fact that the primary text it wishes to unify and simplify was written by a woman. What Auerbach calls "minor, unimpressive, random events"—measuring a stocking, conversing with the maid, answering the phone—can all be identified as conventional women's activities. "Great changes, exterior turning points, and catastrophes" have been the stuff of heroic male literature. Even plot itself—up until *Madame Bovary*, at least—has been conceived as the doings of those who do not stay at home—that is, men. Auerbach's urge to unify and simplify is an urge to resubsume female difference under the category of the universal, which has always been unavowedly male. The random, the trivial, and the marginal will simply be added to the list of things all men have in common.

If "unification and simplification" is the privilege and province of the male, it is also, in America, the privilege and province of the white. If the woman's voice, to be authentic, must incorporate and articulate division and self-difference, so, too, has Afro-American literature always had to assume its double-voicedness. As Henry Louis Gates, Jr., puts it in "Criticism in the Jungle":

> In the instance of the writer of African descent, her or his texts occupy spaces in at least two traditions—the individual's European or American literary tradition, and one of the three related but distinct black traditions. The "heritage" of each black text written in a Western language, then, is a double heritage, two-toned, as it were. Each utterance, then, is double-voiced. (123, 125)

This is a reformulation of W. E. B. DuBois's famous image of the "veil" that divides the black American in two:

> The Negro is a sort of seventh son, born with a veil, and gifted with second sight in this American world,—a world which yields him no true self-consciousness, but only lets him see himself through the revelation of the other world. It is a peculiar sensation, this double-consciousness, this sense of always looking at one's self through the eyes of others, of measuring one's soul by the tape of a world that looks on in amused contempt and pity. One ever feels his twoness—an American, a Negro; two souls, two thoughts, two unreconciled strivings; two warring ideals in one dark body, whose dogged strength alone keeps it from being torn asunder.
> The history of the American Negro is the history of this strife,—this longing to attain self-conscious manhood, to merge his double self into a better and truer self. (214–15)

James Weldon Johnson, in his *Autobiography of an Ex-Colored Man*, puts it this way:

> This is the dwarfing, warping, distorting influence which operates upon each and every colored man in the United States. He is forced to take his outlook on all things, not from the view-point of a citizen, or a man, or even a human being, but from the view-point of a *colored* man. . . . This gives to every colored man, in proportion to his intellectuality, a sort of dual personality. (403)

What is striking about the above two quotations is that they both assume without question that the black subject is male. The black woman is totally invisible in these descriptions of the black dilemma. Richard Wright, in his review of *Their Eyes Were Watching God*, makes it plain that for him, too, the black female experience is nonexistent. The novel, says Wright, lacks

> a basic idea or theme that lends itself to significant interpretation. . . . [Hurston's] dialogue manages to catch the psychological movements of the Negro folk-mind in their pure simplicity, but that's as far as it goes. . . . The sensory sweep of her novel carries no theme, no message, no thought. (25–26)

No message, no theme, no thought: the full range of questions and experiences of Janie's life are as invisible to a mind steeped in maleness as Ellison's Invisible Man is to minds steeped in whiteness. If the black man's soul is divided in two, what can be said of the black woman's? Here again, what is constantly seen exclusively in terms of a binary opposition—black versus white, man versus woman—must be redrawn at least as a tetrapolar structure:

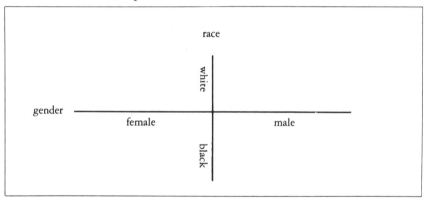

In the case of a black woman the four quadrants are constantly being collapsed into two. Hurston's work is often called nonpolitical simply because readers of Afro-American literature tend to look for confrontational racial politics, not sexual politics. If the black woman voices opposition to male domination, she is often seen as a traitor to the cause of racial justice. But if she sides with black men against white oppression, she often winds up having to accept her position within the Black Power movement as, in Stokely Carmichael's word, "prone." This impossible position between two oppositions is what I think Hurston intends when, at the end of the novel, she represents Janie as acquitted of the murder of Tea Cake by an all-white jury but condemned by her fellow blacks. This is not out of a "lack of bitterness toward whites," as one reader would have it (Davis 116), but rather out of a knowledge of the standards of male dominance that pervade both the black and the white worlds. The black crowd at the trial murmurs, "Tea Cake was a good boy. He had been good to that woman. No nigger woman ain't never been treated no better" (276). As Janie's grandmother puts it early in the novel:

> Honey, de white man is de ruler of everything as fur as Ah been able tuh find out. Maybe it's some place way off in de ocean where de black man is in power, but

we don't know nothin' but what we see. So de white man throw down de load
and tell de nigger man tuh pick it up. He pick it up because he have to, but he
don't tote it. He hand it to his womenfolks. De nigger woman is de mule uh de
world so fur as Ah can see. (29)

In a persuasive book on black women and feminism entitled *Ain't I a Woman*,
Bell Hooks (Gloria Watkins) discusses the ways in which black women suffer from
both sexism and racism within the very movements whose ostensible purpose is to
set them free. Watkins argues that "black woman" has never been considered a
separate, distinct category with a history and complexity of its own. When a
president appoints a black woman to a cabinet post, for example, he does not feel
he is appointing a person belonging to the category "black woman"; he is appointing
a person who belongs both to the category "black" and to the category "woman"
and is thus killing two birds with one stone. Watkins says of the analogy often
drawn—particularly by white feminists—between blacks and women:

> Since analogies derive their power, their appeal, and their very reason for being
> from the sense of two disparate phenomena having been brought closer together,
> for white women to acknowledge the overlap between the terms "blacks" and
> "women" (that is, the existence of black women) would render this analogy un-
> necessary. By continuously making this analogy, they unwittingly suggest that to
> them the term "women" is synonymous with "white women" and the term "blacks"
> synonymous with "black men." (8)

The very existence of black women thus disappears from an analogical discourse
designed to express the types of oppression from which black women have the most
to suffer.

In the current hierarchical view of things, this tetrapolar graph can be filled in
as follows:

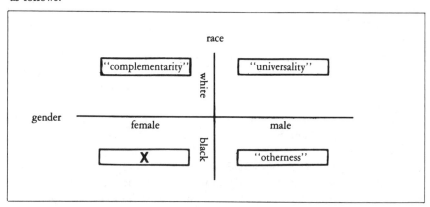

The black woman is both invisible and ubiquitous: never seen in her own right but
forever appropriated by the others for their own ends.

Ultimately, though, this mapping of tetrapolar differences is itself a fantasy of
universality. Are all the members of each quadrant the same? Where are the nations,

the regions, the religions, the classes, the professions? Where are the other races, the interracial subdivisions? How can the human world be totalized, even as a field of divisions? In the following quotation from Zora Neale Hurston's autobiography, we see that even the same black woman can express self-division in two completely different ways:

> Work was to be all of me, so I said. . . . I had finished that phase of research and was considering writing my first book, when I met the man who was really to lay me by the heels. . . .
> He was tall, dark brown, magnificently built, with a beautifully modeled back head. His profile was strong and good. The nose and lips were especially good front and side. But his looks only drew my eyes in the beginning. I did not fall in love with him just for that. He had a fine mind and that intrigued me. When a man keeps beating me to the draw mentally, he begins to get glamorous. . . .
> His intellect got me first for I am the kind of woman that likes to move on mentally from point to point, and I like for my man to be there way ahead of me. . . .
> His great desire was to do for me. *Please* let him be a *man!* . . .
> That very manliness, sweet as it was, made us both suffer. My career balked the completeness of his ideal. I really wanted to conform, but it was impossible. To me there was no conflict. My work was one thing, and he was all the rest. But I could not make him see that. Nothing must be in my life but himself. . . . We could not leave each other alone, and we could not shield each other from hurt. . . .
> In the midst of this, I received my Guggenheim Fellowship. This was my chance to release him, and fight myself free from my obsession. He would get over me in a few months and go on to be a very big man. So I sailed off to Jamaica [and] pitched in to work hard on my research to smother my feelings. But the thing would not down. The plot was far from the circumstances, but I tried to embalm all the tenderness of my passion for him in *Their Eyes Were Watching God*.
>
> (*Dust Tracks* 260–88)

The plot is indeed far from the circumstances, and, what is even more striking, it is lived by what seems to be a completely different woman. While Janie struggles to attain equal respect within a relation to a man, Zora readily submits to the pleasures of submission yet struggles to establish the legitimacy of a professional life outside the love relation. The female voice may be universally described as divided, but it must be recognized as divided in a multitude of ways.

There is no point of view from which the universal characteristics of the human, of the woman, of the black woman, or even of Zora Neale Hurston can be selected and totalized. Unification and simplification are fantasies of domination, not understanding.

The task of the writer, then, would seem to be to narrate both the appeal and the injustice of universalization, in a voice that assumes and articulates its own, ever-differing self-difference. In the opening pages of *Their Eyes Were Watching God* we find, indeed, a brilliant and subtle transition from the seduction of a universal language through a progressive deuniversalization that ends in the exclusion of the protagonist herself. The book begins:

> Ships at a distance have every man's wish on board. For some they come in with the tide. For others they sail forever on the horizon, never out of sight, never

landing until the Watcher turns his eyes away in resignation, his dreams mocked to death by Time. That is the life of men.

Now, women forget all those things they don't want to remember, and remember everything they don't want to forget. The dream is the truth. Then they act and do things accordingly.

So the beginning of this was a woman, and she had come back from burying the dead. Not the dead of sick and ailing with friends at the pillow and the feet. She had come back from the sodden and the bloated; the sudden dead, their eyes flung wide open in judgment.

The people all saw her come because it was sundown. . . . (9)

At this point Janie crosses center stage and goes out, while the people, the "bander log," pass judgment on her. The viewpoint has moved from "every man" to "men" to "women" to "a woman" to an absence commented on by "words without masters," the gossip of the front porch. When Janie begins to speak, even the universalizing category "standard English" gives way to the careful representation of dialect. The narrative voice in this novel expresses its own self-division by shifts between first and third person, standard English and dialect. This self-division culminates in the frequent use of free indirect discourse, in which, as Henry Louis Gates, Jr., points out,[1] the inside-outside boundaries between narrator and character, between standard and individual, are both transgressed and preserved, making it impossible to identify and totalize either the subject or the nature of discourse.

Narrative, it seems, is an endless fishing expedition with the horizon as both the net and the fish, the big one that always gets away. The meshes continually enclose and let escape, tear open and mend up again. Mrs. Ramsay never finishes the brown stocking.[2] A woman's work is never done. Penelope's weaving is nightly reunraveled. The porch never stops passing the world through its mouth. The process of de-universalization can never, universally, be completed.

Notes

[1] See Gates's discussion of *Their Eyes Were Watching God* as what he calls (à la Barthes) a "speakerly text," in *The Signifying Monkey*.

[2] I wish to thank Patti Joplin of Stanford University for calling my attention to this fact.

Domination and Desire

A Feminist-Materialist Reading of Manuel Puig's *Kiss of the Spider Woman*

LAURA RICE-SAYRE

To approach textual analysis from a feminist-materialist perspective demands an initial clarification of three basic questions raised by that perspective: How is materialist feminism constituted? How does feminist materialism differ from or resemble other materialist (usually Marxist) approaches? And finally, what sorts of texts are to be included in this analysis from the outset? Feminism, construed in its most general sense, has been understood as synonymous with women's studies—a field that might include women studying anything and anyone studying women; construed in its narrowest sense, it has been seen as a struggle for career opportunity waged by women who are white, Western, and bourgeois. This latter view of feminism is best summed up by the question Bell Hooks asks in *Ain't I a Woman*: Why are all women white and all blacks men? The charge that the feminist movement is solely a white middle-class phenomenon stems from the fact that feminism has in large part replicated the asymmetry of power relations found in masculinist social formations. White bourgeois feminism has universalized the "woman question": being limited to the private sphere of the home and the family and forced into meaningless consumerism to fill up idle hours hardly describes the oppression of Afro-American women, of women migrant workers, or of the vast majority of third-world women, for example. This myopia operates along class, race, caste, ethnic, and cultural lines. The "white solipsism" of this middle-class feminism, characterized by Adrienne Rich in her "Disloyal to Civilization" as the tendency "to think, imagine, and speak as if whiteness described the world" (299), stems less from individual failure and prejudice than from the fact that in many ways this feminism exists within the same institutionalized structures of dominance as does masculinist culture—asymmetrical access to economic, political, legal, religious, educational, and media resources—and unwittingly reproduces them. And as a limited vision of feminism, it has led those excluded to insist on the centrality of their concerns to the feminist project—such as racism (Audre Lorde), ethnic perspectives (Nira Yuval-Davis and Floya Anthias), compulsory heterosexuality (Adrienne Rich), cultural imperialism (Maria C. Lugones and Elizabeth V. Spelman), and so on. At their worst, these separate perspectives on feminism have led critics to see any claim for a general, unified feminism as bogus, as an erasure of the concrete differences among women in the name of a universality that is in reality another form of domination. This rejection of any commonality among feminists has the drawback of reproducing the radical alterity that has for so long been the mainstay of gender differentiation founded on ideas of binary opposition.

The denial of universality has grown out of the insistence of feminists on the personal as political, or in more materialist terms, the insistence on praxis, on the daily living experiences of women. In her "Toward a Phenomenology of Feminist Consciousness," Sandra Lee Bartky points out that "feminists are not aware of different things than other people; they are aware of the same things differently" (429). The grounding of feminism in practice has revealed that "feminism" includes women of color, third-world women, various ethnic groups, homosexuals, bisexuals, various age groups who see the same facts differently given their specific historical and cultural perspectives. At best, these differences have led to a reexamination of oppression as domination and of commonality as a community that would valorize difference not as alterity but as a dialectic source of liberating power. Catharine MacKinnon makes a specific parallel between Marxist theory and feminist theory when she states,

> Sexuality is to feminism what work is to marxism: that which is most one's own, yet most taken away. . . . [In Marxism, work] is that activity by which people become who they are. Class is its structure, production its consequence, capital its congealed form and control its issue. . . . As work is to marxism, sexuality to feminism is socially constructed yet constructing, universal as activity yet historically specific, jointly comprised of matter and mind. . . . Heterosexuality is its structure, gender and family its congealed forms, sex roles its qualities generalized to social persona, reproduction a consequence, and control its issue. (1–2)

Recent feminist-materialist studies have challenged the universality of the Marxist category of "production" and have begun to study, rather, the structures of domination. Isaac Balbus, in his *Marxism and Domination*, argues that

> production (now understood as technological domination), sexual domination, and political domination are elements of a whole or a totality characterized by an exclusively instrumental mode of symbolizing the relationship between the self and the "natural," sexual and political others with whom/which it relates—a mode, in short, in which self and other are related as subject to an object. . . . At bottom, the movements against sexual, political and technological domination are one movement, the movement to transcend the existing Instrumental mode of symbolization and to create authentically reciprocal relationships . . . within which these others are recognized as subjects in their own right. (7–8)

And in *Money, Sex and Power*, Nancy Hartsock examines the ways in which a theorization of power (both as domination and alternatively as the liberating energy of community) "would give an account of how social institutions have come to be controlled by only one gender; it would locate the points at which conflicts between women and men are generated and make clear the relations between individual intentional actions and structural constraints" (254). I cite MacKinnon, Balbus, and Hartsock to demonstrate that materialist feminism does imply a specific liberatory project: by foregrounding gender, we reexamine the specific sociohistorical differences in our concrete experience both as they have been constituted as structures of domination and asymmetrical alterity and as they offer—especially through an emphasis on nurturing and community—a vision of an alternative social formation that would valorize both difference and cooperation.

Feminist-materialist textual analysis, then, suggests not just literary but social criticism. It challenges not only the canon from which women have been so long excluded but also the elevation of some genres over others. Feminist-materialist criticism includes the serious study of the social function of popular genres that take the place of high art in the reading habits of so many (several hundred million copies of romances are sold each year now). In addition the study of how the gendered nature of language erases, trivializes, or marginalizes women involves the study of all sorts of texts—literary, legal, anthropological, historical, political, and so on. Further, this sort of approach from the perspective of gender leads to the study of the silencing of women (as in Tillie Olsen's *Silences*). Finally, the study of differences may lead one to question the assumed centrality of the study of written texts given that so many women worldwide are illiterate and can author or transmit only oral texts. A feminist-materialist approach to textual analysis, then, foregrounds gender and difference. The critic may be either male or female, the text may be authored by males or females, and the subject of the text may be men or women. In an effort to demonstrate how gender, not biological sex, is at issue, I have chosen to do a feminist-materialist analysis of a third-world text written by a man about two men, Manuel Puig's *Kiss of the Spider Woman*.

> —Something a little strange—that's what you notice, that she's not a woman like all the others. She looks fairly young, twenty-five, maybe a little more, petite face, a little catlike, small turned-up nose. The shape of her face, it's . . . more roundish than oval, broad forehead, pronounced cheeks too, but then they come down to a point, like with cats.
> —What about her eyes?
> —Clear, pretty sure they're green, half-closed to focus better on the drawing. She looks at her subject: the black panther at the zoo, which was quiet at first, stretched out in its cage. (3)

This exchange, which opens Puig's novel, takes place between Luis Alberto Molina, a thirty-seven-year-old sexual offender, sentenced to eight years' imprisonment for corruption of minors, and Valentin Arregui Paz, a twenty-six-year-old urban guerilla who has been held for three years under the executive power of the Argentine Government and is "awaiting judgment" on the charge that he "promotes disturbances" and "instigates revolution." While they share the prison cell, Molina relates the plots of six sentimental B movies to Valentin to pass the time, replacing the degraded daily terror of life under an authoritarian regime with the more entertaining but equally perverse tinsel of Hollywood. The continuing dialogue between Molina and Valentin begins as a mere exchange of variously critical, sarcastic, and defensive commentaries on the films and develops into an examination by each of his cellmate's complexity and, further, into an acute self-examination that is at times implied by silences in the dialogue and at times by interior monologues. Theirs is an investigation into how the self is constituted and how human relations are limited by repressive social institutions, and its depth is demonstrated by contrasting their private search, on the one hand, with the shallow character developments of the movie plots and the press release about one of the movies, presented in the footnotes, and, on the other, with the inhumane, distant bureaucratic investigation of Molina as reported by a secret-service surveillance team that echoes the elitist tone of Puig's footnotes on the possible physical and psychoanalytic origins of homosexuality. In the midst of these cultural narratives, which embody the law of the father inscribed in the two prisoners, Molina and Valentin carry off a mental jailbreak. They move from the exchange of competitive and mutually exclusive points of view to a dialogue that, through a slow and painful uncovering of socially constructed bias and repression, reveals the valuable differences of perspective each brings to their relation. Finally, they develop a bond based on the power of each to contribute to their community and to resist the coercive authority of the structures of dominance that have imprisoned them.

Although at first the movie narratives seem to be at the center of the novel—the *mise en abyme*, as it were—it is less their substantive content than the act of interpretation to which they give rise that is the key event of the novel. This focus on interpretation is emphasized by other forms of interpretation in the novel—dialogues analyzing the movie narratives themselves, searching interior monologues, official investigations, Nazi analysis of social ills, scientific psychoanalytic research. The revolutionary Valentin at first disciplines himself to approach the study of the social system by means of monastic study, even, for instance, leaving Molina alone in an agony resulting from poisoned food that the authorities had planned to give Valentin so that Molina could pump the weakened revolutionary and act as their stoolie. But by the end of the novel, Valentin realizes he has learned more about how domination works itself out in the social system from Molina and his movies than he ever will from the texts of the revolutionary canon, which had made him deny the sensual and emotional lives of both himself and others.

Ironically, critics have often tended to ignore the revolutionary growth both Molina and Valentin are undergoing, perhaps because their analysis divorces the text from the world that produced it. In the case of Puig's *Kiss of the Spider Woman*, most critics have taken refuge in a formalist discussion of the plurality of styles, the multiple play of discourses, and the polysemic qualities of the text and have tended to ignore or even deny the political content and form the novel's dialogue embodies. Francine Masiello's treatment in "Jail House Flicks: Projections by Manuel Puig," a fine formalist essay, is an example of the critical extraction of the text from its political context:

surely contrived to startle an audience that follows what is fashionable, and *perhaps* designed to draw attention to Argentina's deplorable political situation (the novel is currently banned in Puig's country of origin), *El beso de la mujer araña* tells a relatively simple and at times awkward story about a homosexual and a political activist detained in Villa Devoto prison of Buenos Aires.   (15–16; emphasis added)

This merely token recognition of the foundations of the novel—its investigation of the identical origins of civic and sexual repression in the ideology and structures of domination—leads otherwise perceptive critics not only to take refuge in formalist criticism but to misread the plot of the novel. Masiello, noting that "Puig makes no attempt to conceal his sympathies for Molina who turns out to be the innocent hero of the novel," finds Valentin to be "described as an inept and rhetorical youth, responsible, in the final analysis, for the death of his friend" (16). In interpreting the plot in this fashion, she reverses Puig's message by reinforcing a "star" system, by making Molina the "hero," by refusing to recognize what Molina undergoes before making his own choice to carry a message to Valentin's comrades (he does not do so out of a coercion-submission dynamic), by ignoring how Valentin must grow in order to learn to treat Molina as an individual ("I learned a lot from you, Molina. . . . Molina, promise me you won't let anybody push you around" [261]), and finally by failing to recognize that political and sexual oppression are not two mutually exclusive operations. Masiello writes:

> The real revolution, Puig implies, comes not from class struggle, as Valentin would suggest, but rather from sexual liberation, designed to free the individual from the constraints of bourgeois society. . . . Puig thus modifies a potential denunciation of institutionalized repression to focus instead on the personal reality of characters and the ideology of sexual politics.   (16–17)

The attempt to divorce the political from the sexual and the individual from the institutional leads not to a partial reading but to a misreading, as it severs the content from the context in which the novel was written and then severs the style from the content ("Language emerges as the [novel's] central protagonist," Masiello concludes [23]). This formalist criticism suggests that the social concerns out of which the novel grew are merely additive to the formal style of the work. It is, to the contrary, precisely the assumption that cultural criticism is simply additive to formalist literary criticism that novels like Puig's ought to make us examine.

Puig himself has emphasized this cultural context when talking in interviews about *Kiss of the Spider Woman*. In an interview with Ronald Christ, he explained that through the various liberation movements—liberation from military authoritarian regimes in Argentina, the civil rights movement, women's liberation struggles—he came to understand how the personal was political and how his own individual "failure" to "embody authority" (53) might not be a failure so much as a rejection of larger, socially institutionalized repressions:

> **Puig:** What helped me mainly were all the liberation movements that have taken place lately, in Argentina as well as here. The women's liberation movement is one of the most

important things that ever happened. At first women thought that they had to be weak, frail, in order to *be*, especially when searching for sexual pleasure. That was the big trap, the big lie.

Christ: How is this awareness reflected in *The Buenos Aires Affair*?

Puig: When I wrote *Rita Hayworth*, I still believed in Clark Gable as a force of Nature. I thought it was a cruel Nature that had made this strong man and those weak Harlows but that was, in fact, Nature's law. Now I am convinced that Clark Gable is an historical-cultural product, not Nature's creature. In *The Buenos Aires Affair*, I tried to explore the final consequences of the "frail" attitude in women, which is masochism.

Christ: So that novel is an earlier step in the development because woman does not realize the sado-masochistic basis of the relationship?

Puig: Yes. But in the fourth book, she realizes it! [that is, Molina realizes it in *Kiss of the Spider Woman*].

Christ: What does that mean for you?

Puig: For me it means a lot. It means almost everything because I myself have always rejected the role of the authoritarian male. There was something that I hated about it even though I thought that it was natural. I hated it in spite of its apparently being Nature's decision. Now I consider the rejection of authority, which has cost me so much trouble throughout my life, an unconscious rebellion, but a healthy one.   (60–61)

Puig's *Kiss of the Spider Woman* brings to the surface the learned masochism of Molina and the learned aggression of Valentin and allows them, through their discussion of these same formations in the films, to explore the operations of domination. In addition, the reader who listens in on this dialogue is pulled into the exploration of domination by yet another textual means, the scholarly footnotes that refer less to the specifics of the textual dialogue than to the social text of oppression in which the narrative unfolds.

Sexual and political polarity seem to define the positions of Molina and Valentin in their opening discussion of the film about the panther woman (based on Jacques Tourneur's horror film *Cat People*). Molina's eye picks out seductive details of fabric and style—"Her stockings glitter, that kind they turned inside out when the sheen went out of style, her legs look flushed and silky, you can't tell if its the stockings or her skin" (4)—embodied in the film presentation while Valentin rides roughshod over them to get to what he sees as the message—"a real piece," he says (5). Molina sees the unconsummated union between the panther woman and the architect, her new husband, as doomed by the mythic past ("the legend is that the race of panther women never died out and remains hidden in some corner of the world, and they all seem like normal women, but if a man happens to kiss any of them, the woman can turn into a savage beast" [13]). Identifying with the "hotshot" psychiatrist in the movie, a fellow possessed of both a pimp's pencil-line mustache and the idea that he can cure the heroine by initiating her to sex, Valentin gives a clinical explanation; "Well I think she's frigid, she's afraid of men, either that or she has some idea about sex that's really violent, and so she invents things" (15). Valentin's views on the film have more intellectual depth than Molina's sentimental investment, but Valentin is guilty of setting the gentle Molina up by speaking to this sensibility. After asking Molina to describe how he imagines the architect's late mother to have been ("I don't know, a really good person. A lovely lady, who gave her husband every happiness and her children too, always managing everything perfectly"), Valentin comes in for the "consciousness-raising" kill:

> —Yes, always impeccable. Perfect. She has her servants, she exploits people who can't do anything else but serve her, for a few pennies. And clearly, she felt very happy with her husband, who in turn exploited her, forced her to do whatever he wanted, keeping her cooped up in a house like a slave, waiting for him—
> —Listen . . .
> —waiting for him every night, until he got back from his law firm, or from his doctor's office. And she was in perfect agreement with the whole system, and she didn't rebel, and she fed her own son the same crap and now the son runs smack into the panther woman. Good luck with that one.   (16–17)

We sympathize with Molina when he gets angry with Valentin for demeaning him because of his longing for a mother "full of affection," and we understand his feeling of betrayal at Valentin's arrogant breaking of the community the film narrative has created between them: "Why break the illusion for me, and for yourself too? What kind of trick is that to pull?" (17). And Valentin's pontificating the next day about denying all sensuality and all emotional investment in order to serve the revolutionary cause better does not make him any more sympathetic. Yet when Molina narrates the second film in the book, we are led to reconsider Valentin's condemnation of Molina's sentimentality.

The Nazi propaganda film *Her Real Glory* depicts the love affair between the cabaret star Leni Lamaison and a high-ranking officer of the occupation forces of the Third Reich. Different members of the French maquis are depicted as, first, a black marketeer "butcher, with a pointy head, and one of those tiny caps sitting on the back of his scalp" ("like a rabbi," Valentin points out); second, "a clubfoot; one of his shoes has a giant block under it, almost like a hoof, made out of silver"; and finally, a man with "a face like a murderer's, kind of cross-eyed looking, a criminal's face, but retarded too" (48–49). Molina, transported by the spectacle of the film, by its silver gardens, its white fountains, its fairy-tale houses, says, "if I had the chance to choose one film to see all over again, it would have to be this one" (56). When Valentin asks if he doesn't realize that it is "a Nazi piece of junk," Molina argues that he likes it—even given the propaganda—because "it's well made, and besides it's a work of art" (56)—that is, in formalist terms, it is exempt from social and cultural analysis. Molina's uncritical outpouring of sentimentality becomes suddenly less innocent than it first had seemed. But it is not Molina's sentimental nature that is at fault here so much as the system that directs desire toward perverse ends—and it is here that kitsch and propaganda meet.

Puig prepares us for this ever more complex exploration of the connections among emotion, politics, and sexuality in an earlier exchange that occurs when Valentin complains that Molina is "oversensitive":

> —So what am I supposed to do about it? That's how I am, very sentimental.
> —I'll say. It sounds just like a . . .

—What are you stopping for?

—Nothing.

—Say it, I know what you were going to say, Valentin.

—Don't be silly.

—Say it, like a woman, that's what you were going to say.

—Yes.

—And what's so bad about being soft like a woman? Why is it men or whoever, some poor bastard, some queen, can't be sensitive, too, if he's got a mind to?

—I don't know, but sometimes that kind of behavior can get in a man's way.

—When? When it comes to torturing?

—No, when it comes to being finished with the torturers.

—But, if men acted like women there wouldn't be any more torturers.

—And what would you do without men?

—You're right. They're mostly brutes, but I like them.

—Molina . . . But you did say if they all acted like women then there wouldn't be any torturers. You've got a point there, a flimsy one, but still, it's a point.

—Nice of you to say so.

—What do you mean nice?

—Nice and uppity. (29)

This exchange between the cellmates brings into relief how imprisoned they both are by culturally conditioned sexuality. Valentin is embarrassed by his criticism that Molina is "like a woman" because it points to the reactionary idea that to be female is to be inferior. As a revolutionary, Valentin recognizes his hypocrisy in using "woman" as an aspersion, yet he catches Molina out when he demonstrates that Molina's version of the "female role" valorizes an attraction to violent masculinity and contains the masochistic within it. This particular gender deployment, which makes females weak and dependent and males brutal and domineering, leads to the creation of the "couple" as an insufficient whole constructed of two flawed halves. Through the interpretation and analysis of the B-movie plots, the prisoners begin to explore both the failures of the existing gender system and the possibility for a more liberating human community.

The press releases from Tobias-Berlin Studios attached to the narration of the Nazi superproduction *Her Real Glory* illuminate this investigation by demonstrating that sexual "liberation" and political freedom are not inevitably linked. Although the film and the release are creations of Puig's imagination, they are typical of the genre, and the statements attributed to leaders like Hitler and Goebbels are historically accurate:

> Our ideal of beauty must forever be one of healthy fitness. . . . Her single mission is to be beautiful and bear the sons of the world. A woman who bequeaths five sons to the *Volk* has made a greater contribution than that of the finest woman jurist in the world. Because there is no place for women in politics within the ideological context of National Socialism, inasmuch as to drag women into the parliamentary sphere, where they pale, is to rob them of their dignity. (84)

The Nazi conception of womanhood had its roots in the movement for sexual "liberation" in the earlier Weimar Republic. As Atina Grossmann documents in her "The New Woman and the Rationalization of Sexuality in Weimar Germany," the birthrate, which had been dropping since 1870 in Germany, was taken seriously after World War I when the decline was perceived to have hit the working class—the producers of laborers and soldiers. The new woman was needed to replace this loss of manpower, and, given the increase in studies of frigidity, a new man with a better technique was also in demand. Production was explicitly linked to reproduction. The scientific management of Taylorism entered the bedroom as well as the workplace as Grossmann demonstrates by quoting Margarete Kaiser's *Die Liebe als Kunst*, a Weimar sex manual:

> Most important is the expression of life rhythms in the rhythms of the erotic. . . . people whose lives take place unrhythmically, who can show no regularity in their work process, their time distribution, their production, their leisure and their sleep, also tend to practice unrhythmic, inconsistent, jerky coital motions. (Grossman 164)

The liberation of sexuality put to use by the fatherland is a far cry from the gender liberation Molina and Valentin are beginning to explore. And Puig underlines the complexity of gender formation in the other series of footnotes, which begins at this point in the novel and explores theories of the origins of homosexuality and, eventually, of sexuality per se. Puig has commented that his novel is intended to be blatantly didactic:

> I needed, in this novel, to give a summary of all that had been researched on sexual exploitation, "roles," etc. . . . Finally the didactic play of appending footnotes to conform with the events in the novel occurred to me. . . . I believe that people need a "digest" on sexual politics, because the average reader has to struggle a lot to reach the essence of a text by Marcuse or Reich. Also the elitist pedantry of the style of these authors—although not intentional—seemed to me quite reactionary. And this is precisely what I intended to do in the novel, or if you prefer, in the margin of the novel; to give this material intelligible form in everyday language. (Díez 26)

Like the psychoanalysts, Valentin needs to recognize his own elitism ("You're so damn pedantic," Molina tells him. "I'd like to see how I don't come up to your level" [62]). Both Molina and Valentin recite film scripts to themselves that reflect this need for self-examination. Angry at Valentin for finding his film narrations trivial—in comparison to the revolution—and for assuming in however disguised a fashion that he is an uneducated, lower-class "faggot," Molina tells himself the story of *The Enchanted Cottage*, where after the "second worthless world war" a scar-faced aviator, no longer handsome, marries an ugly orphaned servant girl and they find happiness. "To put it simply," the blind old narrator of the film tells them, "you are beautiful to one another, because you love each other so and thus see nothing but your souls" (111). Only the jaundiced eye of the world outside the enchanted cottage can destroy this love story. At the end of his interior monologue about the film Molina thinks, "I won't tell him any more of the films I like the most, they're just for me, in my mind's eye, so no filthy words can touch them, this son of a bitch and his pissass of a revolution" (112).

But Molina, nurturant as he is, relents when Valentin, in his turn, finally falls ill from poisoned food. He tries to take Valentin's mind off his agony by telling him the sort of film "men" are supposed to like, one of the "Le Mans/Indianapolis Racing Car" genre. In this narrative the "playboy son of one of those wealthy [South American] landowners with the big banana plantations" rejects his parents' lifestyle but ends up trying to rescue his father from the guerillas. This story brings Valentin to speak of his own mother: "My mother is the kind of woman who's very . . . very difficult, that's why I don't talk about her much. She's never liked my ideas, she believes she's entitled to everything she owns" (121). This nexus of privilege, struggle, and family ties leads into Valentin's own interior monologue, which concerns the death of the father, the infidelity of the mother, and the revolt of the son. Valentin envisions the son as

> a fellow who joins up with the guerillas in the mountains, . . . a fellow who doesn't want to mix his blood with the blood of an Indian, a fellow who feels ashamed about all his feelings, . . . a fellow who doesn't know how to make up for his faults, a fellow who leads a guerilla assault against the plantation, . . . a fellow who opens fire on his own home, a fellow who opens fire on his own flesh and blood. (146)

Valentin's realization is that he betrays his class and family in embracing the cause and betrays the cause in remaining in large part a middle-class intellectual outsider still inscribed with all the biases of his upbringing. He begins also to recognize that he is sexist and inhumane as well (he longs for Marta, a bourgeois girl with "class," and he belittles Molina). Molina suffers a parallel monologue about self-doubt as he pictures himself as "the white nurse" (164), "the night nurse who is inexperienced" (171), "the poor nurse, so unlucky, they assign her to a patient on the critical list and she doesn't know how to keep him from dying or killing her" (172).

At this point in the text the movie plot—Molina's rendition of Tourneur's *I Walked with a Zombie*—and the psychoanalytic footnotes both comment on the force of the inscription of society's laws on the self and on the extent of this interior colonization, which is such a large part of the unconscious self. *I Walked with a Zombie* has at its center a theme all the movies share: the control of our destinies by forces outside our own personal wills—inherited myths, war efforts, parental approval, class bias. We are inscribed by laws we may feel are alien to our more intelligent, humane, and generous selves, and yet these laws make up a large part of the submerged self we discover on reflection. Valentin discovers himself to be elitist and aggressive. He represses his joy in life in order to carry on an ascetic study of "revolution." Puig's footnotes on Freud state: "repression, in general terms, can be traced back to the imposition of domination of one individual over others, this first individual having been none other than the father. Beginning by such domination, the patriarchal form of society was established, based on the inferiority of the woman and the intensive repression of sexuality" (151). And Puig adds, "Otto Rank considers the long development, which runs from paternal domination to a powerful system of state run by men, to be a prolongation of the same primary repression, whose purpose is the increasingly pronounced exclusion of women" (152). Valentin's monologue reveals his recognition that as an aggressive revolutionary he is part freedom fighter, part executioner: "the learned executioner's cortex, factory girl heads roll, zombie heads, impressive gaze of the learned executioner down upon the poor innocent cortex of a chick from suburbia, of a fag from suburbia . . . the learned executioner obeys an order which comes from no one knows where" (188). Valentin's guilt, like that of many revolutionary intellectuals, stems from his persistent class prejudice; he recognizes that the working class (Molina, Gabriel) does not share his revolutionary vision, and he feels impotent in the face of these interior and exterior contradictions.

The key to what Valentin and Molina must learn about the imbrication of political and sexual repression by the exercise of domination is in Puig's final psychoanalytic footnote on Anneli Taube's *Sexuality and Revolution*:

> The rejection which a highly sensitive boy experiences toward an oppressive father—as symbol of the violently authoritarian, masculine attitude—is a conscious one. The boy, at the moment when he decides not to adhere to the world proposed by such a father—use of weapons, violently competitive sports, disdain for sensitivity as a feminine attribute, etc.—is actually exercising a free and even revolutionary choice inasmuch as he is rejecting the role of the stronger, the exploitative one. Of course, such a boy could not suspect, on the other hand, that Western civilization, apart from the world of the father, will not present him with any alternative model for conduct in those first dangerously decisive years . . . other than his mother. And the world of the mother—tenderness, tolerance, and even the arts—will turn out to be much more attractive to him, especially because of the absence of aggressivity: but the world of the mother, and here is where his intuition would fail him, is also the world of submission, since the mother is coupled with an authoritarian male, who only conceives of conjugal union as subordination of the woman to the man. (207–08)

The final dialogues between Molina and Valentin demonstrate a dawning recognition that the authoritarian government and the prison bureaucracy are only embodiments of a larger social ill: a society based on aggression and humiliation. Valentin realizes that the real revolution for Molina will be first to recognize his own worth:

> —I mean that if you enjoy being a woman . . . you shouldn't feel any the less because of it.
> — . . .
> —I don't know if you follow me . . . how do you see it?
> — . . .
> —I just mean that you don't have to make up for it with anything, with favors, or excuses. You don't have to . . . submit.
> —But if a man is . . . my husband, he has to give the orders, so he will feel right. That's the natural thing, because that makes him the . . . the man of the house.

—No, the man of the house and the woman of the house have to be equal with one another. If not, their relation becomes a form of exploitation.

—But then there's no kick to it . . . The kick is in the fact that when a man embraces you . . . you may feel a little bit frightened.

—No, that's all wrong. Whoever put that idea in your head? It's absolutely wrong.

—But that's the way I feel.

—You don't have to feel that way, you've been fed an old wives tale by whoever filled your head with that nonsense. To be a woman you don't have to be . . . a martyr. (243–44)

And when Molina is released from prison, he does begin to discover his own worth. When chastised by his "godfather" for his sexually deviant behavior, Molina apparently asserts his right to be as he is, because the godfather replies, "You never spoke to me in that tone before, is that what you learned in prison?" (267). Molina goes on to find a job, to release himself from his humiliating attraction to Gabriel and, finally, to reach Valentin's friends—although he knows he is being watched. It is significant that Molina becomes a political martyr and that Valentin is tortured sexually. The prison paramedic says, "The way they've worked you over is unbelievable. Those burns in the groin . . . It will take weeks to heal up" (276). Valentin's thoughts in the final chapter evidence the growth he has undergone; he realizes that sexual liberation and political freedom depend on two modes of action: the identification and dismantling of domination and the creation, in its place, of a community based on a respect for difference rather than on coercion and alterity.

Political Criticism

TERRY EAGLETON

There are two familiar ways in which any theory can provide itself with a distinct purpose and identity. Either it can define itself in terms of its particular *methods* of enquiry, or it can define itself in terms of the particular *object* that is being inquired into. Any attempt to define literary theory in terms of a distinctive method is doomed to failure. Literary theory is supposed to reflect on the nature of literature and literary criticism. But just think of how many methods are involved in literary criticism. You can discuss the poet's asthmatic childhood, or examine her peculiar use of syntax; you can detect the rustling of silk in the hissing of the *s*'s, explore the phenomenology of reading, relate the literary work to the state of the class struggle, or find out how many copies it sold. These methods have nothing whatsoever of significance in common. In fact they have more in common with other "disciplines"—linguistics, history, sociology, and so on—than they have with each other. Methodologically speaking, literary criticism is a nonsubject. If literary theory is a kind of "metacriticism," a critical reflection on criticism, then it follows that it too is a nonsubject.

Perhaps, then, the unity of literary studies is to be sought elsewhere. Perhaps literary criticism and literary theory just mean any kind of talk (of a certain level of "competence," clearly enough) about an object named literature. Perhaps it is the object, not the method, which distinguishes and delimits the discourse. As long as that object remains relatively stable, we can move equably from biographical to mythological to semiotic methods and still know where we are. But . . . literature has no such stability. The unity of the object is as illusory as the unity of the method. "Literature," as Roland Barthes once remarked, "is what gets taught."

Maybe this lack of methodological unity in literary studies should not worry us unduly. After all, it would be a rash person who would define geography or philosophy, distinguish neatly between sociology and anthropology, or advance a snap definition of "history." Perhaps we should celebrate the plurality of critical methods, adopt a tolerantly ecumenical posture and rejoice in our freedom from the tyranny of any single procedure. Before we become too euphoric, however, we should notice that there are certain problems here too. For one thing, not all of these methods are mutually compatible. However generously liberal-minded we aim to be, trying to combine structuralism, phenomenology, and psychoanalysis is more likely to lead to a nervous breakdown than to a brilliant literary career. Those critics who parade their pluralism are usually able to do so because the different methods they have in mind are not all that different in the end. For another thing, some of these "methods" are hardly methods at all. Many literary critics dislike the whole idea of method and prefer to work by glimmers and hunches, intuitions and sudden perceptions. It is perhaps fortunate that this way of proceeding has not yet infiltrated medicine or aeronautical engineering, but even so one should not take this modest disowning of method altogether seriously, since what glimmers and hunches you have will depend on a latent structure of assumptions often quite as stubborn as that of any structuralist. It is notable that such "intuitive" criticism, which relies not on "method" but on "intelligent sensitivity," does not often seem to intuit, say, the presence of ideological values in literature. Yet there is no reason, on its own reckoning, why it should not. Some traditional critics would appear to hold that other people subscribe to theories while they prefer to read literature "straightforwardly." No theoretical or ideological predilections, in other words, mediate between themselves and the text: to describe George Eliot's later world as one of "mature resignation" is not ideological, whereas to claim that it reveals evasion and compromise is. It is therefore difficult to engage such critics in debate about ideological preconceptions, since the power of ideology over them is nowhere more marked than in their honest belief that their readings are "innocent." It was Leavis who was being "doctrinal" in attacking Milton, not C. S. Lewis in defending him; it is feminist critics who insist on confusing literature with politics by examining fictional images of gender, not conventional critics who are being political by arguing that Richardson's Clarissa is largely responsible for her own rape.

Even so, the fact that some critical methods are less methodical than others proves something of an embarrassment to the pluralists who believe that there is a little truth in everything. (This theoretical pluralism also has its political correlative: seeking to understand everybody's point of view quite often suggests that you yourself are disinterestedly up on high or in the middle, and trying to resolve conflicting viewpoints into a consensus implies a refusal of the truth that some conflicts can be resolved on one side alone.) Literary criticism is rather like a laboratory in which some of the staff are seated in white coats at control panels, while others are throwing sticks in the air or spinning coins. Genteel amateurs jostle with hard-nosed professionals, and after a century or so of "English" they have still not decided to which camp the subject really belongs. This dilemma is the product of the peculiar history of English, and it cannot really be settled because what is at stake is much more than a mere conflict over methods or the lack of them. The true reason why the pluralists are wishful thinkers is that what is at issue in the contention between different literary theories or "nontheories" are competing ideological strategies related to the very destiny of English studies in modern society. The problem with literary theory is that it can neither beat nor join the dominant ideologies of late industrial capitalism. Liberal humanism seeks to oppose or at least modify such ideologies with its distaste for the technocratic and its nurturing of spiritual wholeness in a hostile world; certain brands of formalism and structuralism try to take over the technocratic rationality of such a society and thus incorporate themselves into it. Northrop Frye and the New Critics thought that they had pulled off a synthesis of the two, but how many students of literature today read them? Liberal humanism has dwindled to the impotent conscience of bourgeois society: gentle, sensitive, and ineffectual; structuralism has already more or less vanished into the literary museum.

The impotence of liberal humanism is a symptom of its essentially contradictory relationship to modern capitalism. For although it forms part of the "official" ideology of such society and the "humanities" exist to reproduce it, the social order within which it exists has in one sense very little time for it at all. Who is concerned with the uniqueness of the individual, the imperishable truths of the human condition, or the sensuous textures of lived experience in the Foreign Office or the boardroom of Standard Oil? Capitalism's reverential hat tipping to the arts is obvious hypocrisy, except when it can hang them on its walls as a sound investment. Yet capitalist states have continued to direct funds into higher education humanities departments, and though such departments are usually the first in line for savage cutting when capitalism enters on one of its periodic crises, it is doubtful that it is only hypocrisy, a fear of appearing in its true philistine colours, which compels this grudging support. The truth is that liberal humanism is at once largely ineffectual and the best ideology of the "human" that present bourgeois society can muster. The "unique individual" is indeed important when it comes to defending the business entrepreneur's right to make profit while throwing men and women out of work; the individual must at all costs have the "right to choose," provided this means the right to buy one's child an expensive private education while other children are deprived of their school meals, rather than the rights of women to decide whether to have children in the first place. The "imperishable truths of the human condition" include such verities as freedom and democracy, the essences of which are embodied in our particular way of life. The "sensuous textures of lived experience" can be roughly translated as reacting from the gut—judging according to habit, prejudice and "common sense" rather than according to some inconvenient, "aridly theoretical" set of debatable ideas. There is, after all, room for the humanities yet, much as those who guarantee our freedom and democracy despise them.

Departments of literature in higher education, then, are part of the ideological apparatus of the modern capitalist state. They are not wholly reliable apparatuses, since for one thing the humanities contain many values, meanings, and traditions which are antithetical to that state's social priorities, which are rich in kinds of wisdom and experience beyond its comprehension. For another thing, if you allow a lot of young people to do nothing for a few years but read books and talk to each other then it is possible that, given certain wider historical circumstances, they will not only begin to question some of the values transmitted to them but begin to interrogate the authority by which they are transmitted. There is of course no harm in students questioning the values conveyed to them: indeed it is part of the very meaning of higher education that they should do so. Independent thought, critical dissent and reasoned dialectic are part of the very stuff of a humane education; hardly anyone . . . will demand that your essay on Chaucer or Baudelaire arrives inexorably at certain preset conclusions. All that is being demanded is that you manipulate a particular language in acceptable ways. Becoming certificated by the state as proficient in literary studies is a matter of being able to talk and write in certain ways. It is this which is being taught, examined, and certificated, not what you personally think or believe, though what is thinkable will of course be constrained by the language itself. You can think or believe what you want, as long as you can speak this particular language. Nobody is especially concerned about what you say, with what extreme, moderate, radical, or conservative positions you adopt, provided that they are compatible with, and can be articulated within, a specific form of discourse. It is just that certain meanings and positions will not be articulable within it. Literary studies, in other words, are a question of the signifier, not of the signified. Those employed to teach you this form of discourse will remember whether or not you were able to speak it proficiently long after they have forgotten what you said.

Literary theorists, critics, and teachers, then, are not so much purveyors of doctrine as custodians of a discourse. Their task is to preserve this discourse, extend and elaborate it as necessary, defend it from other forms of discourse, initiate newcomers into it, and determine whether or not they have successfully mastered it. The discourse itself has no definite signified, which is not to say that it embodies no assumptions: it is rather a network of signifiers able to envelop a whole field of meanings, objects and practices. Certain pieces of writing are selected as being more amenable to this discourse than others, and these are what is known as literature or the "literary canon." The fact that this canon is usually regarded as fairly fixed, even at times as eternal and immutable, is in a sense ironic, because since literary critical discourse has no definite signified it can, if it wants to, turn its attention to more or less any kind of writing. Some of those hottest in their defense of the canon have from time to time demonstrated how the discourse can be made to operate on "nonliterary" writing. This, indeed, is the embarrassment of literary criticism, that it defines for itself a special object, literature, while existing as a set of discursive techniques which have no reason to stop short at that object at all. If you have nothing better to do at a party you can always try on a literary critical analysis of it, speak of its styles and genres, discriminate its significant nuances or formalize its sign systems. Such a "text" can prove quite as rich as one of the canonical works, and critical dissections of it quite as ingenious as those of Shakespeare. So either literary criticism confesses that it can handle parties just as well as it can Shakespeare, in which case it is in danger of losing its identity along with its object: or it agrees that parties may be interestingly analysed provided that this is called something else: ethnomethodology or hermeneutical phenomenology, perhaps. Its own concern is with literature, because literature is more valuable and rewarding than any of the other texts on which the critical discourse might operate. The disadvantage of this claim is that it is plainly untrue: many films and works of philosophy are considerably more valuable than much that is included in the "literary canon." It is not that they are valuable in different ways: they could present objects of value in the sense that criticism defines that term. Their exclusion from what is studied is not because they are not "amenable" to the discourse: it is a question of the arbitrary authority of the literary institution.

Another reason why literary criticism cannot justify its self-limiting to certain works by an appeal to their "value" is that criticism is part of a literary institution which constitutes these works as valuable in the first place. It is not only parties that need to be *made* into worthwhile literary objects by being treated in specific ways, but also Shakespeare. Shakespeare was not great literature lying conveniently to hand, which the literary institution then happily discovered: he is great literature because the institution constitutes him as such. This does not mean that he is not "really" great literature—that it is just a matter of people's opinions about him—because there is no such thing as literature which is "really" great, or "really" anything, independently of the ways in which that writing is treated within specific forms of social and institutional life. There are an indefinite number of ways of discussing Shakespeare, but not all of them count as literary critical. Perhaps Shakespeare himself, his friends and actors, did not talk about his plays in ways which we would regard as literary critical. Perhaps some of the most interesting statements which could be made about Shakespearean drama would also not count as belonging to literary criticism. Literary criticism selects, processes, corrects, and rewrites texts in accordance with certain institutionalized norms of the "literary"—norms which are at any given time arguable and always historically variable. For though I have said that critical discourse has no determinate signified, there are certainly a great many ways of talking about literature which it excludes, and a great many discursive moves and strategies which it disqualifies as invalid, illicit, noncritical, nonsense. Its apparent generosity at the level of the signified is matched only by its sectarian intolerance at the level of the signifier. Regional dialects of the discourse, so to speak, are acknowledged and sometimes tolerated, but you must not sound as though you are speaking another language altogether. To do so is to recognize in the sharpest way that critical discourse is power. To be on the inside of the discourse itself is to be blind to this power, for what is more natural and nondominative than to speak one's own tongue?

The power of critical discourse moves on several levels. It is the power of "policing" language—of determining that certain statements must be excluded because they do not conform to what is acceptably sayable. It is the power of policing writing itself, classifying it into the "literary" and "nonliterary," the enduringly great and the ephemerally popular. It is the power of authority vis-à-vis others—the power relations between those who define and preserve the discourse and those who are selectively admitted to it. It is the power of certificating or noncertificating those who have been judged to speak the discourse better or worse. Finally, it is a question of the power relations between the literary-academic institution, where all of this occurs, and the ruling power interests of society at large, whose ideological needs will be served and whose personnel will be reproduced by the preservation and controlled extension of the discourse in question.

I have argued that the theoreticallly limitless extendability of critical discourse, the fact that it is only arbitrarily confined to "literature," is or should be a source of embarrassment to the custodians of the canon. The objects of criticism, like those of the Freudian drive, are in a certain sense contingent and replaceable. Ironically, criticism only really became aware of this fact when, sensing that its own liberal humanism was running out of steam, it turned for aid to more ambitious or rigorous critical methods. It thought that by adding a judicious pinch of historical analysis here or swallowing a nonaddictive dose of structuralism there, it could exploit these otherwise alien approaches to eke out its own dwindling spiritual capital. The boot, however, might well prove to be on the other foot. For you cannot engage in an historical analysis of literature without recognizing that literature itself is a recent historical invention; you cannot apply structuralist tools to *Paradise Lost* without acknowledging that just the same tools can be applied to the *Daily Mirror*. Criticism can thus prop itself up only at the risk of losing its defining object; it has the unenviable choice of stifling or suffocating. If literary theory presses its own implications too far, then it has argued itself out of existence.

This, I would suggest, is the best possible thing for it to do. The final logical move in a process which began by recognizing that literature is an illusion is to recognize that literary theory is an illusion too. It is not of course an illusion in the sense that I have invented the various people I have discussed [above]: Northrop Frye really does exist, and so did F. R. Leavis. It is an illusion first in the sense that literary theory, as I hope to have shown, is really no more than a branch of social ideologies, utterly without any unity or identity which would adequately distinguish it from philosophy, linguistics, psychology, cultural and sociological thought; and secondly in the sense that the one hope it has of distinguishing itself— clinging to an object named literature—is misplaced. . . . But this is not exactly the point. The point is whether it is possible to speak of "literary theory" without perpetuating the illusion that literature exists as a distinct, bounded object of knowledge, or whether it is not preferable to draw the practical consequences of the fact that literary theory can handle Bob Dylan just as well as John Milton. My own view is that it is most useful to see "literature" as a name which people give from time to time for different reasons to certain kinds of writing within a whole field of what Michel Foucault has called "discursive practices," and that if anything is to be an object of study it is this whole field of practices rather than just those sometimes rather obscurely labeled "literature." I am countering the theories set out . . . not with a *literary* theory, but with a different kind of discourse—whether one calls it of "culture," "signifying practices," or whatever is not of first importance—which would include the objects ("literature") with which these other theories deal, but which would transform them by setting them in a wider context.

But is this not to extend the boundaries of literary theory to a point where any kind of particularity is lost? Would not a "theory of discourse" run into just the same problems of methodology and object of study which we have seen in the case of literary studies? After all, there are any number of discourses and any number of ways of studying them. What would be specific to the kind of study I have in mind, however, would be its concern for the kinds of *effects* which discourses produce, and how they produce them. Reading a zoology textbook to find out about giraffes is part of studying zoology, but reading it to see how its discourse is structured and organized, and examining what kind of effects these forms and devices produce in particular readers in actual situations, is a different kind of project. It is, in fact, probably the oldest form of "literary criticism" in the world, known as rhetoric. Rhetoric, which was the received form of critical analysis all the way from ancient society to the eighteenth century, examined the way discourses are constructed in order to achieve certain effects. It was not worried about whether its objects of enquiry were speaking or writing, poetry or philosophy, fiction or historiography: its horizon was nothing less than the field of discursive practices in society as a whole, and its particular interest lay in grasping such practices as forms of power and performance. This is not to say that it ignored the truth value of the discourses in question, since this could often be crucially relevant to the kinds of effect they produced in their readers and listeners. Rhetoric in its major phase was neither a "humanism," concerned in some intuitive way with people's experience of language, nor a "formalism," preoccupied simply with analyzing linguistic devices. It looked at such devices in terms of concrete performance—they were means of pleading, persuading, inciting and so on—and at people's responses to discourse in terms of linguistic structures and the material situations in which they functioned. It saw speaking and writing not merely as textual objects, to be aesthetically contemplated or endlessly deconstructed, but as forms of *activity* inseparable from the wider social relations between writers and readers, orators and audiences, and as largely unintelligible outside the social purposes and conditions in which they were embedded (see my *Walter Benjamin*, pt. 2, ch. 2).

Like all the best radical positions, then, mine is a thoroughly traditionalist one. I wish to recall literary criticism from certain fashionable, newfangled ways of thinking it has been seduced by—"literature" as a specially privileged object, the "aesthetic" as separable from social determinants, and so on—and return it to the ancient paths which it has abandoned. Although my case is thus reactionary, I do not mean that we should revive the whole range of ancient rhetorical terms and substitute these for modern critical language. We do not need to do this, since there are enough concepts contained in [contemporary] literary theories . . . to allow us at least to make a start. Rhetoric, or discourse theory, shares with Formalism, structuralism, and semiotics an interest in the formal devices of language but like reception theory is also concerned with how these devices are actually effective at the point of "consumption"; its preoccupation with discourse as a form of power and desire can learn much from deconstruction and psychoanalytical theory, and its belief that discourse can be a humanly transformative affair shares a good deal with liberal humanism. The fact that "literary theory" is an illusion does not mean that we cannot retrieve from it many valuable concepts for a different kind of discursive practice altogether.

There was, of course, a reason why rhetoric bothered to analyze discourses. It did not analyze them just because they were there, any more than most forms of literary criticism today examine literature just for the sake of it. Rhetoric wanted to find out the most effective ways of pleading, persuading, and debating, and rhetoricians studied such devices in other people's language in order to use them more productively in their own. It was, as we would say today, a "creative" as well as a "critical" activity: the word "rhetoric" covers both the practice of effective discourse and the science of it. Similarly, there must be a reason why we would consider it worthwhile to develop a form of study which would look at the various sign systems and signifying practices in our own society, all the way from *Moby-Dick* to the Muppet show, from Dryden and Jean-Luc Godard to the portrayal of women in advertisements and the rhetorical techniques of Government reports. All theory and knowledge, as I have argued previously, is "interested," in the sense that you can always ask why one should bother to develop it in the first place. One striking weakness of most formalist and structuralist criticism is that it is unable to answer this question. The structuralist really does examine sign systems because they happen to be there, or if this seems indefensible is forced into some rationale—studying our modes of sense making will deepen our critical self-awareness—which is not much different from the standard line of the liberal humanists. The strength of the liberal humanist case, by contrast, is that it is able to say why dealing with literature is worthwhile. Its answer, as we have seen, is roughly that it makes you a better person. This is also the weakness of the liberal humanist case.

The liberal humanist response, however, is not weak because it believes that literature can be transformative. It is weak because it usually grossly overestimates this transformative power, considers it in isolation from any determining social context, and can formulate what it means by a "better person" only in the most narrow and abstract of terms. They are terms which generally ignore the fact that to be a person in the Western society of the 1980s is to be bound up with, and in some sense responsible for, the kinds of political conditions [we are living with]. Liberal humanism is a suburban moral ideology, limited in practice to largely interpersonal matters. It is stronger on adultery than on armaments, and its valuable concerns with freedom, democracy, and individual rights are simply not concrete enough. Its view of democracy, for example, is the abstract one of the ballot box, rather than a specific, living, and practical democracy which might also somehow concern the operations of the Foreign Office and Standard Oil. Its view of individual freedom is similarly abstract: the freedom of any particular individual is crippled and parasitic as long as it depends on the futile labor and active oppression of others. Literature may protest against such conditions or it may not, but it is only possible in the first place because of them. As the German critic Walter Benjamin put it, "There is no cultural document that is not at the same time a record of barbarism" ("Edward Fuchs" 359). Socialists are those who wish to draw the full, concrete, practical applications of the abstract notions of freedom and democracy to which liberal humanism subscribes, taking them at their word when they draw attention to the "vividly particular." It is for this reason that many Western socialists are restless with the liberal humanist opinion of the tyrannies in Eastern Europe, feeling that these opinions simply do not go far enough: what would be necessary to bring down such tyrannies would not be just more free speech, but a workers' revolution against the state.

What it means to be a "better person," then, must be concrete and practical—that is to say, concerned with people's political situations as a whole—rather than narrowly abstract, concerned only with the immediate interpersonal relations which can be abstracted from this concrete whole. It must be a question of political and not only of "moral" argument: that is to say, it must be *genuine* moral argument, which sees the relations between individual qualities and values and our whole material conditions of existence. Political argument is not an alternative to moral preoccupations: it is those preoccupations taken seriously in their full implications. But the liberal humanists are right to see that there is a *point* in studying literature, and that this point is not itself, in the end, a literary one. What they are arguing, although this way of putting it would grate harshly on their ears, is that literature has a *use*. Few words are more offensive to literary ears than "use," evoking as it does paperclips and hair driers. The Romantic opposition to the utilitarian ideology of capitalism has made "use" an unusable word: for the aesthetes, the glory of art is its utter uselessness. Yet few of us nowadays would be prepared to subscribe to *that*: every reading of a work is surely in some sense a use of it. We may not use *Moby-Dick* to learn how to hunt whales, but we "get something out of it" even so. Every literary theory presupposes a certain use of literature, even if what you get out of it is its utter uselessness. Liberal humanist criticism is not wrong to use literature, but wrong to deceive itself that it does not. It uses it to further certain moral values, which as I hope to have shown are in fact indissociable from certain ideological ones, and in the end imply a particular form of politics. It is not that it reads the texts "disinterestedly" and then places what it has read in the service of its values: the values govern the actual reading process itself, inform what sense criticism makes of the works it studies. I am not going to argue, then, for a "political criticism" which would read literary texts in the light of certain values which are related to political beliefs and actions; all criticism does this. The idea that there are "nonpolitical" forms of criticism is simply a myth which furthers certain political uses of literature all the more effectively. The difference between a "political" and "nonpolitical" criticism is just the difference between the prime minister and the monarch: the latter furthers certain political ends by pretending not to, while the former makes no bones about it. It is always better to be honest in these matters. The difference between a conventional critic who speaks of the "chaos of experience" in Conrad or Woolf, and the feminist who examines those writers' images of gender, is not a distinction between nonpolitical and political criticism. It is a distinction between different forms of politics—between those who subscribe to the doctrine that history, society, and human reality as a whole are fragmentary, arbitrary, and directionless, and those who have other interests which imply alternative views about the way the world is. There is no way of settling the question of which politics is preferable in literary critical terms. You simply have to argue about politics. It is not a question of debating whether "literature" should be related to "history" or not: it is a question of different readings of history itself.

The feminist critic is not studying representations of gender simply because she believes that this will further her political ends. She also believes that gender and sexuality are central themes in literature and other sorts of discourse, and that any critical account which suppresses them is seriously defective. Similarly, the socialist critic does not see literature in terms of ideology or class struggle because these happen to be his or her political interests, arbitrarily projected on to literary works. He or she would hold that such matters are the very stuff of history, and that in so far as literature is an historical phenomenon, they are the very stuff of literature too. What would be strange would be if the feminist or socialist critic thought analyzing questions of gender or class was merely a matter of academic interest— merely a question of achieving a more satisfyingly complete account of literature. For why should it be worth doing this? Liberal humanist critics are not merely out for a more complete account of literature: they wish to discuss literature in ways which will deepen, enrich, and extend our lives. Socialist and feminist critics are quite at one with them on this: it is just that they wish to point out that such deepening and enriching entails the transformation of a society divided by class and gender. They would like the liberal humanist to draw the full implications of his or her position. If the liberal humanist disagrees, then this is a political argument, not an argument about whether one is "using" literature or not.

I [have] argued . . . that any attempt to define the study of literature in terms of either its method or its object is bound to fail. But we have now begun to discuss another way of conceiving what distinguishes one kind of discourse from another, which is neither ontological nor methodological but *strategic*. This means asking first not *what* the object is or *how* we should approach it, but *why* we should want to engage with it in the first place. The liberal humanist response to this question, I have suggested, is at once perfectly reasonable and, as it stands, entirely useless. Let us try to concretize it a little by asking how the reinvention of rhetoric that I have proposed (though it might equally as well be called "discourse theory" or "cultural studies" or whatever) might contribute to making us all better people. Discourses, sign systems, and signifying practices of all kinds, from film and television to fiction and the languages of natural science, produce effects, shape forms of consciousness and unconsciousness, which are closely related to the maintenance or transformation of our existing systems of power. They are thus closely related to what it means to be a person. Indeed "ideology" can be taken to indicate no more than this connection—the link or nexus between discourses and power. Once we have seen this, then the questions of theory and method may be allowed to appear in a new light. It is not a matter of starting from certain theoretical or methodological problems: it is a matter of starting from what we want to *do*, and then seeing which methods and theories will best help us to achieve these ends. Deciding on your strategy will not predetermine which methods and objects of study are most valuable. As far as the object of study goes, what you decide to examine depends very much on the practical situation. It may seem best to look at Proust and *King Lear*, or at children's television programmes or popular romances or avant-garde films. A radical critic is quite liberal on these questions: he rejects the dogmatism which would insist that Proust is always more worthy of study than television advertisements. It all depends on what you are trying to do, in what situation. Radical critics are also open-minded about questions of theory and method: they tend to be pluralists in this respect. Any method or theory which will contribute to the strategic goal of human emancipation, the production of "better people" through the socialist transformation of society, is acceptable. Structuralism, semiotics, psychoanalysis, deconstruction, reception theory, and so on—all of these approaches, and others, have their valuable insights which may be put to use. Not all literary theories, however, are likely to prove amenable to the strategic goals in question: there are several . . . which seem to me highly unlikely to do so. What you choose and reject theoretically, then, depends upon what you are practically trying to do. This has always been the case with literary criticism: it is simply that it is often very reluctant to realize the fact. In any academic study we select the objects and methods of procedure which we believe the most important, and our assessment of their importance is governed by frames of interest deeply rooted in our practical forms of social life. Radical critics are no different in this respect: it is just that they have a set of social priorities with which most people at present tend to disagree. This is why they are commonly dismissed as "ideological," because "ideology" is always a way of describing other people's interests rather than one's own.

No theory or method, in any case, will have merely one strategic use. They can be mobilized in a variety of different strategies for a variety of ends. But not all methods will be equally amenable to particular ends. It is a matter of finding out, not of assuming from the start that a single method or theory will do. One reason why I [am] not [ending] this [piece] with an account of socialist or feminist literary theory is that I believe such a move might encourage the reader to make what the philosophers call a "category mistake." It might mislead people into thinking that "political criticism" was another sort of critical approach from those I have discussed, different in its assumptions but essentially the same kind of thing. Since I have made clear my view that all criticism is in some sense political, and since people tend to give the word "political" to criticism whose politics disagrees with their own, this cannot be so. Socialist and feminist criticism are, of course, concerned with developing theories and methods appropriate to their aims: they consider questions of the relations between writing and sexuality, or of text and ideology, as other theories in general do not. They will also want to claim that these theories are more powerfully explanatory than others, for if they were not there would be no point in advancing them as theories. But it would be a mistake to see the particularity of such forms of criticism as consisting in the offering of alternative theories or methods. These forms of criticism differ from others because they define the object of analysis differently, have different values, beliefs, and goals, and thus offer different kinds of strategy for the realizing of these goals.

I say "goals," because it should not be thought that this form of criticism has only one. There are many goals to be achieved, and many ways of achieving them. In some situations the most productive procedure may be to explore how the signifying systems of a "literary" text produce certain ideological effects, or it may be a matter of doing the same with a Hollywood film. Such projects may prove particularly important in teaching cultural studies to children, but it may also be valuable to use literature to foster in them a sense of linguistic potential denied to them by their social conditions. There are "utopian" uses of literature of this kind, and a rich tradition of such utopian thought which should not be airily dismissed as "idealist." The active enjoyment of cultural artifacts should not, however, be relegated to the primary school, leaving older students with the grimmer business of analysis. Pleasure, enjoyment, the potentially transformative effects of discourse is quite as "proper" a topic for "higher" study as is the setting of Puritan tracts in the discursive formations of the seventeenth century. On other occasions what might prove more useful will not be the criticism or enjoyment of other people's discourse but the production of one's own. Here, as with the rhetorical tradition, studying what other people have done may help. You may want to stage your own signifying practices to enrich, combat, modify, or transform the effects which others' practices produce.

Within all of this varied activity, the study of what is currently termed "literature" will have its place. But it should not be taken as an a priori assumption that what is currently termed "literature" will always and everywhere be the most important focus of attention. Such dogmatism has no place in the field of cultural study. Nor are the texts now dubbed "literature" likely to be perceived and defined as they are now, once they are returned to the broader and deeper discursive formations of which they are part. They will be inevitably "rewritten," recycled, put to different uses, inserted into different relations and practices. They always have been, of course; but one effect of the word "literature" is to prevent us from recognizing this fact.

Such a strategy obviously has far-reaching institutional implications. It would mean, for example, that departments of literature as we presently know them in higher education would cease to exist. Since the government, as I write, seems on the point of achieving this end more quickly and effectively than I could myself, it is necessary to add that the first political priority for those who have doubts about the ideological implications of such departmental organizations is to defend them unconditionally against government assaults. But this priority cannot mean refusing to contemplate how we might better organize literary studies in the longer term. The ideological effects of such departments lie not only in the particular values they disseminate, but in their implicit and actual dislocation of "literature" from other cultural and social practices. The churlish admission of such practices as literary "background" need not detain us: "background," with its static, distancing connotations, tells its own story. Whatever would in the long term replace such departments—and the proposal is a modest one, for such experiments are already under way in certain areas of higher education—would centrally involve education in the various theories and methods of cultural analysis. The fact that such education is not routinely provided by many existing departments of literature, or is provided "optionally" or marginally, is one of their most scandalous and farcical features. (Perhaps their other most scandalous and farcical feature is the largely wasted energy which postgraduate students are required to pour into obscure, often spurious research topics in order to produce dissertations which are frequently no more than sterile academic exercises, and which few others will ever read.) The genteel amateurism which regards criticism as some spontaneous sixth sense has not only thrown many students of literature into understandable confusion for many decades but serves to consolidate the authority of those in power. If criticism is no more than a knack, like being able to whistle and hum different tunes simultaneously, then it is at once rare enough to be preserved in the hands of an elite, while "ordinary" enough to require no stringent theoretical justification. Exactly the same pincer movement is at work in English "ordinary language" philosophy. But the answer is not to replace such disheveled amateurism with a well-groomed professionalism intent on justifying itself to the disgusted taxpayer. Such professionalism, as we have seen, is equally bereft of any social validation of its activities, since it cannot say why it should bother with literature at all other than to tidy it up, drop texts into their appropriate categories, and then move over into marine biology. If the point of criticism is not to interpret literary works but to master in some disinterested spirit the underlying sign systems which generate them, what is criticism to do once it has achieved this mastery, which will hardly take a lifetime and probably not much more than a few years?

The present crisis in the field of literary studies is at root a crisis in the definition of the subject itself. That it should prove difficult to provide such a definition is, as I hope to have shown . . ., hardly surprising. Nobody is likely to be dismissed from an academic job for trying on a little semiotic analysis of Edmund Spenser; they are likely to be shown the door, or refused entry through it in the first place, if they question whether the "tradition" from Spenser to Shakespeare and Milton is the best or only way of carving up discourse into a syllabus. It is at this point that the canon is trundled out to blast offenders out of the literary arena.

Those who work in the field of cultural practices are unlikely to mistake their activity as utterly central. Men and women do not live by culture alone, the vast majority of them throughout history have been deprived of the chance of living by it at all, and those few who are fortunate enough to live by it now are able to do so because of the labor of those who do not. Any cultural or critical theory which does not begin from this single most important fact, and hold it steadily in mind in its activities, is in my view unlikely to be worth very much. There is no document of culture which is not also a record of barbarism. But even in societies which, like our own as Marx reminded us, have no time for culture, there are times and places when it suddenly becomes newly relevant, charged with a significance beyond itself. Four such major moments are evident in our own world. Culture, in the lives of nations struggling for their independence from imperialism, has a meaning quite remote from the review pages of the Sunday newspapers. Imperialism is not only the exploitation of cheap labor power, raw materials, and easy markets but the uprooting of languages and customs—not just the imposition of foreign armies, but of alien ways of experiencing. It manifests itself not only in company balance sheets and in air bases, but can be tracked to the most intimate roots of speech and signification. In such situations, which are not all a thousand miles from our own doorstep, culture is so vitally bound up with one's common identity that there is no need to argue for its relation to political struggle. It is arguing against it which would seem incomprehensible.

The second area where cultural and political action have become closely united is in the women's movement. It is in the nature of feminist politics that signs and images, written and dramatized experience, should be of especial significance. Discourse in all its forms is an obvious concern for feminists, either as places where women's oppression can be deciphered or as places where it can be challenged. In any politics which puts identity and relationship centrally at stake, renewing attention to lived experience and the discourse of the body, culture does not need to argue its way to political relevance. Indeed one of the achievements of the women's movement has been to redeem such phrases as "lived experience" and "the discourse of the body" from the empiricist connotations with which much literary theory has invested them. "Experience" need now no longer signify an appeal away from power systems and social relations to the privileged certainties of the private, for feminism recognizes no such distinction between questions of the human subject and questions of political struggle. The discourse of the body is not a matter of Lawrentian ganglions and suave loins of darkness, but a *politics* of the body, a rediscovery of its sociality through an awareness of the forces which control and subordinate it.

The third area in question is the "culture industry." While literary critics have been cultivating sensibility in a minority, large segments of the media have been busy trying to devastate it in the majority; yet it is still presumed that studying, say, Gray and Collins is inherently more important than examining television or the popular press. Such a project differs from the two I have outlined already in its essentially defensive character: it represents a critical reaction to someone else's cultural ideology rather than an appropriation of culture for one's own ends. Yet it is a vital project nevertheless, which must not be surrendered to a melancholic Left or Right mythology of the media as impregnably monolithic. We know that people do not after all believe all that they see and read; but we also need to know much more than we do about the role such effects play in their general consciousness, even though such critical study should be seen, politically, as no more than a holding operation. The democratic control of these ideological apparatuses, along with popular alternatives to them, must be high on the agenda of any future socialist program (see Raymond Williams for some interesting practical proposals in this respect).

The fourth and final area is that of the strongly emergent movement of working-class writing. Silenced for generations, taught to regard literature as a coterie activity beyond their grasp, working people over the past decade in Britain have been actively organizing to find their own literary styles and voices (see The Republic of Letters). The worker writers' movement is almost unknown to academia and has not been exactly encouraged by the cultural organs of the state; but it is one sign of a significant break from the dominant relations of literary production. Community and cooperative publishing enterprises are associated projects, concerned not simply with a literature wedded to alternative social values, but with one which challenges and changes the existing social relations between writers, publishers, readers, and other literary workers. It is because such ventures interrogate the ruling *definitions* of literature that they cannot so easily be incorporated by a literary institution quite happy to welcome *Sons and Lovers*, and even, from time to time, Robert Tressell.

These areas are not alternatives to the study of Shakespeare and Proust. If the study of such writers could become as charged with energy, urgency, and enthusiasm as the activities I have just reviewed, the literary institution ought to rejoice rather than complain. But it is doubtful that this will happen when such texts are hermetically sealed from history, subjected to a sterile critical formalism, piously swaddled with eternal verities, and used to confirm prejudices which any moderately enlightened student can perceive to be objectionable. The liberation of Shakespeare and Proust from such controls may well entail the death of literature, but it may also be their redemption.

I shall end with an allegory. *We* know that the lion is stronger than the lion tamer, and so does the lion tamer. The problem is that the lion does not know it. It is not out of the question that the death of literature may help the lion to awaken.

The Death of Mrs. Dalloway

Two Readings

EDWARD MENDELSON

Thesis

Everyone knows what happens in the final lines of *Mrs. Dalloway*. Peter Walsh and Sally Seton have been sitting together at Clarissa Dalloway's party, talking about their friend and hostess, while Clarissa has removed herself to a little room to ponder the death of Septimus Warren Smith. Peter is about to follow Sally, who has stood up to say goodnight to Richard Dalloway. Then it happens:

> "I will come," said Peter, but he sat on for a moment. What is this terror? what is this ecstasy? he thought to himself. What is it that fills me with extraordinary excitement?
> It is Clarissa, he said.
> For there she was.   (296)

Everyone knows Clarissa has reentered her drawing room, where Peter at last sees her. All the book's scholars and critics know it. All its readers know it. Evidently its author knew it also. But a close reading of the book proves that everyone is mistaken. Clarissa does not return to her party, does not come within view of Peter Walsh, because, about a dozen pages earlier, Clarissa died.

Virginia Woolf herself pointed toward this fact about the book—toward this secret, which the book kept hidden even from its author—in an introduction she wrote for a Modern Library reprint published in 1928, three years after the book first appeared. She began by considering a reader's desire to learn the connection between an author's life and an author's work—"For nothing is more fascinating than to be shown the truth which lies behind those immense façades of fiction. . . ." To show this truth adequately, she went on, would require "not a page or two of preface but a volume or two of autobiography." In place of those volumes she offered something more limited:

> Of *Mrs. Dalloway* then one can only bring to light at the moment a few scraps [in fact she brings forth only two], of little importance or none perhaps; as that in

the first version Septimus, who is later intended to be her double, had no existence; and that Mrs. Dalloway was originally to kill herself, or perhaps merely to die at the end of the party. Such scraps are offered humbly to the reader in the hope that like other odds and ends [which the introduction does not supply] they may come in useful.   (vi)

The two truths behind the fiction that Virginia Woolf offers are implicitly a compound truth: the sacrifice of Septimus occurs in order that Clarissa might live. Critics and readers have always taken this to be the case. Yet a close reading demonstrates that the offered victim was inadequate, that the sacrifice failed.

Clarissa's death does not make nonsense of the final lines of the book. On the contrary: only her death can make sense of the precise sequence of events recorded in those lines. In that sequence, Peter Walsh is aware of his terror and ecstasy—which he wonders at—*before* he is aware of Clarissa's presence. This sequence is consistent with the rest of the book—consistent, that is, with the terms and conditions of personal experience established throughout the preceding pages—only if Clarissa's presence is not an ordinary physical presence but something very different. Exactly what form her presence takes is indicated by an extensive pattern of evidence, a pattern accessible only to close reading.

This pattern depends, first of all, on the book's rigorous treatment of time. As the narrative follows its characters through the course of a single day, it is careful to maintain its temporal progress. The narrative never turns back on itself, never retraces its steps in such a way as to turn from, say, Peter Walsh at 3:00 in the afternoon to Clarissa Dalloway at five minutes to the hour. The rule applies to the larger order of the book (which Virginia Woolf first planned to call *The Hours*) as well as to the local order of its individual paragraphs. When Peter, for example, arrives at Clarissa's house at 3:00, "Big Ben was beginning to strike, first the warning, musical; then the hour, irrevocable" (177). Peter has time for one quick thought—"Lunch parties waste the entire afternoon"—before the narrative shifts to Clarissa inside, where she listens to the bells chiming. She has time for two paragraphs of thoughts before the chiming ends; and in fact the full chime of Big Ben, both the musical "warning" and the striking of "the hour," takes well over half a minute, more than enough time for the action that the narrative reports as occurring during this interval. At other moments in the book, the narrative includes glimpses of various characters as a single hour strikes: "twelve o'clock struck as Clarissa Dalloway laid her green dress on her bed, and the Warren Smiths walked down Harley Street" (142). But in each such instance, the forward impetus of the narrative is unchecked. Even in the book's most elaborate shifts in perspective, it follows the practice Joyce established in the "Wandering Rocks" chapter of *Ulysses*—the book on which much of the form of *Mrs. Dalloway* is modeled—and continues its progress through time.

Even the book's frequent flashbacks never impede this progress. When a scene from, say, Clarissa's youth occurs in the narrative, it is summoned up for remembrance by the thoughts of a character recalling it in the present moment. And in the one extended variant on this procedure, the book's account of the life of Septimus Warren Smith, an account that is not localized in the recollection of any of the characters, it is in effect the narrative itself that remembers—and Virginia Woolf takes the trouble to leave enough of an interval in the course of the narrative to permit the recollection to be reported without any suggestion that present narrative time has somehow stopped.

So there is something anomalous, and hitherto unnoticed, about the sequence of events in the last dozen or so pages of the book—at least, there is an unnoticed anomaly in the way those pages are normally read. Shortly before that final sequence, in the eleventh of the book's twelve sections,[1] Clarissa withdraws to the little room, meditates on the death of Septimus Warren Smith, and then resolves to return to her party, specifically to return to two of her guests: "She must find Sally and Peter" (284). With this she leaves the little room, the eleventh section of the book ends— and Clarissa disappears from the book entirely, not to reappear until a dozen pages later, in the final lines of the twelfth and concluding section.

All during those dozen pages, Peter and Sally wonder aloud where Clarissa might be. Six pages after she leaves the little room, Peter asks, "Where was she, all this time?" Sally, two pages later, wonders, "Why did Clarissa not come and talk to them?" After two more pages, Sally adds that "Really she must go, if Clarissa did not come soon." Clarissa had resolved to return to them and had made that resolution many minutes before: every detail of the book's treatment of time makes clear that Clarissa's decision to find Peter and Sally precedes their questions about where she might be. As Peter himself asks, "But where is Clarissa?"

Where indeed? Peter had already, some hours before, found cause for apprehension about Clarissa, so much so that he even imagined her death. At 11:30 in the morning, as the bells of St. Margaret's sounded "Some grief for the past . . . some concern for the present," Peter had suddenly thought about Clarissa's uncertain health:

> She has been ill. . . . It was her heart, he remembered; and the sudden loudness of the final stroke tolled for death that surprised in the midst of life, Clarissa falling where she stood, in her drawing-room. No! No! he cried. She is not dead! (75)

This vision of her death follows, by a few sentences, a report of Peter's strong imaginative sense of her presence:

> It is Clarissa herself, he thought, with a deep emotion, and an extraordinarily clear, yet puzzling recollection of her, as if this bell had come into the room years ago. . . . (74)

"It is Clarissa, he thought": the words that will recur in the book's final sentences occur here, associated not with the physical presence of Clarissa but with an imaginative sense of her remembered presence—and in a paragraph that also imagines her death.

As early as the fifth paragraph in the book, the narrative had called attention to Clarissa's "heart, affected, they said, by influenza." Later, the narrative reports that "Since her illness she had turned almost white," and in the very next sentence, "she had a sudden spasm, as if, while she mused, the icy claws had had the chance to fix in her" (54). Throughout her day, in fact, Clarissa's thoughts touch on death. She thinks of those killed in the war; she recalls the dirge from *Cymbeline*. But she finds some consolation, perhaps, in the thought that one who dies might survive in another who lives: "somehow in the streets of London, on the ebb and flow of things, here, there, she survived. Peter survived, lived in each other . . ." (12). Later in the book his thought expands into a

> transcendental theory which, with her horror of death, allowed her to believe . . . that since our apparitions, the part of us which appears, are so momentary, compared with the other, unseen part of us, which spreads wide, the unseen might survive, *be recovered somehow attached to this person or that.* . . . (231–32; emphasis added)

There may be a sense in which the narrative itself believes this theory. The large emotional direction of the book seeks an event that might overcome the isolation separating Peter and Clarissa. Clarissa repeatedly thinks back to the love, "the fun," she lost when she gave up Peter Walsh for Richard Dalloway, and she repeatedly justifies to herself the emotional limits of her marriage. Peter thinks repeatedly of the past he knew with Clarissa and of the time when, recognizing that she would marry Richard, he left her and England. His obscure dream of a solitary traveler and of the giant female figure at the end of the traveler's ride ("if he can conceive of her, then in some sort she exists, he thinks" [85]) is interpreted by the book's narrator as a dream of Clarissa. Clarissa is the goal of Peter's solitary journey, and now, on the day of the book's action, Peter has returned to England from half a world away and sought her out. But until the three final lines of the book all his attempts to communicate with her are frustrated, flawed by misunderstanding, baffled by convention—although in years past, "They had always this queer power of communicating without words" (90).

Now, the sequence of events in the final paragraphs is as follows. After waiting in vain for Clarissa to come and talk with them, Sally stands up to make her farewells to Richard Dalloway. Peter remains seated. Then, he asks himself what is this terror, what is this ecstasy, what is it that fills him with extraordinary excitement? Only after asking these questions does he find an answer: "It is Clarissa, he said." And only after he names her does the narrative give a local habitation to her name: "For there she was" (296). To put the matter in more general terms: Peter first experiences emotion, then identifies its source, and only then apprehends the source as present. Or to put it more simply still: response first, recognition afterward.

This sort of sequence occurs elsewhere in *Mrs. Dalloway*, but only under specific circumstances. It occurs, for example, in the opening pages, when Clarissa wonders, "But what was she dreaming as she looked into Hatchards' shop window? What was she trying to recover? What image of white dawn in the country . . ." (12).

It occurs again when Peter Walsh, at 11:30, hears the bells of St. Margaret's and remembers Clarissa coming down the stairs. In this instance, Peter experiences emotions associated with that memory, but he is puzzled about the source of those emotions: "why had he been so profoundly happy when the clock was striking?" (75). Part of the answer lies in the fact that in *Mrs. Dalloway*, this sort of puzzlement, this sequence of emotion prior to recognition (or without recognition at all), occurs only when the object of one's emotion is not physically present to the senses.[2] In contrast, whenever anyone in the book has an emotion about something physically present and accessible, the object is perceived and identified first, and only then does the emotion follow—for example, in the various emotional responses to the important-looking motorcar that moves through the book's opening pages. (And in any instance where something is physically present but cannot be identified, it produces no emotional response at all—as in the case of the illegible skywriting that different characters try unsuccessfully to interpret.) The only instances in the book where characters are puzzled by their own emotions are those instances where the source of that emotion is physically absent.

This might be called one of the Fictional Laws of *Mrs. Dalloway*. Another is the law of temporal sequence specifying that events (including recollections of the past) occurring in the day of the book's action are reported in the narrative in the same sequence as their implied occurrence. So if one makes the normal assumption that Peter Walsh's terror and ecstasy in the final lines of the book are the consequence of the physical return of Clarissa to her party—her arrival in the doorway of her drawing room—then it must follow that Virginia Woolf established these two fictional laws, and treated them as irrefragable for some 280 pages of her book, only to abandon them in the last dozen pages. But if these laws are consistent from beginning to end, if Virginia Woolf was as consistent in *Mrs. Dalloway* as, in different ways and with different laws, she was consistent in all her other serious novels, then the final lines call for an interpretation entirely different from the normal one.

That interpretation can be stated largely in words taken from the book itself. The church bells that struck throughout the narrative "tolled for death that surprised in the midst of life, Clarissa falling where she stood," soon after the excitement of her resolution to find Sally and Peter. She dies of a failure of "her heart, affected, they said, by influenza." Soon after her death, as Clarissa herself had imagined, "the unseen part of us, which spreads wide," finds its chance to "survive, be recovered somehow attached to this person or that"—attached to Peter, in fact, as she had also imagined: "She survived. Peter survived, lived in each other." "There was an embrace in death." When Peter asks "What is this terror? what is this ecstasy? . . . What is it that fills me with extraordinary excitement?," his questions have their special climactic force because he has never been filled by anyone's unseen presence before. Only after having asked himself what has happened to him does he recognize whose presence he has responded to, and where that presence has come to rest.

It is Clarissa, he said.

For there she was.

Antithesis

The trouble with this interpretation is that it makes sense of the final lines of the book by making nonsense of everything else. The great emotional thrust of the book is one that moves not toward Clarissa's defeat by death but toward her triumph over it. In Woolf's previous novel, *Jacob's Room*, the central figure had died just before the final paragraphs. In *Mrs. Dalloway* Woolf abandoned her intention to make the central figure suffer an identical fate and offered Septimus Warren Smith as a surrogate. If a close reading of the book seems to demonstrate that Clarissa dies after all, that the sacrificial offering was inadequate to the death required by the author's vision, this does not prove that the book refused to obey its author's conscious intent. It indicates instead what is wrong with close reading.

Contemporary criticism, especially in its more self-conscious territories, tends to favor close readings over readings made from what might be called the middle distance. Psychoanalytic criticism, for example, searches out the symptomatic detail that betrays the hidden interior of a text or its author. Deconstructive criticism searches out the contradictory rhetorical figures that wreak havoc on a work's implicit claims to coherence and consistency. In each case, as in many others, behind the critical method lies an unexamined assumption. This is the assumption that the minuscule detail and the hidden pattern—revealed only when an expert investigator approaches a book with specialized instruments of interpretation—are more revealing, more telling, than the texture and pattern revealed when a book is read with instruments of interpretation similar to those that both author and reader use in making sense of their daily experience. The assumption that close reading approaches the ultimate truth (or, more often, the ultimate untruth) of a book is a prejudice much like the antibourgeois prejudice of avant-garde writers who emerged from the nineteenth- or twentieth-century bourgeoisie. This sort of prejudice assumes that whatever happens on the scale of experience in which we live and act cannot possibly matter much, that what happens in remote or inaccessible regions matters a great deal more. From this prejudice grew the middle-class artist's assumption that workers were closer to "life," and aristocrats closer to "art," than the middle classes could ever be. From this prejudice has grown the critical assumption that close readings of a few isolated sentences (at one extreme of scale) or studies of massive cultural ideologies (at the other) are more likely to reach the truth than are studies of a book as a whole or of the whole of an author's work. The habit of thought—as ancient as Plato and not uncommon among the educated—that supposes that events on the subatomic scale (e.g., the Heisenberg uncertainty principle) or on the cosmological scale (e.g., the dissolution of matter into black holes) are ultimately more real than events that occur on the middle level of human experience is a habit of thought that refuses attention to the ethical and emotional acts that occupy by far the greater portion of human lives. It is a habit of thought that has consequences in the lives of those who adhere to it and in societies that honor it. As aristocratic fantasies and *nostalgie de la boue* are both forms of self-contempt, so is a commitment to close reading as the privileged mode of interpretation.

Like most forms of self-contempt, it confuses a part of the truth with the whole. The individual details of a book, its moments of local disorder, no more determine the larger shape of that book than the awkward unbalanced shapes of individual stones determine the form of a gothic tower. Many of the separate details of *Mrs. Dalloway*—its separate stones—weight the narrative with the burden of Clarissa's death. But when set in the larger form of the book, these small indications of her death combine in a way that contradicts their individual weight—as the combined stones of the tower rise above the original disordered heap. All the indications of Clarissa's death combine to make her final refusal of death all the more triumphant.

That triumph follows a moment of nearly total defeat. When Clarissa, alone in the little room, contemplates the news of Septimus's suicide, she begins with simple resentment that death should have been brought indecorously into her party. "The party's splendour fell to the floor. . . . What business had the Bradshaws to talk of death at her party?" (280). But the vulnerability of her party to the shadow of death reveals precisely what is lacking in that party and in all the values that Clarissa had honored when she organized it. She has no close relations with any of the invited guests. Of the two persons present who matter most to her, one, Sally Seton, was not even invited: she happened to be in London and came after hearing about the party from someone else. The other, Peter Walsh, is there only because he happened to pay a call on Clarissa earlier in the day. Everyone else at the party, everything else about it, amounts to a deadening shroud concealing what Clarissa thinks of as the "thing there was that mattered":

> A thing there was that mattered; a thing, wreathed about with chatter, defaced, obscured in her own life, let drop every day in corruption, lies, chatter. This he [Septimus] had preserved.   (280)

Through his choice of death over mental servitude, Septimus preserved the thing that mattered from the defacing touch of Sir William Bradshaw, from the touch that Clarissa thinks of as power without love, thought without care. And thinking of Septimus's defiance, Clarissa feels the contrast with her own acceptance:

> Somehow it was her disaster—her disgrace. It was her punishment to see sink and disappear here a man, there a woman, in this profound darkness, and she forced to stand here in her evening dress. She had schemed; she had pilfered. She was never wholly admirable. She had wanted success. Lady Bexborough and the rest of it.   (282)

"And once," she concludes, "she had walked on the terrace at Bourton," walked there with Sally Seton, felt the emotions she had abandoned for the sake of success, for her parties, for Lady Bexborough and the rest of it.

But now Septimus has reminded her of the worth of that which she had "let drop every day in corruption, lies, chatter." Now, because of his example, "She felt glad that he had done it. . . . He made her feel the beauty; made her feel the fun. . . . She must assemble. *She must find Sally and Peter*" (283–84; emphasis added).

She does find them. Close reading can prove to its own satisfaction that an impossibly long interval comes between her decision to seek them out and her entrance into Peter's awareness. But anyone who knows about parties from personal experience as well as from novels knows that a hostess cannot cross a room without being stopped for idle conversation by those she meets along the way. A middle-distance reading recognizes that for all Clarissa's newfound resolve, she remains part of the social world whose limits she now acknowledges: she is still the wife of Richard Dalloway. Her triumph is partial: it occurs on the limited scale possible within her daily experience, but that is the scale that matters to her and to the book's implied readers—a scale no less significant than any other.

Yet if the discoveries made possible by close reading have no special privilege in themselves, neither is any context in which they might be understood self-evidently privileged either. In practice, every reader makes a personal decision about the context relevant to the local details of a novel. That context could conceivably be found anywhere along the scale extending from the adjacent words on the page to the universe. In practice, the scale chosen reflects a reader's idea of the limits and possibilities of personal choice. If a reader believes that personality is an illusion, that what matters are the anonymous powers of language or society, then the context of a book's local details will be the system of language or the patterns of thought imposed by psychology or the state. If a reader believes in unbounded existential freedom, then the context will be the deliberate choices that supposedly produced the book's every syllable. Most readers choose a context somewhere in between. The following paragraph offers an account of *Mrs. Dalloway* that results from one such choice, and it is presented in the knowledge that any other account of the book's local details will be different.

The book's intimations of Clarissa's mortality, then, stand as survivals in the final text of an intention consciously but incompletely abandoned. (To return to the architectural metaphor, many gothic buildings retain some of the outline and detail of the abandoned Romanesque buildings whose sites they occupy.) Largely invisible among the dense textures of the book, its earlier plan still gives the finished work some of its form and language. Clarissa's victorious resolve in the book's final page corresponds to its author's resolve to triumph over both the earlier design of her book and the mood that helped shape that design. The fatal strain that persists in the book makes Clarissa's achievement—and Virginia Woolf's—all the more impressive. The dirge from *Cymbeline* proves, as it does in the play, to be a prelude to renewed life. The question whether Woolf knew explicitly that she had written into her narrative all the hidden local conflicts of this larger struggle is an empty one. Writers write better than they know. If their powers are great enough, then the details in their work that are shaped outside their powers—shaped by the unconscious forces of psyche, genre, language—serve their chosen design.

Notes

¹ The divisions, each marked by a line space in the text, are apparent in all British editions; in the setting used in all American editions some of the line spaces are absent, evidently lost in the course of the confusion that normally attends transatlantic publication. In the text of the American editions, the eleventh section begins with the break visible on page 250 and ends where a break *should* be—and is to be found at the corresponding point in all British editions—between the fourth and fifth lines on page 284.

² Near the start of the book, a moment before Big Ben strikes, Clarissa feels an "indescribable pause; a suspense" (4), but Woolf emphasizes that this is the result of Clarissa's "having lived in Westminster—how many years now? over twenty," and is the effect of nothing more mysterious than habit.

Heresy and the Question of Repetition

Reading Kierkegaard's *Repetition*

ROBERT POGUE HARRISON

Despite a current awareness among critics that the problem of style is a philosophical problem in Kierkegaard's works, there persists a temptation to "read through" the rhetorical overlay of his texts in order to arrive at the underlying concepts. The procedure stems from a desire to vindicate the philosophical dignity of Kierkegaard's thought and to rescue it from modes of expression that come dangerously close to being "literary." Kierkegaard remains a philosopher. At least the impressive bulk of scholarship that surrounds his name declares as much.[1] In the case of *Repetition*, the work I will be dealing with here, the critical routine is still idealistic to a naive degree. Critics have proposed divergent interpretations of what Kierkegaard means by repetition, but they have consistently searched for a syncretic idea lurking in the folds of this ironic, "whimsical" essay. Here I will try to show how repetition is neither an idea nor another existential category but the irreducible difference between expression and the immanence of a meaning that never gets produced in the discursive fabric. This difference lies beyond the calibrated distinctions between philosophy and literature and situates Kierkegaard's reader within the more radical difference of repetition as a mode of "suspended" discourse.

In a polemic addressed to Professor Heiberg, a Danish Hegelian, Kierkegaard remarked that he wrote *Repetition* "not in a learned manner, still less in a manner so scientific that every teller in our philosophical bank could say 'one, two, three' " (*Repetition* xviii). Heiberg was among the first ever to read the book, and we may excuse this idealist who could count to three (thesis, antithesis, synthesis) for having been misled by its desultory style. It is curious that Kierkegaard could not do the same, given the declaration of Constantine Constantius—the narrator and pseudonymous author of *Repetition*—that a serious author should "write in such a way that the heretics cannot understand what he writes" (131). To prevent heretics from understanding one's discourse and then to reproach a heretic for misunderstanding it seems an inconsistent attitude, but perhaps the notion of heresy will have to be reconsidered in this context. Heresy is an act of choosing. It remains the trademark of criticism: critics, who inevitably decide the meaning of what they read, repeat the heresy at every turn. To avoid the heresy might mean renouncing the hope of thematizing the meaning of repetition. The following investigation will decide to what extent this is possible, for the fall back into heresy may be not only inevitable but also "repetitionary," which could also explain why *Repetition* remains Kierkegaard's most misunderstood work.

Repetition tells the story of a young man who falls in love, undergoes a crisis, and abandons his beloved for the *idea* of love. The psychologist narrator Constantine finds in this melancholy youth an opportunity to study the patterns of a higher spirituality: "The idea was in movement in the young man's love, and for that reason I was interested in him" (43). Through Constantine's eyes we watch the young man transcend his beloved and transform her into an object of recollection. Recollection figures here as a category of poetic consciousness: it consists in poetic recuperation of the loss of immediate presence. Although the beloved lies near at hand, the young man longs for her from a remote spiritual distance. Constantine declares: "In the dawn of love the present and the future strive with one another in order to acquire an eternal impression, and this act of recollection is precisely the counter-current of eternity flowing back into the present" (40). Recollection, then, is the elliptical return of a dislocating projection forward, resulting in a collision between opposing orders: the present and future, the possible and actual. It brings on a crisis in the young man that we can call the crisis of literal values: the idea of the beloved transports him so deeply into the temporal ecstasies that it no longer corresponds to the person from whom it was abstracted. According to Constantine, this idealization belongs to the essence of poetry: "The man who is not enthusiastically convinced that the idea is the vital principle in love, and that for this, if need be, one must sacrifice life, yes, even love . . .—such a man is banned from poetry" (43). In the poetic, recollective act, the beloved is reborn for the young man as a figure. This breakthrough of her figurative value haunts his relation to her, so much so that even in her presence he has to recollect the idea she has become for him. The contradictions of recollection torment him with increasing intensity, especially because of the deception they entail for the girl he loves: "The girl was and remained his darling . . . although he was near losing his mind with agonizing dread at the monstrous untruth which only served to imprison her more. In reality her existence or non-existence was in a certain sense of no importance to him" (41). The stress heightens until one day, beside himself with desperation, the young man leaves Copenhagen to avoid the person he loves.

His departure marks a second stage in his psychological itinerary. Resolved on the idea, he turns himself over to the freedom of poetry, which transfigures the world in recollection. But poetic recollection only prepares the way for spiritual repetition. Having fled the confines of a literal world and suffered the contradictions of recollection, the young poet is now ready to discover repetition as authentic transcendence. This happens in an illuminating flash as he reads the story of Job in the Bible. In the figure of Job he discovers the religious category of human trial. Job becomes his hero and displaces the figure of the beloved in his imagination. Whereas she had merely projected him beyond literal values, Job offers him an explicit definition of fate as radical contingency. Job, says the young man, experiences repetition "once all *conceivable* human certitude pronounced it impossible" (117). The trial between God and Job takes place: the latter loses his case yet also wins it "for the fact that he lost his case *before God*" (117). In short, Job represents a mysterious reconciliation between existential contingency and providential necessity; and the biblical story, emblematically linking the temporal order to the order of eternity, becomes an analogy for the meaning of repetition.

This notion of repetition as a surrender to temporal finitude, with the human subject blindly seeking its origin in eternity, sounds familiar. It sounds "Kierkegaardian." It permits us to place repetition alongside other focal words in Kierkegaard's religious lexicon: faith, absurdity, despair, infinite resignation, and so forth. Furthermore, it allows us to thematize repetition as a noetic concept. The question we raise now is whether *Repetition* makes such thematizations impossible, or better, heretical.

The young man does not have the last word on repetition. In fact, the narrator's rhetorical strategies urge us to recognize the lover's self-deception. The lover thinks he discovers repetition, but in truth he only discovers more poetry. To bear out the claim I will point to narrative strategies that prohibit a thematization of repetition in terms of the young man's spiritual conversion. What the young man takes as revelation we must take as another ironic fold in the overall narrative. This becomes clear when we remember that the second part of *Repetition* consists almost exclusively of the letters that the vanished lover sends to Constantine, whom he calls his "silent confidant." However, just before the climax—that is, just before the lover's last dramatic letter—Constantine interrupts the epistolary flow with a brief interlude in which he announces his skepticism about the poet's religious conversion. Not only does Constantine attribute the lover's dithyrambic spirituality to poetic and erotic confusion, he also anticipates the lover's last letter in a way that deflates its climactic rhetoric about his revelation concerning repetition. In the following quotations I place side by side passages from Constantine's interlude and passages from the lover's last letter:

Constantine: What he is suffering from is a misapplied melancholy magnanimity for which there is properly no place but in a poet's brain. He expects a thunderstorm . . ., perhaps he means a nervous apoplexy. He is the sort of man that says "Whole battalion right-about face!" instead of facing right-about himself, which can be expressed in another way: the girl must be got out of the way. (121)

Young Man: She is married—to whom I do not know, but when I read it in the paper it was as though I had a touch of apoplexy. . . . Here I have repetition, I understand everything and existence seems more beautiful than ever. It came as a thunderstorm after all. (125)

Constantine: Whether, when that event he is counting on has come about, he would want to give it a religious expression—that's his affair, I have no objection. (121)

Young Man: I am again myself . . . only spiritual repetition is possible, although in the temporal life it is never so perfect as in eternity, which is the true repetition. (126)

Constantine: Though the girl had made a fool of him right before his eyes, he would have thought it magnanimity on her part. (123)

Young Man: It came as a thunderstorm after all, though I owe its occurrence to her magnanimity. (125)

The critic and translator Walter Lowrie, taking his cue from Kierkegaard's own remarks about *Repetition*, was among the first to write Constantine off as a cynic, a decadent, a mere aesthete who remains excluded from the religious depths fathomed by the young man by the end of the book.[2] Since then most interpretations of *Repetition* have maintained severe prejudices against Constantine; in fact critics readily accept Lowrie's suggestion that Kierkegaard drew a self-portrait in the young man, whose experience so much resembles Kierkegaard's rupture with his fiancée Regina. These prejudices must be finally vaporized. The passages I have placed side by side reveal the extent to which Constantine circumscribes the young man's consciousness up to the very end. He maintains that the lover's consciousness is "raised to the second power" in the ostensible conversion but misses the mark with regard to repetition. Why? The poet's recollective temper, we gather, has a shortcoming. Take, for example, a crucial remark of Constantine early on in the book: "This potentiated act of recollection is the external expression of love at the beginning, it is the token of a real love. But on the other hand an ironic elasticity is requisite in order to make use of it. This he lacked, his soul was too soft for it" (48). The young man lacks irony. He remains a poet striving for analogical continuity between the oppositions that haunt a recollective consciousness: future and present, possible and actual, figurative and literal, eternal and temporal. He is looking for the "eternal expression" of love, for the enunciatory act resolving the temporal discontinuities that brought about the crisis of recollection. For this reason the story of Job enchants his poetic imagination: it represents a poetic, but specious, synthesis of oppositions. It stands as the pure metaphor conjoining incongruous orders of being insofar as Job's trial with God figures as a supreme exchange between divorced ontological domains. Recollection, which began with a loss, which insisted on loss, finds an overhasty consolation in the story of Job's recompense.

The young man understands repetition as restoration, yet he lacks irony. An ironic consciousness cannot share his compulsion for analogy or his faith in revelation in the enunciatory, scriptorial act; on the contrary, irony militates against revelation by withholding or suspending meaning in an apophantic discourse that is inherently differential, disjunctive, double. Irony is the ongoing subversion of a tertiary, synthetic language of revelation, and we find it precisely in the narrative play of *Repetition*. The question, of course, is: Who is Constantine, the ironic narrator who veils and reveils the meaning of repetition?

Constantine is the voice of repetition. We gather as much from his name—Constantine Constantius—and the hesitation critics have shown with regard to this narrator is curious.[3] One must listen to the silence of this "silent confidant," which distinguishes itself from the verbose earnestness of the young man "who had not the strength to take irony's vow of silence, not the power to keep it; and only a man who keeps silent amounts to anything" (48). What is at stake in this sort of silence? Why is it a strength? To what extent does Constantine's irony—resolved on as a vow of silence—coincide with repetition? The following passage may reveal the direction in which we must look for these answers. Constantine states:

> He who knows how to keep silent discovers an alphabet which has as many letters as the one commonly in use, so that he can express everything in this thieves' Latin, so that there is no sigh so profound that he has not the laughter which corresponds to it in thieves' Latin, and no prayer so importunate that he has not the witticism which redeems the claim. For him there will come an instant when it is as though he were about to lose his reason. But this is only a moment, though it is a dreadful moment. . . . If one endures this madness one is sure to conquer it. (48)

The passage provides something of a manifesto for Constantine's writing style. It tells us that his silence never gives way to reticence but constitutes itself in a language of its own.[4] It also implies that an ironic silence risks giving way to delirium. With characteristic subtlety, Constantine alludes to his own name when he speaks of the necessity to endure that moment of madness, in other words to "stand firm" (*constans*) in moments of dread. The laughter and concealments of irony, therefore, are part of a discursive game that plays over an abyss.

That abyss is time. More precisely, time's futurity. The "profound sigh" of the poet and the "importunate prayer" of the parson are modes of appeal to that futurity, and once again we are not surprised to find that they are elocutionary appeals, full of earnest eloquence. Constantine rejects such eloquence in favor of an ironic language that relates to the future in terms of silence. In his own words: "Death possesses marvelous powers of persuasion; if only one will not contradict it but will let it have its own say, then it persuades in an instant, so that never has anyone had a word to object or longed for the eloquence of life" (81). While Constantine's ironic alphabet travesties the eloquence that does not let death "have its own say," its underlying silence, persuaded by the rhetoric of death as the limit of all enunciation, acknowledges the uncircumscribability of time in the alphabet of any language whatsoever. The thieves' Latin of irony dramatizes in parodic repetition the inadequacies of eloquent Latin to bring the outstanding terms of time within the boundaries of its rhetoric, be it the rhetoric of the poet or of the parson.

Or even, for that matter, of the philosopher. "Repetition," says Constantine, "is a recollection forwards." It is not an idea recollected backward, in the Platonic sense, but a temporal projection forward that resists the closure of representation and its backward recollection. We may extend the implications. Metaphysical discourse brings time to a closure within the parameters of ideal representation. Hegelian idealism, for example, against which *Repetition* is written, deprives time of its essence as eventuality. Repetition has to do precisely with that eventuality, but metaphysics in general cannot deal with it: "Repetition is the *interest* of metaphysics, and at the same time the interest upon which metaphysics founders" (53). Constantine's polemic with the language of idealism, the systematic totalization of idealism, points to the outstanding futurity whose opacity can only be recollected forward, that is to say, nonmetaphysically.

When Constantine journeys to Berlin hoping to repeat his past experience in that city, the enterprise fails. Things are different the second time around, and there is no repeating in the sense of re-presenting the has-been. This noncoincidentality dramatizes time's introduction of difference into repetition. Constantine's name dramatizes the same failure of coincidence in repetition: Constantine Constantius. What is at work in Constantine's irony, therefore, is a resignation to the nonfinalized and differential eventuality of time. However, in this context resignation speaks more to the point in its etymological sense: *resignare*, which means "to remove the seal." To apply a seal means to declare or claim as one's own: the signatures of metaphysics upon truth, for instance. Constantine's resignation *unseals* the future, removes the seals of appropriation by remaining silent about that which "outstands" his discourse: the repetition that representation as such cannot appropriate as the selfsame insofar as it figures as the expropriation of presence and re-presence in speech. If representation is an adequation of *res* and *signa*, repetition is the disadequation of apophantic utterance and immanent significance. Repetition is irony, if by irony we understand the discursive repetition of time's differential terms. By writing in such a way "that the heretics cannot understand what he writes," Constantine does not just conceal a noetic concept in the code language of his ironic narrative; his ironic silence about the meaning of repetition is rather a repetition of time's undisclosed terminal meaning. His narrative repeats but does not represent temporal reality. Stated otherwise, it wants to avoid reflexivity and to become methectic—that is, to participate in, in order to bring about in the discursive fabric, a repetition of finitude. It re-petitions, as it were, the deferred possibility of death by drawing the reader into its ironic suspension.

But Constantine knows that reading remains a heretical activity. The heretic resists suspension and decides the meaning of the issue in question, seals off the horizon of irony and reduces repetition to a manageable idea with thetic content. While Constantine cannot preclude such heresy, he manages nevertheless to laugh at it in advance in his "thieves' Latin." We should remark here that irony's laughter has an acute sense of the farce. The allusion is to a long passage in part 1 of *Repetition* where Constantine enlarges on the virtues of the farce over and against tragedy. The farce, he contends, reaches degrees of authenticity unavailable to tragic performances precisely because both actors and audience, in strict complicity, never forget that "this is a farce!" If the ruses of representation efface the production of representation in tragedy, the farce exaggerates that production so that laughter can resound in the hollowness of representation.

Repetition itself is a farce, the farce of Constantine's narrative spectacle as he makes a mockery of the language of metaphysics or the parson's "importunate prayers."

As for the young poet, Constantine declares that he "brought him into being," put him on stage, so to speak (134). The young poet is perhaps the most clownish figure of all: earnest, verbose, and credulous. And if we remember that most critics have taken this figure seriously as Kierkegaard's self-portrait and as the voice of a higher spirituality, we can begin to see how the reader of this book also turns into one more clownish figure on Constantine's stage.

Constantine, of course, is the principal actor here, but his is the voice audible behind the scene. In his own words: "Every burlesque actor must have a voice which is audible from behind the scenes, so that he may thus prepare the way for himself" (69). And again: "One has not gone to the theater as a tourist, or as an aesthetic spirit, or as a critic, but if possible as though it were a matter of no importance" (70). Constantine's narrative offers itself as though it were a matter of no importance, but the seriousness of his farce comes from the fact that something absents itself from the stage of representation:

> Thus it was I lay back in my loge, cast aside like the clothing of a bather, flung beside the stream of laughter . . . which foamed past me incessantly. I could see nothing but the vast expanse of the theater, hear nothing but the din in the midst of which I dwelt. Only now and then did I raise myself, look at Beckmann and laugh so heartily that for very fatigue I sank down again beside the foaming stream. This in itself was blissful, and yet I sensed the lack of something.   (71)

The passage fastens on the age-old metaphor for time, the metaphor of the river. After joining the waves of laughter, Constantine lies back in his loge and senses the lack of something: the lack at the heart of representation. In the same passage Constantine declares, "Go on thou spectacle upon the stage of life, which no one calls a comedy, no one a tragedy, because no one knows the end!" (81). Death as the end of the spectacle eludes the stage. The "lack of something" on the stage of representation is the terminal destiny of time, and the narrative of *Repetition* resolves on this lack through Constantine's vow of silence, which repeats on a scriptorial plane temporality's defiance of an inclusive circuit of referentiality. The recollective poet also senses the "lack of something," yet his recollection lacks irony. To lack irony means to lack repetition, which petitions the lack that temporalizes finitude and keeps it recollecting forward in a spectacle where "no one knows the end." Irony repeats by maintaining a concealment in its discourse, the way *Repetition* finally withholds a revelation of what is meant by its own title.

How, then, are we to read this work? As a philosophical treatise or a piece of literature? If the philosophical work is one whose discursive ambition is to explicate and demonstrate the truth-value of propositions, then *Repetition* leaves philosophy aside. If the literary work strives for a maximum resonance in the recesses of the unspoken, then a text like *Repetition* becomes a work of literature. But if literature means aesthetic transfiguration at the expense of rigorous thought and if philosophy means raising the question of truth, then it remains up to the critics to decide the difference in the case of *Repetition*. They will be neither the first nor the last to repeat the heresy.

Notes

[1] Kierkegaard ensnares critics in conceptual, "philosophical" discourse, but some have pursued a more literary approach to his works. See Mackey; Grimsley; Spanos, who uses Kierkegaard to elaborate a theory of literary interpretation; and Caws ("Winging It"), who places Kierkegaard's *Repetition* as a frame around a discussion of the swan motif in the poetry of Baudelaire, Mallarmé, Yeats, and Neruda.

[2] In his journals, Kierkegaard refers to repetition as a "religious category" and declares that "Constantine Constantius therefore can proceed no further. He is shrewd, an ironist, resists the interesting but is unaware that he himself is caught in it" (*JP* III 3794 [*Pap.* IV A 169] n.d., 1844). But the question remains to what extent Kierkegaard repeats Constantine's irony whenever he sits down to write. To what extent is Constantine a mask behind which there is no "proper" face?

[3] It is all the more curious in the case of a critic like Mackey, who remains attentive to Kierkegaard's literary strategies yet still claims that Constantine's life "is a retreat into the eternity of recollection" (19).

[4] Cf. Nietzsche: "It is my favorite art and malice that my silence has learned not to betray itself through reticence" ("On the Mount of Olives," *Thus Spoke Zarathustra* 286). For the development of this paradox into a new poetics, see Harrison.

Style and the Extreme Situation

ANGUS FLETCHER

Literary style lives and breathes exactly in that space, that interval, where the text meets the reader. The first thing we encounter, with any text, is its style. *Style* names the front, the arming, of the text. Yet not every individual style affronts the reader to make its point. Some styles are deliberately neutral or easy and perspicuous. Only those that concern me here, Patagonian word games as I call them, styles in extremis, affront by their strangeness.

A critical concern with such matters is not new. Longinus theorized about rhetorical excess in his treatise *On the Sublime*. The ancient rhetorician Demetrius said: "Metaphor is dangerous." Poetry threatens sense, science and logic. Plato's visionary manias, including the poet's, partake of a similar danger and risk. And if we isolate the most powerfully idiosyncratic styles, the oddest of odd mixtures, we again find ourselves on hazardous ground. What follows is a sidelong inquiry into these hazards and their darker purpose.

Style, a planetary term, wanders about like a monad: sometimes it refers to artistic technique; sometimes to manner, manners, and mannerisms; sometimes to these functions seen diachronically, sometimes to their synchronic description; sometimes to an innate or mastered skill of performance; sometimes to flair and sensibility; sometimes to rhetorical effects (the deictics of "point" and "statement," as with interior decoration or the color of a Maserati); sometimes to notions of harmony, control, elegance, economy, taste, and what in American slang is sometimes called "class"—John O'Hara said that *Across the River and into the Trees* had "real class." Finally, style is often loosely used to indicate structural principles—we find this with writings on architecture—though more properly it should point to the architectonics of the work, as Sir Philip Sidney stated long ago.

Reflection on the wide variety of common uses of the term suggests that we should not seek to entrap the word *style*. We should work simply in the field of its wandering, as with any other planetary term. We must accept the openness of the field. Middleton Murry once observed that "a discussion of the word Style, if it were pursued with only a fraction of the rigour of a scientific investigation, would inevitably cover the whole of literary aesthetics and the theory of criticism" (3). True, and a similar balooning occurs when style becomes the object of specific analytic study. Some years ago, reviewing Nils Erik Enkvist's *Linguistic Stylistics*, Samuel R. Levin observed this field diffusion:

> Stylistics is a large and sprawling field. Marks have been left upon it by rhetoricians, dialectologists, literary critics, factor analysts, aestheticians, linguists, information theorists, textual critics, statisticians, psychologists, and computer technicians—to give a partial list. Stylistics evokes such a wealth and diversity of responses because it offers a variety of purchase points for its consideration and discussion. . . . From this complexity in the empirical state of affairs [there is a text, this text was written by someone under certain conditions of time, place, and circumstance and is read by another under different conditions of time, place, and circumstance (the foregoing being obviously simplified)], there arise both the manifold definitions of style (and hence also of stylistics) and their typical failure to represent [style] to everyone's satisfaction.   (467)

Fundamentally, Levin is reminding us of the eternal war between subjective response and objectively determinable features of text and context. I believe we invoke style in order to play between these two domains (as Levin too believes), and so long as we recognize that there is no magic way to escape this maze except to stay active within it, we shall not suffer too much anxiety.

In ordinary social situations this anxiety is more or less painful—one does what one can, to achieve a modicum of stylistic individuality and harmony. If a lady and gentleman arrive at a formal occasion wearing egregiously informal costumes, they do threaten the assembly; but the degree of threat implied by the egregious is always proportional to the tightness of the group, and groups have complex ways of rejecting and assimilating a wide range of eccentricities, a wide range of humors. Any group that can openly admit the threat of "difference from the group norm" will always feel less anxious. Interesting cases among writers who transgress a social norm occur when there is a strong professional unity of correct style, as when Erich Segal, a classical scholar, wrote *Love Story*, or—a more interesting case—when William Gass, a philosopher, dazzles and dances in the ballroom of the personal essay.

In the following pages there will, however, not be much in the way of social analysis, though such an inquiry would naturally flow from certain notions that arise. For present purposes I keep my notion of style rather loose. Let's say it refers, in what follows, to the rhythmic articulation of a surface; it links with structure only insofar as it faces or bodies forth that structure. But in any case style is not structure; rhythmic, it always implies movement, motion, vibration, vibrance—the segmentation and continuity of flow. Nor is it mechanical; machines, however complex their motions, have no style in a significant sense. Machines eject style from process. As Schleiermacher saw, the problem of style must include the less effable problem of manner. *Manner* names an almost hidden aspect (a paradox, therefore) of what's going on somewhere close to the immediate surface of the work of art. A subsurface ripple. Just under the surface, so to speak, the manner of a work talks back and forth to the innards and the outer membranes.

To be told that manner, if not style, shows itself "just beneath the surface" of the artwork may strike the reader as mystical. I have no desire to be mysterious. All I have in mind is that one can objectively extract from any text the features of syntax, lexis, and so on, and this extraction occurs precisely at the surface of the work. But as Levin's review of Enkvist maintained, the responses of readers so vary and complicate their own processing of surface features that "something" stylistic occurs that cannot be deduced merely from an assembly of the extracted features. We today may not yet be in any position to account exactly for that something, but we are aware it occurs. My impression of Schleiermacher's hermeneutic project, after the 1805 *Aphorisms*, is that he gives what I am calling a "just beneath the surface" function to the interpreter's play of mind, a play corresponding to a similar play that partly generated the text to be read. A later aphorism, dated Friday, 23 March 1810, virtually says that the reader must look inside the author's mind: "(1) Combining the objective and the subjective so that the interpreter can put himself 'inside' the author. (2) On understanding the author better than he understands himself . . ." (64). Schleiermacher sees that writing occurs in a mental context, a context where the "mental" role of words is not clearly definable but where we should never neglect our uncertainty as to what authors are thinking of when choosing their words, because surely they think of something besides or beyond those mere words and the choices to be made among available words.

The process I have just called "thinking" is the unclear part of the poetic or hermeneutic labor, and I cannot clarify what it consists in. But the marvellous articulation of the poem, the speech, the play, the novel, the essay, and the like— this working of words involves feelings in the activity Hart Crane used to call "poetic logic." And logic suggests thought, albeit thought conditioned by emotional climate. Thus Schleiermacher observes,

> The coherence of the leading ideas [of the work] is recognized along with the author's peculiar view of the subject matter of the work. The coherence of the secondary representations is to be recognized from the relationship between the author's ability to use ideas and the subject matter of the work—with the interest he had in one thing or another, especially during the preparation of the work, and therefore with the entire relation of his personality to the work. Consequently, it is especially important to trace, in addition to the actual train of thought, the sequence of the leading and secondary ideas as they are interwoven. (155)

What follows in Schleiermacher's draft is a sketchy outline of questions that arise when we ask, in effect, how an author finds a style or manner of expression to get "leading thoughts" across. The philosopher distinguishes a wide range of authorial situations and verbal capacities that enable—but may also interfere with—this task. The complexity of the artist's task (and the interpreter's) lies in the understanding of an ever-shifting interplay between leading thoughts and the means of "secondary representations"—it is the mental interplay, not the linguistic elements as such, that needs to be considered.

On this basis we are justified in speculating about the subsurface activity of the verbal artifact, as if indeed we might try to understand authors better than they understood themselves. We never shall, of course, but we may act as if we could. The task, we admit, is impossible. Yet we undertake it, in part for the sake of interpreting any specific work, but also—and this is necessary too—that we may begin to see how a theory of any type of work may be produced. In this case theory will lift the notion of style to a higher level of generality than is required for its use in connection with the specific work. To grasp style technically, to extract stylistic features, we need only record what is in a work, linguistically, and how it is set forth as narrative, drama, argument, and so on. But to grasp a particular style of a particular work as belonging to the larger domain where style is a basic purpose of making texts (or speeches) in general, we shall have to think about authors' mental, emotional, and spiritual states as they undertake the practice of art. In terms of those odd touches of manner that so interested Schleiermacher, we shall have to shift from idiosyncrasies of style to styles of idiosyncrasy.

Style and idiosyncrasy have long been associated terms. The *idio-synkrasis* (the "odd, peculiar, or strange mixture") rests on a yet deeper sense of the term, the mix of *ta idia* ("things that are one's own; one's private affair"). Tradition woos us with the idea that style may be understood in terms of that which marks it, namely the personal idiosyncrasy of the author's literary manner. But do we understand much about oddness itself, about the conditions and nature of excess that is marked or signaled as the expression of some overpowering privacy? Idiosyncrasy itself is the obscure aspect of the problem of style. We need, as Mary Ann Caws has suggested, to examine styles of idiosyncrasy before we can be sure we are ready to speak of the idiosyncrasies of style. The two phrases are not quite symmetrically reversible. Idiosyncrasies of literary style occur and persist in any author's work for reasons that go beyond the mere literarity of that work, reasons that involve "extreme situations." In my own shorthand I call these situations Patagonian, and their writing I call Patagonian word games—after the early and modern explorers of that "uttermost part of the earth." Patagonia, the metaphorical Patagonia, names a state of mind and feeling virtually entrapped in the regions of deep paradox.

To introduce some notions of this entrapment (and escape?) I have chosen to discuss two apparently different authors, whose works are strange, with a strangeness that tests the larger implications of the problem of style.

My first case, then, is the last known letter written by the English poet John Clare. We presume that someone addressed the letter for him; about exactly how the letter was sent or what exactly its text responded to, we cannot and will surely never know. We only know that Clare wrote the letter, in his own hand, with his own pen, and signed it. The letter went to James Hipkins, an "unknown inquirer from the outside world," as the editors call him, about whom we know nothing except that this letter was indeed sent to him. At the time of transmission, 8 March 1860, John Clare was an inmate of Saint Andrew's Asylum, Northampton. He had been in that asylum, by this date, for some twenty years.

Clare was doubtless crazy, lucid at intervals. He thought he had two wives—the first was nonexistent; he suffered from other wilder hallucinations. His madness was tragic. To James Hipkins he wrote as follows:

DEAR SIR

    I am in a Madhouse & quite forget your Name or who you are You must excuse me for I have nothing to communicate or tell of & why I am shut up I don't know I have nothing to say so I conclude

Yours respectfully
JOHN CLARE (309)

Odd this certainly is—also, is it not humorous? It would make a fitting document for the final pages of *Jokes and the Unconscious* or Freud's late essay *Humor.*

We can begin by asking where, in the letter, any stylistic oddity resides. Surely, on the plane of genre, where the writer has somehow twisted the form chosen, the genre "personal letter." Frame analysis gives the following:

> Opening salutation (Dear Sir)
>> the text proper
>>> transition element (so I conclude)
>>>> closing salutation (Yours respectfully)
>>>> signature (John Clare)

Genre normalizes. The older manner of personal correspondence was generally more formal than our own, but a more or less formal salutation tends to frame any letter—a "letter" is what is thus framed.

In this case the closing "Yours respectfully" rings peculiarly odd—an empty shell of decorum, proper to communicating with a friendly stranger and yet here eccentric to the main text. Body and limbs are somehow not working together as they should. At least, frame and text interact in a weird, slightly spastic fashion, as if Clare (without expressly intending it) were asking James Hipkins (and now us) to consider what indeed respect and regard amount to, when directed to a correspondent from "the uttermost part of the earth." Normal retroactivity, re-specting and re-garding, are all rendered baseless.

Having claimed that Clare (witting or not—it hardly matters) has achieved an oddness in relation to generic frame—the standard letter form, we could equally wish to argue that he is not so very deviant after all—and on quite ordinary grounds. The personal letter permits a loose and infinitely open and variable shaping of its matter. Of all genres it is, with the private diary, capable of greatest un-self-consciousness about the writer's own thought connections, feelings, language, and unbuttoned self.

Byron, for example, says whatever he pleases in his letters. He moves freely at lightning speed from one item to another. His spirit, what Schleiermacher understood as the entire relation of personality to work, is such that the oddest mixtures cohere. Passion and brilliant verbal adolescence override any pedantic need for reasons and explanations; Byron just lets things happen. John Clare, who hallucinated at times that he was Lord Byron, had always gone his lordship one better in the matter of epistolary form and style: he typically punctuates with dashes; he omits the period

at the close of every paragraph of his letters, which is not so surprising as at first
it appears—there are scarcely any periods at all in his correspondence, early or late.
Clare, like Byron, knew this to be part of a style. To Chauncy Townshend, he had
written in 1820 that "Letter writing is a thing I give no brush of correction or
study too—tis just set down as things come to my 'tongue's end'." Clare had never
constructed or composed his letters. He allowed the tumble of streaming thought
to take its own way. Point and punctuation were not for him.

Their absence or mystification still constitute a style, however. The chosen frame
"personal letter" permits this choice.

Analogously, throughout the vast territories of literature forms abound, to enable
the framing of different idiosyncrasies of style. The drama directly controls voice
and distributes voices among different characters; so, more narrowly, the voices
resound in the dramatic monologue and its introspective precursor, the Shakespearean
soliloquy; so also the personal essay; so the novel; so also the lyric, especially in its
modern deformities—one could extend the list of permissive forms far and wide.

The opposite applies in technical writing, which tends to rinse out the oddness
of the author's own private mannerisms. Is oddness then the enemy of the technical,
where standardized, repeatable, numberable language use is the final goal? Perhaps.
The current of such discourse does seem to drift away from or against the current
of individual differences, at least in normal science. Only when science reaches out
to the edges of its unknown does its language begin to acquire a more poetic—that
is, idiosyncratic—flavor. The real language of science—mathematics—becomes no
less idiosyncratic as the data to be explained become more and more extreme, as
they approach the status of "naked singularities."

All this is only to say that much concerning idiosyncratic styles can be done by
analysis of frames and norms and by deviance from them.

As a goal or purpose or hidden agenda, however, idiosyncratic style (occurring
for my purposes in nontechnical imaginative literature) is rather a kind of self-
expression, interesting in and for itself.

Starting from norm and deviation, we get idiosyncrasies of style. But starting
from the manner itself, we get into the problem of styles of idiosyncrasy. This
second field overarches the first and forces us to speculate more freely about the
normality and oddness of oddness.

In this light one notices that John Clare's letter presents a parodoxical conniption
of oddness. At first hearing or first reading, the note to Hipkins is a shock. But to
what, exactly, in our expectations is it a shock? The question arises as to what makes
for a normal communication emanating from an insane asylum. Let me quote the
letter again.

DEAR SIR

    I am in a Madhouse & quite forget your Name or who you are You must
excuse me for I have nothing to communicate or tell you of & why I am shut up
I don't know I have nothing to say so I conclude

                              Yours respectfully
                              JOHN CLARE

This time, the letter appears perfectly sane. Clare states that communication itself is puzzling to him, which is surely the most analytically intelligent sort of reflection, given his state. What, he asks, should he talk about, given that in "prison," as he elsewhere called the asylum, there is no "about." That's why the letter appears to come from beyond the grave. It is *outre tombe*. In higher style it might have been penned by a resident of the inferno, or Dante's limbo. The effect is ghostly. The dangerous linguistic site, as Foucault would call the asylum, is a first-order Patagonian locus; the asylum defeats communication, and the extreme situation is actual and objective. It could be located: Saint Andrew's Asylum, Northampton (in the Midlands), in the year 1860, on the eighth day of March.

The question that counts, however, is just how Clare relates to this objectivity of site. If we decide that Clare (an author who, like Hölderlin, wrote some of his most powerful poems while certifiably "mad") remains painfully clearheaded and perspicuous about his extremity, then we shall have discovered a paradox of writing in the extreme situation. The more perspicuous and incisive Clare's vision of his state, the more lucidly he expresses his own insanity. If he were not mad, he would make small talk. It's true, he may only have lost his short-term memory, so far as anything this letter alone can tell us. Yet we suspect a madness of some kind—the madness of an undue or misplaced or displaced perspicuity. (This condition, we are told, characterizes certain forms of schizophrenia—the splitting allows moments of clarity to alternate with moments of darkness.) Perhaps only the rhythm of repetition in this letter provides the clue. My method has been to trust the text completely, and I am left with the impression that whatever is most illuminated about Clare's letter is what feels like madness.

There is a factor of naming and lost naming, which in due course I want to bring into my speculations. For the moment it suffices to point out the local, situational aspect of Clare's oddness—the Patagonian aspect of things here. A double-binding linguistic event (the mutual antagonism of frame and textual body) makes it impossible for us to decide where lie the edges between inside and outside Clare's word space, his "asylum." The letter shows its author searching for that boundary, which he cannot find, because he is on it. "Give me a place to stand, and I will move the world." The arrested liminality is complete. It can only generate more of the same. Utter oddness comes to be absolute sameness.

Postmodernist criticism tends to discover such documents and then to erect virtually metaphysical capriccios around their inscrutable self-contradictions. We do better to recall that Clare is objectively anchored in fact, when he writes, "I am in a Madhouse." This clearly stated avowal is the base for all the subsequent disorientation. It would have been less disturbing to us, had Clare written, "They claim this is a madhouse . . . I know better; but they won't let me out, because I am indeed mixed up, and a nuisance." No, not so. He says, "I am in a Madhouse," and goes on to make some brief remarks about how it all works in a madhouse. For these reasons we are drawn to emphasize the letter genre, which is the vestigial frame of Clare's sanity, that structure still persisting from a world outside the asylum. Only on a higher level of interpretation, when we jump the whole question of this letter's meaning up to a higher perspective, do we discover that there is no way of knowing whether in Gödelian terms the letter is inconsistent or incomplete. In the realm of language it appears that a system can oscillate forever between the two states of lack. Sometimes Clare's letter seems complete but inconsistent; sometimes consistent, but incomplete. Gödel's proof could now be renamed "Clare's Final Madhouse Theorem." Gödel's proof applies to any situation extreme enough to raise questions about man's actual relations to the more intransigent paradoxes of self-reflexivity. As with Bruce Chatwin's journey "in Patagonia," we can ask if Clare's mental and physical state prevents any resolution of the endless Gödelian debate.

What needs to be hammered home is that with any valid case of extremely odd mixture, of deep idiosyncrasy, we cannot tell where to look for the origin of the oddness. Shall we look in mind (the "inner"), or in situation (the "outer")? The two are confounded. Absolute oddness melts and merges the solid ground of difference. Stylistic suicide is the next and final step, and I follow classical stylistic wisdom in this regard: classical stylists have always said that any pervasive and exaggerated trait of style will undermine its initially delightful or animating effect; it will kill the effect it was intended to produce. With Clare, of course, the problem of style has gone right out of orbit. We can still speak of a problem of style correctly, in this case, only because of the almost studied perfection of the way Clare uses genre frame and his own easy epistolary rhythms to effect his escape from earth's gravitation. It's as if he had waited many years to be able to write this perfect "letter from an asylum." The letter is a supreme fiction. It defies augury. It is a tale of cock and bull. It goes nowhere.

Transition to a Description of the Opposite Case of Odd Mixtures

Antinomies are boring, infinitely replaceable by one another, but they are useful and apparently irresistible to humans. A structuralist could make up a nice list of binary oppositions to cover Clare's letter, and it would generate nice arguments about the writer and his writing. Instead of a grid of binaries I shall now resort to a single one that seems applicable to the problem of writing in general: either the author's mind is too full of words or too empty. By words I mean words that the author can use. Shakespeare uses about thirty thousand words in his canon, Racine about two thousand. The one is perhaps too "full of words," the other too "empty of words." Instead of saying, then, that authors are either inside their lexica or outside them, I shall say that they are either filled or emptied by them. (There might be a useful analogy to be drawn from the art of cuisine.) Relatively, this is only to say that full/empty is only the extreme situation of the classical stylist's principle of a natural economy of literary means—that is, the "nothing too much" of ancient Greek wisdom.

Clare's case suggests a dictionary bled white. Earlier he had loved earth, its creatures, its pools, streams, bushes, thorns, and rinds—he tells us in one prose piece how the bark of trees in spring "kindles" into a new birth every year. Clare the naturalist, whether in poem or prose, achieves a miraculous passivity for years, standing empty before nature, letting it fill him, letting it instigate a play of his mind—the naming game. He bows before nature. Ashbery's prose poem, "For John Clare," salutes the clarity of this homage: "Kind of empty in the way it sees everything, the earth gets to its feet and salutes the sky" (35). Earth-Clare is also empty in the way he sees everything. He looks and bows to the sky, as to his own reflection in a mirror, and knows his own emptiness.

In Peter Neumeyer's *Homage to John Clare*, itself a Patagonian work, there is a footnote on emptiness and the poet in his madness:

> During the asylum years there was a period of time during which Clare would capitalize the initial letters of words,—later he would write in a code omitting all vowels. In 1860 [the year of our letter]—very late in his life, when much of his reason had deserted him—he attributed his inability to write to the fact that "they have cut off my head, and picked out all the letters of the alphabet—all the vowels and consonants—and brought them out through my ears; and they want me to write poetry! I can't do it." (21)

That's what I mean by emptiness, and if you must go to a schizophrenic to find it in extremis, of course that's where and how far you must go.

You go to art movements like minimalism, or to the greater emptiness of Beckett, to a work like Beckett's *Sans*, which reduces the story of Job to a series of twenty-four revolving paragraphs that turn round and round on slight additions and subtractions made on the ground of its first paragraph:

> Ruins true refuge long last towards which so many false time out of mind. All sides endlessness earth sky as one no sound no stir. Grey face two pale blue little body heart beating only upright. Blacked out fallen open four walls over backwards true refuge issueless. (7)

My sense is that while all the phrasal units recur in some form or other, the generative phrase is "only upright," that is, a deprivation not preventing a sense of deprivation. One is held, in short, without.

The other side of the coin is the case of excessive fullness, a fullness that might result from any number of *engloutissements*.

The case I choose is the fullness of a certain kind of charm: the charm of idle curiosity. The example is John Aubrey (1626–97), the celebrated, slightly mad antiquarian biographer of Elizabethan and seventeenth-century men and women. Anthony Wood, rival and contemporary, called Aubrey "roving and maggoty-headed." His mind, from his youngest years, was a kind of informational sluice. Friends expected him to fall and break his neck, running downstairs to catch one last anecdote from a departing guest. Despite a lifelong serious interest in mathematics and science, he instinctively chose to chronicle the uncountable odd bits of gossip that alone could show that X or Y actually lived and breathed. Aubrey could accept the most dubious evidence. He gathered stories as if he intended to live forever, and the *Brief Lives* treats over 425 individuals. Why so many lives? one wonders, until one recalls that Aubrey mourned the loss or transformation of a whole world, the England as it existed before the Civil War. Science and scientific learning fascinated him, but the pervasive tone of his *Lives* is nostalgic royalism, with its belief that the ancient magic of "the land" was the chief support of permanent worth.

Aubrey never published the *Lives*. Each biography is in principle incompletable, hence consistent at least with its open-ended mode of production. The manuscripts agglomerated while to the main pages of a given life were added the later marginalia, the "one more story" that would confer actuality, for certain, on its subject. There could never be too many stories, no matter how tangential or even absurd they might look to a more analytic biographer. For Aubrey was collecting materials sufficient to furnish an old curiosity shop. The abiding mood is one of almost overpowering affection for his subjects. Like Herodotus, on his humbler plane, he is the curator of legend.

Thus, of Dr. Ralph Kettel, the president of Trinity College, Oxford (1563–1643), he writes:

> He dyed a year after I came to the Colledge, and he was then a good deal above 80, and he had a fresh ruddy complexion. He was a tall well-growne man. His gowne & surplice & hood being on, he had a terrible gigantique aspect with his sharp grey eyes.
> . . .One of the Fellowes (in Dr. Francis Potter's time) was wont to say that Dr. Kettel's braine was like a Hasty-Pudding, where there was Memorie, Judgmente and Phancy all just so jumbled together. If you had to doe with him, taking him for a Foole, you would have found in him great subtlety and reach; *e contra*, if you treated him as a Wise man you should have mistaken him for a Foole. . . .
>
> . . .He was irreconcileable to long haire; called them hairy Scalpes, and as for Periwigges (which were then very rarely worn) he beleeved them to be Scalpes of men cutte off after they were hang'd, and so tanned and dressed for use. When he observed the Scholars haire longer than ordinary (especially if they were Scholars of the House) he would bring a paire of Cizers in his Muffe (which he commonly wore) and woe be to them that sate on the outside of the Table. I remember he cutt Mr. Radford's haire with the knife that chipps the bread on the Buttery Hatch, and then he sang (this is in the old play of *Gammer Gurton's Needle*):
>
> > And was not Grim the Collier finely trimm'd?
> > Tonedi, Tonedi.
>
> Mr. Lydell, said he, how do you decline tondeo? Tondeo, tondes, Tonedi?
> He was constantly at Lectures and Exercises in the Hall, to observe them, and brought along with him his Howerglasse; and one time, being offended with the Boyes, he threatened them that if they did not doe their exercise better, he would bring an Howerglasse two hours long. . . .   (181–86)

Aubrey recalls, too, that during the Civil War a Parliament soldier broke in, while Kettel lectured on rhetoric, and smashed his hourglass.

Aubrey loves an eccentric. One movement of his thought is away from the center of normal behavior. His own life, reported in Oliver Lawson Dick's Aubreyan introduction to the 1949 edition of *Brief Lives*, never went right and smooth until he had lost his considerable fortune—a series of incurable erotic and monetary bafflements preceded Aubrey's later complete enslavement by antiquarian obsession. So he tends to notice how obsessions may rule human lives. Of William Outram he notes only that he was "a tall spare leane pale consumptive man; wasted himself much, I presume, by frequent preaching" (cii). Aubrey, as Dick says, had such a reductive and epithetic skill "that he could conjure a living being out of a mere *list* of facts," thus: "Mrs. Abigail Slope, borne at Broad Chalke, near Salisbury, A.D. 1648. Pride; lechery; ungratefull to her father; married; runne distracted; recovered." And another such list:

> Richard Stokes, M.D. His father was Fellow of Eaton College. He was bred there and at King's College. Scholar to Mr. W. Oughtred for Mathematiques (Algebra). He made himself mad with it, but became sober again, but I feare like a cracktglasse. Became a Roman-catholique: maried unhappily at Liege, dog and catt, etc. Became a Sott. Dyed at Newgate, Prisoner for debt 1681.   (cii)

The sequence "runne distracted–recovered" fascinates Aubrey. Equally fascinating to him are body language and those windows to the soul, the eyes, of which he has the portraitist's keen awareness—for instance, James Bovey, Esquire: "a dark hazell eye" (33); Venetia Digby: "Her face, a short ovall; dark browne eie-browe about which much sweetnesse, as also the opening of the eie-lids" (101); Sir Walter Raleigh: "He had a most remarkable aspect, an exceedingly high forehead, long-faced and sour eie-lidded, a kind of pigge-eie" (255). The eyes of his friend Thomas Hobbes elicited an unusually lengthy description:

> He had a good eie, and that of a hazell colour, which was full of Life and Spirit, even to the last. When he was earnest in discourse, there shone (as it were) a bright live-coale within it. He had two kinds of looks: when he laugh't, was witty and in a merry humour, one could scarce see his Eies; by and by, when he was serious and positive, he open'd his eies round (i.e. his eie-lids.) He had midling eies, not very big, nor very little.   (154)

That such physical details are not trivial in Aubrey's work is to be seen in the recurrence of the eye motif. To the following picture of the poet John Denham, the motif gives a culminating focus:

> Sir John Denham was unpolished with the smallpox; otherwise a fine complexion. He was of the tallest, but a little incurvetting at his shoulders, nor very robust. His haire was but thin and flaxen, with a moist curle. His gate was slow, and was rather a Stalking (he had long legges). His Eie was a kind of light goose-grey, not big, but it had a strange Piercingnesse, not as to shining and glory, but (like a Momus) when he conversed with you he look't into your very Thoughts.   (91)

Quoting Aubrey for a systematic recurrence will give a skewed impression of his method. His method is to pursue the curious fact. Thus of Denham he further tells us that the poet suffered a seizure of ecstatic madness, during which he went to visit the king "and told him he was the Holy Ghost." "Runne distracted–recovered" applies here too (Denham recovered), but the charm of the curious detail was to persist beyond recovery: "His 2nd Lady had no child: was poysoned by the hands of the Countess of Rochester, with Chocolate" (93).

Poisoned with chocolate! "How these curiosities would be quite forgott, did not such idle fellowes as I am putt them downe" (lxxxiii). "I have nothing to say so I conclude[,] Yours respectfully. . . ." Too full of words, too empty of words, the two worlds of the ground of oddness.

Yet to leave the matter here is to materialize the problem of style unduly. Something underlies this excessive emptiness and fullness, some kind of epistemic rule is governing the vacuity and the plethora. Otherwise there would be no resultant manner in Clare or Aubrey. What can we say of the problem of searching for such a rule? We can certainly see that style and manner are not mere matters of an itemized lexical numerosity; otherwise Aubrey would be plethoric merely as the Hammacher Schlemmer catalog is plethoric, the latter being odd and itemized enough to represent the word bank of any plethoric odd mixture of stylistic elements, in short, style as gadget list:

> The World's Only Travel Steam Iron—La Valtromplina Nut and Bean Roaster—The Electronic Wine Guide—The English Heated Towel Stand—The Electric Shoe-Buffing Wand—The Rotating Electronic Chef—The Blomberg Solarium—The Osake Electric Massage/Stereo Chair—The Self-Adjusting Wide-Mouth Toaster—The Infrared Yard Sentry—The Wellington Boot Jack—The Best-Designed Travel Iron—The Sculler's Ergometer—Le Petit Electric Mincer—Electrically Heated Socks—Talking Clock—The Sonic 2000 Rodent Eliminator—The World's Best Corkscrew—The Nantucket Steamer—The Classic Syphon—Genuine Ostrich Plume Telescoping Duster—Squirrel-Proof Bird Feeder—The Talking Scale—The Double Wedge Electric Log Splitter—Solid Brass Spyglass—The Hammacher Schlemmer Winter Supplement—The Suburban Consumer—The Narcissism of Small Differences—The Anxiety of Influence—The Deconstruction—The Selfconsuming Artifact—The Fizzle—The Blanchot Folie Du Jour—The Misfits—The Original Maldoror Song Book—The Professional's Costume Stilts—The Hammacher Schlemmer Winter Supplement—The Definite Article—The Indefinite Article—The Alchemist—The Shifter—The End.

One can make a bad poem out of any list, or a good one. As by the same token, one can make good or bad poetry, develop a strong or feeble style, out of any truly reductive sequence of ideas such as we found in John Clare's letter. The pile of stuff or the reductive formula needs its appropriate manner, even when this pile or reduction is strange. Choice of topic is only the opening move. Here we must reach out toward a further speculation.

> But as the wind the waters stir
> The mirrors change and flye   (Clare, "A Song")

> The sea whispers me (Whitman, *Song of Myself*)

The list of greatest poems, plays, novels, discourses, and so on does not easily come to include works written with highly idiosyncratic style. What is most valuable to us lies more in the middle range. No one denies that *Finnegans Wake* is amazing. Yet there is a human scale of values according to which a handful of Shakespeare sonnets is worth more than the whole *Wake*. If, however, it became possible for average intelligent readers to read the *Wake* without struggle, then the *Wake* might even surpass Shakespeare.

The value of the most eccentric works falls on another scale, yet it is not easy to say exactly what that scale measures. It seems to measure a literary activity akin to the production of the sublime, hence a Patagonian word game. One aspect of the sublime is its self-reflexive encounter with the means of its own coming into being. The characteristic trait of sublime works is the way they affront us with their medium. An Alpine poem, say, will thrust on us rock words, cataract words, ice words, mass words, and so on. Such language is never drawn from the lexicon of ordinary speech, because that vocabulary would stop or deflate the elemental connection between the special (odd) words and their idea (in the poem). Or, to put it another way, ordinary language returns vision to the field of history and the irreversible passage of time, that field where we all live.

The superordinate category is the rhetoric of extreme situations, the sublime being only one such modality, the picturesque another, dada and *humour noir* another, Calvino's "cosmicomic" style another, and so on. What all strong idiosyncrasies of style have in common is a peculiar, undue thoughtfulness. Serious odd mixture is intended to show forth the almost verbal activity lying "just beneath the surface" of the work. The style, instead of being natural or transparent, is designedly opaque, but in a special sense: the aim is to produce a language that, instead of communicating something, reveals its own elemental laws and rhythms. Thus Clare's letter in effect draws on the logic of the liar's paradox (Epimenides the Cretan announces, "All Cretans are liars"). Aubrey's *Brief Lives*, it could be shown, draws on the logic of various paradoxes of infinity. Anthony Wood perceived the latter clearly. When Aubrey asked Wood, "Is my English style well enough?," the testy Oxonian replied, "'Tis well. You should never ask these questions, but do them out of hand. *You have time enough*" (ci). Wood, an extremely intelligent if bitter man, saw that Aubrey wrote in such fashion that for him there would always be time enough, since his whole method made the passage of time an issue in the work and in its coming into being. Only by doing too much could Aubrey know what would be enough. Which is another way of saying that an Aubrey is always testing something more fundamental than the materials (in his case, antiquarian data) at hand. Rather, he is testing the possibility of even doing antiquarian collection and narrative, testing a deeper logic.

The idiosyncratic author embeds the logical issue right in the utterance of this text, just beneath the surface, and thus leads the reader to notice always how the text is being uttered, to notice a certain opacity of the text. That's what strikes the reader of Whitman's and Poe's verses. Every odd stylistic mixture has a way of saying, like a child, "Look at me!" With Whitman, for example, one has to master the oddness, until one can read through its opacity of participles, anaphoras, tone clusters, and so on and only then discover that on a certain plane of philosophic discourse Whitman is as clear as a bell. Hart Crane is a lesser Whitman, in this regard, but he was quite right to claim that he worked according to a "poetic logic" that only his baroque extravagance of diction could veil and reveal. A fortiori these remarks apply to Mallarmé and to Rimbaud.

Although he does not explain exactly how this works, as I too have failed to explain exactly how it works, Edward Sapir tried to describe what is really going on at the outer reaches of idiosyncrasy. In "Language and Literature," the final chapter of his *Language*, Sapir draws a contrast between scientific and imaginative literature or discourse:

> There is really no mystery in the distinction. . . . A scientific truth is impersonal, in its essence it is untinctured by the particular linguistic medium in which it finds expression. It can as readily deliver its message in Chinese as in English. (223)

Sapir, who here regards thought as "nothing but language denuded of its outward garb," is of course thinking about a properly verbal scientific expression. He knew what Galileo had taught, that in the stricter sense numbers and mathematics constitute the natural language of science. Thus he goes on:

> The proper medium of scientific expression is therefore a generalized language that may be defined as a symbolic algebra of which all known languages are translations. One can adequately translate scientific literature because the original scientific expression is itself a translation. Literary expression is personal and concrete, but this does not mean that its significance is altogether bound up with the accidental qualities of the medium. (223–24).

The poet's Vichian use of myth would bear out this last statement, as would the Borgesian view of basic metaphors (for him the labyrinth is one). Sapir continues:

> A truly deep symbolism, for instance, does not depend on the verbal associations of a particular language but rests securely on an intuitive basis that underlies all linguistic expression. The artist's "intuition," to use Croce's term, is immediately fashioned out of a generalized human experience—thought and feeling—of which his own individual experience is a highly personalized selection. The thought relations in this deeper level have no specific linguistic vesture; the rhythms are free, *not bound, in the first instance*, to the traditional rhythms of the artist's language. (224; emphasis mine)

"In the first instance" seems to mean at some level of "thought relations" where a style evolves. Sapir wants to contrast two kinds of author, two styles, the normal and the odd. Two Sapirian instances of the normal, Shakespeare and Heine, achieve transparency and a kind of natural manner. They seem to have "known subconsciously to fit or trim the deeper intuition to the provincial accents of their daily speech. In them there is no effect of strain." Oddness, by contrast, does show strain. Sapir continues:

> Certain artists whose spirit moves largely in the non-linguistic (better, in the generalized linguistic) layer even find a certain difficulty in getting themselves expressed in the rigidly set terms of their accepted idiom. One feels that they are unconsciously striving for a generalized art language, a literary algebra, that is related to the sum of all known languages as a perfect mathematical symbolism is related to all the roundabout reports of mathematical relations that normal speech is capable of conveying. Their art expression is frequently strained, it sounds at times like a translation from an unknown original—which, indeed, is precisely what it is.
>
> These artists—Whitmans and Brownings—impress us rather by the greatness of their spirit than the felicity of their art. Their relative failure is of the greatest diagnostic value as an index of the pervasive presence in literature of a larger, more intuitive linguistic medium than any particular language. (224)

With the classic artist of a natural economy of style, the very opposite is true, while there is little sign of struggle to reach back and down to Sapir's deeper level. With Heine, he observes, "one is under the illusion that the universe speaks German" (225). The linguistic material, the opacity of the poet's medium, "disappears," to use Sapir's word. Whereas with the artist of the odd mixture this sense of linguistic material, linguistic lumber, increasingly pushes to the foreground.

There is then method in the madness of the odd manner. It is, on Sapir's view of Whitman and Browning, virtually a research project into theoretical linguistics— Chomsky *avant la lettre*. Our conclusion must then be that the idiosyncratic style provides the testing ground of that "literary algebra" which subtends any style, of any kind, including the classic style. Only by going to the verge of meaning can one discover the norms of meaning; only if someone twists and distends and extrudes and dilates the primary materials of discourse can it be seen where the normal styles are naturally at work and how these styles articulate the surfaces and subsurfaces of texts.

Taking a larger view of idiosyncrasy, I find it relates closely to the prophetic, which in turn always implicates the writer and reader, speaker and listener, in a consideration of thresholds—and, one might add, in the balancing of the too much and the too little, not as quantities but as qualities. Late in this century we have no comfortable terms with which to describe these relations. Pater, who thought deeply about such matters, wrote in his essay "On Style" that mind and soul need to be distinguished.

> Hard to ascertain philosophically, the distinction is real enough practically, for they often interfere, are sometimes in conflict, with each other. Blake, in the last century, is an instance of preponderating soul, embarrassed, at a loss, in an era of preponderating mind. As a quality of style at all events, soul is a fact, in certain writers—the way they have of absorbing language, of attracting it into the peculiar spirit they are of, with a subtlety which makes the actual result seem like some inexplicable inspiration. By mind, the literary artist reaches us, through static and

objective indications of design in his work, legible to all. By soul, he reaches us, somewhat capriciously perhaps, one and not another, through vagrant sympathy and a kind of immediate contact. (22)

We might instance others along with Blake. Our present critical activities have enabled us to decode authors like Blake—Frye's great career began in just such fashion, with a desire to decode a prophetic canon. What might be called High Deconstruction is a prophetic mode of reading. We have come to appreciate those authors in whom there are grounds for such reading. Prophecy is the search for veiled, not buried, meaning, and it requires what Sapir called a "generalized linguistic," an underlying and yet not entirely lost order of language—perhaps only the memory of a lost harmony.

I should not leave my reader with the idea that authors like Clare and Aubrey, Whitman and Browning, were mad semioticians in search of a universal language. Though Gertrude Stein, just about the oddest of all authors who ever published, does often appear to follow that star. What I mean to say, as Stein might and indeed did sometimes say, is that certain authors force the fundamental question as to why and how they can be writing in the first place, as if they doubted their right to exist, as authors. Ben Jonson's aggressive and epochal publication of his *Works* (1616) betrays an intense self-doubt in this regard. Of all works for the theater written by Englishmen *The Alchemist* is, I think, by design lexically the most estrangingly strange; it has to be so, because Jonson in that play—which Coleridge called our most perfect comedy—discovered a deeper algebraic system (alchemy) through which he could explore the question, What indeed are the styles of idiosyncrasy? Whatever be our final answer, we can at least say they will result from some attempt to speak across a wide gap, as John Clare wrote his strange letter to "an unknown inquirer from the outside world."

Critical theory seeks to understand the gap across which the idiosyncratic author speaks. Recent critical parlance identifies various kinds of aporia, deep meaningless pits, pits of nonmeaning, various nothings. These appear to be moments in the discourse where the author reaches a final blanked-out area, where the "poetic logic" has led the text to a double bind, to a finally undecidable issue. Often such issues are contained in a single term—let's say, the "whiteness" of the whale in Melville, or the "perfect whiteness of the snow" of "the shrouded human figure," the final vision in *The Narrative of Arthur Gordon Pym*. A more radical example, one of the deepest in our literature, is given by the letter "O" in the play *Othello*. By the time we reach Mallarmé we discover that Sterne's blank page is scarcely framable, anymore, by the containing book or genre. With Mallarmé and the surrealists later, *the frame is blank*. Aporia is no longer the product of a certain line of discursive motion; it is now the process of that motion. In that state of thought and poetics we still in part share a certain terror: of frameless extremism.

The preceding pages have, I think, been speaking to such problems in a slightly less philosophical way than is usual. The kind of threatening gap that Clare and Aubrey illustrate has a look of the childish about it, as if they were children who could not "communicate" with grownups. Learning to speak, the child has either too few or too many words. I have not shown this, but I believe that the child's early and continuing encounters with language provide the model for Patagonian word games. Further research should reveal whether this is true or not.

The analogy between idiosyncrat and child has one final, furthering consequence: both are engaged in a struggle to acquire an adequate metalanguage for their expressive purposes. In this light extreme oddness seems to come from a defect of metalinguistic fluency. Hence the struggle! By contrast, normality in style, as elsewhere, seems to imply a power of drawing easily at all times on multiple systems of linguistic self-regulation, namely on the perspective powers of metalanguage.

On Ghosts and Prime Numbers

SUSAN STEWART

What is the matter with ghosts? Why don't they go back to the anonymous sleep of the earth? Why don't they fly around in asexual flocks like angels, their robes radiant and blinding? Who needs their transparency and noise, their particulars and opinions, their transgressions and unfinished resolves?

Lafcadio Hearn writes at the beginning of *Some Chinese Ghosts*, "in preparing [these] legends I sought especially for *weird beauty*" (vii). And it is the weird beauty of ghosts, of idiosyncrasy in general, and of the preceding essay by Angus Fletcher in particular, that I will follow in these remarks.[1] If style is the veil or membrane, the surface stretched over the truth, can I assume that style's appearance here as the weird and incongruous, the odd mixture, will lead to a revelation of some other, some discourse yet unread and unreadable, a lost city, a first place, a horror unimagined? Incongruous metonymy; incongruous metaphor. What is the way out of the cultivation of eccentricity here? I will try to turn the key of the pragmatic.

Thus I will begin with the broadest questions: What is the relation of idiosyncrasy to what it is not? What is the relation of idiosyncrasy to a notion of social totality? Not just odd mixtures, selectivity, the infinity of elements and combinations offering themselves for consumption; rather, the odd mixture is foregrounded against the velvet curtain of the proper, the classical, the balanced mixture of the normal and its seemingly smooth functioning. Here we have the problem of levels of analysis—take, for example, the idiosyncratic text, whose oddness might emerge out of its relation to the spatial and temporal, to the social, and to the conventions of art, of literature, of narrative, of an author's oeuvre, of a given work itself. What is the proper scale of the lacuna or the blot? There is some problem of pattern here, of expectation thwarted, but there also is always the problem of context in the sense that context itself is emergent in the articulation of difference that idiosyncrasy brings forth. We know this context through both accidents and mistakes-on-purpose. We name a context not only through what it includes or permits but through its exclusionary practices as well.

Furthermore, the whole that is left out of the idiosyncratic universe, that background or shadow which lies behind it, is consequently totalized or made more than the sum of its parts by idiosyncrasy—in other words, the very particularity of idiosyncrasy allows the generalization of the normal; the out-of-sequence gives shape to the sequence; the in-focus permits the out-of-focus; the boundary defines the territory; the aberration deflects the proper form. In one sense we are at the place where the baroque and the grotesque, by perpetual motion, invent the absent place of the classical. But in another, we are talking about the conditions for knowledge and, inseparably, the conditions for a structure of knowledge. I am thinking of Foucault's point, in *Discipline and Punish*, that each individual has a place and each place an individual. Within what Foucault calls "disciplinary space,"

> one must eliminate the effects of imprecise distributions, the uncontrolled disappearance of individuals, their diffuse circulation, their unusable and dangerous coagulation; it [disciplinary space] was a tactic of anti-desertion, anti-vagabondage, anti-concentration. Its aim was to establish presences and absences, to know where and how to locate individuals, to set up useful communications, to interrupt others, to be able at each moment to supervise the conduct of each individual, to assess it, to judge it, to calculate its qualities or merits. It was a procedure, therefore, aimed at knowing, mastering and using. (143)

Idiosyncrasy must be displayed within social space, must be categorized and managed, for, as part of a range of categories—the eccentric, the deviant, the criminal—that name the problematic, idiosyncrasy helps give integrity and power to that social space.

Thus it might be fruitful to look at idiosyncrasy not in terms of a constant content but in terms of a constant function—the function of marginalization in the articulation of the social whole. In this sense, marginalization legitimates, necessitates, structures, the order of that whole. It has long been noticed that the idiosyncratic is necessary because it serves as an outlet or exit (here we have an overheated social organism); but we must also consider how the idiosyncratic defines the place and status of the normal and, on its far side, defines those practices that might be termed truly deviant and thus in need of normalization and correction. Let me put this another way: idiosyncrasy and eccentricity are managed through narrative and a discourse of normalization; those aberrations on the far side of idiosyncrasy are managed, as unspeakable crimes, through the ineffability and indirect gaze of the Panopticon.

If we assume that, like all notions, the idiosyncratic is articulated through a discourse, we might look further at the genres of the idiosyncratic. A quick survey would suggest, in addition to riddles and liminal phases of ritual, such marginal and marginalizing forms as travel writing, the examination, the interview, the circus, the carnival, the freak show, and—perhaps most significantly because most pervasive—gossip. What all these forms have in common is the authority of the third person and the rubric of normalization on this side, from this point of view—the point of view of the individual perceiving subject, gazing on an object that defines that viewer's own subjectivity. The idiosyncratic occupies a space-time, more often than not, of the private room in the public square. As much as any other odd dimension of *In Patagonia*, Chatwin's continual "dropping in" and "walking into" the private worlds of his "objects" increases through the text in its startling quality. Only the "Boers" refuse him. But his desires are always distant, his contact limited to the view, his strongest feelings attached to the dead and their piecemeal ruins or souvenirs; continually "acted upon," Chatwin is the still center of the maelstrom of history, an observer whose back seems to face a precipice. The methodology of Chatwin's book, as with all travel writing, is the estrangement of objects. What is visible, what is surface, reveals its interiority through the process of narrative. At the risk (but not realization) of contamination and of dissolving the boundary of their subjectivity, travel writers are able to internalize a profoundly external view. Thus narrators are marked off from their views and at the same time internalize those views. In travel writing particularly this view is doubly mediated by the narrative voice, which "translates" a distant and distanced object—an object that has no context, as far as we know, other than that of the narrative voice that legitimates or authenticates it. Hence Chatwin's delight in subjecting the familiarity of historical "fact" to the estranging context of his own narrative construction. The investment we have in Chatwin's subjectivity is emphasized by the investment we have in the reality of *In Patagonia*'s fantastic. Should we find the book, like much early travel writing and early anthropology, to be "really" a fiction, we would consider Chatwin a fraud or a fake. Here we see that the idiosyncratic is profoundly tied to the natural and authentic in its articulation of the subject, and we see as well our insistence that the last frontier be a material rather than mental entity.

In all its genres, the idiosyncratic is constituted through a discourse of the gaze, a gaze mediated, constrained, and distanced simultaneously—a gaze that seeks objectification and thus always grazes on the surface of things. Here we find the structure of voyeurism, the structure of perversion, the process of "going the long way around" as Lacan describes it: "[The subject] is there as pervert and is situated only at the culmination of the loop"—the object is the gaze itself—that is the subject, which attains it. It is not that the object, the observed, is surprised by the subject looking through the keyhole; rather it is that the subject is surprised by the unsuspected and hidden gaze; "The gaze is this object lost and suddenly refound in the conflagration of shame, by the introduction of the other" (*Concepts* 182). Our view of the idiosyncratic is always such a sidestepping, side-glancing; we go to the freak show in terror and anticipation of reciprocity, the reciprocity that would break our subjectivity into pieces and hence confirm our conviction of its original wholeness. There is no outlook from within idiosyncrasy—instead of self-consciousness, we find a mirrored surface.

Thus the idiosyncratic is always subject to, but not vulnerable to, this desiring/ disapproving gaze. The idiosyncratic goes on without being affected by context and thus on the one hand approaches a heroic ideal, a subject oblivious to—and thus somehow transcendent to—history; on the other hand, it takes on the qualities of perversion by which it is defined—the perversely stubborn, the perversely attached, the perversely motivated. In the voyeur's mirror we might recall as well the "whimsical" roundaboutness of the fetishist (note here the etymology of *whim* as "the female pudend") or the retentiveness of the hoarder, who, in a bid for authenticity, desperately attempts to keep inside and outside, body and soul, subject and system, one.

Here we see the bad straits we travel if we begin to confuse the observer and observed, the diagnostician and the symptom. It follows then that the discourse of the idiosyncratic should not itself be idiosyncratic—the idiosyncratic is handled, conventionally, by the scientist, the explorer, the expert, the authority. In this way the idiosyncratic—that which always resists abstraction—is subjected to abstraction, even if its proper category is idiosyncrasy itself. Thus we tread a fine line between manners and mannerisms in social life. Idiosyncrasy of person is often manifested in the way one walks, answers the phone, behaves at parties, handles reciprocity and obligations. The mannerism always maps itself on an etiquette that defines the style of a class; the mannerism is the individual manifestation, and thus exaggeration, of an abstraction. Who is allowed to be idiosyncratic, and who is required to be idiosyncratic? In a brute sense, we could say that the rich are eccentric, the poor are crazy, and the latter's craziness, unlike the former's eccentricity, is always categorizable and redeemable. We might think of the discourse of contemporary advertising, which mass-markets luxury goods under slogans of uniqueness and individuality that can only be understood within the metonymic process of consumption—a process where the economy's "thinning out" at the top is imagined as divine selection. Just as elites are "filled in" by their particular anecdotes, so Bakhtin writes "[the] zone surrounding the important characters of the novel is stylistically, profoundly idiosyncratic" (320). But on closer look such discrimination does not appear only at the highest point on the social scale; as Foucault reminds us, the characteristics of idiosyncrasy appear at the boundaries of "the average": high and low, rich and poor. Foucault contends that individualization shifts historically:

> In regimes like the feudal one, individuality was most highly marked at the top. The more one exercised power, the more one was marked as an individual—by honors, prestige, even by the tombs in which burial takes place. In a disciplinary regime, individualization is descending. Through surveillance, constant observation, all those subject to control are individualized. . . . The dossier replaces the epic. (159)

The dossier rescues us; the institution confines our uncategorizability. But what Angus Fletcher reminds us of here is the possibility of the extreme situation, the situation absolute in its refusal of context, its refusal of normalization. Perhaps what is so disturbing about the texts of Chatwin and Clare is their idiosyncratic "presentation" of idiosyncratic "points of fact." As Victor Shklovsky has reminded us, *Tristram Shandy* is "the most typical novel of world literature" in that it directly negates and thus clearly foregrounds all the novelistic conventions available to Sterne. We might conjecture that a novel about Shandyism written in a Shandyistic style would more closely approximate the complete estrangement of the object that Fletcher is describing. For a concrete example we might imagine the translation of *In Patagonia* into Lunfardo. It would be a defining quality of such an absolutely idiosyncratic literature that it not be admitted into the canon. I suspect our veneration of Chatwin and Clare as "strange" writers stands in a different relation to the canon than does our interest in a writer such as Amanda Ros (Anna Margaret McKittrick), who is generally regarded as a literary curiosity. Yet Ros's exaggeration of the conventions of the romance and gothic novel is coupled, we might remember, with a truly idiosyncratic style. Here are the opening lines to *Irene Iddesleigh*: "Sympathize with me indeed! . . . Ah no! Cast your sympathy on the chill waves of troubled waters; fling it on the oases of futurity; dash it against the rock of gossip; or better still, allow it to remain within the false and faithless bosom of buried scorn." Hyperbole, systematic use of misplaced modifiers, relexification (i.e., "south" could mean a man's trousers or hell in her lexicon), allegorical naming practices (in *Helen Huddleston* important characters are named Sir Christopher Currant, the Duke of Greengage, and Sir Peter Plum, Madam Pear, Mrs. Strawberry, and Lily Lentil), and an anti-conventional thematics (the state of the body after death was a preoccupation in her writing) place Amanda Ros out of the tradition, a tradition she never belonged to anyway, "remaining largely ignorant of the mass of English literature and the works of her contemporaries" (Somerville-Large 251; see his whole discussion of Ros [246-54]). Her work cannot be taken as parody once we grant it a kind of irreducible originality. To take this a bit further, we might say that a truly idiosyncratic literature would have no system of allusions, no intertextuality; it would be readable in only one way and would thus refuse the multiplicity necessary for the construction of the social, the construction of audience.

I am not surprised that in thinking of such an absolute singularity of interpretation, we have ended up in the place of schizophrenia. For on a closer look, the idiosyncratic is not a negation; it is not in the business of inverting the social order. The extreme edge of idiosyncrasy is not the most antisocial; it is the most remote or asocial—the figure of the hermit, *L'enfant sauvage*, the "natural" or "animal" human. Here is another sense in which the idiosyncratic is naturalized, tied to the authentic, the true-to-oneself. The *OED*'s major definitions of the idiosyncratic are (1) due to individual disposition and (2) by inherent peculiarity of constitution. We rarely refer to our own idiosyncrasies, but, when we do, we call them "our ruling passions," "our weaknesses"—those natural drives pulling us away from the social center of things. Yet there is a "natural" balance to be maintained in this formulation, a balance between voluntary and involuntary behavior, between consciousness and self-consciousness. When we describe the "duck lady" or "the grate man" why do we not say "It's just their way of doing things?" Do we say that a behavior is voluntary whenever it can afford or legitimate its own defining context? It becomes apparent that this "natural boundary" is not coterminous with the body of the subject; rather, this boundary is maintained by a legitimating discourse tied to authority, license, and power.

We have reached a far edge of the margin that is idiosyncrasy; let's move back to the other side, the center from which idiosyncrasy is defined. The nonidiosyncratic, it seems, cannot have any examples. We see what has happened to Horatio here—the anecdote, the narrative, makes him remarkable. Just as the idiosyncratic, as I suggested earlier, resists abstraction, so does the normal resist exemplification, for it is the function of narrative either to make different or to typify strangeness (here we might think of Hegel's anatomy of tragedy as ways of being outside); otherwise we are in danger of being in the worst of bad ends—the "so what?" If the normal is exemplified, it is exemplified as an abstraction: in other words, it appears as parody or stereotype. The normal when manifested always undermines itself: transvestitism, the nerd poster, the WASP handbook, thick powder, and the unbearable weighting of surface—these are the characteristics of the normal displayed. Through them we see the perhaps even more profound idiosyncrasy of the normal, and this "exposed view" can only serve the interests of another normal, an outside that is part of another convention either wanting to come in or wanting to remain outside in an absolute sense. Here we might remember Freud's point in *Civilization and Its Discontents* regarding the "narcissism of minor differences" (68). Forms of *blason populaire* serve, he contends, to bind a community in love by letting others receive the manifestation of their aggression.

But we should consider not only the normalizing function of the idiosyncratic in the discourses of common sense or everyday life but also its analogous function in what Kuhn calls "normal science." Here idiosyncrasy in turn remarks on a failure of methodology. *Idiolect* (the notion of the sum total of an individual's speech) and *idiopathy* (a primary disease), for example, are unabstractable, unexaminable categories within which to place unabstractable, unexaminable phenomena, phenomena "out of the blue," phenomena with unaccounted-for causes or origins. In another time and place, like John Clare's, we would most likely say that such ideas come in an unmediated fashion from God. Our impulse indeed is to "deal" the idiosyncratic into the "normal deck of cards"—when we encounter idiosyncrasy, something must be done.

If we put aside for a moment the question of an absolute—that is, unreadable—idiosyncrasy, we must think of idiosyncrasy in relation to modes of representation and in relation to history—we must think of idiosyncrasy in relation to style. Specifically, we see subjects acting on their lives as art in particular historical periods and the various modes of such action differing significantly between periods: the slightly academic form of Renaissance self making; nineteenth-century dandyism; the notion of "life-style" and its relation to the contemporary ideology of social mobility. Again I want to underline here the total social function of the idiosyncratic. We might recall that one of the definitions of a crank is "a person subject to fads," but we might also recall, perhaps from the social domain of personal experience, that it is virtually impossible to start a fad by oneself, particularly if one is generally regarded as a crank.

Our notion of idiosyncrasy as the basis for style may be seen as an inheritance of Saussurean linguistics—here performance struggles against a uniform competence, situation against tradition, speech against language, exception against norm. But universal grammars themselves go in and out of style, and we might conclude, in the profoundly anachronistic style of Bakhtin, that the normal itself is a kind of utterance that is contextualizable and particularizable. Bakhtin concludes that "it is precisely the diversity of speech, and not the unity of a normative shared language, that is the ground of style" (308). Thus the idiosyncratic does not seem the same kind of problem if we contextualize it within the social and historical dimensions of its emergence and if we place the nonidiosyncratic in social life rather than in some transcendent or universal order.

Hegel helps us take note of such historical differences in his discussion of the idiosyncratic at the close of volume 1 of *The Philosophy of Fine Art* (394–405). Here he distinguishes *manner* (the specific and consequently accidental idiosyncrasies of the artist) from, first, *style* (the mapping of the particularity of the work onto the necessary conditions of the type of the work or genre) and, second, *originality* (the inspired state both personal to the artist and in a form adequate to the universal notion of the ideal). Although we might contend that the personal, the authorial, the particular is the foundation for style, our contention itself has a particular historical context from which it emerges to differ with Hegel. Yet Hegel, too, was aware of cultural differences with regard to his position. His statement on the artistic uses of odd mixtures might well serve as an epigraph to Chatwin's book:

> A common idea of originality is simply the stringing together of so many curiosities, things which this particular individual and no other could perpetuate or even faintly imagine. That is, however, merely idiosyncrasy gone mad. No other people on earth are more original in this meaning of the term than the Englishmen, a country where everyone prides himself on committing some folly or other, which no man in his senses is likely to repeat and then fondly imagines his performance to be original. (400–01)

We have before us, perhaps, the most typical travel book of English literature. Thus we can attribute a function to the idiosyncratic: we can account for it. But in doing so, have we chosen a disciplinary style? Is there an extra place at the table, a diary never to be read, a floor missing from the skyscraper, a tomb now suddenly empty?

Note

[1] This paper was originally delivered in response to Angus Fletcher's "Style and the Extreme Situation" at the conference of the International Association for Philosophy and Literature, University of Iowa, May 1984.

Terms

A list of key terms used in this volume, with parenthetical references to representative authors who use them.

analogy (Mil)
anaphora (Ch, Ma)
anasemia (CC, Mil)
aporia (F)
apostrophe (Mil)
apposition (Mil)
architectonics (F)
autotelic (Ch)
blanked-out area (F)
catachresis (Mil)
channel (Ch)
circumlocution (Mil)
close reading (Me)
closure (R)
code (Ch)
cognitive reading (Mi)
conative (G)
condensation (CC)
constative language (CC)
contextual (A)
contexture (J)
contiguity (J)
conversion (Ma)
deconstruction (Jo)
descriptive (MB)
design (Me)
deuniversalization (Jo)
deviation, deviance (A, R)
disadequation (H)
disjunction (H)
dislocation (Mil)

displacement (Mil)
economy of style (F)
ekphrasis (R)
embedding (Ch)
emitter (Ch)
emptiness (F)
energy (Ja)
epimone (E)
epistemic rules (F)
epistemological criticism (Co)
exchange (W)
exfoliation (Ja)
extreme situations (F)
extrinsic (K)
fictionality (MB)
fictional laws (Me)
figures (R, E)
frame analysis (F)
fullness (E, F)
gender (RS)
heresy (H)
historical specificity (Ma)
hypersign (R)
idiolect (R)
idiosyncrasy (F, H)
illocutionary situation (Ch)
immanentist reading (MB)
incantation (W)
incision (G)
intentions (H, Ja)
interpretant (R)

Contributors

Jaime Alazraki teaches Spanish American literature at Harvard University. He is the author of *Poética y poesía de Pablo Neruda*, *Jorge Luis Borges*, and *En busca del unicornio: Los cuentos de Julio Cortázar*, among others, and is chiefly interested in problems of narrative.

Mary Ann Caws teaches French, English, and comparative literature at the Graduate School and Hunter College of the City University of New York, codirects the Peyre Institute for the Humanities, and coedits *Dada/Surrealism*. She is past president of the Modern Language Association. Her books include *The Eye in the Text: Essays in Perception, Mannerist to Modern*; *A Metapoetics of the Passage: Architextures in Surrealism and After*; and *Reading Frames in Modern Fiction*.

Ross Chambers teaches French and comparative literature at the University of Michigan. His interests lie in French and European literature of the modern period (with special attention to the mid–nineteenth century) and in literary and critical theory (especially narrative). His most recent book is *Story and Situation: Narrative Seduction and the Power of Fiction*.

Cynthia Chase teaches English literature at Cornell University. She is the author of *Decomposing Figures: Rhetorical Readings in the Romantic Tradition* and essays on Freud and on Wordsworth and other Romantic writers in *Diacritics*, *Studies in Romanticism*, *PMLA*, and the *Oxford Literary Review*.

Robert Greer Cohn teaches French literature at Stanford University. He is the author of *The Writers' Way in France*, *Toward the Poems of Stéphane Mallarmé* and of books on Rimbaud, Mallarmé's *Igitur*, and *Un coup de dés*.

Terry Eagleton teaches English literature at Wadham College, Oxford University. His books include *The Rape of Clarissa: Writing, Sexuality, and Class Struggle in Samuel Richardson*; *Walter Benjamin: Criticism and Ideology*; *Marxism and Literary Criticism*; *Literary Theory: An Introduction*; and *The Function of Criticism*.

Deborah Esch teaches English literature at Princeton University. She has published readings of Romantic and post-Romantic texts and is presently completing a book on the senses of the past in Henry James.

Angus Fletcher teaches English literature at Lehman College and at the Graduate School of the City University of New York. He is the author of *Allegory: Theory of a Symbolic Mode* and *The Prophetic Movement: An Essay on Spenser*, and he edited *The Literature of Fact*. His recent interests are in liminality and labyrinths.

Sandra Gilbert teaches English literature at Princeton University. With Susan Gubar, she has coauthored *The Madwoman in the Attic: The Woman Writer and the Nineteenth-Century Literary Imagination* and coedited both *Shakespeare's Sisters: Feminist Essays on Women Poets* and *The Norton Anthology of Literature by Women: The Tradition in English*. She has also published a study of the poems of D. H. Lawrence; her most recent volume of poems is *Emily's Bread*.

Thomas M. Greene teaches English and comparative literature at Yale University. His most recent book is *The Light in Troy: Imitation and Discovery in Renaissance Poetry*. A gathering of his essays, *The Vulnerable Text: Essays on Renaissance Literature*, is forthcoming.

Robert Pogue Harrison teaches Italian literature at Stanford University. He is preparing a work on Dante's *Vita nuova*.

Thomas H. Jackson teaches English literature at Bryn Mawr College and edits *Poesis*, a journal of contemporary poetry. He is the author of *The Early Poetry of Ezra Pound* and works in English Renaissance literature as well as in contemporary American and British poetry.

Barbara Johnson teaches French and comparative literature at Harvard University. She is the author of *The Critical Difference: Essays in the Contemporary Rhetoric of Reading* and *Défigurations du langage poétique*, the editor of *The Pedagogical Imperative: Teaching as a Literary Genre*, the translator of Jacques Derrida's *Dissemination*, and is working on translations of Mallarmé's prose writing.

John W. Kneller teaches French literature at Hunter College and the Graduate Center of the City University of New York. He was Editor in Chief of the *French Review*, coauthored *Introduction à la poésie française* with Henry A. Grubbs, and now cochairs the Peyre Institute at the Graduate Center.

James Lawler teaches French literature at the University of Chicago. He is the author of *The Language of French Symbolism*, *The Poet as Analyst: Essays on Paul Valéry*, and *René Char: The Myth and the Poem* and the editor of a Valéry anthology. He is the founding editor of *Dalhousie French Studies*.

Felix Martinez-Bonati teaches Spanish and comparative literature at Columbia University. In English he has published *Fictive Discourse and the Structures of Literature* and several articles on theoretical topics. His work in Spanish on Cervantes has been appearing in *Dispositio*.

Giuseppe Mazzotta teaches Italian literature at Yale University. His concerns are medieval and Renaissance Italian literature as well as questions of aesthetics. His publications include *Dante: Poet of the Desert* and *The World at Play: A Study of the Decameron*. He is at present working on a book entitled *Petrarch and the Myth*.

Edward Mendelson teaches English and comparative literature at Columbia University. He is the author of *Early Auden* and of many essays on modern literature and culture; he has edited books on Thomas Pynchon and on the Western epic and dramatic tradition, as well as collections of works by W. H. Auden and Thomas Hardy. He is currently writing a book on later Auden and on studies of narrative.

J. Hillis Miller teaches English and comparative literature at Yale University. He is the author of a number of books and articles on nineteenth- and twentieth-century English and American literature and on literary theory. His most recent books are *Fiction and Repetition: Seven English Novels* and *The Linguistic Moment: From Wordsworth to Stevens*. He is at work on *Ariadne's Thread*, a book on narrative theory, and a book on the ethics of reading.

Earl Miner teaches comparative literature and Japanese literature at Princeton University. He is the author of *The Cavalier Mode from Jonson to Cotton*, *Dryden's Poetry*, *The Japanese Tradition in English and American Literature*, and the coauthor and coeditor of many books on Japanese poetry.

Laura Rice-Sayre teaches English literature at Oregon State University. She is working on feminism and on the theory of perception. At present she is preparing a book on *The Poetics of Parody* and coediting a sourcebook on modern art and literature.

Michael Riffaterre teaches French and English literature at Columbia University. He is the author of *Essays in Structural Stylistics*, *The Semiotics of Poetry*, *The Production of the Text*, and, most recently, *Intertextuality*. He is the coauthor of *Literature and Reality* and the editor of *Romanic Review*.

Susan Stewart teaches English literature at Temple University. She is the author of *Nonsense: Aspects of Intertextuality in Folklore and Literature*; *On Longing: Narratives of the Miniature, the Gigantic, the Souvenir, the Collection*; and a book of poetry, *Yellow Stars and Ice*. Her articles have appeared in *Critical Inquiry*, *MLN*, *Journal of American Folklore*, and her poems in *Poetry*, *American Poetry Review*, *Paris Review*, *Georgia Review*.

Helen Vendler teaches English literature at Harvard University. She is the author of *Yeats' Vision and the Later Plays*, *On Extended Wings: Wallace Stevens' Longer Poems*, *The Odes of John Keats*, and *Wallace Stevens: Words Chosen Out of Desire* and the editor of the *Harvard Book of Contemporary American Poetry*.

Frank J. Warnke teaches comparative literature at the University of Georgia. He is the author of *Versions of Baroque: European Literature in the Seventeenth Century* and *European Metaphysical Poetry*. He has edited John Donne's *Poetry and Prose* and is the coeditor of *Seventeenth Century Prose and Poetry* and the *Princeton Encyclopedia of Poetry and Poetics*.

Works Cited

Abraham, Nicolas. "L'écorce et le noyau." *Critique* 24 (1968): 162–81.

Alaya, Flavia. "The Ring, the Rescue, and the Risorgimento: Reunifying the Brownings' Italy." *Browning Institute Studies* 6 (1978): 1–41.

Alazraki, Jaime. *La prosa narrativa de Jorge Luis Borges.* 2nd ed. Madrid: Gredos, 1974.

Alonso, Amado. "Borges, narrador." *Materia y forma en poesía.* Madrid: Gredos, 1960. 368–80.

Angenot, Marc. "L'intertextualité: Enquête sur l'émergence et la diffusion d'un champ notionnel." *Revue des sciences humaines* 189 (1983): 122–35.

Anthias, Floya, and Nira Yuval-Davis. "Contextualizing Feminism—Gender, Ethnic and Class Divisions." *Feminist Review* 15 (1983): 62–75.

Ashbery, John. "For John Clare." *The Double Dream of Spring.* New York: Ecco, 1976.

Aubrey, John. *Brief Lives.* Ed. O. L. Dick. Ann Arbor: U of Michigan P, 1962.

Auden, W. H. *Collected Poems.* Ed. Edward Mendelson. New York: Random, 1976.

———. *The English Auden.* Ed. Edward Mendelson. New York: Random, 1977.

Auerbach, Erich. *Mimesis: The Representation of Reality in Western Literature.* New York: Anchor-Doubleday, 1957.

Augustine, Saint. *Confessions.* Corpus Christianorum, series latina 37. Turnhout: Brepols, 1981.

———. *Contra academicos.* Corpus Christianorum, series latina 29. Turnhout: Brepols, 1981.

Austin, J. L. *How to Do Things with Words.* New York: Oxford UP, 1965.

Austin, Lloyd J. "Mallarmé and Gautier: New Light on 'Toast funèbre.'" *Balzac and the Nineteenth Century.* Ed. D. G. Charlton, J. Gaudon, and Anthony R. Pugh. Leicester: Leicester UP, 1972. 335–51.

Avalle-Arce, Juan Bautista. "*La gitanilla.*" *Cervantes* 1 (1981): 9–17.

Aynesworth, Donald. "A Face in the Crowd: A Baudelairean Vision of the Eternal Feminine." *Stanford French Review* 5 (1981): 327–39.

Bachofen, J. J. "The Three Mystery Eggs." *Myth, Religion, and Mother Right: Selected Writings of J. J. Bachofen.* Trans. Ralph Manheim. Bollingen Series. Princeton: Princeton UP, 1967. 24–30.

Bakhtin, Mikhail. *The Dialogic Imagination.* Ed. Michael Holquist. Trans. Caryl Emerson and Michael Holquist. Austin: U of Texas P, 1981.

Balbus, Isaac D. *Marxism and Domination: A Neo-Hegelian, Feminist, Psychoanalytic Theory of Sexual, Political, and Technological Liberation.* Princeton: Princeton UP, 1982.

Balmary, Marie. *Psychoanalyzing Psychoanalysis: Freud and the Hidden Fault of the Father.* Baltimore: Johns Hopkins UP, 1982.

Barthes, Roland. *Critique et vérité.* Paris: Seuil, 1966.

———. *S/Z.* Paris: Seuil, 1970.

Bartky, Sandra Lee. "Toward a Phenomenology of Feminist Consciousness." *Social Theory and Practice* 3 (1975): 425–39.

Bashō, Matsuo. *The Narrow Road through the Provinces.* Miner, *Japanese Poetic Diaries* 157–97.

———. "A Record of the Unreal Hermitage." Odagiri and Miner 309–12.

Baudelaire, Charles. *Œuvres complètes.* 2 vols. Ed. Claude Pichois. Paris: Gallimard, 1975.

Beckett, Samuel. *Sans.* Trans. Beckett. London: Calder, 1970.

Benjamin, Walter. "Edward Fuchs, Collector and Historian." *"One-Way Street" and Other Writings.* London: NLB, 1979.

———. "On Some Motifs in Baudelaire." *Illuminations.* New York: Schocken, 1969. 155–200.

———. "Schicksal und Charakter." *Gesammelte Schriften.* 5 vols. Frankfurt am Main: Suhrkamp, 1974. 2.1: 171–89.

———. "Über einige Motive bei Baudelaire." *Charles Baudelaire: Ein Lyriker im Zeitalter des Hochkapitalismus.* Frankfurt am Main: Suhrkamp, 1969. 111–64.

Benveniste, Emile. *Problèmes de linguistique générale*. 2 vols. Paris: Gallimard, 1966, 1974.

Bersani, Leo. *The Death of Stéphane Mallarmé*. Cambridge: Cambridge UP, 1982.

Bidez, J., ed. *Vie de Porphyre*. Gant, Belg.: van Goethen, 1913.

Blöcker, Günther. *Heinrich von Kleist oder das absolute Ich*. Berlin: Argon, 1960.

Blodgett, Harold W., and Sculley Bradley, eds. Leaves of Grass: *Comprehensive Reader's Edition*. By Walt Whitman. New York: New York UP, 1965.

Borges, Jorge Luis. "Encuentro con Borges." With James E. Irby. *Vida universitaria* (Monterrey, México) 12 Apr. 1964: 7–16.

———. "Elementos de preceptiva." *Sur* (Buenos Aires) 7 April 1933: 158–61.

———. *Historia universal de la infamia*. Buenos Aires: Tor, 1935.

———. *El idioma de los argentinos*. Buenos Aires: Gleizer, 1928.

———. *Labyrinths: Selected Stories and Other Writings*. Ed. Donald A. Yates and James E. Irby. New York: New Directions, 1962.

———. *Other Inquisitions*. Trans. Ruth L. C. Simms. New York: Washington Square, 1966.

———. "*Paradiso*, XXXI, 108." *Dreamtigers*. Trans. Mildred Boyer and Harold Morland. Austin: U of Texas P, 1964.

———. *A Universal History of Infamy*. Trans. Norman Thomas di Giovanni. 1935. New York: Dutton, 1979.

Bowring, Richard. "Japanese Diaries and the Nature of Literature." *Comparative Literature Studies* 18 (1981): 167–74.

Brasher, Thomas L., ed. *The Early Poems and the Fiction*. By Walt Whitman. New York: New York UP, 1963.

Brody, Jules. "Critique littéraire et crise post-structuraliste: Essai de consolation." *French Forum* 1 (1976): 177–84.

Browning, Elizabeth Barrett. Aurora Leigh *And Other Poems*. Introd. Cora Kaplan. London: Women's, 1978.

———. *Casa Guidi Windows*. Ed. Julia Markus. New York: Browning Inst., 1977.

———. *The Complete Works of Elizabeth Barrett Browning*. Ed. Charlotte Porter and Helen A. Clarke. 6 vols. New York: Crowell, 1900; New York: AMS, 1973.

———. *Elizabeth Barrett to Mr. Boyd*. Ed. Barbara McCarthy. New Haven: Yale UP, 1955.

———. *The Letters of Elizabeth Barrett Browning*. Ed. Frederic G. Kenyon. 2 vols. New York, 1899.

———. *The Poetical Works of Elizabeth Barrett Browning*. Ed. Harriet Waters Preston. Cambridge Edition. 1900. Rpt. with introd. by Ruth M. Adams. Boston: Houghton, 1974.

Cassirer, Ernst. "Heinrich von Kleist und die Kantische Philosophie." *Idee und Gestalt*. Berlin: Cassirer, 1924. 159–202.

Caws, Mary Ann. "A Double Reading by Design: Breughel, Auden and Williams." *Journal of Aesthetics and Art Criticism* 41 (1983): 323–30.

———. "Winging It; or, Catching Up with Kierkegaard and Some Swans." *Yale French Studies* 66 (1984): 83–90.

Cervantes Saavedra, Miguel de. *La gitanilla. Novelas ejemplares*. Ed. Francisco Rodriguez Marín. Clásicos Castellanos. Madrid: Espasa-Calpe, 1965. 3–130.

Chambers, Ross. "Parole et poésie." *Poétique* 37 (1979): 56–62.

———. "Pour une poétique du vêtement." *Michigan Romance Studies* 1 (1980): 18–46.

———. *Story and Situation*. Minneapolis: U of Minnesota P, 1984.

Chatman, Seymour, ed. and introd. *Literary Style: A Symposium*. New York: Oxford UP, 1971.

Chatwin, Bruce. *In Patagonia*. New York: Summit, 1977.

Chevigny, Bell Gale. *The Woman and the Myth: Margaret Fuller's Life and Writings*. Old Westbury: Feminist, 1976.

Christ, Ronald. "An Interview with Manuel Puig." *Partisan Review* 44 (1977): 53–61.

Churchill, Kenneth. *Italy and English Literature 1764–1930*. London: Macmillan, 1980.

Clare, John. *The Letters of John Clare*. Ed. J. W. Tibble and Anne Tibble. New York: Barnes, 1970.

Claudel, Paul. *Cahiers Paul Claudel I*. Paris: Gallimard, 1959.

Claudel, Paul, and André Gide. *Correspondance: 1899–1926*. Paris: Gallimard, 1949.

Cohn, Dorrit. "Kleist's *Marquise von O . . .*: The Problem of Knowledge." *Monatshefte* 67 (1975): 129–44.

Cohn, Robert Greer. *Mallarmé: Igitur*. Berkeley: U of California P, 1981.

——. *Modes of Art*. Stanford French and Italian Studies. Saratoga: Anma Libri, 1975.

——. *L'œuvre de Mallarmé: Un coup de dés*. Paris: Librairie des Lettres, 1951.

——. *The Poetry of Rimbaud*. Princeton: Princeton UP, 1973.

——. "A Poetry-Prose Cross." *The Prose Poem in France*. Ed. Mary Ann Caws and Hermine Riffaterre. New York: Columbia UP, 1983. 136–63.

——. *Toward the Poems of Mallarmé*. Berkeley: U of California P, 1980.

Coleman, Dorothy. *Maurice Scève: Poet of Love*. Cambridge: Cambridge UP, 1975.

Coleridge, Samuel Taylor. *Biographia Literaria*. Ed. J. Shawcross. 2 vols. Oxford: Oxford UP, 1907. Vol. 2.

Constans, François. "Artémis, ou les fleurs du désespoir." *Revue de littérature comparée* 14 (1934): 337–71.

Cooper, Helen. "Working into Light: Elizabeth Barrett Browning." *Shakespeare's Sisters: Feminist Essays on Women Poets*. Ed. Sandra M. Gilbert and Susan Gubar. Bloomington: Indiana UP, 1979. 65–81.

Dällenbach, Lucien. *Le récit spéculaire*. Paris: Seuil, 1977.

Dante Alighieri. *De vulgari eloquentia*. Ed. Aristide Marigo. Firenze: Sansoni, 1969.

——. *La divina commedia secondo l'antica vulgata*. Ed. Giorgio Petrocchi. 4 vols. Milano: Mondadori, 1966–67.

Davis, Arthur P. *From the Dark Tower*. Washington: Howard UP, 1974.

de Man, Paul. *Allegories of Reading*. New Haven: Yale UP, 1979.

——. "Anthropomorphism and Trope in the Lyric." *The Rhetoric of Romanticism*. New York: Columbia UP, 1984. 239–62.

——. "Hypogram and Inscription: Riffaterre's Poetics of Reading." *Diacritics* 11.4 (1981): 17–35.

——. "The Rhetoric of Temporality." *Blindness and Insight: Essays in the Rhetoric of Contemporary Criticism*. Minneapolis: U of Minnesota P, 1983. 187–228.

Derrida, Jacques. *De la grammatologie*. Paris: Minuit, 1967.

——. *Spurs: Nietzsche's Styles/Epérons: Les Styles de Nietzsche*. Trans. Barbara Harlow. Chicago: U of Chicago P, 1979.

——. " Fors." Pref. to *Cryptonymie: Le verbier de l'homme aux loups*. By Nicolas Abraham and Maria Torok. Paris: Flammarion, 1976. 7–82.

Dickinson, Emily. *Complete Poems of Emily Dickinson*. Ed. Thomas Johnson. Boston: Little, 1960.

Díez, Luys A. "*El beso de la mujer araña*: Parabola de la represion sexual." *Campo de l'arpa* 40 (1977): 23–36.

Douglas, Mary. *Purity and Danger*. London: Routledge, 1966.

Dreyfus, Hubert, and Paul Rabinow. *Michel Foucault: Beyond Structuralism and Hermeneutics*. 2nd ed. Chicago: U of Chicago P, 1983.

DuBois, W. E. B. *The Souls of Black Folk*. Franklin 207–389.

Eagleton, Terry. *The Rape of Clarissa*. Minneapolis: U of Minnesota P, 1982.

——. *Walter Benjamin; or, Towards a Revolutionary Criticism*. London: NLB, 1981.

Eikhenbaum, Boris. "How Gogol's *Overcoat* Is Made." 1919. Todorov, *Teoría* 159–76.

——. "The Theory of the Formal Method." *Russian Formalist Criticism: Four Essays*. Ed. Lee T. Lemon and Mario J. Reis. Lincoln: U of Nebraska P, 1965. 99–139.

Eliot, T. S. "Baudelaire." *Selected Essays, 1917-1932.* New York: Harcourt, 1950.

Ellis, John M. *Heinrich von Kleist: Studies in the Character and Meaning of His Writings.* Chapel Hill: U of North Carolina P, 1979.

El Saffar, Ruth. *Novel to Romance: A Study of Cervantes' Novelas ejemplares.* Baltimore: Johns Hopkins UP, 1974.

Empson, William. *The Structure of Complex Words.* Ann Arbor: U of Michigan P, 1967.

Erdman, David. "Coleridge, Wordsworth, and the Wedgwood Fund." *Bulletin of the New York Public Library* 60 (Sept.–Oct. 1956): 425–43, 487–507.

Erikson, Erik. "The Dream Specimen of Psychoanalysis." *Journal of the American Psychoanalytic Association* 2 (1954): 5–56.

Fairley, Irene. "On Reading Poems: Visual and Verbal Icons in William Carlos Williams' 'Landscape with the Fall of Icarus.'" *Studies in Twentieth Century Literature* 6 (1981–82): 67–97.

Felman, Shoshana. "Psychoanalysis and Education: Teaching Terminable and Interminable." *Yale French Studies* 63 (1982): 21–45.

Fontanier, Pierre. *Les figures du discours.* Paris: Flammarion, 1977.

Forcione, Alban K. *Cervantes and the Humanist Vision: A Study of Four Exemplary Novels.* Princeton: Princeton UP, 1983.

Foucault, Michel. *Discipline and Punish: The Birth of the Prison.* Trans. Alan Sheridan. New York: Vintage, 1979.

Franklin, John H., ed. *Three Negro Classics.* New York: Avon, 1965.

Freud, Sigmund. *Civilization and Its Discontents.* 1930. Trans. James Strachey. New York: Norton, 1961.

———. "Female Sexuality." Trans. Joan Riviere. *Sexuality and the Psychology of Love.* Ed. Philip Rieff. New York: Collier, 1963. 194–211.

———. *The Standard Edition of the Complete Psychological Works of Sigmund Freud.* Ed. James Strachey. 24 vols. London: Hogarth, 1953–68.

———. *Totem and Taboo.* 1913. *The Basic Writings of Sigmund Freud.* Trans. and ed. A. A. Brill. New York: Modern Library, 1938. 807–930.

Fries, Thomas. "The Impossible Object: The Feminine, the Narrative." *MLN* 91 (1976): 1295–326.

Frye, Northrop. *Anatomy of Criticism: Four Essays.* Princeton: Princeton UP, 1957.

Gallop, Jane. *The Daughter's Seduction: Feminism and Psychoanalysis.* Ithaca: Cornell UP, 1982.

Gates, Henry Louis, Jr. "Criticism in the Jungle." *Black American Literature Forum* 15 (1981): 123–27.

———. *The Signifying Monkey.* New York: Oxford UP, 1986.

Gautier, Théophile. "Notice." *Les fleurs du mal.* By Charles Baudelaire. Paris: Calmann-Lévy, 1901.

Gelpi, Barbara. "*Aurora Leigh*: The Vocation of the Woman Poet." *Victorian Poetry* 19.1 (1981): 35–48.

Genette, Gérard. *Figures of Literary Discourse.* Trans. Alan Sheridan. New York: Columbia UP, 1982.

———. *Figures III.* Paris: Seuil, 1972.

Geninasca, Jacques. *Analyse structurale des Chimères de Nerval.* Neufchâtel: Baconnière, 1971.

———. *Les Chimères de Nerval.* Paris: Larousse, 1973.

———. *Une lecture d' "El Desdichado."* Archives des Lettres Modernes 59. Paris: Minard, 1965.

Gérard, Albert S. "Images, structure et thèmes dans 'El Desdichado.'" *Modern Language Review* 58 (1963): 507–15.

Gilbert, Sandra M., and Susan Gubar. *The Madwoman in the Attic: The Woman Writer and the Nineteenth-Century Literary Imagination.* New Haven: Yale UP, 1979.

Gilman, Charlotte Perkins. *Herland.* 1915. New York: Pantheon, 1979.

Glen, Heather. *Vision and Disenchantment: Blake's* Songs *and Wordsworth's* Lyrical Ballads. Cambridge: Cambridge UP, 1983.

Goebel, G. "Bemerkungen zu Topic and Comment bei einigen Gedichten Baudelaires." *LiLi: Zeitschrift für Literaturwissenschaft und Linguistik* 4 (1974): 65–90.

Goethe, Johann Wolfgang von. *Faust.* Ed. Cyrus Hamlin. Trans. Walter Arndt. Norton Critical Edition. New York: Norton, 1976.

———. *Faust.* Vol. 3 of *Werke.* Hamburger Ausgabe. 14 vols. Hamburg: Wegner, 1972.

———. *Faust: Les textes en deux langues.* Paris: Gibert, 1947.

Goncourt, Edmond, and Jules Goncourt. *Journal.* 22 vols. Vol. 2: *1856–1858.* Ed. Robert Ricotte. Monte Carlo: Editions de l'Imprimerie Nationale de Monaco, 1956.

Greene, Thomas. *The Light in Troy: Imitation and Discovery in Renaissance Poetry.* New Haven: Yale UP, 1982.

———. "Styles of Experience in Scève's *Délie.*" *Yale French Studies* 47 (1972): 57–75.

Grimsley, Ronald. *Kierkegaard: A Biographical Introduction.* New York: Scribner's, 1973.

Grossman, Atina. "The New Woman and the Rationalization of Sexuality in Weimar Germany." *Powers of Desire: The Politics of Sexuality.* Ed. Ann Snitow, Christine Stansell, and Sharon Thompson. New York: Monthly Review, 1983.

Gubar, Susan. "*She* in *Herland*: Feminism as Fantasy." *Coordinates: Placing Science Fiction and Fantasy.* Ed. George E. Slusser, Eric S. Rabkin, and Robert Scholes. Carbondale: Southern Illinois UP, 1983. 139–49.

Guillaume, Jean, ed. Les chimères *de Nerval: Edition critique.* Bruxelles: Palais des Académies, 1966.

Gutwirth, Madelyn. *Madame de Staël, Novelist: The Emergence of the Artist as Woman.* Urbana: U of Illinois P, 1978.

Halliday, M. A. K. "Linguistic Function and Literary Style: An Inquiry into the Language of William Golding's *The Inheritors.*" Chatman 330–65.

Hammond, Mac. "On the Grammar of Wallace Stevens." *The Act of the Mind: Essays on the Poetry of Wallace Stevens.* Ed. Roy Harvey Pearce and J. Hillis Miller. Baltimore: Johns Hopkins UP, 1965. 179–84.

Harari, Josué V., and D. F. Bell, eds. *Hermes: Literature, Science, Philosophy.* Baltimore: Johns Hopkins UP, 1982.

Harrison, Thomas J., ed. *The Favorite Malice: Ontology and Reference in Contemporary Italian Poetry.* New York: Out of London, 1983.

Hartman, Geoffrey. "The Interpreter: A Self-Analysis." *The Fate of Reading.* Chicago: U of Chicago P, 1975. 3–19.

Hartsock, Nancy. *Money, Sex and Power: Toward a Feminist Historical Materialism.* New York: Longman, 1983.

Hassoun, Jacques. "Variations psychanalytiques sur un thème généalogique de Heinrich von Kleist." *Romantisme* 8 (1974): 54–63.

H. D. [Hilda Doolittle]. *Tribute to Freud: Writing on the Wall, Advent.* New York: McGraw, 1975.

Hearn, Lafcadio. *Some Chinese Ghosts.* Boston: Little, 1906.

Hegel, Georg Wilhelm Friedrich. *Enzyclopädie der philosophischen Wissenschaften.* Leipzig: Lasson, 1905.

———. *The Philosophy of Fine Art.* 4 vols. Trans. F. P. B. Osmaston. New York: Hacker, 1975. Vol. 1.

Hertz, Neil. "Dora's Secrets, Freud's Techniques." *Diacritics* 13.1 (1983): 65–80.

———. "Freud and the Sandman." *Textual Strategies.* Ed. Josué V. Harari. Ithaca: Cornell UP, 1979. 296–321.

Hooks, Bell [Gloria Watkins]. *Ain't I a Woman.* Boston: South End, 1981.

Huff, R. "Kleist and Expectant Virgins: The Meaning of the 'O' in *Die Marquise von O. . . .*" *Journal of English and Germanic Philology* 81 (1982): 367–75.

Hugo, Victor. *Œuvres complètes*. 18 vols. Ed. Jean Massin. Paris: Club français du livre, 1967–70. Vol. 16.

Hurston, Zora Neale. *Dust Tracks on a Road*. Philadelphia: Lippincott, 1942.

———. "Folklore Field Notes from Zora Neale Hurston." Introd. Robert Hemenway. *Black Scholar* 7.7 (1976): 39–46.

———. *Their Eyes Were Watching God*. 1937. Urbana: U of Illinois P, 1978.

Husserl, Edmund. *Ideas: General Introduction to Pure Phenomenology*. Trans. W. R. Boyce Gibson. London: Allen, 1931.

Jaccottet, Philippe. *Paysages avec figures absentes*. Paris: Gallimard, 1970.

Jacobs, Carol. "The Style of Kleist." *Diacritics* 9.4 (1979): 47–61.

Jakobson, Roman. "The Dominant." *Selected Writings*. 5 vols. s' Gravenhage: Mouton, 1962–81. 3: 751–56.

———. *Essais de linguistique générale*. Paris: Minuit, 1963.

———. "Linguistics and Poetics." Sebeok 350–77.

———. "Poetry of Grammar and Grammar of Poetry." *Lingua* 21 (1968): 597–609.

———. "Two Aspects of Language and Two Types of Aphasic Disturbances." Jakobson and Halle 55–82.

Jakobson, Roman, and Claude Lévi-Strauss. " 'Les chats' de Charles Baudelaire." *L'homme* 2 (1963): 5–21. Rpt. in *Questions de poétique*. Paris: Seuil, 1973.

Jakobson, Roman, and Morris Halle. *Fundamentals of Language*. s' Gravenhage: Mouton, 1956.

James, Henry. "The Art of Fiction." 1884. *Critical Theory since Plato*. Ed. Hazard Adams. New York: Harcourt, 1971. 661–70.

Johnson, Barbara. *Défigurations du langage poétique*. Paris: Flammarion, 1977.

———, trans. "Fors." By Jacques Derrida. *Georgia Review* 31 (1977): 64–116.

Johnson, James Weldon. *The Autobiography of an Ex-Colored Man*. Franklin 391–511.

Johnson, Richard. *Man's Place: An Essay on Auden*. Ithaca: Cornell, UP, 1973.

Kaiser, Margaret. *Die Liebe als Kunst*. Berlin: Ibis, 1932.

Kant, Immanuel. *Die Metaphysik der Sitten*. Vol. 8 of *Werkausgabe*. 12 vols. Ed. Wilhelm Weisschedel. Frankfurt am Main: Suhrkamp, 1968.

Kerényi, Karl. *The Religion of the Greeks and Romans*. London: Thames, 1962.

Kierkegaard, Søren. *Journals and Papers*. Ed. and trans. Howard V. Hong and Edna H. Hong. 7 vols. Bloomington: Indiana UP, 1967–78.

———. *Repetition*. Ed., trans., and introd. Walter Lowrie. Princeton: Princeton UP, 1941.

Klaar, A., ed. Die Marquise von O . . . : *Die Dichtung und ihre Quellen*. Berlin: Propyläen, 1922.

Kleist, Heinrich von. *Sämtliche Werke und Briefe*. Ed. Helmut Sembdner. 2 vols. München: Hanser, 1961.

———. *Werke in einem Band*. Ed. Helmut Sembdner. München: Hanser, 1966.

Knapp-Tepperberg, Eva Maria. "Baudelaire: 'A une passante.' Psychoanalytische Bemerkungen zu einer Textvariante." *Germanisch-Romanische Monatschrift* 24 (1974): 182–92.

Kneller, John W. "The Poet and His Moira: 'El Desdichado.'" *PMLA* 75 (1960): 402–09.

Kommerell, Max. "Die Sprache und das Unaussprechlide: Eine Betrachtung über Heinrich von Kleist." *Geist und Buchstabe der Dichtung: Goethe, Schiller, Kleist, Hölderlin*. Frankfurt am main: Klostermann, 1956. 243–317.

Kristeva, Julia. *Desire in Language: A Semiotic Approach to Literature and Art*. Ed. Leon S. Roudiez. Trans. Thomas Gora, Alice Jardine, and Roudiez. New York: Columbia UP, 1980.

Kuper, Adam, and Alan A. Stone. "The Dream of Irma's Injection: A Structural Analysis." *American Journal of Psychiatry* 139 (1982): 1225–34.

Lacan, Jacques. "Discours de Rome." *Ecrits* 30–113.

———. *Ecrits: A Selection*. Trans. Alan Sheridan. London: Tavistock, 1977.

————. *The Four Fundamental Concepts of Psycho-Analysis*. Ed. Jacques-Alain Miller. Trans. Alan Sheridan. New York: Norton, 1981.

————. *Le moi dans la théorie de Freud et dans la technique de la psychanalyse*. Vol. 2 of *Le séminaire*. Paris: Seuil, 1978.

Lakoff, George, and Mark Johnson. *Metaphors We Live By*. Chicago: U of Chicago P, 1980.

Lanham, Richard. *A Handlist of Rhetorical Terms*. Berkeley: U of California P, 1968.

Laplanche, J., and J.-B. Pontalis. *The Language of Psycho-Analysis*. Trans. Donald Nicholson-Smith. New York: Norton, 1973.

Lausberg, Heinrich. *Elemente der literarischen Rhetorik*. München: Hueber, 1963.

Lawrence, D. H. "The Lemon Gardens." *D. H. Lawrence and Italy*. New York: Compass-Viking, 1972. 32–54.

Lebois, André. *Vers une élucidation des* Chimères *de Nerval*. Archives des Lettres Modernes 1. Paris: Minard, 1957.

Lerner, Isaías. "Marginalidad en las *Novelas ejemplares*. I. *La gitanilla*." *Lexis* 14 (1980): 47–59.

Levin, Samuel R. Rev. of *Linguistic Stylistics*, by Nils Erik Enkvist. *Foundations of Language* 12 (1975): 467–69.

Liu, James J.-Y. *Chinese Theories of Literature*. Chicago: U of Chicago P, 1975.

Lorde, Audre. "The Master's Tools Will Never Dismantle the Master's House." *Sister Outsider*. Trumansberg: Crossing, 1984. 110–13.

Lugones, Maria C., and Elizabeth V. Spellman. "Have We Got a Theory for You! Feminist Theory, Cultural Imperialism and the Demand for 'the Woman's Voice.'" *Women's Studies International Forum* 6 (1983): 573–81.

Luke, David, and Nigel Reeves, trans. The Marquise von O— *and Other Stories*. By Heinrich von Kleist. Harmondsworth: Penguin, 1978.

Lyotard, Jean-François. *Discours, Figure*. Paris: Klincksiek, 1971.

Macdonald, Dwight, ed. *Parodies: An Anthology from Chaucer to Beerbohm—and After*. London: Faber, 1960.

Mackey, Louis. *Kierkegaard: A Kind of Poet*. Philadelphia: U of Pennsylvania P, 1971.

MacKinnon, Catharine A. "Feminism, Marxism, Method, and the State: An Agenda for Theory." *Feminist Theory: A Critique of Ideology*. Ed. Nannerl O. Keohane, Michelle Z. Rosaldo, and Barbara C. Gelpi. Chicago: U of Chicago P, 1982. 1–30.

Magliola, Robert R. *Phenomenology and Literature*. West Lafayette: Purdue UP, 1977.

Mallarmé, Stéphane. *Correspondance*. Ed. Henri Mondor and Lloyd J. Austin. 10 vols. to date. Paris: Gallimard, 1959–.

————. *Œuvres complètes*. Ed. Henri Mondor and G. Jean-Aubry. Paris: Gallimard, 1945.

Mann, Thomas. "Heinrich von Kleist und seine Erzählungen." *Gesammelte Werke*. 20 vols. Frankfurt am Main: Fischer, 1960.

Marchand, Leslie. *Byron: A Biography*. New York: Knopf, 1957.

Masiello, Francine R. "Jail House Flicks: Projections by Manuel Puig." *Symposium* 32 (1978): 15–24.

Masson, Jeffrey Moussaieff. *Freud's Suppression of the Seduction Theory*. New York: Farrar, 1984.

Mauron, Charles. *Le dernier Baudelaire*. Paris: Corti, 1966.

Mazzotta, Giuseppe. "The *Canzoniere* and the Language of the Self." *Studies in Philology* 75 (1978): 271–96.

Mehlman, Jeffrey. "Baudelaire with Freud: Theory and Pain." *Diacritics* 4.1 (1974): 7–13.

————. "Trimethylamin: Notes on Freud's Specimen Dream." *Diacritics* 6.1 (1976): 42–45.

Mendelson, Edward. *Early Auden*. New York: Viking, 1981.

Miller, Philip B. *An Abyss Deep Enough; Letters of Heinrich von Kleist, with a Selection of Essays and Anecdotes*. New York: Dutton, 1982.

Miner, Earl. *Japanese Linked Poetry*. Princeton: Princeton UP, 1979.

————, trans. *Japanese Poetic Diaries*. Rev. ed. Berkeley: U of California P, 1976.

————. "On the Genesis and Development of Literary Systems." *Critical Inquiry* 5 (1979): 339–53, 553–68.

————. "That Literature Is a Kind of Knowledge." *Critical Inquiry* 2 (1976): 487–518.

Miner, Earl, and Hiroko Odagiri, eds. and trans. The Monkey's Straw Raincoat *and Other Poetry of the Bashō School*. Princeton: Princeton UP, 1981.

Moering, Michael. *Witz und Ironie in der Prosa Heinrich von Kleists*. München: Fink, 1972.

Moers, Ellen. *Literary Women*. New York: Doubleday, 1976.

Mommsen, Katharina. *Kleists Kampf mit Goethe*. Heidelberg: Stiehm, 1974.

Monval, Jean. "Deux camarades du Parnasse: Catulle Mendès et François Coppée." *Revue de Paris* 1 Mar. 1909: 73–86.

Müller-Seidel, Walter. "Die Struktur des Widerspruchs in Kleists *Marquise von O. . . .*" *Deutsche Vierteljahrsschrift für Literaturwissenschaft und Geistesgeschichte* 27 (1954): 497–515.

Murry, Middleton. *The Problem of Style*. London: Oxford UP, 1960.

Musset, Alfred de. *Poésies complètes*. Paris: Gallimard, 1941.

Nerval, Gérard de. *Sylvie*. Vol. 1 of *Œuvres*. Ed. Albert Béguin and Jean Richer. Paris: Gallimard, 1956.

Neumeyer, Peter. *Homage to John Clare*. Salt Lake City: Peregrine Smith, 1980.

Nietzsche, Friedrich. "On Truth and Lies in a Nonmoral Sense." *Philosophy and Truth: Selections from Nietzsche's Notebooks of the Early 1870's*. Trans. Daniel Breazeale. Atlantic Highlands: Humanities; Hassocks, Eng.: Harvester, 1979. 79–97.

————. *Thus Spoke Zarathustra*. Trans. Walter Kaufmann. New York: Viking, 1968.

Nightingale, Florence. *Cassandra*. Old Westbury: Feminist, 1979.

Norton, M. D. Herter, ed. and trans. *Sonnets to Orpheus*. By Rainer Maria Rilke. New York: Norton, 1962.

Oehler, D. "Art-névrose: Soziopsychanalyse einer gescheiterten Revolution bei Flaubert und Baudelaire." *Akzente* 2 (1980): 113–30.

Onís, Harriet de, introd. and trans. *The Gypsy Maid. Six Exemplary Novels*. By Miguel de Cervantes Saavedra. New York: Barron's, 1961. 91–162.

Ovid. *Metamorphoses*. Trans. F. J. Miller. Loeb Classical Library. Cambridge: Harvard UP, 1971.

Panofsky, Erwin. "Et in Arcadia Ego: Poussin and the Elegiac Tradition." *Meaning in the Visual Arts: Papers in and on Art History*. Garden City: Doubleday, 1955. 295–320.

Pater, Walter. "Style." *Appreciations, with an Essay on Style*. London: Macmillan, 1944. 5–38.

Paz, Octavio, et al. *Renga: A Chain of Poems*. New York: Braziller, 1972.

Peel, Ellen. "Both Ends of the Candle: Feminist Narrative Structures in Novels by Staël, Lessing, and Le Guin." Diss. Yale U 1982.

Petrarch. "The Ascent of Mont Ventoux." *The Renaissance Philosophy of Man*. Ed. Ernst Cassirer. P. O. Kristeller, and J. H. Randall, Jr. 1948. Chicago: U of Chicago P, 1975. 36–46.

————. *Canzoniere*. Ed. Gianfranco Contini. Annotated by Daniele Ponchiroli. Torino: Einaudi, 1964.

————. *Le rime*. Ed. Giosuè Carducci and Severino Ferrari. Pref. Gianfranco Contini. Firenze: Sansoni, 1960.

————. *Petrarch's Lyric Poems*. Trans. and ed. Robert M. Durling. Cambridge: Harvard UP, 1976.

Pizan, Christine de. *The Book of the City of Ladies*. Trans. Earl Jeffrey Richards. New York: Persea, 1982.

Plath, Sylvia. *Ariel*. New York: Harper, 1965.

Plato. *Theateatus. The Collected Dialogues*. Ed. Edith Hamilton and Huntington Cairns. Princeton: Princeton UP, 1961. 845–919.

"Poetic Aberrations." *Blackwood's* 87 (1860): 490–504.

Pratt, Mary Louise. *Toward a Speech Act Theory of Literary Discourse.* Bloomington: Indiana UP, 1977.

Praz, Mario. *Mnemosyne.* Princeton: Princeton UP, 1970.

Puig, Manuel. *Kiss of the Spider Woman.* 1976. Trans. Thomas Colchie. New York: Vintage, 1980.

The Republic of Letters: Working Class Writing and Local Publishing. London: Comedia, n.d.

Rich, Adrienne. "Compulsory Heterosexuality and Lesbian Existence." *Signs* 5 (1980): 631–60.

———. "Disloyal to Civilization: Feminism, Racism, Gynephobia." *On Lies, Secrets and Silence.* New York: Norton, 1979. 275–310.

Richer, Jean. *Nerval: Expérience et création.* Paris: Hachette, 1963.

Riffaterre, Michael. "Criteria for Style Analysis." *Word: Journal of the Linguistic Circle of New York* 15 (1959): 154–74.

———. "Interpretation and Undecidability." *New Literary History* 12 (1980–81): 227–42.

———. "Intertextualité surréaliste." *Mélusine* (Lausanne) 1 (1980): 27–37.

———. *La production du texte.* Paris: Seuil, 1979.

———. *Semiotics of Poetry.* Bloomington: Indiana UP, 1978.

———. "Syllepsis." *Critical Inquiry* 6 (1980): 625–38.

———. *Text Production.* Trans. Terese Lyons. New York: Columbia UP, 1983.

———. "La trace de l'intertexte." *La Pensée: Revue du rationalisme moderne* 215 (1980): 4–18.

Rilke, Rainer Maria. *Werke.* Ed. Beda Allemann. 3 vols. Frankfurt am Main: Insel, 1966. Vol. 1.

Rinsler, Norma. Introduction. *Les chimères.* By Gérard de Nerval. Ed. Rinsler. London: Athlone, 1973.

Rogers, Samuel. *The Complete Poetical Works of Samuel Rogers.* Ed. Epes Sargent. Boston, 1854.

Rosenblum, Dolores. "Face to Face: Elizabeth Barrett Browning's *Aurora Leigh* and Nineteenth-Century Poetry." *Victorian Studies* 26.3 (1983): 321–38.

Rossetti, Christina Georgina. *The Poetical Works of Christina Georgina Rossetti.* Ed. William Michael Rossetti. London: Macmillan, 1928.

Rousseau, Jean-Jacques. *Emile ou de l'éducation.* Paris: Garnier-Flammarion, 1966.

———. *Œuvres complètes.* 4 vols. Paris: Gallimard, 1959.

Rousseaux, André. "Un déjeuner avec Tristan Derême." *Candide* 12 Aug. 1926: n.p.

———. "Sur trois manuscrits de Gérard de Nerval." *Le monde classique.* Paris: Albin, 1946. 153–65.

Roustang, François. *Dire Mastery: Discipleship from Freud to Lacan.* Baltimore: Johns Hopkins UP, 1982.

Ruegg, Maria. "Metaphor and Metonymy: The Logic of Structuralist Rhetoric." *Glyph* 6 (1979): 141–57.

Ruskin, John. *The Diaries of John Ruskin.* Ed. J. Evans and J. H. Whitehouse. Oxford: Oxford UP, 1956.

———. "Modern Manufacture and Design." Sesame and Lilies *and* The Two Paths. London: Dent, 1906. 136–60.

———. *Ruskin's Letters from Venice 1851–1852.* Ed. J. L. Bradley. New Haven: Yale UP, 1955.

Sapir, Edward. *Language.* New York: Harcourt, 1957.

Scève, Maurice. *The* Délie *of Maurice Scève.* 1544. Ed. I. D. McFarlane. Cambridge: Cambridge UP, 1966.

Schlegel, Friedrich. *Athenaeums-Fragmente. Kritische Schriften* 25–88.

———. *Kritische Schriften.* Ed. Wolfdietrich Rasch. München: Hanser, 1970.

———. "Über die Unverständlichkeit." *Kritische Schriften* 530–42.

Schleiermacher, Friedrich. *Hermeneutics: The Handwritten Manuscripts*. Ed. Heinze Kimmerle. Trans. James Duke and Jack Forstman. Missoula: Scholars, 1977.

Schmidt, Erich. *Richardson, Rousseau and Goethe*. Jena, 1875.

Schneider, Monique. *La parole et l'inceste*. Paris: Aubier, 1980.

Scholem, Gershom G. *Major Trends in Jewish Mysticism*. New York: Schocken, 1946.

Schur, Max. "Some Additional 'Day Residues' of 'the Specimen Dream' of Psychoanalysis." *Psychoanalysis—A General Psychology: Essays in Honor of Heinz Hartmann*. New York: International Universities, 1966. 45–85.

Sebeok, Thomas A., ed. *Style in Language*. Cambridge: MIT P, 1960.

Selig, Karl-Ludwig. "Concerning the Structure of Cervantes' *La gitanilla*." *Romanistisches Jahrbuch* 13 (1962): 273–76.

Sembdner, Helmut. *Heinrich von Kleists Lebenspüren: Dokumente und Berichte der Zeitgenossen*. München: Deutscher Taschenbuch, 1969.

Semple, J. W., trans. *The Metaphysic of Ethics*. By Immanuel Kant. Edinburgh, 1871.

Serres, Michel. *Le parasite*. Paris: Grasset, 1980.

Shklovsky, Victor. "Sterne's *Tristram Shandy*: Stylistic Commentary." *Russian Formalist Criticism*. Trans. and ed. Lee T. Lemon and Marion J. Reis. Lincoln: U of Nebraska P, 1965. 25–57.

Somerville-Large, Peter. *Irish Eccentrics: A Selection*. New York: Harper, 1975.

Soupault, Phillippe, and Pierre Jean Jouve. *Baudelaire*. Paris: Hachette, 1961.

Spanos, William V. "Heidegger, Kierkegaard, and the Hermeneutic Circle: Towards a Postmodern Theory of Interpretation as Dis-closure." *Boundary 2* 4 (1976): 455–88.

Spivak, Gayatri Chakravorty, trans. *Of Grammatology*. By Jacques Derrida. Baltimore: Johns Hopkins UP, 1976.

Staël, Mme de. *Corinne ou l'Italie*. 1807. Ed. Claudine Herrman. Paris: Des Femmes, 1979.

Stamelman, Richard. "The Shroud of Allegory: Death, Mourning and Melancholy in Baudelaire's Work." *Texas Studies in Literature and Language* 25 (1983): 390–409.

Stechow, Wolfgang. *Pieter Brueghel the Elder*. New York: Abrams, 1940.

Steinmetz, Virginia. "Beyond the Sun: Patriarchal Images in *Aurora Leigh*." *Studies in Browning and His Circle* 9.2 (1981): 18–41.

Stevens, Wallace. *The Collected Poems*. New York: Knopf, 1954.

———. *Opus Posthumous*. New York: Knopf, 1957.

Stierle, Karlheinz. "Baudelaires 'Tableaux parisiens' und die Tradition des 'tableaux de paris.' " *Poetica* 6 (1974): 285–322.

Swales, Erika. "The Beleaguered Citadel: A Study of Kleist's *Die Marquise von O. . . .*" *Deutsche Vierteljahrsschrift für Literaturwissenschaft und Geistesgeschichte* 51 (1977): 124–48.

Taplin, Gardner B. *The Life of Elizabeth Barrett Browning*. New Haven: Yale UP, 1957.

Todorov, Tzvetan. *Mikhaïl Bakhtine: Le principe dialogique*. Paris: Seuil, 1981.

———. "The Place of Style in the Structure of the Text." Chatman 29–39.

———. *The Poetics of Prose*. 1971. Trans. Richard Howard. Ithaca: Cornell UP, 1977.

———, ed. *Teoría de la literatura de los formalistas rusos*. 1965. Trans. Ana Maria Nethol. Buenos Aires: Signos, 1970.

Touponce, William F. "Straw Dogs: A Deconstructive Reading of the Problem of Mimesis in James Liu's *Chinese Theories of Literature*." *Tamkang Review* 9 (1981): 359–86.

Trilling, Lionel. "Art and Neurosis." 1945. *The Liberal Imagination: Essays on Literature and Society*. New York: Doubleday, 1957. 155–75.

Ueda, Makoto. *Matsuo Bashō*. Boston: Twayne, 1970.

Valéry, Paul. *Cahiers*. 29 vols. Paris: Centre National de la Recherche Scientifique, 1957–61. Vol. 22.

———. *Œuvres*. Ed. Jean Hytier. 2 vols. Paris: Gallimard, 1957, 1960.

Vergil. *Georgics*. *Virgil*. Trans. H. Rushton Fairclough. Loeb Classical Library. Cambridge: Harvard UP, 1974.

Versluys, Kristiaan. "Three City Poets: Baudelaire, Rilke, Verhaeren." *Revue de littérature comparée* 54 (1980): 283–307.

Vinogradov, V. V. "Sobre la tarea de la estilística." Todorov, *Teoría* 81–84.

Warminski, Andrzej. "A Question of an Other Order: Deflections of the Straight Man." *Diacritics* 9.4 (1979): 70–78.

Warner, William. *Chance in the Text of Experience: Freud, Nietzsche, and Shakespeare's* Hamlet. Ithaca: Cornell UP, 1986.

Weiss, Hermann F. "Precarious Idylls: The Relationship between Father and Daughter in Heinrich von Kleist's *Die Marquise von O. . . ."* *MLN* 91 (1976): 538–42.

Wharton, Edith. "An Alpine Posting Inn." *Italian Backgrounds.* New York: Scribner's, 1905. 3–14.

Whitehead, Alfred North. *Science and the Modern World.* 1932. New York: Free, 1967.

Williams, Raymond. *Communications.* London: NLB, 1962.

Williams, William Carlos. *Complete Collected Poems.* New York: New Directions, 1938.

———. *Imaginations.* Ed. Webster Schott. New York: New Directions, 1970.

———. *Pictures from Brueghel: Collected Poems 1950–1962.* New York: New Directions, 1962.

Wolff, Hans M. *Heinrich von Kleist: Die Geschichte seines Schaffens.* Bern: Francke, 1954.

Woolf, Virginia. "Aurora Leigh." *The Second Common Reader.* New York: Harcourt, 1932. 182–92.

———. *Flush: A Biography.* New York: Harcourt, 1933.

———. Introduction. *Mrs. Dalloway.* By Woolf. New York: Modern Library, 1928.

———. *Mrs. Dalloway.* New York: Harcourt, 1925.

Wordsworth, William. *Poems.* Ed. John O. Hayden. 2 vols. New York: Penguin, 1977.

———. *The Poetical Works of William Wordsworth.* Ed. Ernest de Selincourt and Helen Darbishire. 5 vols. Oxford: Clarendon, 1940–49.

———. *The Prose Works of William Wordsworth.* Ed. W. J. B. Owen and J. W. Smyser. 3 vols. Oxford: Clarendon, 1974.

Wordsworth, William, and Samuel Taylor Coleridge. *Lyrical Ballads.* 1798. Ed. W. J. B. Owen. Oxford: Oxford UP, 1969.

Wright, Richard. "Between Laughter and Tears." *New Masses* 5 Oct. 1937: 25–26.

Yuasa, Nobuyuki. *Bashō: The Narrow Road to the Deep North and Other Travel Sketches.* Harmondsworth: Penguin, 1966.